T0314161

"FOLLOW THE FLAG"

"FOLLOW THE FLAG"

A History of the
Wabash
Railroad
Company

H. Roger Grant

NORTHERN ILLINOIS UNIVERSITY PRESS / DEKALB

A Book in the

RAILROADS IN AMERICA

Series

H. ROGER GRANT AND JAMES A. WARD, *General Editors*

© 2004 by Northern Illinois University Press

Published by the Northern Illinois University Press, DeKalb, Illinois   60115

Design by Julia Fauci

Library of Congress Cataloging-in-Publication Data

Grant, H. Roger, 1943–

"Follow the flag" : a history of the Wabash Railroad Company / H. Roger Grant.

p.   cm.

Includes bibliographical references and index.

ISBN 0-87580-328-8 (hardcover : alk. paper)

1. Wabash Railroad—History. I. Title.

HE2791.W183G73 2004

385'.0977—dc22

2004004278

To

Thomas H. "Tom" Dearinger

Contents

Preface

I have long found it amazing that the Wabash Railroad has never been the subject of a serious book-length study. Here was a company that from the 1880s to the 1960s operated between some of America's largest cities: Buffalo, Chicago, Detroit, Kansas City, St. Louis and Omaha. As such, the Wabash occupied a unique position by running east *and* west of *both* Chicago and St. Louis, the nation's two principal rail terminals. Yet I do not mean to suggest that this strategic railroad has been completely overlooked. However, for more than fifty years the focus of railfan publications has been pictorial and not textual. In the early 1960s, though, a longtime Wabash employee, J. Orville Spreen, wrote several publishers, asking them whether they would be interested in a history of a "prominent mid-western railroad." Unfortunately, Spreen's project withered, yet fortunately his extensive research materials later were deposited with the Western Historical Manuscript Collection at the University of Missouri—St. Louis. His papers constitute the largest single holdings of diverse Wabash items.

Historians have missed a golden opportunity to explore a major American railroad. The Wabash developed into a significant interregional carrier, contributing mightily to the development of its multistate service territory and becoming an important player in the industry. Even though the company descended into several lengthy bankruptcies, it never sank to the status of a truly woebegone property or the butt of cruel and tasteless jokes. It would not be farfetched to argue that the Wabash is a highly representative American railroad. The company grew out of antebellum efforts by state governments to shatter the tyranny of isolation with the iron horse. Although the particular experience of the Northern Cross Railroad, the first unit of the Wabash, ended unhappily for Illinois taxpayers in the 1840s, other segments appeared during the next several decades and encountered better fates.

It would be Jay Gould, a giant of nineteenth century railroading, who in the 1880s assembled the modern Wabash system. Although Gould encountered difficulties, and the Wabash did not always prosper, this skilled capitalist had the good sense to see that this carrier entered strategic railroad centers, including Chicago and Omaha, which ultimately provided strength. Unlike some contemporary roads, the Wabash was much more stem than branch and twig and certainly did not run from "nowhere to nowhere in particular." The company not only was an active participant in the era of system building, it entered the twentieth century in an optimistic and expansive mood. Management endeavored to make the railroad an attractive avenue for people and goods and told the public that it was wise to "Follow the Flag." The road participated fully in what business historian Albro Martin has aptly called the second building of American railroads. Unfortunately, George Gould, Jay Gould's son and principal heir to his vast transportation and communication empire, lacked the talents of his father. As a result, the Wabash suffered, most of all from a costly building foray into Pittsburgh, Pennsylvania. Despite the setback, the property reorganized and pushed ahead, but with repeated challenges. Neither the industry nor the Wabash was immune from the sting of harsh progressive era regulatory statutes; intermodal competition, first from electric interurbans and then motor vehicles, particularly automobiles; two disruptive wars and several severe economic downswings; and later the albatross of archaic labor work rules. After World War II, the Wabash coped reasonably well with its problems and rightly considered itself to be one of America's better railroads. It dieselized and adopted other replacement technologies that brought about much-needed trimming of costs and enhanced efficiencies. The company prospered and gained acclaim for its sleek streamliners and its dependable and often fast "Red Ball" freight trains. Then the Wabash became a "fallen flag." As railroad consolidations intensified, the company fortuitously entered the orbit of the Norfolk & Western Railway, a prosperous and determined carrier. Differing from some neighbors, the twilight years of the Wabash were not dominated by corporate instability, bankruptcy and economic heartache.

Authors usually have personal stories to explain why they selected their topics. I am no exception. I enjoy working on railroad company histories, especially their human dimensions. I found the personal side of the Wabash exceedingly fascinating, especially its network of company hospitals and the shopmen's strike of 1922. Creating a well-researched and readable book that appeals to an audience that is both professional and popular provides me with enormous satisfaction. Moreover, I like carriers that I can visualize. I certainly can do this with portions of the Wabash. It was one of three steam roads that once served my hometown of Albia, a small county seat in southern Iowa. I must admit that the Wabash locally lacked the pizzazz and the majesty of the Burlington Route, with its *Zephyr* streamliners, yet it was a reliable carrier with a punctual early morning and late evening passenger run that provided me with some memorable train-watching moments. I can still recall those big, black 2-8-2's Wabash steam locomotives and, later, the brightly painted blue and white diesels that powered the daily single freights as they snaked through town. I often watched the train that came up "from the South" with a string of forty or fifty cars that its crew would leave for the Minneapolis & St. Louis Railway (M&StL). An hour or so later this important interchange partner would take these freight cars to the Twin Cities and other points north. And daily the reverse pattern occurred; the M&StL always left a substantial train for the Wabash to handle southbound for Kansas City, St. Louis and other destinations. There was always that mid-morning and late-afternoon banging and clanking of couplers and repeated whistling, indicating that the Wabash freight had either arrived or would soon leave town.

The Wabash has disappeared as a corporation, along with much of the trackage that I once knew. Portions of the "Good Ole Wabash," however, remain in active service, providing valuable arteries for modern freight commerce between Kansas City, St. Louis and Detroit. For decades, this railroad loomed large in the lives of thousands of Americans, and my book may keep alive some aspects of its rich past.

Acknowledgments

I have received assistance from an array of organizations, institutions and individuals. Without their aid, this book would have been impossible. First of all, several members of the Wabash Railroad Historical Society (WRHS), including Craig Berndt of Indianapolis, Indiana, James Holmes of Bolingbrook, Illinois, James Holzmeier of Brashear, Missouri, Vance Lischer of Olivette, Missouri, and Gary Roe of Fort Worth, Texas, shared with me a variety of historical data and provided insights into their much-adored "fallen flag" carrier.

I also thank Mary Ann Mullady, assistant corporate secretary of the Norfolk Southern Corporation, for directing me through the Wabash materials, especially minute books, that are housed in the railroad's archives in Atlanta, Georgia. Similarly, I am grateful to Robert W. Kimmons and his friendly staff at the Wabash Memorial Hospital Association in Decatur, Illinois, for permitting me to examine a wide assortment of hospital and employee materials; Nancy Masten of the Miami County Museum in Peru, Indiana, for helping me better understand the Wabash in this one-time shop and division-point town; and Don Snoddy, former head of the Union Pacific Museum in Omaha, Nebraska, and his daughter Elizabeth Snoddy, who assembled Wabash documents that are contained in the archives of the Union Pacific Railroad.

I am also grateful for the efforts of Ron Goldfeder, collections assistant at the Museum of Transportation in Kirkwood, Missouri, who provided me access to the papers of Wabash Railroad president Arthur Atkinson and an assortment of Wabash and predecessor company documents; Clayton McGahee, an archivist for the Virginia Tech Digital Library and Archives in Blacksburg, Virginia, who made available minute books of Wabash predecessor carriers and brought my attention to a collection of Wabash materials, mostly from the 1920s; Jacqueline ("Jackie") Pryor, archivist for the Railway & Locomotive Historical Society in Sacramento, California, who scoured her collections for Wabash materials; and Doris Wesley, who works for the Western Historical Manuscript Collection at the University of Missouri—St. Louis, who guided me through the J. Orville Spreen Collection and later processed my photographic orders. Zelli Fischetti, at the Western Historical Manuscript Collection, allowed me to view correspondence in the partially processed T. J. Moss Tie Company papers. The staffs of the Mercantile Library in St. Louis, Missouri, especially Gregory Ames, and the Hagley Museum and Library in Wilmington, Delaware, most of all Christopher Baer, helped tremendously. These two institutions provided me with generous fellowships and attractive housing arrangements, easing my research efforts. Personnel at the Illinois Commerce Commission in Springfield; Lake Forest College Library, Lake Forest, Illinois; Missouri Historical Society in St. Louis; Newberry Library in Chicago; St. Louis Public Library; and State Historical Society of Missouri in Columbia also enhanced my knowledge of the Wabash and its many predecessors.

As usual, the talented interlibrary loan staff of the R. M. Cooper Library at Clemson University made a significant contribution. Because I live far from the service territory of the former Wabash Railroad, I needed professional assistance in locating a wide range of printed book and article materials, newspapers, and other imprints on microfilm. Reference personnel at the University of

Georgia Libraries in Athens helped as well.

Clemson University should be acknowledged for accelerating the process of writing. I received a sabbatical for the academic year 2002–2003. This allowed me to remain free from classroom activities and other time-consuming responsibilities associated with a modern institution of higher education.

Many individuals provided assistance: James A. Bistline, Alexandria, Virginia; O. K. Blackburn, St. Louis, Missouri; Paul Brothers, University of Alabama at Tuscaloosa; Arthur D. Dubin, Highland Park, Illinois; James Geyer, Greenville, South Carolina; the late John F. Humiston, Olympia Fields, Illinois; J. David Ingles, *Trains,* Waukesha, Wisconsin; William S. Kuba, Cedar Rapids, Iowa; Robert McMillan, Jacksonville, Florida; Professor J. Parker Lamb, University of Texas at Austin; Steve Parsons, Sparta, Illinois; John Shedd Reed, Chicago, Illinois; Charles H. Stats, Oak Park, Illinois; Dr. Augustus J. Veenendaal, Jr., Institute of Netherlands History, The Hague, the Netherlands; and David M. Young, Wheaton, Illinois.

I am especially indebted to Professor Don L. Hofsommer, St. Cloud State University, St. Cloud, Minnesota, for supplying materials and reviewing a draft of the manuscript. Similarly, Professor Richard Saunders, Jr., my colleague at Clemson University, shared research information and commented on a portion of the work. Professor Keith L. Bryant, Jr., a former colleague at the University of Akron and a distinguished railroad scholar who resides in Bryan, Texas, gave the manuscript close scrutiny, making scores of valuable suggestions. James Holzmeier also provided a careful examination of the manuscript. So, too, did I benefit from an unidentified reader for the Northern Illinois University Press.

Finally, my family has contributed to this work. My daughter, Julia, a budding young professional fund-raiser, has always encouraged me to pursue my interests in railroad history, and my wife, Martha, has given me everything I could ever ask for and much more. In a score of book acknowledgments I have noted that she *always* has been my best critic, and this work is no exception. Even though my stepfather, Thomas Dearinger (1900–1968), had no idea that I would ever study the Wabash, his almost daily observations of this railroad in Monroe County, Iowa, provided him with a font of knowledge about the Des Moines line. Over the years, he happily shared with me his interest in the road. Tom had grown up in Lovilia, a village on the Wabash, where his father, who operated a general mercantile business, had been affected by its presence, and later Tom's Mobil Oil bulk plant abutted the joint Burlington-Wabash tracks in Albia. From him I understood why Lovilians, rather than Albians, were usually more oriented toward St. Louis than they were toward Chicago and why the Wabash was such an important freight railroad.

"FOLLOW THE FLAG"

The Wabash Emerges East of the Mississippi River

THE NORTHERN CROSS AND THE SANGAMON & MORGAN

Almost a decade before the ten-ton locomotive *Pioneer* chugged and clanked over the fragile rails of the initial stretch of the Galena & Chicago Union Railroad, the first railroad to serve Chicago and the earliest component of the vast Chicago & North Western Railway System, a similarly Lilliputian engine, the *Rogers,* on November 8, 1838, puffed and snorted along an equally primitive Northern Cross Railroad, the oldest unit of the Wabash Railroad. The distances were approximately the same. The *Pioneer* pulled a short train crammed with dignitaries along a ten-mile stretch of track from the city of Chicago to the Des Plaines River; the *Rogers* trundled its notables over an eight-mile span between the village of Meredosia, located on the Illinois River in Morgan County, and Dickinson Lake, then the end of track.[1]

The similarities between these two pioneer companies include more than the parallels between their maiden runs. Both the

Locomotive No. 143 of the Toledo, Wabash & Western Railroad and its engineer and fireman pose at an unidentified location (probably the Springfield, Illinois, engine house) around 1870. This stately American 4-4-0-type engine, with its gigantic oil-burning headlight, served as the company's principal motive power for both freight and passenger runs. In 1869 the Schenectady Locomotive Works built No. 143, and the engine remained in service until the mid-1880s. (Author's Coll.)

Galena & Chicago Union and Northern Cross projects grew out of the burning desire of Illinois citizens to reduce their isolation. Geography blessed portions of the state with several navigable rivers, including the mighty Illinois, access to Lake Michigan and the Great Lakes, and a terrain in some areas suitable for construction of long-distance canals. Nevertheless, huge sections of Illinois were remote from any natural or possible artificial waterways. By the 1830s and 1840s, all-weather roads remained rare, with many settlers forced to use trails that originally had been fashioned by wild animals or Indians. These primitive arteries were occasionally improved with crushed rock or crudely cut halves of trees or rough-hewn wooden planks. Although travel conditions in the winter might be acceptable, when the frozen and snow-covered ground permitted usage of sleighs and sleds, other seasons brought "freshets" and floods, muddy ruts and choking dust. Rutted roads were particularly troublesome, and at times dangerous. When the roads filled with water, wagons became struck and sometimes overturned.[2]

Understandably, politicians, those seismographs of public tremors, eventually responded, realizing the critical need for improved transportation arteries and knowing that the state's population was about to reach the one-half million mark. They fully sensed the enthusiasm for better commercial intercourse as result of an enthusiastic internal improvement convention held in 1836 at Vandalia, then the state capital. Governor Joseph Duncan ably captured the feelings of these assembled representatives, when he asked rhetorically: "When we look abroad and see the extensive lines of intercommunication penetrating almost every section of our sister states, when we see the canal-boat and the locomotive bearing, with seeming triumph, the rich productions of the interior

to the river, lakes and ocean, almost annihilating burden, time and space, what patriot bosom does not beat high with a laudable ambition to give to Illinois her full share of those advantages which are adorning her sister States, and which a munificent Providence seems to invite by the wonderful adoption of our whole country to such improvements?"[3]

In 1837, legislators took action. They overwhelmingly endorsed "An Act to Establish and Maintain a General System of Internal Improvements." This commitment, startling to some nonresidents, prompted the *American Railroad Journal* to editorialize that it "must surely satisfy those who are still incredulous as to the high destinies of that young State." Part of the legislative response would be better water commerce, which led to construction of the ninety-seven-mile-long Illinois & Michigan Canal between Chicago (Lake Michigan) and La Salle (Illinois River), opening in 1848. Yet, in addition to "ditches" and improved river channels, the newly invented railroad would be the capstone of their grand scheme of transportation improvements.[4]

Illinois lawmakers saw railroads as their *principal* magic carpet for what would surely be a glorious future. They would have the best transport network that could possibly be obtained. These men were well aware that a variety of railroads had become part of the landscape of prosperous and well-settled Eastern and Southern states, including Maryland, Pennsylvania and South Carolina. Although the South Carolina Canal & Rail Road Company spanned the 136 miles between the seaport of Charleston and the Savannah River community of Hamburg, making it the world's longest rail route, this transport technology remained novel and experimental. By 1840, there existed only a scattering of lines nationwide, and they lacked the standardization and precision of operation to come in later years. When Illinois decided to build railroads, only one line existed in the states and territories of the Old Northwest. In April 1833 the Legislative Council of Michigan Territory had made a monumental decision by incorporating the Erie & Kalamazoo Rail Road (E&K) and authorizing it to build from the Maumee River (Toledo) to the Kalamazoo River "by the power and force of steam, animals, or any mechanical or other power, or of any combination of them." In 1834, survey work began, and construction followed late the next year. About a year later, the primitive pike opened, using horsepower between its two terminals, Toledo and Adrian, Michigan, a distance of thirty-three miles. Although the iron horse subsequently became the motive power, the E&K never reached its intended destination, 180 miles away, remaining merely a tap line for Toledo.[5]

The Illinois act called for massive and expensive railroad building. If implemented, 1,342 miles of line would be constructed at a cost exceeding $10 million. Specifically, the Central Railroad would link Cairo, near the confluence of the Ohio and Mississippi rivers with Vandalia, Decatur and Bloomington to a point at or near the terminus of the Illinois & Michigan Canal and northward to Galena with a branch from Shelbyville to the Indiana border; the Southern Cross Railroad would stretch from Alton on the Mississippi River to Mount Carmel on the Indiana border via Edwardsville and Salem with an extension to Shawneetown, and the Northern Cross Railroad would run from Quincy through Meredosia, Jacksonville, Springfield, Decatur and Danville to Indiana, where it would connect with the Wabash & Erie Canal. The measure also designated other railroads to crisscross the state, including one from Bloomington to Mackinaw,

where it would diverge to Peoria and Pekin.[6]

Even though blatant political logrolling and sectionalism shaped the measure, there still would be supervisory controls. The act created as part of an expanded state bureaucracy "fund commissioners," chosen by the legislature, who would raise the necessary investment money through disposal of internal improvement bonds. These three "practical and experienced financiers," qualities required by law, would work closely with the seven commissioners of public works, who each represented a state judicial district.[7]

In hindsight, it is amazing that *any* state-railroad project moved much beyond the planning stage. "Instead of building trial railroads, completing them, deriving experience from them, and possibly obtaining revenue for further construction the legislature permitted sectional jealousy to dictate," observed an early student of the internal improvement act. "All construction work was begun as nearly simultaneously as possible and carried along at about the same." This strategy, thought lawmakers, would reduce fear that one community or section would reap the advantages of rail service before others could receive it. Yet the policy enormously diminished prospects for any major accomplishments. Moreover, the times soon proved inauspicious for railroad building, already realized by knowledgeable individuals to be inordinately capital intensive and risky. Although Illinois possessed limited state debt and had a rapidly growing population, a devastating financial panic in 1837 burst upon the country. Throughout the nation, especially in the "West," hundreds of banks failed and money and credit tightened. Citizens rightly worried about their economic well-being and wondered whether their future lay at the end of parallel rails.[8]

Even though lawmakers tried to spend

public funds equitably on internal improvements, especially for railroads, and even though the economy dramatically weakened after the Panic of 1837, the Northern Cross still took shape. Political maneuvering had resulted in a provision that became part of the authorizing legislation, namely, that the Northern Cross project should have *first* priority. According to the statute, "It shall be the duty of the board of commissioners to contract for the immediate construction, so soon as located, of all railroads or parts thereof contemplated between Quincy and the Wabash [River], as lies between Jacksonville in Morgan county, Springfield in Sangamon county, Decatur in Macon county, and Danville in Vermilion county; thence to the state line in Vermilion county in a direction to Lafayette in Indiana, at such point as the commissioners of this State and of Indiana may agree to cross the same." If this language had not existed, the Northern Cross probably would not have been the first steam-powered common carrier railroad in Illinois.[9]

On May 11, 1837, survey crews began their work. These hardy men encountered their greatest challenges finding an acceptable route through the rugged terrain east of Meredosia. "More than one hundred miles of experimental line [were] surveyed by Mr. [James M.] Bucklin [chief engineer] and the engineers under his charge, with a view to ascertaining the best route for said road," reported Murry McConnel of Jacksonville, a public works commissioner. "Notwithstanding all these difficulties [through the Illinois River bluffs at Meredosia], notwithstanding the almost constant rains in this part of the country in the month of June, the engineers completed the location of the road between Jacksonville and the river . . . a sufficient time before the tenth of July [1837] to enable all persons wishing to make contract

upon said road to obtain all necessary information relative thereto."[10]

While surveyors staked the twenty-mile route between Meredosia and Jacksonville, another locating party reconnoitered the largely level countryside between Jacksonville and Springfield, experiencing no major difficulties along this thirty-five-mile stretch. But establishing the location of the future railroad through the relatively remote northern part of Jacksonville annoyed residents, who vociferously demanded that this technological wonderment pass through the heart of their county-seat community. After considerable wrangling, the commission reluctantly authorized a resurvey and ran track through the public square, a victory that Jacksonville citizens subsequently regretted.[11]

Once the surveyors had completed their tasks, the state awarded construction contracts. The process moved quickly. On July 10, 1837, a local consortium received approval to build approximately fifty-five miles of track, with a gauge of four feet nine inches, to be fitted with "strap rail" and the necessary rolling stock.[12]

In what became a typical event throughout the antebellum phase of American railroad building, a gala ceremony occurred with the start of construction. "Ground was first broken at Meredosia [on August 1] . . . with great ceremony and in the presence of a vast concourse of citizens," recorded a local Jacksonville historian. "Speeches were made by Mr. J. E. Waldo and Hon. O. M. Long. Mr. Daniel Waldo was selected to dig the first shovelful of dirt, which he did amidst the shouts of the multitude. This labor so exhausted himself and the multitude that no more work was done that day."[13]

The drudgery of creating the right-of-way began in earnest. When one considers that laborers did most of the grading with pick, shovel and wheelbarrow, it is impressive that by September 1838 these men, many of whom had been recruited from the Louisville, Kentucky, area because of a shortage of local workers and enticed to the project by good wages and "eight jiggers of whiskey a day," had excavated more than 6,000 cubic yards of dirt and had thrown up more than 14,000 cubic yards for earthen embankments. And they had readied about two miles for track laying. State payment records reveal that construction continued even through the winter season. By December 1838, grading crews had nearly completed their work between Meredosia and Jacksonville, and only eight miles remained unfinished on the section between Jacksonville and Springfield.[14]

Significantly, track-laying gangs mostly kept up with the grading, installing in January 1838 the first timbers for this "wooden railroad." Because the state opted for cheaper strap or "flat" rail, rather than recently introduced iron "U" or "T" rail, wood consumption ran high. The strap rail option was popular where construction funds were limited, especially during hard times. It meant attaching twenty- to twenty-five-foot strips of two-and-one-half-inch-wide and five-eights-inch-thick iron, a yard of which weighed thirteen pounds, to longitudinal red or white oak "stringers" that were fastened by metal "joining plates" to eight-foot-long cedar ties and secured by ordinary twenty-penny cut nails. Workers spaced these ties every five or six feet, placing them on twelve-inch-wide and four-inch-thick wooden ground timbers or "mud sills" that rested atop the graded roadbed.[15]

Although economical and relatively easy to install, strap rail had drawbacks. The most troublesome was that occasionally the iron worked loose and curled up under the weight of a passing train. These "snake heads" might then pierce a passenger coach floor and injure or even kill its occupants or damage or possibly derail a freight car, halting the train for an extended period. It is not surprising that, by the 1840s, some states—including New York, in 1847—outlawed this rail for safety reasons. And this type of rail required almost constant maintenance. Resembling contemporary plank roads, the untreated wood needed frequent replacement.[16]

Most people who were involved with the Northern Cross, including members of the Board of Public Works, seemed pleased with the construction process. Although some technical problems developed, track continued to advance from Meredosia toward Jacksonville. By July 1838, laborers arrived in Morgan City, approximately the halfway point, and by the end of the year they entered Jacksonville.[17]

Even before the Northern Cross reached Morgan City and Jacksonville, the Morgan County seat, residents of the Meredosia area saw the billowing wood smoke of the railroad's first locomotive, a diminutive teakettle, manufactured in Newark, New Jersey, by Rogers, Ketchum & Grosvenor. Although ordered for service in South Carolina and originally called the *Experiment,* the engine was rejected by the initial customer for unknown reasons, and it arrived at the dock in Meredosia on board the steamboat *Quincy.* The cost was high, amounting to approximately $7,400, which included $1,000 for its lengthy sea and river journey. Renamed the *Rogers,* this locomotive, once fully assembled and operational, hardly resembled those engines built just a few years later; it lacked a cab, pilot, bell and whistle and had only a single pair of thirty-six-inch drivers.[18]

The locomotive operated on that second Thursday of November in 1838 and soon pushed and pulled construction trains, but revenue service did not begin until the summer of 1839. An announcement placed in the *Springfield Journal* on July 6, 1838, by John E. Tolfree, the railroad's superintendent, read:

> Two trips daily between Meredosia and Morgan City, on that division of the Northern Cross Rail Road, comprised between Meredosia on the Illinois River and the town of Morgan City, (a distance of twelve miles) having been completed by the Contractors, and accepted by the Board of Public Works on the part of the State. Trains of cars will commence running on Monday the 8th instant, for the transportation of passengers and freight—the cars will arrive at and depart from Meredosia at the hours of 7 o'clock A.M. And 2 o'clock P.M.—returning, the trains will leave Morgan City at the hours of 9 o'clock A.M. And 4 o'clock P.M. In connection with the Rail Road, a line of post coaches will run twice every day between Morgan City and Jacksonville, leaving the Depot at Morgan City, on the arrival of the trains, and arriving in Jacksonville in time for passengers to take the daily line, which will run between Jacksonville and Springfield. . . . Thus the entire distance between Meredosia and Springfield will be readily and pleasantly performed by daylight. Every facility conducive to comfort and convenience will be furnished by the Superintendent of the Rail Road . . . and it is hoped that one or more packets may be induced to run daily between St. Louis, Alton and Meredosia.[19]

In the fall of 1839, when the entire line was finished, residents of Jacksonville no longer needed to board a stagecoach to Morgan City to reach the Northern Cross for the sixteen-mile, seventy-five-cent ride to Meredosia and the Illinois River. An operating railroad finally at hand was reason for rejoicing. There was something special about the arrival of the first train, and most denizens of the Jacksonville community flocked to the public square to honor the iron horse. What followed was not exactly what these well-wishers had anticipated. "The public square was filled with teams, and when the engine steamed into the square making all the noise possible, there was such a stampede of horses as was never before heard of, nearly every team breaking loose, and at least one-third of the vehicles in the county were broken, and many of the people were as much scared as the horses at the steaming monster as it came rushing into the square."[20]

Train service between Jacksonville and Meredosia was at best pedestrian. Company officials allowed their slow-moving trains—they reached only ten to fifteen miles per hour on the trip—pulled by either the wheezy *Rogers* or the newly acquired *Illinois*, built by Matthias W. Baldwin in Philadelphia, to stop virtually anywhere to pick up and discharge freight and passengers. These mixed freight and passenger or "accommodation" runs barely met the needs of patrons. Shippers of freight had to accept the open, four-wheel gondola, which during the early years of American railroading was the standard freight car. If cargo required protection from the elements, canvas covers and leather straps had to be used. Probably less popular were the road's two spartan eight-wheeled passenger or "pleasure" cars. "The seats ran along each side, like those of the omnibus, and the coaches were equally destitute of any and every other appliance for the comfort or conveyance of the traveler, other than to sit down and 'hang-on'—if he could. . . . [A] sudden lurch of the coach would often slide a sitter half the length of the coach and land him, or her, with a gruesome bump in the middle of the floor." Regardless of whether the equipment was acceptable, the Northern Cross became a mostly, although not always, dependable all-weather artery for residents of Jacksonville and the immediate vicinity.[21]

One early journey between Jacksonville and Meredosia left a lasting impression on many Jacksonville residents. Always eager to boost revenues, the Northern Cross offered a special excursion trip to the Illinois River and promised ticket holders that they would be home by early evening. A Jacksonville resident related this account of the ill-fated summertime outing that he had gathered from a participant:

The train . . . consisted of two common passenger cars and several [empty] sand cars. The excursionists had a merry time at the river, and in fact were enjoying themselves so much that they did not get started on the return *voyage* until about sundown. Then came the tug of war—the engine was by no means a powerful one, the grade was rather steep [leaving Meredosia], and in the language of our informant, "every time they came to a leaf or a twig on the track, the engine couldn't pull them over, and all hands were obliged to get out and *push*." Of course they made but little headway, and when midnight came they had accomplished but half the distance. At this juncture the conductor slyly unfastened the coupling which joined the cars, and away went the engine with the two passenger cars [sans the sand cars], leaving a terribly enraged crowd. . . . The engine and favored few arrived in Jacksonville about daylight, and then it [engine] started back after the remainder of the load. When they reached the place where the remaining cars had been left, the engineer found that they had all been pried off the track, and thrown into a ditch by the maddened passengers, who were, in consequent, obliged to walk home.[22]

Officials of the Northern Cross badly wanted to reach Springfield, site of the newly relocated state capital and a commu-nity that promised a source of considerable freight and passenger business. Although the capital city enjoyed regular stagecoach service and the occasional steamboat plied the shallow and snag-infested Sangamon River, a railroad would greatly facilitate long-distance travel. Residents could take the steamcars to Meredosia and from there passenger packets to St. Louis and other river ports.[23]

But by the time the Northern Cross had reached Jacksonville, prospects for an extension eastward had dimmed. A depressed economy had made it difficult for Illinois to sell bonds for its internal improvement projects, including the partially built road. By December 1840, all railroad construction in the state, with two minor exceptions, had been suspended; in fact, work on the Northern Cross had stopped in March.[24]

Just as the Northern Cross had benefited from earlier political logrolling, it took advantage of its current status, namely, that it was a functioning railroad of nearly fifty-six miles rather than a largely paper proposal. Internal improvement advocates in the legislature cogently argued that this project must be completed, at least to Springfield. When it was, net revenues would surely cover most or all of the building and operating costs. A majority of lawmakers agreed, and on February 17, 1841, a measure went into effect to underwrite with state canal bonds the remaining construction. Workers returned to the unfinished route, completed the grading and installed track between Jacksonville and Springfield. They also built various support facilities, including a turntable in Springfield and three 1,000-gallon water tanks to slake the thirst of the road's two iron horses.[25]

Two months after the line's completion in October 1841, scheduled freight and passenger service commenced. Quantities of flour, grain, lumber, pork and sand regularly moved over the road. Trains also hauled a variety of smaller shipments. J. C. Zabriskie

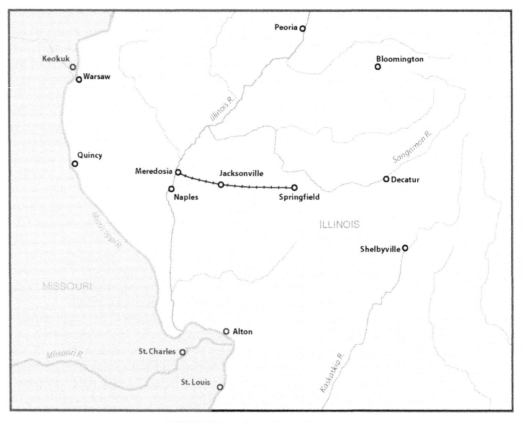

NORTHERN CROSS RAILROAD

of Springfield, for example, sent three trunks to Jacksonville, and J. E. Mitchell shipped 1,500 wooden barrel staves. And every month hundreds of passengers "took the cars" with some making the arduous twenty-three-hour rail-water trip between Springfield and St. Louis. Likely these tenacious travelers found the steamboat *Mungo Park,* which regularly called at Meredosia, more comfortable than the omnibus-like passenger equipment of the Northern Cross.[26]

Better days anticipated by backers of Illinois's first railroad did not happen. Even with the Springfield extension and the accompanying increase in overall business, revenues were disappointing. The sluggish economy forced reductions in freight and passenger charges. Significantly, too, construction expenses had been excessive, partially the result of high wages because of chronic labor shortages. The entire cost, including track, rolling stock and improvements, reached approximately $800,000, with the price tag of the Meredosia to Jacksonville segment totaling $436,233. This translated into about $14,500 per mile, substantially exceeding what other roads in the Old Northwest had cost by 1840. Their construction bills ranged between $7,000 and $12,000 per mile.[27]

Along the Northern Cross, public opinion grew for Illinois to privatize the railroad.

"We are every day more and more satisfied that works of this character never ought to be under the control of the State," editorialized a Springfield newspaper in March 1842. "[T]hey are likely to be managed with far less economy in the hands of the State than by private individuals." Public officials generally agreed. "The expense of keeping it in operation owing to the breaking of locomotives and other fixtures and having to send either to Cincinnati or St. Louis for the principal repairs, I was induced to lease the same to the highest bidder," opined Fund Commissioner J. D. Whiteside. And in May 1842 the state leased to a private group the entire property, including its rolling stock, for the modest annual sum of $10,300.[28]

Leasing the Northern Cross may have been popular, but it did not guarantee that the railroad would prosper, or even function. Almost immediately the first group of leaseholders gave up on the line and willingly paid a penalty to do so. In July 1842, however, the state signed another agreement with a new party, and this time the annual rate was for four years at $10,000 per annum. Once again, though, the lessees decided that the Northern Cross was anything but a money machine and forfeited their contract, paying what largely amounted to one year's rental fee. With this second setback, sentiment increased for public officials to *sell* the railroad. But before the state could dispose of what was rapidly becoming both an embarrassment and a transportation slum, it entered into still another lease, this one covering only from September 1843 to April 1844 for a mere $2,000.[29]

Until the state sold the Northern Cross at auction on April 26, 1847, additional leases were made, for less and less money. At the same time, the property itself declined precipitously. At first, train speeds dropped to six miles per hour between Springfield and Jacksonville and to four miles per hour over the remainder of the route. Then, in 1844, because of a lack of overall maintenance on the motive power, three or four mules, and occasionally oxen, walking in tandem, replaced the two iron horses. "Stage coaches dashed by in a cloud of dust," noted one commentator, and soon passenger service ended. Weeds choked the tracks, and at times farmers removed the strap iron from the longitudinal stringers for use as sled runners or for other purposes. Though management occasionally ordered repairs, only intermittent shipments of freight moved at a snail's pace over the rickety line.[30]

In 1847 public ownership of the Northern Cross mercifully came to an end. In February, a legislative act ordering its sale contained an important caveat: "If the corporation [Northern Cross] shall not, within three years from the passage of this act, repair the Road to the Illinois River, so that the same may be safely used for the transportation of persons and property thereon by the force of steam, the sale authorized by this act shall be void." Illinois coffers, however, received a pittance of $21,000—in state-issued bonds and not cash—for an investment that had been more than thirty-five times greater. Moreover, operating revenues had never paid operating costs and at times fell far short.[31]

The purchaser, Nicholas H. Ridgely, a prominent Springfield "capitalist" and speculator, gladly paid the winning price, even though he had expected the Northern Cross to sell for less. Held on the steps of the capitol building, the auction at first attracted only Ridgely and the curious, and it appeared that his initial offer of $10,000 would take the railroad. Ridgely's hope evaporated when a "Col. Johnson" entered the bidding, apparently representing "parties in St. Louis." Seeing that his bargain-basement bid might not take the railroad, Ridgely sought out Johnson and learned that his rival would receive a commission if he were victorious. The resourceful Ridgely asked the Colonel, "Would you not as soon receive a commission from Springfield as St. Louis?" Johnson replied, "Certainly, that is satisfactory," and walked away from the crowd. The next day, a satisfied Ridgely gave the Colonel a check for $1,000 "for his commissions."[32]

Ridgely quickly made the most of his auction triumph. He soon sold an interest to businessmen and area boosters Thomas Mather of Springfield and James Dunlap of Jacksonville. With the state's blessings, the new owners reorganized the property as the Sangamon & Morgan Railroad Company and went to work with the rehabilitation. At the time they embarked on these betterments, the Northern Cross was a shambles. The locomotives had been discarded, and local residents had helped themselves to much of the iron and usable lumber. "There was not much left of the road except the bed," commented one writer, "and that was in a fearfully bad condition."[33]

Before the railroad could be renewed to operable standards, Mather, representing the three principal investors, traveled to New York City and sold control of the property. The deal amounted to $100,000 and gave them "a large profit." The new owner was Robert Schuyler, "who was then deemed the great railroad manager of the country." Mather, Dunlap and Ridgely, however, retained some stock and remained involved in the road's operations.[34]

Management of the Sangamon & Morgan undertook major improvements. Before train service resumed on July 22, 1849, locally hired laborers relocated the line that had pierced downtown Jacksonville, returning it to the original survey route north of the commercial center. Also, Naples, a community on the Illinois River, four miles below Meredosia, soon became the second western terminus. This town was better situated and appeared to be much more alive than Meredosia. Moreover, it was relatively easy for track-layers to reach Naples because they could use the abandoned right-of-way of a three-and-a-half-mile animal-powered railroad between Naples and Bluffs, east of Meredosia, that after its opening in July 1837 had operated only briefly. The Sangamon & Morgan wisely embraced standard gauge and opted for iron "U" rail rather than strap metal and subsequently replaced it with "T" rail, adopting the best track technology of the times. Crews installed mostly tough red cedar ties and happily discovered that the roadbed was reasonably "well-settled." And the railroad acquired suitable motive power, three modern American-type (4-4-0) locomotives from Rogers, Ketchum & Grosvenor: *Pioneer*, *Sangamon* and *Morgan*. Later a similar locomotive, *Springfield*, arrived from the same manufacturer. Additional freight cars and more comfortable passenger coaches were also purchased. Other betterments occurred, including refurbished station, engine and water facilities.[35]

Train operations on the Sangamon & Morgan, the self-proclaimed "Sangamon River Road," largely resembled those of the Northern Cross during its short heyday. A typical timetable appeared in the January 7, 1850, issue of the *Springfield State Journal*: "A train of Freight Cars with Passenger Car attached, will leave Springfield every day at 8 A.M. (Sundays excepted), Jacksonville 11.18, and arrive at Naples at 1 o'clock 30 P.M. Leave Naples at 11 o'clock 11 A.M., Jacksonville 1.42 P.M., arriving at Springfield at 5—from and Monday next, until further notice." Once more, patrons encountered a mixed train that likely transported lading identical to what the Northern Cross had handled. Again there was a connecting water option. At Naples, travelers destined for St. Louis might board one of two steamboats operated by the Naples Packet Company, organized in 1848, the *Time and Tide* and the *Anthony Wayne,* both light-draft side-wheelers.[36]

But these movements over the Sangamon & Morgan held some important differences. Train service now had become largely dependable. More powerful locomotives pulled freight and passenger cars over a more durable roadway. The "snake heads" that once stopped or even derailed trains had become only unpleasant memories. Moreover, the public viewed the company favorably, realizing that its predecessor was highly experimental and undoubtedly launched too soon in the "demonstration period" of railroad construction.

GREAT WESTERN

As did hundreds of other railroads of the antebellum period, the Sangamon & Morgan underwent a reorganization. On February 13, 1853, its backers won legislative approval to create "The Great Western Railroad Company." Like both the Northern Cross and the Sangamon & Morgan, this property had the legal right to extend eastward to Indiana and anticipated strategic canal and railroad connections to eastern and intermediate points. A name change and new securities issued to predominantly Eastern investors seemingly enhanced prospects for significant expansion.[37]

The Great Western accomplished much. By November 1856 the road had added 120 miles to its original line, reaching Indiana via Decatur and Danville. Of great import, the road made two connections with the rapidly developing Illinois Central (IC) Railroad, which on September 27, 1856, completed its 705-mile north-south "system," making it the longest railroad in the world. At Decatur, the Great Western met the Cairo-to–Galena-Dunleith stem, and at Tolono it met with the "branch" (and much later the IC's mainline between Chicago and New Orleans) from near Centralia through Urbana and Kankakee to Chicago. Both interchange points, especially the latter, helped the Great Western attract much-needed "bridge" or overhead traffic by "forming a very direct through route to Chicago."[38]

The new line construction completed by the Great Western surely surprised few observers. After all, prior to the Panic of 1857 a rash of railroad building swept large sections of the country, especially in the South and West. Crews were especially active in the five states of the Old Northwest. Indeed, by decade's end mileage in Illinois reached an impressive 2,790 miles; in 1850 it had stood at only 111. And for the West as a whole, trackage skyrocketed 768 percent. By 1860 the East, South and West had roughly equal railroad mileage.[39]

Survey and construction work between Springfield and Danville posed few major problems. One surveyor recalled that, in December 1852, he found the "country was sparsely settled after leaving the Sangamon river at Rivertown, a trackless, treeless, houseless prairie presented itself as far as the eye could reach." At times, however, the terrain became broken by meandering streams and stands of timber along flood plains. Because of the nature of the topography, construction crews found their jobs relatively easy, except in places that required large bridges, most notably across the Sangamon and Vermillion rivers, and in the valleys of some waterways that necessitated sizeable earthen fills. Also, Great Western personnel were able to use about twenty miles of grading between Decatur and Danville that contractors for the state had undertaken for the Northern Cross.[40]

Of course, forging the Great Western was not entirely pleasant. Arguably, the worst construction experience involved not an

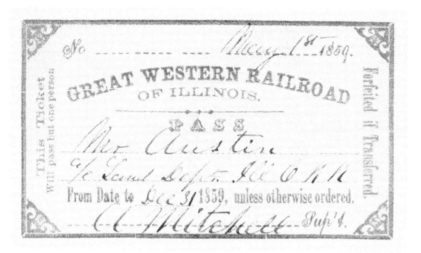

Typical of the style of annual passes railroads issued for free transportation before the 1870s is this frank presented in 1859 by officials of the Great Western Railroad of Illinois to employees and friends, including ministers, journalists, politicians and railroaders. (Author's Coll.)

engineering challenge but rather a near war between German and Irish laborers who worked separately on dirt embankments near Stevens Creek east of Decatur. According to one reminiscence, "The close proximity of these two gangs caused constant friction and bloody fights were numerous." When rumors spread that the Germans planned to "exterminate" the often unruly Irish, the latter immediately responded by gathering up their picks, shovels and shillelaghs and organizing an attack on the former's camp. This anticipated violence so alarmed residents of Decatur, a county-seat community of 1,500, that about twenty-five of them hurriedly armed themselves with "rusty muskets taken from the courthouse" and intervened. Although this show of force averted bloodshed, some arrests for disorderly conduct followed, and tensions remained high, especially after the Irish workers "got full of bad whisky." Once the Stevens Creeks project ended, most of the Germans dispersed, although some of the sons of the Emerald Isle remained in the Decatur area to work for the railroad.[41]

After the line opened, the Great Western moved quickly to serve one of the potentially richest agricultural sections of the Mid-

west. The carrier built a variety of railroad structures, warehouses and commercial sidings. The anticipated increase in business led to additions to its fleet of steam locomotives, most of which came from Rogers, Ketchum & Grosvenor, and expansion and upgrading of its freight and passenger equipment. In 1854, for example, the company acquired "four passenger, two mail and baggage, and ninety-four freight cars."[42]

Although these betterments were needed, business and revenues soon slipped unexpectedly. Several bad crop years in central Illinois and, most of all, the hard times that immediately followed the Panic of 1857, which were particularly severe in the state, promoted a reorganization, creating what officially became known as the "Great Western Rail Road of 1859." Once again the gyrations of agriculture and the business cycle negatively affected one of the embryo companies destined to become a core unit of the Wabash Railroad Company.[43]

Operations of the second Great Western largely resembled the first. The scope of service was nearly identical, although, as in the past, lack of traffic at times reduced freight-train movements just as business expansion promoted new regularly "time-carded" or "extra" trains. From its operating headquarters in Springfield, the road typically dispatched three trains daily except Sunday in each direction between State Line (7.2 miles east of Danville) and Springfield; they consisted of a "Mail & Express," a "Mixed" and a "Freight." One fewer train, a freight, operated between Springfield and Meredosia and Naples. Speeds for the passenger train averaged twenty miles per hour, somewhat faster than other movements.[44]

Yet some important changes occurred. These involved bridging the Illinois River at Meredosia in 1860, making it possible to interchange with the independent Quincy & Toledo Railroad (Q&T), which three years earlier had opened a thirty-three-mile route westward from the Illinois River to Camp Point, Illinois. Later, the Great Western gained trackage rights over the Q&T and leased the Illinois & Southern Iowa Rail Road (I&SI), which in 1863 completed its thirty-mile line northwestward from Clayton to Carthage. These relationships allowed penetration of more developing agricultural lands in western Illinois and a strategic interchange at Camp Point with the Northern Cross *Rail Road* (a component of the evolving Chicago, Burlington & Quincy Railroad), which gave access to Quincy and the considerable commerce of the Mississippi River. The Quincy connection also allowed the Great Western to reach by ferry the recently opened Hannibal & St. Joseph (H&StJ), permitting a direct rail linkage to the Missouri River and western overland wagon trains at St. Joseph, Missouri.[45]

For the six years of its corporate life, the Great Western Rail Road of 1859 performed relatively well financially. In its first annual report, the corporate secretary listed net earnings of $104,375.58, although this amount was insufficient to pay interest on its bonds *and* a "reasonable" dividend on its stock. Despite the company's limited financial resources, the tone of this document was correctly optimistic: "The road traverses one of the most fertile sections of the state—much of the land, even in its immediate vicinity, is yet unsettled—we may therefore reasonably expect . . . a corresponding increase of local traffic, and when . . . the lines between our western terminus and the Hannibal and St. Joseph shall have been finished, we shall undoubtedly secure a fair share of thorough business." Fortunately for debt and equity owners local business improved and the strategic H&StJ connection became operable. Also, during the Civil War years both on-line and interline freight and passenger traffic generated additional income.[46]

Shortly after cessation of hostilities between the North and South, the Great Western Rail Road of 1859 participated in one of America's first great railroad mergers. This union created the 522-mile Toledo, Wabash & Western Railway Company (TW&W), forming a direct, through line between Toledo, Ohio, and the Mississippi River.

TOLEDO, WABASH & WESTERN

Although the State of Illinois had owned the ill-fated Northern Cross Railroad that led to its more successful private successor roads, the companies that in 1865 merged with the Great Western lacked any heritage of public sponsorship. In the early 1850s the principal components of what became the eastern portion of the TW&W emerged. On August 31, 1852, the Lake Erie, Wabash & St. Louis Railroad (LEW&StL) won incorporation in Indiana. The following year saw the organization of the Toledo & Illinois Railroad (T&I) in Ohio. Although both carriers had separate officials and directors, they were interconnected or "associated," sharing the same objective of uniting Toledo, "being the most important port on [Lake Erie] west of Buffalo," with the Great Western and connecting "at some point near the eastern limits of Illinois, to be mutually agreed upon" with the Terre Haute & Alton Railroad to gain access to St. Louis. Their backers fully grasped the prime location of their projected route: "*Nature* has marked the Wabash Valley as the *best route* of a great commercial thoroughfare (by Rail Road) from the cities of Boston and New York to St. Louis." Specifically, the T&I would build the seventy-four miles of line largely through the Maumee River valley in Ohio, and the LEW&StL would construct the 241-mile segment mostly along the Wabash River in Indiana. Between Toledo and Lafayette, Indiana, this route would generally parallel the busiest

Early in the development of American railroads, companies often did not issue a printed schedule for public consumption. Most carriers, however, did produce "For the Government and Information of Employees Only" timetables, or what became known as employee or operating schedules. Besides a schedule for freight and passenger trains, these publications included various rules, critical for operating safety. (Author's Coll.)

NOTE.—Read Special Rules—changes have been made.

GREAT WESTERN RAIL ROAD.

TIME TABLE NO. 17.

For the Government and Information of Employees only.

To take effect on Sunday, November 3rd, 1861, at Noon.

No Train will be allowed to leave a Station before its time as per this Table.

GOING WEST.

STATIONS.	Total Distance from State Line	†No. 1. MIXED.	†No. 2. MIXED.	†No. 3. Freight.	†No. 4. Mail & Express.
STATE LINE		4.00 A.M		6.45 A.M.	12.40 P.M.
Danville	7.2	4.32 "		7.21 "	1.00 "
Bryant	9.8	4.45 "		7.35 "	1.07 "
Catlin	13.2	5.08 "		7.54 "	1.15 "
Fairmount	26.1	5.30 "		8.30 "	1.36 "
Homer	24.8	6.00 "		9.05 "	1.55 "
Sidney	32.9	6.26 "		9.35 "	2.15 "
Philo	37.5	6.50 "		10.00 "	2.25 "
TOLONO	43.2	7.15 " ar / 7.30 " lv		10.30 " ar 11.00 " lv	2.40 "
Sadorus	47.7	7.52 "		11.25 "	2.55 "
Ivesdale	53.9	8.17 "		11.58 "	3.11 "
Bement	66.1	8.45 "		12.30 P.M. ar 1.00 " lv	3.29 "
Cerro Gordo	68.8	9.25 "		1.45 "	3.52 "
Oakley	73.9	9.42 "		2.09 "	4.04 "
Sangamo	75.6	9.52 "		2.21 "	4.11 "
DECATUR	80.6	10.15 " / 10.25 " lv		7.50 " ar 3.10 " lv	4.26 "
Wyckles	83.3	10.55 "		3.56 "	4.39 "
Harristown	88.1	11.05 "		3.56 "	4.46 "
Niantic	92.5	11.25 "		4.15 "	4.58 "
Illiopolis	96.5	11.40 "		4.38 "	5.10 "
Lanesville	102.2	12.02 P.M.		5.10 "	5.26 "
Mechanicsburg	105.3	12.16 "		5.25 "	5.35 "
Dawson	108.2	12.26 "	12.45	5.42 "	5.42 "
Jamestown	112.5	12.45		6.00 "	5.55 "
SPRINGFIELD	119.5	1.15 "		1.30 P.M.	6.15 " ar 6.20 " lv / 6.39 P.M.
St. L. A. & C. Junc.	121.5			1.44 "	6.25 "
Sanger	125.5			2.09 "	6.40 "
Curran	128.4			2.15 "	6.50 "
Bates	132.5			2.35 "	7.00 "
Berlin	135.9			2.51 "	7.10 "
Island Grove	138.9			3.05 "	7.20 "
Alexander's	142.5			3.23 "	7.30 "
Orleans	144.5			3.35 "	7.33 "
JACKSONVILLE	153.0			4.15 " ar 4.30 " lv	8.00 "
Jones' Switch	159.5			5.00 "	8.22 "
Chapin	163.3			5.26 "	8.32 "
Morgan City	164.8			5.35 "	8.41 "
Neely's	167.9			5.52 "	8.51 "
Van Gundy's	169.9			6.05 "	8.58 "
Naples	174.7			6.39 P.M.	9.20 "
Meredosia	176.9				9.25 P.M.

GOING EAST.

STATIONS.	Distances between Stations	No. 5. Mail & Express.	No. 6. Freight.	†No. 7. MIXED.	†No. 8. MIXED.
STATE LINE		3.50 A.M.	5.35 P.M.		10.20 P.M
Danville	7.2	3.10 "	4.55 "		9.50 "
Bryant	2.6	3.02 "	4.36 "		9.35 "
Catlin	3.3	2.52 "	4.15 "		9.20 "
Fairmount	6.9	2.34 "	3.35 "		8.45 "
Homer	6.7	2.14 "	2.50 "		8.10 "
Sidney	6.1	1.56 "	2.15 "		7.35 "
Philo	4.6	1.41 "	1.45 "		7.11 "
TOLONO	5.7	1.28 "	1.10 " lv 12.45 " ar		6.42 "
Sadorus	4.5	1.12 "	12.21 a.m.		6.15 "
Ivesdale	6.2	12.55 "	11.58 "		5.45 "
Bement	6.2	12.36 "	11.30 " lv 11.00 " ar		5.16 "
Cerro Gordo	2.7	12.11 A.M.	10.05 "		4.25 "
Oakley	4.1	12.00 "	9.42 "		4.04 "
Sangamo	2.7	11.51 "	9.30 "		3.50 "
DECATUR	5.0	11.36 "	9.00 " lv 8.40 " ar		3.20 " lv 3.10 " ar
Wyckles	4.6	11.25 "	8.15 "		2.48 "
Harristown	2.9	11.18 "	8.01 "		2.33 "
Niantic	4.4	11.05 "	7.40 "		2.16 "
Illiopolis	4.	10.52 "	7.21 "		1.?? "
Lanesville	5.7	10.35 "	6.56 "		1.? "
Mechanicsburg	3.1	10.26 "	6.40 "		1.20 "
Dawson	2.9	10.19 "	6.25 "		1.06 "
Jamestown	4.3	10.05 "	6.05 "	12.45	12.45 "
SPRINGFIELD	7.	9.45 " lv 9.40 " ar	5.30 A.M	11.55 A.M	12.15 P.M
St. L. A. & C. Junc.	2.	9.30 "			11.45 "
Sanger	4.	9.20 "			11.26 "
Curran	2.9	9.11 "			11.11 "
Bates	4.1	9.00 "			10.51 "
Berlin	3.4	8.50 "			10.35 "
Island Grove	2.6	8.42 "			10.21 "
Alexander's	4.	8.32 "			10.04 "
Orleans	2.3	8.25 "			9.59 "
JACKSONVILLE	8.2	8.00 "			9.10 " lv 8.60 " ar
Jones' Switch	6.5	7.46 "			8.15 "
Chapin	3.8	7.28 "			7.52 "
Morgan City	1.5	7.22 "			7.44 "
Neely's	3.1	7.12 "			7.26 "
Van Gundy's	2.	7.06 "			7.11 "
Naples	4.5	6.45 "			6.45 A M
Meredosia	7.	6.45 P.M.			6.45 A M

The FULL FACE figures denote meeting and passing Stations.

SPECIAL RULES

Mr. C. H. Speed, at Springfield, is authorized to run trains by telegraph, and all engineers and conductors will report themselves at every telegraph station before leaving.

Philo, Ivesdale, Sangamo, Wyckles, Harristown, Lanesville, Sanger, Curran, Island Grove, and Jones' Switch, are flag Stations, at which Nos. 4 & 5 must stop when signaled, and Agents must be careful and give the proper signal in time; same with Nos. 1 and 8.

Mixed Trains will be entitled to the road over Freight Trains, but will keep out of the way of Passenger Trains.

Nos. 1 and 8 will stop only on signal for passengers at Bryant, Fairmount, Sidney, Philo, Ivesdale, Sangamo, Wyckles, Harristown and Lanesville.

The speed of all Trains must not exceed six miles per hour, across Vermillion and Sangamon Bridges.

The dampers of the ash pan must be closed when crossing all bridges, and all bridges must be crossed at a speed not exceeding 6 miles an hour. *The speed through towns must not exceed six miles an hour,* and through Springfield and Decatur, *five miles per hour.*

The clock in the Depot, at Springfield, will be taken as the standard time. Conductors and Engineers will compare their watches daily.

†Daily, Sunday excepted. No. 5 Daily, but will run to Springfield on Saturday, and leave there on Sunday night.

A. HARDY, Train Master.   **F. W. BOWEN, Sup't.**

section of the 468-mile Wabash & Erie Canal, considered to be one of the supreme follies of the "canal mania" that swept the Old Northwest in the 1830s.[47]

The leaders of the LEW&StL and T&I railroads resembled their counterparts on the Great Western; they were mostly local bankers, merchants and professionals. The head of the LEW&StL, Albert White, hailed from Lafayette and his counterpart on the T&I, William Barker, resided in Toledo. The directors of the T&I were nearly all local entrepreneurs from Toledo; however, those on the LEW&StL were somewhat more geographically diverse. Several lived in the Empire State, the most prominent being Troy resident Russell Sage, who later had an extensive career in railroad development, especially with Midwestern carriers, and became a longtime friend and business associate of railroad builder and organizer Jay Gould.[48]

Construction of the LEW&StL and T&I proceeded with dispatch. In early 1854, the companies reported that "maps, profiles, plans, drawings and specifications of the Road, bridges, &c., &c., have been made and filed. Rights of way, with inconsiderable exceptions, have been obtained along the whole route, and station and machine grounds have been secured at all the principal points, including most valuable grounds at Toledo."[49]

Typical of so many railroad-building projects of the era, the LEW&StL and T&I relied on local financial support. As early as June 23, 1852, railroad supporters gathered for a "Rail Road Convention" in Logansport, Indiana, where they discussed matters of finance, leading to units of government and individuals investing liberally in the trans-Indiana line. It was common for a county or township to subscribe to company stock and occasionally to invest in corporate bonds. Also, property owners frequently made donations and concessions for rights-of-way,

station grounds and the like, all designed to make certain that their community captured the iron horse. Again, the logic was clear and sound: "Rapid development of a new country is only possible through a system of railroads, affording speedy, regular, safe and economical transportation."[50]

Contractors, subcontractors and their employees, a combination of area residents and itinerant Irish laborers, encountered few major difficulties. They had to slice through some densely wooded areas along the Maumee River and build through several miles of wetlands west of Fort Wayne. Also, during the summer of 1854, scores of workers contracted "Asiatic Cholera," causing some deaths. The most challenging grading occurred along scattered portions of the central and western sections of the LEW&StL, most notably a series of rock cuts in the vicinity of Logansport. Yet the line featured "remarkably even grades and easy curves." Several important and "expensive" bridges were required, but none demanded special engineering or heroic construction efforts. Track gangs, who installed iron "T"-rail, moved swiftly after completion of the roadway and bridges. The section between Toledo and Fort Wayne, a distance of ninety-four miles, opened for revenue service on August 1, 1855, and by the end of January 1856, residents of Wabash, Indiana, 136 miles from Toledo, heard the screeching whistle of the locomotive. On June 18, 1856, the first train steamed into Lafayette, signaling for 203 miles of completed line. By August 1 crews had spiked down an additional thirty-nine miles of rail to forge the connection at the Illinois border with the Great Western. Crowed the LEW&StL-T&I, "The whole work has been done in the most perfect and permanent manner, so as to make it in all respects a first class Road."[51]

Even before the first work train reached the Great Western at State Line, leaders of the companion LEW&StL-T&I roads had decided to merge officially. Because the companies had common financial ownership (occasionally referred to as the "Toledo Associates"), it made little corporate sense to remain separate. For all practical purposes, the T&I functioned as the "eastern division," while the LEW&StL served as the "western division." A moving force behind this adroit union was a major investor, Azariah Boody. Educated in the common schools of Massachusetts, he lived for several years in Rochester, New York, where he engaged in farming and served briefly as a Whig member of the U.S. Congress before relocating to New York City to "engage in the construc-

tion of railroads, canals, and bridges." Much to Boody's satisfaction, on September 23, 1856, the "great consolidation" took place without difficulty. The new 242-mile carrier sported an appropriately descriptive corporate name, the Toledo, Wabash & Western Rail Road Company.[52]

Almost immediately the TW&W generated a respectable freight and passenger business. Former canal towns became railroad towns as the carrier developed its presence in Fort Wayne, the largest on-line community, Peru, Logansport and Lafayette. Rapidly the TW&W sapped traffic from the dying Wabash & Erie Canal, an occurrence that may have saddened some Hoosier residents.

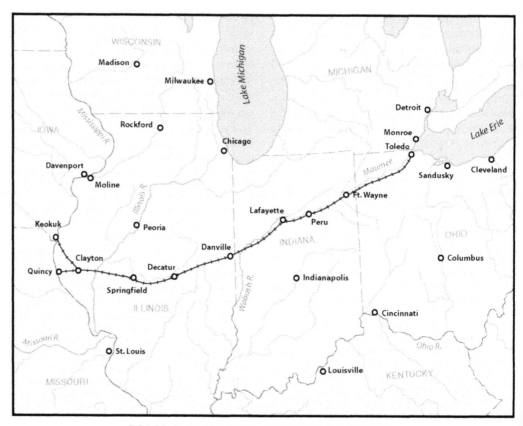

TOLEDO, WABASH & WESTERN RAILROAD

After all, Indiana lawmakers had opted for the canal over the railroad for egalitarian reasons: any person could own or use a canal boat, but only a private corporation could operate a train. Not only did the TW&W take away canal business, but its presence also stimulated more traffic. Management, therefore, had good reason to be strongly optimistic: "The Toledo, Wabash and Western Railroad is destined to do a business, which can find its limit only in the carrying capacity of the Road." Though this assertion contained much truth, the devastating Panic of 1857 forced a swift and "friendly" reorganization. A shuffling of charters ensued, with the original T&I briefly becoming the Toledo & Wabash Railroad Company of *Ohio* with the LEW&StL portion assuming the corporate name of the Wabash & Western Railway Company of *Indiana*. Shortly, thereafter, on October 8, 1858, a combined corporation emerged, the Toledo & Western Rail Road Company (T&W).[53]

The T&W prospered. Business grew appreciably, spurred on by better economic times, an increasing regional population, improved rail connections and the outbreak of the Civil War. Train movements were more frequent than on the former TW&W, which had only single daily-except-Sunday freight and passenger runs. At times several T&W freight trains traveled daily over the line, and at least two passenger trains paid daily calls at its thirty-nine stations in Indiana and Ohio. By the early 1860s, rolling stock had increased to handle traffic demands; at the end of 1861 the road owned thirty-five American-type locomotives, twenty-eight mail, baggage and passenger cars and 654 pieces of freight equipment.[54]

In the spring of 1861 armed conflict brought more than an increase in business to support federal troops and such betterments as improved port facilities in Toledo. War helped to alter permanently earlier patterns of interregional trade. Before completion of the Erie Canal in October 1825, and the hundreds of miles of "ditches" that subsequently laced Ohio, Indiana and Illinois, agriculturalists and other shippers in the Old Northwest typically used the Ohio and Mississippi rivers to reach the deep-water outlet at New Orleans. Although canals made for a more direct flow of goods on an east-west axis via the Great Lakes, the conflict, which for several years closed the lower Mississippi to boat traffic, led to railroads largely superseding both river and canal transport. "The [T&W] performed outstanding service to our country in providing a quick, efficient route for the transportation of much-needed food for the armies from the central West to the East," observed one writer in the 1950s. Once Union forces reopened the Mississippi to trade from the Old Northwest, shippers frequently failed to revert to their prewar ways of transport. Wheat, corn, livestock and other products of thousands of farmers continued to travel the "Wabash Valley Line."[55]

The merger in June 1865 of the Toledo & Wabash with the Great Western forming the *second* Toledo, Wabash & Western *Railway* (rather than *Rail Road*) involved additional properties. Two western Illinois shortlines participated, the Q&T and the I&SI, both of which had had close corporate ties with the Great Western (see page 15). The latter road had recently built a few miles from its northern terminus at Carthage to a connection with the Toledo, Peoria & Warsaw Railroad at Elvaston, Illinois, that gave access to Hamilton (East Keokuk), eleven miles away, on the Mississippi River. Ferry service and later a bridge at Hamilton made possible a link to Keokuk, Iowa. This bustling Hawkeye State city, situated near the confluence of the Des Moines and Mississippi rivers, had become headquarters of the Des Moines Valley Rail Road (née Keokuk, Fort Des Moines & Minnesota Rail Road). Its iron rails stretched northwestward, reaching the Iowa capital, Des Moines, in August 1865, 162 miles away.[56]

The *new* TW&W seemed to impressed everyone. "We venture to say that [the merger] is not equaled in importance by any similar movement in the Western States," editorialized the *American Railway Times,* a leading trade publication. "Opening a direct unbroken line from the most Western point on Lake Erie to the Mississippi, a distance of *four hundred and eighty-nine miles,* of uniform [standard] gauge and without change of cars, it furnishes for business between those waters far superior to any other route, and presents the longest continuous line of Railroad under one management in the United States."[57]

By operating from northwestern Ohio through Indiana and Illinois, the TW&W took advantage of strategic interchange points, which had grown more numerous since the first trains traversed Great Western and LEW&StL-T&I rails. Connections with the IC at Decatur and Tolono remained especially important, but the one with the Chicago, Alton & St. Louis Railroad (Alton) at Springfield emerged as perhaps the most vital. The Alton link provided the best route from Lake Erie and Toledo to reach Mississippi River commerce and the developing market and rail gateway of St. Louis.[58]

Dependence on railroads by a growing population in the Midwest remained nearly universal; public roads continued to be deplorable. "Chief drawbacks are the bad roads," observed a Dutch traveler who visited central Illinois in 1866. "Roads are difficult to improve." The lack of alterative transportation (except along enhanced waterways) filled TW&W coffers by expanding local and bridge traffic. At the company's annual meeting, held on October 2, 1867, at corporate headquarters in Toledo, shareholders were content, confident of ever better future performances. "The reports and exhibits

of accounts presented to the meeting, showing the condition of the finances of the company, and also a history of the operations of the road in its several departments for the past year, were regarded by the stockholders as being highly favorable and indicative of marked success and prosperity," reported the *Toledo Commercial.* "The stockholders have the gratification of finding that the business and revenues of the road have been constantly and steadily increasing over that of any preceding year." Black ink flowed. The gross income for calendar year 1868, for example, reached $4,013,207, or $203,854 more than the previous year, and net income totaled $1,123,588, an improvement of $101,117 over 1867. Yet these figures could have been more impressive if rate wars had not erupted. "The prevalence of a most vicious competition at all principal cities at the East during a large portion of the year, for the through traffic, and carried to an extent as to involve a positive loss upon the business done, has seriously depressed the aggregate earnings of our own line, and I dare say it has that of all others," observed the astute president Boody, a man who continued to shape the road. "It is to be much regretted that harmony and community of interest between the various lines, furnishing outlets to common points or markets, cannot be more permanently established in these matters, so that these frequent and disastrous conflicts for business might be avoided." This was not to be.[59]

With adequate operating income and no floating debt, the TW&W attempted to keep up with modern railroad technology. In the late 1860s it expanded its fleet of motive power, acquiring in 1869 "first-class" locomotives. Five of these American types came from the Schenectady Locomotive Works and five from the Pittsburg Locomotive Works. These state-of-the-art engines burned soft coal rather than cord wood. At the time of their purchase, workers in the company's machine shops in Fort Wayne, Springfield and Toledo were busily adapting the remaining wood-fired locomotives to coal. "We have converted a large number of engines from wood-burners into coal-burners," reported management in early 1870, "so that from our present equipment of 115 engines, 81 are now consuming coal." This fuel was readily available, including from mines in the Danville area, and was more convenient and less expensive to use than wood. And, of course, the newest locomotives burned coal.[60]

While TW&W track crews laid heavier replacement iron rails, they also began to install rails made of steel on some track. In 1869, workers spiked down four and a half miles of these thirty-foot sections on the mainline as part of the company's commitment to steel. A few years later, the road bought from a French manufacturer steel for much of the mainline. At the time, few railroads used steel rails, largely because they were expensive and somewhat experimental. The first Bessemer steel plant, located in Sheffield, England, did not open until 1860, and the cost of shipping and tariff duties after 1862 limited sales to American railroads. In the United States by the late 1860s, steel rails accounted for only about 1 percent of total rail production. As the weight and speed of locomotives increased and heavier loads were carried in larger cars, however, enormous wear on the iron "T"-rails, especially on curves, made rail "failure" a common occurrence. Steel rails held considerable promise, and the TW&W was willing to pioneer in the use of this replacement metal.[61]

A healthy ledger, a modern plant and a promising future placed the TW&W leadership in an expansive mood. Through construction and lease arrangements, the company increased its mileage considerably. Without question, the most important addition to its "system" took place in August

1870, with acquisition of the newly finished Decatur & East St. Louis Rail Road Company (D&EStL). Although not strongly displeased with the Alton connection in Springfield, TW&W officials recognized the importance of the rising St. Louis as a rail center and considered it vital to have their own route there. In 1869 and 1870, the D&EStL built a well-engineered and well-constructed 109-mile northeast-to-southwest "air-line" route that connected the cities in its corporate name and provided entry into St. Louis, where it could serve both local and interchange traffic. Because of "the gentle lay of the country," building costs were "comparatively light." Incorporated in early 1867, the D&EStL had always been in the orbit of the TW&W; backers of the former had agreed to purchase the latter as soon as it opened. The arrangement worked out well, for with the D&EStL in hand, the TW&W no longer needed to dispatch traffic destined for St. Louis via the Alton, ending tenant status that at times delayed train movements. Also, the TW&W could serve local patrons, including those in Edwardsville, Litchfield and Taylorville, who lived in a "country thickly settled, thoroughly cultivated, and regarded as the richest and most productive in the State of Illinois." Regular passenger service into the St. Louis gateway began on October 3, 1870. The road's day trains between St. Louis and Toledo carried "new and elegant passenger coaches," and its night trains featured "the much celebrated and popular Pullman and Gates and Wagner lines of palace sleeping coaches." Moreover, the TW&W could rightly boast that it was the only St. Louis road that reached the Great Lakes east of Chicago.[62]

The newly opened D&EStL benefited, too, from a short feeder, the Madison County Railroad (MC). This approximately ten-mile-long road had its origins in one of the first railroad projects in Illinois, the Mount

Carmel & Alton Rail Road, launched in January 1836. Only a portion of the grading between the communities of its name ever occurred. Then after the Civil War the property became the MC. Within two years, it succeeded in opening. "The last rail was put in place yesterday [February 5, 1868]," announced the *Edwardsville Intelligencer,* "and the locomotive came in amongst us with a very becoming and graceful gait." In August 1877 this Edwardsville–to–Edwardsville Crossing pike formally entered the Wabash system.[63]

About the time the TW&W took control of the D&EStL, it leased the fifty-two-mile Hannibal & Naples Railroad (H&N). This action gave the TW&W still another connection with the Mississippi River and rail lines in the trans-Mississippi West. Unlike the D&EStL, the smaller H&N had a long, hardscrabble past. In February 1857 civic-minded residents of Pike County, Illinois, and Hannibal, Missouri, won incorporation from the state of Illinois for the aptly named Pike County Rail Road, designed to cross the county, linking the Mississippi River, opposite Hannibal, with the Great Western Railroad at Naples. "We are anxious to build the Pike County Rail road," noted its sponsors, "and we are willing to make any contract or arrangement with the Great Western Rail road Company that will enable us to do so with such means as we can raise along the line of the road and in Hannibal." When built, the H&N would establish an important route between Hannibal and the Father of Waters and Eastern markets. Even though the regional economy was depressed, by 1861 approximately $350,000 had been subscribed to the road's common stock, including $200,000 from the City of Hannibal and $70,000 from the townships along the projected line. From its inception until being sold at a sheriff's sale on May 18, 1865, this venture struggled mightily to become more

than a paper road. Considerable grading and bridge work took place, but efforts to complete the roadbed and to lay rail failed. A shortage of resources and the outbreak of hostilities stymied the project. Not long after peace returned, however, a revitalized H&N sought to finish the job. At first funding proved inadequate, but Hannibal officials agreed to purchase $150,000 of H&N stock if Pike County would acquire an equivalent amount. After delays and considerable political maneuvering, approval came from Pike County voters at a special election held on Christmas Eve, 1867. Pike Countians also endorsed funds for a six-mile stub from Maysville, thirteen miles west of Naples, to Pittsfield. Although incorporated as the Louisiana & Pike County Railroad, the H&N took control of this appendage through a long-term lease agreement. Delays in awarding the construction contract meant that actual building could not begin until late November 1869. At last the road, including the Pittsfield line, was finished, and on February 11, 1870, the first excursion train made its way over an often hill-and-dale profile.[64]

At the November 1871 stockholders meeting, the TW&W officially agreed to enter into several expensive, additional long-term leases. Altogether, they produced another 254 miles of line and involved four carriers. The reasoning for expansion was clear: "The primary object in securing possession of these new roads was to attract to our own line a large and increased share of the growing business of new and productive sections of country lying immediately west of us," announced the company. "And secondarily to anticipate rival lines in the occupation of territory naturally tributary to our own road, and thus prevent the diversion of an important traffic, which if left untrammeled would inevitably seek the advantages of our own shorter and more eligible route." The TW&W was hardly alone in attempting to protect its territory and hence its balance sheets. Scores of emerging regional and interregional systems during the Gilded Age were doing the same.[65]

East of the Mississippi River the TW&W leased three recently completed roads: Pekin, Lincoln & Decatur Railroad (PL&D), Lafayette, Muncie & Bloomington Railroad (LM&B) and Lafayette, Bloomington & Mississippi Railroad (LB&M). The first of these, the PL&D, spanned the sixty-seven miles from the TW&W at Decatur in a northwesterly direction to the central Illinois towns of Lincoln and Pekin. This allowed the company to serve more than a half-dozen thriving communities in a fertile agricultural region and to gain access to several key carriers, mostly through connections at Pekin. The two other roads, the thirty-six-mile LM&B and the eighty-mile LB&M, jointly formed a new east-west route between the TW&W at Lafayette and Bloomington, Illinois, via such Illinois towns as Gibson, Paxton and Hoopeston. Like the PL&D, the LM&B-LB&M traversed productive agricultural lands and offered additional interchange opportunities. The TW&W anticipated that all of these properties, especially the latter two, would send large quantities of grain to Toledo for lake shipments to the East, especially to mills in Buffalo and Rochester. And it was hinted that the LM&B-LB&M would in time operate an even greater mileage, ultimately stretching from Muncie, Indiana, to the Mississippi River at Keokuk.[66]

Part of this leasing binge included short-term control of a railroad *west* of the Mississippi River. What the TW&W acquired in this case was the seventy-mile Hannibal & Central Missouri Railroad (H&CM). Although the H&CM was about to stretch westward from Hannibal to Moberly, in north-central Missouri, its promoters anticipated additional construction, likely to

Kansas City along the southern bank of the Missouri River. But even a truncated H&CM gave the TW&W access at Moberly with the North Missouri Railroad (soon the St. Louis, Kansas City & Northern Railroad) and valuable admittance to the Show-Me State and regions beyond, especially north and west. The TW&W held high hopes for the H&CM and its connecting carriers. Large quantities of grain, for example, were expected to travel to Toledo, or at least to connecting points along the TW&W, just as a plethora of merchandise would move from Eastern to Midwestern or even Western destinations, all made possible by a competitive TW&W–H&N–H&CM route. This iron road became ever more attractive in 1872, when the Hannibal Bridge Company finished its span over the Mississippi River at Aladdin, Illinois, providing a direct connection with the H&N. Unexpected contractual problems, however, developed with the H&CM lease, and the agreement was terminated. In 1873 its owners sold their line to the Missouri, Kansas & Texas Railway ("Katy"), although in the twentieth century the Wabash would recapture this strategic trackage.[67]

As the 1870s took shape, indicators looked encouraging for the TW&W. The *Railroad Gazette,* for one, thought highly of the property. "[F]ew, if any, of the Western railways have, in all human probability, a brighter prospect of financial success than the Toledo, Wabash & Western Railway," observed the publication in June 1870. "And that experience would vindicate the policy which, in 1865, consolidated several lines, naturally and geographically indivisible, into one powerful organization, operating, inclusive of branches, upwards of 520 miles of road." Furthermore, close corporate ties with the Lake Shore & Michigan Southern Railroad (LS&MS) and the New York Central & Hudson River Railroad (NYC&HR) spurred interchange traffic. The TW&W balance sheets benefited from its association with these powerful "Vanderbilt roads."[68]

A brisk business with the Vanderbilt roads was not all that promised a rosy future. Although the H&CM agreement proved temporary, the TW&W still benefited from its direct connection with this new Katy property. The company hoped that its other leased lines would pay for themselves and would protect an extensive, albeit vulnerable, service territory from unwanted competition. The core road seemed as busy as could be expected. "During the past week ending November 14 [1874], this railroad did a heavier freight business than ever before," reported a contributor to the *Railroad Gazette*. "There were 1,158 cars which passed eastward through Danville, Ill., and on the 14th there were eleven freight trains . . . with 245 cars." Many of these freight cars contained grain destined for elevators in Toledo. In 1871 TW&W trains hauled more than 15 million bushels to that busy lake port. The flood of grain to Toledo led to severe storage problems, prompting the company in 1873–1874 to use its subsidiary Wabash Elevator Company to erect a facility with a capacity of 1.2 million bushels. Freight income soared from $2,364,225 in 1867 to $4,311,970 five years later.[69]

The passenger business, however, did not reflect the strong gains made in freight haulage. Revenues remained rather flat from the late 1860s into the early 1870s, with $1,162,764 received in 1872, or about $50,000 less than in 1867. Increased competition caused by the opening of competitive routes and "the superior facilities of rival roads" largely explain a disappointing income performance. Still, management ballyhooed its service, especially after acquisition of the D&EStL and entry into St. Louis: "The Shortest and Only Continuous Route between Lake Erie and the Mississippi." It did more than boast. The company upgraded

equipment and increased speeds. In 1871, for example, it added Pullman car service from St. Louis through Toledo to New York City, via the LS&MS and NYC&HR, and also a sleeper from Quincy to Toledo. In 1873 the TW&W introduced fast service between St. Louis and New York City: "This train runs from St. Louis to Toledo, 432 miles, in 13 hours and 50 minutes. The time through to New York is 38 hours." The previous schedule called for nineteen hours to Toledo and forty-eight hours to New York. A trip that averaged approximately thirty-three miles an hour, including stops, was "ballast scorching" for the day.[70]

Of course, during the early and mid-1870s the Toledo, Wabash & Western endured its share of troubles, disappointments, setbacks and even financial disaster. Fires commonly plagued carriers in the age of steam and wood, and the TW&W had its share of conflagrations. In May 1874, for example, flames engulfed the roundhouse at Springfield, and six months later a fire destroyed the small shop facilities at Clayton, Illinois, on the Keokuk branch. Fire of another type caused inconvenience along the mainline in eastern Indiana. "Sometimes I thought I would suffocate," recalled a veteran Wabash employee who in the early 1870s served as station agent at Roanoke. "The bogs across the prairie between Roanoke and what is now known as Prairie Switch [east of Fort Wayne] was on fire [because of drought] and burned holes six to eight feet deep in the ground, and was on fire or smoldering there for two or three years, making it very dangerous to operate trains." Nothing could be done about the smoke and haze caused by these low-temperature fires; eventually, though, a period of heavy rains doused this annoyance. Severe drought conditions, which began about 1870 and lasted for nearly four years along extended sections of the road, hurt agricultural production and forced the company to make "heavy" expenditures for additional wells, tanks and pumps, particularly in Illinois.[71]

The TW&W also felt the sting of "Granger" agitation. In the early years of the 1870s, the nationwide granger movement seized power in four states of the upper Mississippi River valley, Illinois, Iowa, Minnesota and Wisconsin. Members of the recently formed Patrons of Husbandry, a heretofore mostly social and scientific organization for farmers, supported by a coalition of commercial interests and working through the dominant Republican Party, sought to bring about tough controls over a largely unregulated railroad industry. These reform seekers focused on freight rates, especially those that made noncompetitive short-haul shipments usually more expensive than competitive long-haul ones. Grangers fervently believed that railroads must provide transportation that was inexpensive, convenient and predictable. As in adjoining states where Grangers gained political power, Illinois lawmakers "in the hectic atmosphere created by the farmers' uprising of the winter of 1872–73" passed in May 1873 their "granger codes." They were built upon an 1871 antidiscrimination rate act, which the state's 1870 reform constitution sanctioned, and significantly included creation of a "strong" regulatory agency. This Railroad and Warehouse Commission was designed to ensure that carriers adhered to the "public interest." Soon thereafter, the Illinois attorney general, working on behalf of the commission, successfully brought suit against the TW&W to recover $100,000 on rate overcharges and to force payment of $5,000 in damages. The company would have other unpleasant encounters with the legacy of this consumers' revolt.[72]

As the national and regional economies worsened as the Panic of 1873 ushered in a protracted business depression, TW&W earnings plummeted. The previous year's income stood at $6,000,978; by 1875 it had dropped to $3,948,816, a decrease of 34 percent. A continuation of intermittent rate wars and somewhat unreliable connections for interchange traffic at Toledo also contributed to the troubling economic picture.[73]

In the fall of 1874, management responded as best it could to save money. It consolidated·its five operating divisions into two, and "the principle of reduction of organization to a minimum carried into all departments, whilst purchases and all other expenditures were rigidly revised." On December 1, 1873, general officers took a 20 percent salary cut and all other employees received a similar reduction, scaled according to the amounts of salaries and wages.[74]

Although the TW&W reported publicly that slimming the payroll was received by "officers and employees in the best spirit," the reality was different. Operating and shop personnel howled. Not only did they sustain a sizable wage reduction, but for a three-month period during the summer of 1874 the company actually missed its payroll to shopmen. In October, most workers in the Toledo shops walked out, returning only after management agreed to pay one month's wages and to make "more payment hereafter." Yet the promises were not kept; by spring 1875, during the depths of the depression, the company owed at least four months' pay to most employees. In addition to vocal and written complaints flooding into corporate, divisional and supervisory offices, a few workers, in their anger and frustration, took to committing acts of corporate sabotage. One episode of violence involved attempts in May 1875 to derail a night express train at several places near Jacksonville, Illinois. "Three obstructions, each consisting of a tie cut out so as to fit over the rails and chained fast to the track with a heavy chain [were used]. Fortunately the night was not exceptionally dark, and in each case the obstruction was seen in time to stop the train without damage." Entry of the TW&W into bankruptcy in February 1875 calmed some employees, who expected that the court-appointed receiver would quickly honor all their claims. Others were not so certain.[75]

By early 1875, the optimism that company personnel, investors and the public once had in the TW&W had largely evaporated. Admittedly, the railroad was wonderfully situated and had the potential of becoming a stellar property. As Ossian D. Ashley, a TW&W director who chaired a stockholders protective committee, reminded fellow shareholders in 1876: "It may be safely assumed . . . from the extraordinary agricultural richness of the country tributary to this line of road, that . . . [it] can scarcely fail, from local business alone, to develop within a few years . . . a traffic large and profitable enough to pay interest upon its debt and satisfactory dividends upon its stock." Added Ashley, "But as a trunk line, connecting with all of the important thoroughfares running east and west, the Wabash is far more promising and valuable than is generally supposed, and it needs but judicious and intelligent direction to take rank with any trunk road in the United States."[76]

Why than did the TW&W fall into receivership? There is no mistake that the hard times triggered by the Panic of 1873 adversely affected the company's balance sheets. If the economy had remained healthy, the TW&W might never have sought court protection from its creditors. Recurring rate wars, poor cooperation from connecting roads in expediting interchange traffic, particularly from the Vanderbilt lines, and intermittent periods of drought and the resulting decrease in traffic collectively diminished income.

Management, though, was not blameless. The earlier leases for feeder and connecting roads came at too high a price. The TW&W faced an obligation to pay 7 percent interest on the bonded debt of each property. This annual bill totaled a whopping $3,942,000. "To control traffic," admitted one director, "very onerous contracts and leases were made." Yet he placed these expensive lease agreements in context. "Some of these errors were natural and incidental to a period of exaggerated public opinion, in regard to railway property, which led many persons of experience and sagacity astray, and cannot be fairly criticized without due consideration of the time during which, and the circumstances and conditions under which, they were committed."[77]

Not only did these leases prove burdensome during a time of crushing depression, but they may have come about for reasons other than solely for traffic protection. There can be no denying that management understandably worried about possible incursions by other roads into its home territory. During the Gilded Age and after, thousands of miles of rail line were constructed for reasons of economic self-preservation, a normal corporate response to the competitive challenges of the time. But some directors, and likely other top-ranking personnel in the Boody administration, were infected with a gambling mentality, so much a part of the 1870s. Speculators grew rich and binged on credit. "I wasn't worth two cents two years ago," remarks a character in *The Gilded Age,* the popular satirical novel by Mark Twain and Charles Dudley Warner. "Now I owe $2 million." Apparently capitalists used the high-priced leases to bolster gross traffic, which had a beneficial, albeit short-term impact on the price of their TW&W shares. "Its stock has been the football of speculation for a number of years," noted one financial authority. This feeder traffic was too costly, and funds spent on some or all of the leases could have been used for reduction of fixed costs and ongoing betterments.[78]

Whether the product of speculation or economic conditions, bankruptcy was real. Becoming "financially embarrassed" meant that the TW&W could not make a large interest payment that came due on February 1, 1875. As with other railroad bankruptcies, a judge named a receiver to keep the trains running and to supervise a reorganization. In the case of the TW&W the receiver was the distinguished lawyer, soldier and politician, Jacob Dolson Cox. A member of the Oberlin College class of 1850, Cox quickly became a prominent Ohio attorney. As soon as the Civil War began, however, he left his law practice to serve the Union as a brigadier general of the Ohio volunteers. Cox soldiered with distinction in several major campaigns, including the Battle of Antietam and Sherman's march to the sea. Following the war, he served one term as Republican governor of his home state and then as secretary of interior in the first U. S. Grant administration. But after only eighteen months, he resigned his cabinet post because he detested the political assessments levied upon federal employees and the rampant "spoils" practices, especially evident in his department. At the time of his selection as TW&W receiver, Cox resided in Toledo, where a few years earlier "this man of impeccable honesty and good business sense" had been elected to the TW&W presidency, following the resignation of Boody. During his tenure as receiver, Cox would win election to the House of Representatives as a Liberal (reform) Republican, and served a single term between 1877 and 1879.[79]

Bright, hardworking and scrupulously honest, General Cox brought about a fair and speedy reorganization. The final agreement, endorsed by investors, Cox and the court, extinguished both common and preferred stock amounting to $15 million, canceled the unprofitable leases of the PL&D, LM&B and LB&M railroads and ended interest on about $6 million of bonds. On June 10, 1876, the court-ordered sale of the TW&W, under Cox's supervision, took place in Toledo and laid the foundation for formation of the highly viable Wabash Railway Company. This successor carrier, a union on January 10, 1877, of the Wabash Railway Company of Illinois, Wabash Railway Company of Indiana and Wabash Railway Company of Ohio, prospered, with net earnings exceeding $1 million in 1877 and amounting to more than $1.5 million in 1878. These figures would have been even stronger had not persistent rate wars eroded revenues. Yet the Wabash Railway would operate for less than two years, becoming one of the two principal units that through merger with the St. Louis, Kansas City & Northern Railway Company created the Wabash, St. Louis & Pacific Railway Company. It would be this consolidated and well-positioned road that would be led by the foremost railroad leader of the Gilded Age, Jay Gould.[80]

The Wabash Emerges West of the Mississippi River

NORTH MISSOURI

The appearance of a predecessor firm to the Wabash Railroad west of the Mississippi River took somewhat longer than it did in the Old Northwest. It was past midcentury before the iron horse even arrived west of the Mississippi. On August 20, 1852, an excited crowd gathered at the St. Louis waterfront to watch dock hands unload from the steamboat *Tuscumbia* the twenty-two-ton locomotive *Pacific,* a product of the Taunton Locomotive Works in Massachusetts. Four months later, this archetypical American standard-type (4-4-0) locomotive made its maiden run over the newly installed five miles of broad-gauge (5′ 6″) iron rails of the Pacific Railroad Company (of Missouri) between downtown St. Louis and suburban Cheltenham, making this the first railroad operation in the state.[1]

While construction crews of the Pacific Railroad headed for Jefferson City and beyond, building the initial stem of the future Missouri Pacific Railway, and its promoters fantasized about a transcontinental line extending westward from St. Louis, the first segment of the Wabash in Missouri

A locomotive that served the earliest hauling needs of the North Missouri Rail Road was No. 19, originally known as the *Minnesota*. Built in 1852 by Swinburne & Smith, eight years later the North Missouri scrapped this broad-gauge 4-4-0. The *Minnesota* allegedly pulled the first train from St. Louis to St. Charles. (Author's Coll.)

appeared. On August 2, 1855, after nearly thirteen months of somewhat sporadic construction, the North Missouri Railroad Company opened nineteen miles of broad-gauge (5′ 6″) line between Second and North Market streets in St. Louis and a ferry landing on the Missouri River opposite St. Charles, the former state capital. Backers of this road hoped that in the foreseeable future it would reach the Iowa border, or even Minnesota. Now, with train service, residents of St. Charles happily found themselves twenty-one miles closer to St. Louis than by the circuitous Missouri-Mississippi water route.[2]

Even though residents of Illinois beat Missourians to the iron horse by nearly a decade and a half, there had been discussions earlier about the possibilities of railroads in Missouri. When it came to railroad promotion in the Midwest, the Mississippi River was hardly a fault line. As early as April 20, 1835, a gathering in St. Louis of representatives from eleven Missouri counties had contemplated internal improvement of various sorts, but most of all railroads. They knew that they could not continue to rely on steamboats and stagecoaches. River levels were unpredictable, and the waterways often froze over during the long and severe winters. Also, the state's deplorable network of roads permitted limited stagecoach service, with the only routes being from St. Louis to Jefferson City, St. Charles to Palmyra, Fulton to Fayette and Fayette to Independence. A growing and hardly unexpected sentiment for bringing the railroad to the state, aptly described as "speculative intoxication," led members of the General Assembly in Jefferson City, during the two-week period between January 23 and February 6, 1837, to grant articles of incorporation for seventeen railroads with an aggregate capital stock of nearly $8 million. But the subsequent severe and lengthy depression pre-vented these chartered dreams from immediately taking more tangible forms. Not until the economic picture brightened in the mid-1840s did it appear likely that railroads would become part of the Missouri landscape.[3]

During the formative period of railroading in Missouri, officials shunned direct public ownership and management. They did not wish to repeat the disasters that had happened elsewhere when states had entered the railroad business; there would be no money-losing Northern Cross embarrassment for them. Yet politicians knew that a growing Missouri, which by 1850 boasted a population of 682,044, nearly double the 1840 figure, needed railroads to enhance wealth and lessen the tyranny of distance. Because of the success of the Illinois & Michigan Canal and the Galena & Chicago Union Railroad and connecting rail projects, they feared that Chicago and cities beyond their borders might monopolize the expanding trade with the West. The state, and most of all St. Louis, could no longer expect prosperity to rest on the steamboat traffic of the Mississippi and Missouri rivers. Moreover, these elected officials realized that local promoters lacked capital of their own and found it difficult, if not impossible, to attract outside investment dollars.[4]

Missouri sought to promote railroad construction through attractive financial arrangements. Although the federal government provided a land grant to the Pacific Railroad (125,000 acres) and a much more valuable one to the developing Hannibal & St. Joseph Railroad (H&StJ) (611,323 acres), railroads still needed state assistance, as they had during the canal and early railroad era, especially for projects that failed to receive congressional largesse or to attract substantial capital from private investors. Missouri responded in a thoughtful way—namely, by "loaning" bonds to the most promising companies. The credit of the state was good, and these government obligations generally sold at par or above, certainly at higher levels than bonds issued by these infant carriers. To protect taxpayers, Missouri took a first lien on the railroad. In the several acts passed in the 1850s, bond authorizations exceeded $19 million, with $4.5 million earmarked for the North Missouri. Politicians could take satisfaction in knowing that by January 1859, their financial support had led to construction of 614 miles of line, including the soon-to-be completed transstate H&StJ between the river cities of its corporate name.[5]

The promoters of the evolving North Missouri creatively assembled a largely satisfactory financial package. In addition to the state bonds, they cobbled together funds from municipal and county bond sales and stock subscriptions from local governments and private investors. Various parcels of donated real estate "along the route, [and] at or near points where stations and depots have been located" also aided their efforts.[6]

The process of arranging financing had been ongoing for some time. At the North Missouri Railroad Convention, held in St. Charles on November 10, 1852, nearly two years after the railroad's official incorporation, matters such as routing and the wherewithal to make it possible were painstakingly discussed. Advocates needed to be in agreement about how the road, chartered to "pass up the divide between the tributaries of the Mississippi and Missouri river or as near as may be possible to the Iowa line" would be achieved. "Mixed" public and private financing, they believed, would enable them to accomplish their goal.[7]

Even before this assembly convened, proponents of the North Missouri, who hailed from nearby localities, especially St. Louis, considered it to be economically viable. Prospects for strong traffic patterns seemed assured. "The North Missouri road running near midway between the Missouri and Mississippi rivers, one of which is closed by ice from one to three months of the year, the other closed by ice and low water for five or six months of the year and of dangerous navigation the other six months;—we say the North Missouri road must take nearly all the business of the country lying between these rivers," exclaimed one diehard enthusiast. "This will be accomplished by plank and macadamized roads, combined with a judicious system of well located and permanently constructed branch railroads connecting the river and country towns with the central trunk road, which terminates at St. Louis, a great and growing market, and which will always be adequate to the purchase of all the surplus produce: fish, furs and peltries of the vast country from the mouth of the Missouri river to the Yellow Stone, and across to the Hudson's Bay." This backer surely assumed that everyone realized that the North Missouri would tap a fertile and well-watered agricultural area where producers lacked access to water transport and where public roads were often little more than unimproved trails.[8]

One matter that weighed heavily on the minds of representatives from St. Louis and St. Louis County involved protecting and developing their commercial livelihoods. And these sentiments would translate into substantial monetary commitments, ranging from nearly $1 million from private stock subscriptions to $1.75 million from the city and county of St. Louis. Not conceding that Chicago was "nature's metropolis" of the Midwest, St. Louisians sought to exploit their own community's economic power in the hinterlands, including the vast region to the north and west. Explained the *St. Louis Pilot:*

The efforts now being made at the North and East to divert from this State a large portion of our most valuable trade and to build up Chicago at the expense of St. Louis, should induce our people to co-operate to prevent this result. In order to counteract these efforts, the early completion of the North Missouri road is indispensably necessary, and if we are wise we will throw aside all local prejudices or preferences, and concentrate all our means (both State and individual) upon pushing on the road to the Iowa line. We say this not only in reference to St. Louis, but in reference to the interests of the whole State. It is true that the early completion of this road is vital to the interests of St. Louis, as it will secure to her a trade which is now in danger of being lost. But the whole State is no less interested in securing this trade, which otherwise will go to build up a rival city, inimical to our institutions and opposed to our interests. But in addition to this, the entire road passes through a rich agricultural district of the State which has no other outlet to a market for its surplus productions. The road, when completed, will have no river to compete with it in business, and will have the Hannibal and St. Joseph road as a feeder to it.[9]

Admittedly, Chicago benefited from a benign geography. By the late 1850s, the dozen or so railroads that entered or radiated out from the city encountered few natural barriers. Lake Michigan was simply skirted. More problems existed with marshlands near Chicago and the seasonal lakes and sloughs that dotted the nearby "Grand Prairie" region of Illinois and Indiana. But those who desired to ensure the economic prosperity for St. Louis and its environs and even the State of Missouri did not feel that physical hindrances would stymie their railroad building.[10]

At the time of the St. Charles meeting or in other discussions, there was little worry

expressed about the barrier of the mighty and occasionally erratic Missouri River. It was expected that initially a ferry would carry "broken" freight across the waterway with the expectation that later transfer boats would shuttle freight cars, thus ending the expensive and time-consuming need for unloading and reloading shipments and reducing breakage and theft. Indeed, this is what happened. For the time being, however, there were no plans for a bridge; the costs would be beyond the immediate range of the fledgling company. Fortunately for the North Missouri, once iron rails were laid beyond the "Big Muddy," there were no major rivers to cross, although some bridge and much culvert work would be required.[11]

Construction of the North Missouri moved slowly, but progress was for the most part steady. In August 1857, track reached Warrenton, fifty-eight miles from St. Louis, and in May 1858 it extended to Mexico, Missouri, 107 miles, and by December reached Allen (Randolph County), some 146 miles. Then in February 1859, construction crews arrived in Macon City (Macon), 172 miles from the road's eastern terminus, where they installed an interchange with the 206-mile H&StJ, a road that on February 13, 1859, celebrated the driving of its last spike. The only handicap with this beneficial connection involved a gauge gap; the H&StJ was built to standard width (4' 8 1/2"), whereas the gauge of the North Missouri rails was nine and a half inches wider. The use of a mechanical hoist to shift car bodies between tracks of the two gauges partially remedied the problem.[12]

Although the Panic of 1857 did not adversely affect railroad construction in Missouri as much as it did in the Old Northwest, it still had an impact, and the North Missouri was not immune from these hard times. "This Company has been compelled (owing to the want of funds) to reduce the forces on the Road," noted an official statement in 1858, "and the work has in consequence been greatly retarded." Individuals, most of all, who had subscribed to earlier stock were either slow or had stopped making their installment payments. Still, the North Missouri was taking shape, and the company optimistically proclaimed, "There is no reason to doubt that this Road when finished to the crossing of the Hannibal and St. Joseph Road will prove one of the best paying Roads in the West."[13]

Revenues from initial operations boded well for the company. From its opening in August until September 30, 1855, freight carried by the then nineteen-mile railroad produced a respectable income of $1,825.14, and passenger ticket sales generated $3,328.08. As rails pushed northwestward, income increased steadily. In late fall of 1857, a railroad trade journal indicated that "this road is already illustrating the wonderful developing properties of the iron track through a rich agricultural region." The report continued, "The number of hogs shipped at Florence, in Montgomery county, will be probably over five thousand. A few days ago, seventy-seven car loads were waiting at that point, the rolling stock of that road not being sufficient to take them away as fast as they arrived." The only serious obstacle, other than the economic downturn that came after the Panic of 1857, was crossing the Missouri River in winter. Unlike proponents of the North Missouri, in May 1857 an impartial outside professional maintained that "the falling off in the receipts during the winter months on the freight account, is owing to the obstruction of the Missouri river by ice. The want of a bridge across that river will always be a serious drawback to the earnings of that road."[14]

The early operations of the North Missouri resembled those of nearly all pioneer pikes in the Midwest. A single daily-except-Sunday freight and a daily passenger train usually served its stations. Additional movements occurred during the harvest season or when excursionists took to the rails. The motive power consisted of the ubiquitous wood-burning American-standard locomotive, ideally suited for both freight and passenger service. Duplicating practices on other roads of the antebellum era, North Missouri engines sported such names as *Audrain, Montgomery,* and *Warren* rather than numbers. (The company honored the counties that it served.) And an assortment of box, gondola and "platform" or flat cars, baggage and passenger coaches made up its revenue-generating rolling stock.[15]

The North Missouri busily installed the necessary support facilities. With finite resources, expenditures on structures and equipment were kept to minimal levels. For one thing, the company opted for simple wooden depots rather than erecting more expensive brick or stone structures. On the eve of the Civil War, the road "was not yet in a fully completed condition, being deficient in depot buildings, water stations, . . . and many other things." As with neighboring carriers, when net income climbed to acceptable levels, various betterments, usually of a "more permanent" nature, would then occur.[16]

The appearance of North Missouri freight and passenger trains did for the local economy what its supporters had expected. Optimism reigned, and local populations grew and often prospered. "We hazard nothing therefore in prophezing that when our . . . road is carried to completion," opined a company executive in 1861, "that we shall have advanced a thousand times more in numbers, importance and wealth, then we would without them." Macon City, seat of Macon County and until 1868 the northern terminus, graphically illustrates the positive impact the carrier had on a local economy.

"The completion of the North Missouri Railroad to Macon City caused the town to increase rapidly in population and business," noted the author of a county history in the 1880s. "There were not half houses enough for applicants, and rents were very high. The business men prospered to an extent not surpassed since the road [after the Civil War] was extended northward. Trade extended to Iowa, and our merchants and grocers had a wholesale trade that was large and profitable for a period of 10 years with Northern Missouri and Southern Iowa."[17]

Macon City remained the end of the line for nearly a decade because of the catastrophic disruptions caused by the Civil War. Unlike predecessor roads of the Wabash east of the Father of Waters, the North Missouri found itself in the midst of some of the most intense guerrilla fighting of the lengthy conflict. Virtually none of its 170-mile line was immune from damages wrought by bands of Confederate attackers. And there would be horrible human tragedies as well.[18]

On April 12, 1861, secessionists in Charleston, South Carolina, fired the first guns of what became a great national tragedy. The bloodless and confidence-building victory for the South at Fort Sumter prompted an immediate mobilization of federal troops by the Lincoln administration. The immediate outbreak of hostilities found a badly divided Missouri. While the St. Louis area largely remained loyal to the Union, counties to the south and further west, particularly those that comprised "Little Dixie" in the central part of the state, showed strong sympathies for the rebel cause. Moreover, the state's governor, Claiborne Jackson, stood unabashedly pro-Southern. The commander of the State Guard, General Sterling Price, shared similar views. The governor, in fact, issued an order for 50,000 men to join the State Guard and "resist invasion." Beyond that proclamation, he shocked many

when he demanded that the railroad network of Missouri be destroyed.[19]

Even before fighting erupted, officials of the North Missouri worried about the consequence of Governor Jackson's actions. The company did more than fret; it took direct action. President Isaac Sturgeon boarded a special train to urge citizens at stations between St. Charles and Macon City "to follow their peaceful vocations." And, above all, he exhorted them, "not to create public disturbance, nor to destroy public property, and especially to let the railroad remain uninjured." He went so far as to assure Missourians that, based on conversations with federal military officers in St. Louis, if they remained peaceful "no United States troops would be sent amongst them."[20]

Soon, however, war did come to Missouri. The federal government sought to prevent a rebel takeover by occupying threatened locales and protecting strategic water and rail arteries. At first, the Union strategy proved largely successful. General Nathaniel Lyon secured control of Jefferson City, and his troops speedily took over the major Missouri River crossings and ferries between St. Charles and Kansas City. Then Union forces moved to protect the network of railroads, especially those lines north of the river. Units from Illinois, Iowa and Kansas began guarding rolling stock, bridges and other property that belonged to the H&StJ and the North Missouri.[21]

Even though the federal government for the most part secured northern Missouri, Confederate forces under the command of General Price achieved some successes. In August 1861, badly outnumbered Union soldiers near Springfield lost to the Confederates at the Battle of Wilson's Creek, one of the bloodiest engagements of the war. General Lyon became the first Union general to die in action. Shortly after the Confederates achieved victory in the southwestern corner of the state, Price led his troops north and captured the Union garrison at Lexington, located on the south bank of the Missouri River east of Kansas City. But the federals drove Price south into Arkansas, and there in early March 1862 Union troops won at Pea Ridge, their first decisive victory west of the Mississippi River. It would not be until September 1864 that Price and his seasoned army returned to Missouri, hoping to capture St. Louis and win the state for the Confederacy. At the least, Price expected to keep federal forces tied down, preventing them from reinforcing offensive units in the Deep South. But at Westport, near Kansas City, on October 23 of that year, his troops lost a mighty battle, thus ending organized Confederate military operations in the state.[22]

Although the principal battles of the Civil War occurred at Wilson's Creek, Lexington and Westport, Missouri encountered nearly four years of savage and fierce fighting, mostly guerrilla warfare, with small bands of mounted Confederate raiders attacking any civilian or military target that could aid the Union. This type of warfare began in the summer of 1861 when Confederates or their sympathizers burned the H&StJ bridge that spanned the Salt River, in Shelby County, and inflicted severe damages on the North Missouri by destroying scores of depots, bridges and culverts and miles of telegraph lines. One target was the Red Hill bridge near Warrenton. "About midnight a party of guerrillas rode through the town, proceeded immediately to the Red Hill bridge on the North Missouri Railroad, set fire to the structure, waited until there was no longer any question as to the total destruction of the bridge, and then dashed out of town in the darkness." More devastation followed. According to the North Missouri, "for one hundred miles on the 20th of December, every bridge and culvert was burned; our depots, cars and engines injured, ties and fuel

on the road burnt, the track torn up and the iron bent."[23]

Forces loyal to the Southern cause had good reason to attack the North Missouri. The railroad transported a considerable number of federal troops and at times large volumes of supplies, particularly foodstuffs and horses. Moreover, not long after fighting broke out, Sturgeon ordered all employees to take a "stringent" loyalty oath. The company immediately discharged from service anyone who failed to comply, "an act that greatly incensed the disloyal."[24]

The Union military failed to provide much protection to the highly vulnerable railroad. It is not surprising that the central command decided that it lacked sufficient resources to guard company facilities. Not wanting to give carte blanche to the enemy, its commander, General John Pope, who had replaced Lyon, exasperated by the railroad incendiaries, decided to have local Committees of Safety police the railways. If damages occurred, county governments would be held financially responsible. But this policy accomplished little. Moreover, Pope worsened the situation by seeming to permit his remaining troops to terrorize the civilian population. "When there is added to this the irregularities of the soldiery—such as taking poultry, pigs, milk, butter, preserves, potatoes, horses, and in fact everything they want," wrote an official of the H&StJ to Union authorities, "entering and searching houses, and stealing in many cases; committing rapes on the negroes and such like things—the effect has been to make a great many Union men inveterate enemies." The northern counties were nearly in a state of anarchy, making railroad operations difficult. Military attacks and vandalism, dispirited people and injured economies disrupted service and reduced freight and passenger traffic. The North Missouri conservatively estimated that in 1861 alone it sustained nearly $100,000 in direct war-related damages.[25]

Conditions remained unsettled, yet the North Missouri continued to operate. Maintenance-of-way employees along the line and shop personnel in St. Charles made repairs as best they could. The company dispatched its daily freight and passenger trains. At times, too, it ran "war specials," transporting troops and military materials for the federal government, although at bargain-basement rates.[26]

It was during the closing months of the war that the North Missouri would experience some of its heaviest damage and suffering. In the summer of 1864, a group of Sterling Price's men, led by Captain William "Bloody Bill" Anderson, who possessed a pathological hatred for Unionists, caused widespread havoc. On July 23, Anderson's raiders burned the North Missouri depot at Renick and then pulled down several miles of telegraph wire, but local militiamen and troops of the Seventeenth Illinois Cavalry prevented destruction of the railroad facilities at nearby Allen. In the face of this rebuke, the Confederates merely moved elsewhere in the region. "Again there was a carnival of blood and arson. Houses were burned, home guard units were ambushed, men were shot, scalped, and stripped."[27]

But Anderson and his bushwhackers were about to commit their greatest atrocities. Simultaneous with Price's final assault on Union forces in Missouri, the Anderson guerrillas became active in northeastern and central counties. On the morning of September 27, members of the Bloody Bill band, who had been camping near the Boone County village of Centralia, a station on the North Missouri, entered the town in search of St. Louis newspapers, hoping to learn more about Price's activities. In the course of their visit, they terrorized residents and held them "under guard, thereby preventing intelligence of their presence." A few drunken guerrillas, who had taken advantage of a large quantity of "free" whiskey, set fire to the depot. Then about midday, the westbound passenger train approached the station. Although Jim Clark, the engineer, saw the smoking remains of the depot, he could not reverse, knowing that a gravel train was too close behind. At the Centralia stop, Clark found his foreword movement blocked by ties and other obstructions on the rails. The guerrillas quickly came aboard and forced the passengers out onto the platform and robbed them. On that unfortunate train were twenty-five unarmed Union soldiers. After questioning by Anderson, the furloughed fighters who were attempting to reach their homes in northwestern Missouri and southwestern Iowa, were told to strip, on the weak claim that Anderson's men needed their uniforms. Soon thereafter these twenty-four naked or nearly naked men were gunned down at close range. Also murdered was a German civilian who had the misfortune of wearing military clothing. Unable to speak English, he could not explain his noncombat status. The only Union survivor, though wounded, took shelter under a nearby wooden loading dock. Anderson's men set it ablaze. When flames forced out the trooper, he was shot.[28]

The rampage continued. The guerrillas torched the passenger train and sent it, without a crew, toward Sturgeon. They also tied down the locomotive whistle, allowing everyone within hearing range to know that this was no ordinary day on the North Missouri. It did not take long before a lack of steam halted the westerly movement. "The burning cars sent a column of oily black smoke into the clear noon air, which was observed for miles."[29]

Not long after the "Centralia Massacre," a small force of mounted Union infantry engaged Anderson's men not far from North Missouri rails. More blood flowed. Members of the Thirty-ninth Missouri Infantry found themselves trapped and outnumbered. After a few minutes of fierce fighting, most of these federal soldiers were dead. For some time their slaughter took on an eerie physical presence. "Along side of our road, near Centralia, every traveler may see a long but slightly raised mound in which [are] the remains of about eighty martyrs to the cause of the UNION and LIBERTY."[30]

Bloody Bill and his compatriots took refuge in the hilly and mostly friendly confines of neighboring Howard County. "No better region than this could be selected for guerrilla warfare," reported Union General Clinton Fisk. "The topography of the country and the hearts and consciences of the people are adapted to the hellish work."[31]

Shock and anger among Unionists seemed ubiquitous. In a letter to General William Starke Rosecrans, commander of the Department of the Missouri, a deeply troubled Sturgeon wrote:

> Since the murdering of the unarmed soldiers on our train on Tuesday a week ago and the burning of our cars we have not felt that we could with any safety go beyond Saint Charles with our trains, and the destruction of trains on the Hannibal and St. Joseph Railroad confirms us in the propriety of not attempting to run trains until the road is guarded by a sufficient military force. In the multitude of matters that you have to think of, I feel you will not deem it out of place on my part to make suggestions, even if what I suggest is of no value or has been thought of by you. Three thousand cavalry distributed along our line of road and west of the Hannibal and St. Joseph road, patrolling the road, ever on the march backward and foreword, taking sections of fifty miles for 300 or 400, and scouring the country each side, armed with plenty of heavy revolvers as well as the musket, as the guerrilla bands are, would soon enable us in safety to run our trains. If

we have not horses press them and mount our infantry, and let our men live as guerrillas do, off the country, giving vouchers to the loyal and none to rebel sympathizers. At Wellsville, Mexico, Centralia, or Sturgeon, and at Macon there should be garrisons of infantry, with log-houses or some fortification, so as to defend against a superior force. At Perruque bridge a guard should be kept till all trouble is over; also the bridges just north and south of Mexico should be guarded. We are anxious to move our trains as soon as you can make it safe to do so.[32]

Although Rosecrans did not provide the protection that Sturgeon had suggested, the North Missouri did resume operations. But so did Bloody Bill's guerrillas. On October 14, 1864, Anderson's men attacked Danville, seat of Montgomery County, and then looted nearby New Florence and High Hill and in the process torched the North Missouri depots in these two communities. Yet the military, in a sense, came to the railroad's rescue. While he was leading his guerrilla band on October 27, 1864, near Orrick, Missouri, Union troops ambushed Anderson and riddled his body with bullets. With the death of Bloody Bill and the defeat of Price, the Civil War had mostly come to an end for the embattled North Missouri. The financial setbacks caused by property destruction and losses of business were enormous. In fact, the company estimated that Anderson's raids in September and October alone had cost it about $150,000, almost equal to its net earnings for the fiscal year from March 1, 1863, to February 29, 1864.[33]

After the war clouds dissipated, the North Missouri no longer thought about mere survival. At last a feeling of optimism returned. "The state is now FREE FROM SLAVERY," reported the company in 1866, and "we may reasonably expect a large immigration of free white labor into Northern Missouri."

More people, of course, would surely translate into more business.[34]

The road moved forward in several ways to accommodate the anticipated growth. For one thing, management wisely decided that its track gauge must be altered to standard width of 4' 8 1/2". This decision received the kudos from a firm of consulting engineers: "The North Missouri Company exhibit[ed] prudent forethought and sound judgment in their determination to change their gauge at once, while their road is still *in the early infancy of its business*." Following the Civil War, conversion to standard gauge became common, including roads that served the St. Louis gateway. The Pacific Railroad would do so in 1869, and two years later the Ohio & Mississippi Railway, "The Great Broad Gauge Route," which linked St. Louis with Cincinnati, reduced its 6' 0" gauge to standard width. It took the North Missouri only three days in August 1867 (the fifth through the seventh) to accomplish this task, an investment that allowed equipment to "run direct from St. Louis to St. Joseph."[35]

Just as a lack of standard gauge hindered operations of the North Missouri, so, too, did the absence of a span across the Missouri River at St. Charles. Regauging the 170-mile line, however, was far less expensive, difficult and time consuming than bridging Big Muddy, a treacherous river that had a habit of flooding and shifting channels. A few months after changing its gauge, the North Missouri arranged financing for the much-needed project with the St. Charles Bridge Company. This largely St. Louis syndicate was led by James B. Eads, a self-trained civil engineer who would make possible completion in 1874 of the St. Louis Bridge (Eads Bridge), the first span over the Mississippi River at St. Louis.[36]

In 1865, the North Missouri had taken the first steps for the St. Charles bridge, and within a year the project was officially advertised. The railroad seemed to have received a good plan, one that called for resting a Bollman truss on stone piers, but it was abandoned after the bridge company's chief engineer, C. Shaler Smith, became concerned about its overall stability. After making a detailed series of experiments on the river's strong and at times erratic currents, Smith offered his own proposal, a trellis-girder-type bridge, which found favor. On September 14, 1868, work began.[37]

Laborers initially constructed the eight stone piers. The first two were erected without serious difficulty, but the third posed problems. The supervisory personnel discovered that the rock base in the riverbed was not as solid as expected. After preparing the foundation and beginning the stone masonry work, a flood that swept the lower river in July 1869 destroyed much of what had been accomplished, delaying completion for nine months on the 105-plus-foot-high structure. There were more challenges. A change in the course of the river, which cut away a large portion of the bank on the St. Charles side, threatened three additional piers that had been finished. Fortunately, by fashioning a dike out into the stream, water pressure was reduced. Finally, workers struggled to build the last pier, known as "No. 5." "It was the most difficult and expensive work of the substructure," reported a visiting journalist. "A deposit of sand at the pier site rendered it necessary to scour to a sufficient depth to float the pontoons by means of powerful jets of water. The resistance of friction by the sand in sinking the caisson was unexpectedly great, requiring a pressure of from six to seven hundred pounds to the square foot to keep it in motion."[38]

As work progressed on the piers, laborers prepared the superstructure and approaches. More than 3,500 tons of cast and wrought iron were used for the seven metal spans, each exceeding 300 feet in length, with the

In about 1869, workers take a break from constructing the massive stone piers that would soon support a splendid railroad bridge over the Missouri River at St. Charles. This structure significantly strengthened the operating efficiency of the North Missouri. (Author's Coll.)

longest measuring 321²/₃ feet. The project also necessitated the laying of approximately two miles of track. Finally, on May 29, 1871, the 6,570-foot-long "first high bridge across the Missouri" opened to traffic amid a festive ceremony. It had been a monumental $2.1 million undertaking, and the results were impressive. Observed the *Railroad Gazette:* "The main spans are, we believe, the longest now existing on this continent, with the exception of the Louisville Bridge [over the Ohio River], which has twenty-seven spans, one 400 feet; the rest being each less than 300 feet." The North

Missouri bridge was also a physical beauty. "I went out to St. Charles and saw the finest Bridge that I ever saw," wrote the road's general freight agent to his wife. "It surely is most splendid."[39]

But the St. Charles bridge, which the North Missouri leased for $170,000 annually together with payment of all taxes and assessments upon it and its approaches, was more than a wonderful feat of engineering and an attractive structure; it made the railroad more efficient and strategically significant. Beyond that, it bolstered the St. Louis economy. "The value of the work to St. Louis cannot easily be overestimated," wrote a trade journalist. "So long as the Missouri remained unbridged, that city was so cut off from all the populous and fertile country north of the Missouri River that it could conduct business with it only at a disadvantage."[40]

With the Missouri River Bridge in place, trains of the North Missouri could now extend unimpeded further into the hinterland. By the time the span opened, iron rails already had been pushed well beyond the end of tracks. Between May 8, 1866, and December 2, 1868, work crews under contract with Champlain, Smith & Company, "a firm composed of some of the best known railroad builders in the country," grubbed, graded and installed sixty-five miles of track from Macon northward through Kirksville to the Iowa-Missouri line (Coatesville, Missouri), 234 miles from St. Louis. Though specific objectives had not been publicly announced, the railroad might well use this new line construction to reach a transcontinental carrier in Iowa or even Minnesota and, of course, to tap immediately additional local traffic.[41]

When in July 1868 the iron horse reached Kirksville, seat of Adair County, the community participated in two celebrations. The line was finished by the patriotic Fourth, and two days earlier the local newspaper had promoted this long-anticipated event: "RAILROADS, BRASS BANDS, TOURNAMENTS, HORSE FAIR, FREE RIDES, ain't that enough for one day's amusement? Don't fail to be here." Then on July 18, the North Missouri dispatched a special celebratory excursion train from Macon with an onboard brass band that played "Hail Columbia" and other popular and patriotic tunes at various stops along its thirty-four-mile route. Kirksvillians duly welcomed its arrival. "The train was met by a great crowd and a band. The excursionists were escorted to a nearby grove, where some felicitous speech making was in-

dulged in. The day was exceedingly hot, but every one seemed to enjoy the occasion." Later the company superintendent offered attendees a complimentary ride to Macon and a return trip on the regularly scheduled passenger train from St. Louis, an invitation many accepted. A few days later local residents received long-awaited telegraphic service after line crews installed the final miles of poles and wires.[42]

In another strategic move, the company pushed west toward Kansas City from near Allen, at a place named Moberly, which honored William Moberly, a Randolph County railroad promoter. It also planned to use this line for a possible northwestward extension that would reach the Union Pacific at Council Bluffs, Iowa.[43]

Sensing the commercial value of this emerging junction location, a St. Louis real estate firm, working closely with the North Missouri, platted the town of Moberly and on September 27, 1866, sold the first lot. The eager promoters helped their cause by offering free lots to any neighboring residents of Allen who were willing to relocate, contending that Allen would never prosper in the shadow of the new junction. This

Management of the North Missouri Rail Road proudly incorporated on its 1870 annual pass a drawing of its recently completed bridge over the Missouri River at St. Charles. (Author's Coll.)

became obvious in 1867 when the railroad selected Moberly as a division point. In the early 1870s these promoters scored an even greater victory when they acquired a machine and repair shop after their principal rival, Montgomery City, could not furnish an adequate supply of water. But could it? According to a published report in the early 1890s, Montgomery City in its bid for this coveted railroad prize had hired a well driller "who after going down about 2,500 feet got his tools [stuck] fast, and declared he could not get them out; so Moberly got the shops." Then the writer noted, "But last fall this dry 'spell' made somebody think that possibly the tools could be gotten out: and it was resolved to make a desperate effort. So an expert was employed and put to work. He took out about a bushel of old railroad spikes, a number of old gunny sacks and other rubbish and cleared the hole and found an abundance of water, and the well now . . . is proving a bonanza to the town." Asked the reporter, "Did Moberly hire those spikes dumped in there?" If they did, this act of mischief was fully explainable. The capturing of a large railroad payroll, it was widely believed, would guarantee a community's future.[44]

Moberly's prospects for prosperity seemed assured. The hopes of its promoters were realized; the community grew so rapidly that by 1880, with a population exceeding 6,000, it had become widely known as the "Magic City," and by the mid-1880s it claimed 10,000 residents. By this time, civic boosters bragged that Moberly had become the "largest and by far the most important town between St. Louis and Kansas City."[45]

In the spring of 1866, when the North Missouri started to shape its "West Branch" or "Second Division" from Moberly, it restarted earlier efforts to build other rail lines in the area. The first project, the Chariton and Randolph Rail Road Company (in-corporated in December 1858) proposed to link the North Missouri in Randolph County with Brunswick in Chariton County, but it never evolved much beyond a "hot-air" scheme. And a related project, the Missouri River Valley Railroad Company, formed a year later to build through Carroll and Clay Counties to "any point on the Missouri River in Platte County," was also stillborn. Realizing that the North Missouri already had a construction record, state lawmakers in 1864 willingly consolidated the charters of the Chariton and Randolph and Missouri River Valley railroads with the North Missouri.[46]

Construction of the West Branch went well. The thirty-nine-mile stretch between Moberly and Brunswick, which was begun on May 8, 1866, opened on December 15, 1867, and on October 18, 1868, workers began their labors on three separate segments: twenty-four miles between Brunswick-Carrollton, twenty-five miles between Carrollton-Lexington Junction (then called R&L Junction) and thirty-two miles between Lexington Junction and Birmingham (known as North Missouri Junction). They completed the first project in August 1868, the second one in October 1868 and the third in December 1868. Trackage rights over the Kansas City & Cameron Railroad, an H&StJ affiliate, gave the West Branch access to Harlem (North Kansas City), on the Missouri River, opposite Kansas City, and important rail linkages. "At Harlem . . . direct connections are made with the Missouri Valley railroad for Leavenworth, Atchison, St. Joseph, and thence via Council Bluffs and St. Joseph railroad for Nebraska City, Council Bluffs, and Omaha; at Omaha, with the Union Pacific railroad for Cheyenne, Ogden, and California," proclaimed a company promotional brochure in 1870. "At the western terminus of the road [Kansas City] direct connections are made with the Kansas Pacific railway (formerly known as the Union

Pacific, Eastern Division) for Lawrence, Topeka, Fort Hays, Sheridan, and thence by overland daily stages for Denver, Salt Lake, etc.; also, the Missouri River, Fort Scott, and Gulf railroads, making the shortest line from St. Louis to all points in Kansas."[47]

The North Missouri soon benefited from the first bridge constructed over the Missouri River in Kansas City. The mammoth $1.2 million project of the Kansas City Bridge Company, which featured a draw span of more than 360 feet, opened officially on July 3, 1869. Under the firm's articles of incorporation the North Missouri had the right to use it on equal terms with all other carriers. The annual rental charges of $55,000 were manageable. This bridge provided the St. Louis road with direct access to a rapidly growing Kansas City, which in 1870 claimed a population that exceeded 30,000. This Missouri metropolis not only provided strategic interchange partners, including the Kansas Pacific and the Missouri River, Fort Scott & Gulf railroads, but its expanding commercial and industrial activities, including grain elevators and meatpacking, promised a lucrative traffic. Thus, the North Missouri was becoming less dependent upon local, country business.[48]

Because the North Missouri did not wish to rely wholly on a Harlem interchange for traffic destined to and from the Omaha gateway, it began the process of pushing more directly toward that destination. The initial segment in what ultimately became the "Omaha Line" began as a wholly grassroots project, the Chillicothe & Brunswick Railroad (C&B), chartered in 1864, designed to link these two west-central Missouri communities and provide an immediate tie-in to the H&StJ at Chillicothe. At its founding, times remained difficult because of continued guerrilla incursions into the region, so the C&B remained lifeless until after the war. Sparked by the willingness of taxpayers

of Livingston County in 1867 to purchase $150,000 of stock and a lease arrangement that same year with the North Missouri, the thirty-eight-mile road began to take shape, opening finally on March 1, 1871. To the delight of St. Louisians, some regional traffic followed the North Missouri route rather than going eastward to Chicago via the H&StJ and the Chicago, Burlington & Quincy (CB&Q).[49]

The second portion of the Omaha line began as the St. Louis, Chillicothe & Omaha Railway (StLC&O), organized in July 1868. Because it was less of a hometown road, promoters from prospective on-line communities and St. Louis, with financial ties to the North Missouri, sought to build in a northwesterly direction from a connection with the Chillicothe & Brunswick. At the Iowa line, the StLC&O, renamed the Chillicothe & Omaha Rail Road in June 1869, would connect with a companion Iowa-chartered firm, the St. Louis, Council Bluffs & Omaha Railroad (StLCB&O), that planned to build southeasterly from Council Bluffs. In a subsequent renaming, both the Iowa and Missouri chartered roads took the StLCB&O moniker. The property struggled during the 1870s. Prior to the reorganization of the North Missouri, the StLCB&O had completed only forty-two miles from Chillicothe to Pattonsburg, yet this pike and the Brunswick & Chillicothe Railroad, successor in 1873 to the C&B, generated immediate feeder traffic and offered real hope for future expansion.[50]

The North Missouri also became involved in another road that was taking shape in northwestern Missouri, the St. Louis & St. Joseph Railroad (StL&StJ). Designed by its local backers to operate from Sedalia through Lexington to St. Joseph, the road by 1870 had completed only forty miles of line from North Lexington (north of the Missouri River) to Lathrop and a tie-in with the

Cameron branch of the H&StJ. Beginning in 1869, the North Missouri, which connected with the StL&StJ at R&L Junction, three miles from North Lexington, operated "temporarily the small portion now finished." And North Missouri trains continued to run over the road, even after it reached St. Joseph, a trade center of more than 30,000 inhabitants, seventy-two miles from North Lexington. Indeed, the St. Louis, Kansas City & Northern (StLKC&N), the North Missouri successor company, leased the property during most of its corporate life. St. Joseph and its environs seemed ideally suited for both roads. "All of these rich sections of country, by a strong and energetic management, can be made largely tributary to the trade of this line, as the natural tendency of their business is towards St. Louis, and nothing but the want of commercial enterprise on the part of the merchants of this city will turn it away," observed StLKC&N general superintendent W. R. Arthur in 1875. In time, however, the heir to the StLKC&N, Wabash, St. Louis & Pacific Railway, lost control of an admittedly attractive property. Then, on January 31, 1888, the Atchison, Topeka & Santa Fe Railway at a trustee's sale paid $972,300 for the StL&StJ, and this line became a useful feeder for that sprawling transcontinental railroad system.[51]

Although the extended Macon mainline trackage or "Third Division" terminated in late 1868 at the hamlet of Coatesville, a few feet south of the Iowa border, officials had wished since the inception of the North Missouri to penetrate the Hawkeye State, creating a through line between St. Louis and the upper Midwest. These men had their eyes especially set on two sources of freight traffic. By the 1860s, no one questioned the agricultural richness of the region, least of all the ability of farmers to produce an abundance of corn and livestock, and geologists had identified large, albeit scattered, deposits of commercial-grade coal, especially in the greater Des Moines River valley.[52]

A start, of sorts, was made in the fall of 1865 when a group consisting largely of Iowa railroad promoters received articles of incorporation for their St. Louis & Cedar Rapids Railway (StL&CR), designed to extend from the North Missouri connection to Cedar Rapids, the bustling seat of Lynn County, which promised to become an important railroad hub. Their proposed route of approximately 140 miles would run northward through three growing county-seat towns: Bloomfield, Ottumwa and Sigourney. Short of funds, their dream languished until 1868 when the North Missouri agreed to lease the StL&CR, which gave the Iowa project valuable leverage with lenders.[53]

When the StL&CR was finally able to tap sufficient capital, construction began on the "south end" of the StL&CR. Rails quickly spanned the twenty-two miles from Coatesville to Bloomfield, via Moulton, a newly laid-out community in Appanoose County that honored J. B. Moulton, chief engineer of the North Missouri. Then, in July 1870, crews extended track another twenty-one miles to the market town of Ottumwa, located on the east-west mainline of the Burlington & Missouri River Railroad, which linked Chicago with Council Bluffs, and the Des Moines Valley Railway, a 211-mile road that ran from the Mississippi River at Keokuk to the Iowa capital and beyond to Grand Junction and a tie-in with the expanding Chicago & North Western system. These superb connections may explain why the StL&CR stalled at Ottumwa, although some grading did occur northeast of the city. Also, leaseholder North Missouri surely felt financially constrained after its burst of new line extensions and construction of the St. Charles bridge.[54]

During the "Railway Age," the coming of the iron horse to any community, even one such as Ottumwa that already enjoyed good railroad service, was a special event. The *Ottumwa Courier* contained a page-one article about the opening of its newest and third carrier, the St. Louis & Cedar Rapids:

Pete Ballingall [Ottumwa hotel proprietor] caught us up on last Saturday [July 16, 1870] about 4 P.M. . . . . we listened to his tale of how nice it would be to go over to Bloomfield on a locomotive and return by the first passenger train reaching the Des Moines river [at Ottumwa] on the St. Louis and Cedar Rapids road. Mr. Gamble, of Missouri, Superintendent of track laying, was our Conductor, and Wm. Allen, engineer. . . . We left Bloomfield at 11 o'clock P.M. and arrived here at midnight. Conductor T. M. Quigley brought us through with dispatch and safety, though he passed nearly half the distance over a portion of the road he had never before run. The road is well and substantially built, and the cars run as smoothly upon it where it is surfaced up as upon most of the . . . roads.[55]

Although North Missouri management embraced a philosophy of constructing "stems," it did not disregard the branch line. Such a quintessential appendage opened in October 1867 between Centralia and Columbia. Residents of Columbia, home of the University of Missouri and seat of Boone County, had long sought a railroad. As early as 1857, local residents had received incorporation for their Boone County and Jefferson City Railroad Company (BC&JC), but hard times and four years of war hindered the project. In 1866, the hope of bringing the iron horse to town brightened when BC&JC president D. H. Hickman, a Columbia resident, struck a deal with the North Missouri, allowing it to lease the resulting shortline. With this agreement in hand, Hickman's road turned toward Centralia and the North Missouri rather than southward to Jefferson City

and a connection with the Pacific Railroad. Beginning in May 1866, crews installed twenty-two miles of line and erected the essential support facilities, including depots at Columbia, Hickman and Stevens. Unlike the trackage north of Macon or Brunswick, there was never any intention of additional construction. Nevertheless, the "Columbia Branch" became a valuable feeder.[56]

The 353 miles of line laid down by construction and the 143 miles operated through lease arrangements made the North Missouri an important regional carrier. Although the H&StJ and the Pacific Railroad had made major contributions to the Show-Me State, the North Missouri arguably had accomplished as much as they and some thought even more. In an 1869 essay, "St. Louis and its Railroads," a knowledgeable commentator believed that the "Most prominent among these railroads is the North Missouri." And he anticipated great things for this carrier. "When completed, [it] will be to St. Louis much what the Chicago & Northwestern [sic] is to Chicago, giving it connections, and almost the only railroad connections north of the Missouri River." As he correctly concluded, "The North Missouri is essentially a St. Louis road. It aims to furnish that part of the State north of the Missouri river with railroads to St. Louis. Its lines all run in such directions and with such connections that it cannot well serve any other city. The interests of the North Missouri and St. Louis are identical."[57]

Management attempted as best it could to exploit its advantages, but there were obstacles. At times tonnage was light, often a factor of the annual agricultural cycles and the boom-or-bust nature of farming, which in turn had a direct impact on other businesses. The road, too, during traffic spurts, lacked enough motive power and freight equipment to serve every customer, resulting in thousands of dollars in unrealized revenues.

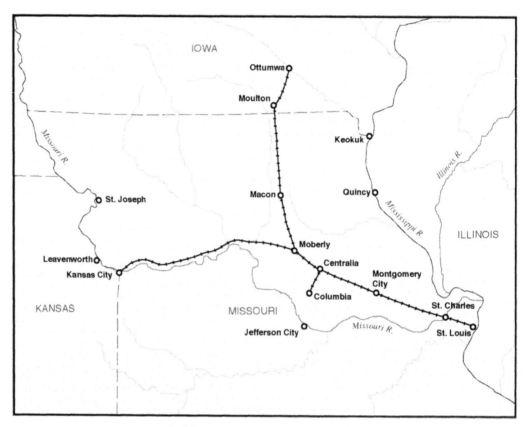

NORTH MISSOURI RAILROAD

The North Missouri was also beginning to lose local monopolies that it had earlier enjoyed. Mexico, the Audrain County government and trade center that was about to get its second railroad, is a case in point. Spearheaded by interests in the Mississippi River community of Louisiana, Missouri, the Louisiana & Missouri River Railroad (L&MR), chartered before the Civil War, began to emerge physically. This local endeavor, however, needed the financial assistance of the Chicago & Alton Railroad, which had its eyes on the Kansas City gateway. In 1870 the Alton, which called itself the "shortest line between St. Louis and Chicago," leased this unfinished project and resumed building westward, helping to make that year the greatest ever for railroad construction to date, 6,145 miles. With this backing, the L&MR not only quickly reached Mexico, but also Cedar City, a village on the north bank of the Missouri River opposite Jefferson City. At Louisiana the L&MR connected with an Alton line for Chicago via a steam-powered transfer boat. No longer did railroad users in the Mexico area, which the North Missouri had served exclusively since 1858, need to rely entirely on their pioneer pike. Perhaps the silver lining came when the Alton asked for trackage rights west to Kansas City, and the North Missouri, eager for this rental income, readily agreed.[58]

THE WABASH EMERGES WEST OF THE MISSISSIPPI RIVER

Although well positioned in a rich and growing agricultural region and a valuable asset for St. Louis, which in 1870 had become the nation's fourth largest city, all was not well for the nearly 500-mile North Missouri Railroad Company, the self-proclaimed "Old Reliable." By 1870 financial troubles mounted. Even before its official reorganization in early 1872, freight and passenger profits had been mixed during much of the previous decade: $74,006 in 1862, $47,515 in 1863, $57,496 in 1864 and $132,479 in 1865. The physical damages inflicted by Confederate forces drained large amounts of money from company coffers, and the war years adversely affected income. The balance sheet would have been decidedly better if the road would have won compensation for war-related losses and had received fair payment from the federal government for the movement of troops and supplies. Indeed, the North Missouri realized less than $350,000 for its services. "Notwithstanding that we were compelled to do the Government business for one-third our regular rates, and at less than the rates paid badly built United States *land grant* roads [H&StJ and Pacific Railroad]," explained president Sturgeon, "the United States has never remunerated this Company in one cent of damages." The only significant public assistance came rather from Jefferson City. In 1865, the Missouri General Assembly released the state lien and authorized the company to issue $6 million of first mortgage bonds to be secured by the mileage already completed. It was this bond money that the North Missouri used for its postwar construction blitz.[59]

Inadequate income, high interest obligations and mounting debt that stemmed from recent construction activities forced restructuring. Moreover, a poor crop year and a shortage of motive power and equipment exacerbated the troubling financial situation. On August 26, 1871, the North Missouri was sold under foreclosure to a veteran New York City investment banker, Morris Ketchum Jesup, who had distinguished himself in the field of railroading. He already served as president and director of Iowa's Dubuque & Sioux City Railroad, which in 1867 the Illinois Central had leased for top dollar. He and his associates at the highly respected M. K. Jesup & Company, which concentrated on southern and western roads, had been watching the North Missouri carefully and saw value in the property. They believed that the railroad, which had cost more than $20 million to build, could be acquired for about half that amount. In this case, Jesup represented holders of the $4 million in 7 percent second mortgage bonds on which interest payments had been missed. As with other railroads, the Jesup firm brought about a speedy and attractive reorganization.[60]

ST. LOUIS, KANSAS CITY & NORTHERN

As the St. Louis, Kansas City & Northern Railway Company, the new road took a name that was fully self-descriptive. After all, the road served two of the Midwest's principal rail centers and had aimed two partially completed arteries northward, one proposed to reach Cedar Rapids or some other Iowa or Minnesota point and the other directed toward the Council Bluffs–Omaha gateway. Compared with contemporary railroads in the Midwest of the early 1870s, the 582-mile StLKC&N (which included its leased lines) was one of the largest. The fact that StLKC&N trains could cross bridges over the Missouri River at both St. Charles and Kansas City added to its value and cohesiveness.

Differing from some of his other railroad interests, Morris Jesup assumed neither an office nor a place on the board of directors of the StLKC&N once the company officially began operations on February 6, 1872. Other prominent railroad leaders did join the carrier. Thomas A. Scott, of Philadelphia, a board member, was the best known. At this time he was vice president of the Pennsylvania Railroad and served as the right-hand man to its dynamic president, J. Edgar Thomson. Scott also led both the Union Pacific and Texas & Pacific railroads. Timothy B. Blackstone became a board member and took on the StLKC&N presidency. Although less prominent than Scott, Blackstone had been since 1864 president of the Chicago & Alton, and would continue in that role until 1899. Also a member of the eleven-member board was Adolphus Meier, who lived in St. Louis and served as president of the Kansas Pacific Railway.[61]

Another notable personage won election to the StLKC&N board: New York banker Solon Humphreys. A contemporary source described him this way: "Sound judgment and fine mind allied with enterprise have made him a successful man." Humphreys had become prosperous as a partner in a New York firm that specialized in the coffee, sugar and tea trade but later branched into railroad securities. He became personally involved in a variety of railroad enterprises, including promotion in the early 1850s of the Ohio & Mississippi, and as a result was no stranger to St. Louis area railroads.[62]

The presence of Scott, Blackstone and Meier signified the strategic importance of the StLKC&N. Scott saw it as a pivotal link between east and west, Blackstone as a prized western outlet for an adjoining trunk carrier and Meier as a valuable eastern connection for his expanding prairie road. "The names of the directors . . . indicate that the new company," commented the *Railroad Gazette*, "will have intimate relations with several connecting lines." This trade organ made much of the fact that Pennsylvania "needs only a line from St. Louis to Kansas City to complete a route in which it has a powerful, if not a controlling, interest from New York to Denver."[63]

Yet the StLKC&N was hardly a perfect road. During its waning years, the North Missouri had not been able to maintain properly and upgrade the physical plant and rolling stock, and some war-related damages had not been wholly repaired. Management agreed that much needed to be done. During its first year of operation, the StLKC&N understandably spent heavily on improving a property that was "very incomplete and imperfect." Pushing forward construction of the shops complex earlier proposed for Moberly received high priority, as did improving rolling stock. "The construction of a system of Repair Shops for Locomotives and Cars at Moberly, which shall be adequate to the wants of your Company, will soon be completed, and will result in reducing largely the cost of Repairs, which have heretofore been made without proper Machinery and Tools," reported president Blackstone in March 1873. And he proudly noted that "20 Locomotives, 5 Passenger Coaches, 150 Box Freight Cars, 150 Stock Cars, 50 Platform Cars and 100 Coal Cars were added by purchase, and 3 Passenger Coaches, 1 mail and Baggage Car, 1 Passenger and Baggage Car, 2 Box Cars, 1 Stock Car, 6 Cabooses and 1 Tool Car were constructed at the Shops of the Company during the year." This upgrading of the physical plant, which in time included a steel rail replacement program and more modern rolling stock, continued.[64]

Part of the strategy to make the StLKC&N a better property involved expansion. Its leadership, which saw four presidents in a span of seven years, collectively felt the need for "more tributary territory and more connections." Prompting this desire for new trackage was the explosion of railroad construction in the region, most notably toward the end of the decade when the economy rebounded nicely from the depression wrought by the Panic of 1873. But as early as 1874 the company complained that "our line, from Moberly to Ottumwa, a distance of only 131 miles, is crossed by six [rail]roads, rendering every important station of that section a competing point and making us dependent on the through business from Iowa for the business of that portion of our line." Unfortunately, the road experienced similar competitive situations elsewhere.[65]

Although the StLKC&N did not blossom like the core North Missouri, it made one vital and widely popular extension when it forged a controlled through line to the Omaha gateway. In the fall of 1879 the StLKC&N completed a seventy-eight-mile segment northwestward from Pattonsburg (near Elm Flats in Daviess County), northern terminus of the leased St. Louis, Council Bluffs & Omaha (the lease arrangement on two occasions during the 1870s had been temporarily interrupted), to the Missouri-Iowa state line. There StLKC&N rails met those of the recently completed and leased Council Bluffs & St. Louis Railway (née St. Louis, Council Bluffs & Omaha), which had been surveyed since the early 1870s. This sixty-six-mile road not only made possible long-distance bridge traffic with the Union Pacific and created the shortest route between Omaha and St. Louis, but it also gave access to the rolling "Blue Grass Country" of southwestern Iowa and Shenandoah, a market and county-seat town that seemed destined to dominate the immediate locality. Again, the appearance of the iron horse spurred local development, showing once more that cheap, dependable transportation conferred upon an area a profitability that heretofore had been limited or largely nonexistent. On October 15, 1879, the first train rolled over the Omaha line.[66]

Two smaller trackage additions had occurred earlier. To facilitate better access to St. Louis, between July 1875 and June 1876 the StLKC&N built an expensive twelve-mile extension from its main stem at Ferguson, Missouri, to the Grand Union Depot at Eighteenth Street in St. Louis. Before this first St. Louis union station opened, both the North Missouri and the StLKC&N passenger trains terminated downtown at Carr Street and the Levee. Appropriately called the "Union Depot Line," the new route "pass[es] through a beautiful country, and running nearly a mile through Forest Park, it will give a handsome and picturesque entrance to the city, and will possess the additional and peculiar advantage, that of eleven principal [public] thoroughfares which it intersects, it goes under or over nine, thereby doing away with much danger and inconvenience to the public, and avoiding great annoyance in movement of trains." There was another expected benefit: "A large and profitable local passenger traffic on this line will be added to our resources."[67]

What may have been one of the region's more convoluted, albeit modest, acquisitions involved lease and then purchase of the fifteen-mile Salisbury & Glasgow Railroad. This branch left the Kansas City line at Salisbury, twenty-one miles west of Moberly, and ran southward through hilly terrain to the Missouri River at Glasgow, "one of the oldest towns in the State, and the centre of considerable business." Just as Columbians wanted a railroad outlet, Glasgowegians sought one, too, and had great expectations. In February 1865, local promoters won incorporation for their Missouri & Mississippi Railroad Company, but their transportation dreams went unfulfilled. Eight years later, this paper road took on new life as the Keokuk & Kansas City Railway Company, and construction began. In May 1875, track reached within less than three miles of Glasgow, and at long last, on November 16, 1875, the iron horse made its triumphal entrance. The building process forced a reorganization, and on January 12, 1877, the shortline became the more descriptive Salisbury & Glasgow Railroad Company. Because the StLKC&N had earlier leased the property from its trustee and soon thereafter gained a financial stake, followed by outright control in May 1877, the legal department of the StLKC&N had the corporate shell of the Salisbury & Glasgow dissolved. Although this appendage supplied traffic to the parent, the StLKC&N monopoly in Glasgow was short lived. The Alton's thrust into Kansas City in 1878–1879, under the banner of the Kansas City, St. Louis & Chicago Railroad, went through Glasgow and at that point crossed the Missouri River, site of the nation's first steel railroad bridge.[68]

While the Alton became a thorn in the side of the StLKC&N, initially the company enjoyed good relations with the Alton and at the same time forged a successful traffic alliance with the Pennsylvania in the east and the Kansas Pacific in the west. When the StLKC&N organized its first board of directors, two members came from the Alton, two from the Pennsylvania and five from the Kansas Pacific. The Alton's preferred interchange partner at St. Louis was the StLKC&N rather than the Missouri Pacific (née Pacific Railroad and Atlantic & Pacific Railroad), and traffic continued to move over the StLKC&N through Mexico. The Pennsylvania-controlled properties, too, found the StLKC&N a cooperative road. But it would be the Kansas Pacific that most heavily relied on the StLKC&N. Its eastbound traffic at Kansas City, some of which traveled over the Central Pacific–Union Pacific via Denver, usually went over StLKC&N rather than Missouri Pacific rails to St. Louis. Indeed, rumors spread in 1875 that there

was about to be a corporate merger between the two roads, inspired by Jay Gould, who in that year became a Kansas Pacific director.[69]

As rate wars flared through the midsection of the nation, these battles affected the StLKC&N. In the mid-1870s, rate skirmishes, especially for passenger traffic, erupted for business between Kansas City and St. Louis, pitting the road against the Missouri Pacific. Although creation of the so-called Iowa Pool (1870–1884) had mostly solved rate conflicts between the Chicago-Omaha lines, the StLKC&N avoided such gentlemen's agreements, and its charges generally reflected its combative environment. When compared with five neighboring roads, the StLKC&N offered shippers some of the region's lowest freight rates even as charges generally fell during the last quarter of the nineteenth century. For instance, the company in 1876 charged 1.10 cents per ton per mile for freight, but by 1879 it was asking only 0.63 cents. Competitors, however, averaged 1.89 cents in 1876 and 1.47 cents in 1879.[70]

Customers had even more to like about the StLKC&N. The general quality of its passenger service far exceeded that of the predecessor North Missouri and ranked highly when compared to competitors. The number of trains dispatched daily over the mainlines was usually three rather than two, and their speeds averaged ten to fifteen miles per hour faster than during North Missouri days. With major connections at Kansas City, which had become a rail rather than stage terminal, and more at St. Louis, convenient travel options existed. There was truth in the promotional statement: "Quicker Time and Better Connections THAN ANY OTHER ROUTE." The company also upgraded its equipment. Not only did new coal-burning locomotives perform better than older wood-burning power, but the road also offered between its principal points an assortment of state-of-the art coaches and sleepers. The railroad understandably did much to publicize this modern rolling stock: "The Improved Equipment of this Road consists of the Westinghouse Improved Automatic Air Brake (the only Line west of the Mississippi River fully equipped with this Brake), Blackstone Platform and Coupler (in many respects an improvement over the Miller Platform and Coupler), [and] Buck's Celebrated Reclining Chair Cars (the only Line running these Cars on all trains)." The StLKC&N further bragged that "The best Pullman Palace Sleeping Cars are run on all night trains" and reminded travelers that "Polite and attentive employees accompany all trains, and will cheerfully render any assistance to passengers."[71]

Public reaction to these betterments was heartening. Members of the St. Louis press corps found the reclining chair cars particularly attractive. According to a report that appeared in 1878, "[These cars have] reversible seats with tall backs, and all the comforts of an easy rocking-chair." In what must have been a publicist's dream, the fourth estate observed that "in these cars passengers are exempt from the annoyance of shiftless and cramping positions, but go bowling over the smooth steel rails with an ease which can only be likened to a ride on scudding banks of clouds."[72]

The StLKC&N also sought to adjust passenger-train schedules to accommodate patrons and boost patronage. While cognizant of the need to make train connections in Kansas City and St. Louis, there were examples of where service at noninterchange stations was made popular. In July 1876, residents of a growing Moberly were delighted to learn that eastbound No. 2, which heretofore had left for St. Louis at 11:00 A.M. would depart at 8:00 A.M., after making a breakfast stop at the company-operated eating house. "This will be a grand thing for Moberly," commented the *Moberly Headlight,* "as our merchants can go to St. Louis on this train,

In the 1870s public passenger schedules reflected the fancy styling frequently selected for other Gilded Age publications. The elaborate St. Louis, Kansas City & Northern Railway timetable of December 1875 ballyhooed service through the rapidly expanding St. Louis gateway. By this time StLKC&N trains used the "Grand Union Depot" at St. Louis and exclaimed that it was "The Shortest Line from the Missouri River TO ALL POINTS EAST." (Author's Coll.)

spend five or six hours in the city and be at home the next morning." The newspaper liked the altered schedule for another reason; it offered an opportunity to snipe at Huntsville, the Randolph County–seat community seven miles west whose courthouse Moberly coveted. "It will also enable people from our delightful suburb, Huntsville, to come to the 'hub' and do a full days work, returning at 4 P.M."[73]

The generally positive public perceptions did not mean that the StLKC&N was a perpetually happy railroad; at times the company experienced aggravating internal personnel problems. One nasty flare-up erupted between workers and managers in 1873. Members of the ten-year-old Brotherhood of Locomotive Engineers (BLE), the nation's first railroad union, left their posts after the company "gave an engine" to a non-BLE engineer. The union demanded that the individual be terminated, but instead W. C. Van Horne, the general superintendent, refused and ordered that all strikers be discharged. Although this "disastrous Engineer's strike" in time was resolved, the company paid dearly, in terms of both diminished employee goodwill and lost revenues.[74]

Although the observation that the "St. Louis, Kansas City & Northern Railway is unquestionably one of the great roads of the continent" smacked of so much braggadocio, its location in a rapidly developing region coupled with its program of modernization, current earnings and overall potential made for attractive securities. Those willing to invest were not limited to Americans; overseas capitalists also liked the company. The "net results of StL,KC&N positive," concluded a Dutch financier in 1879, "and interest on [existing] North Missouri bonds easily earned. . . safe investment, better than most American RRs." Earnings mostly bore out this positive assessment: the balance sheet for 1873 showed gross income of $2,755,194; for 1876 $3,143,866 (after flat earnings for 1874 and 1875) and for 1878 $3,324,496 (again after flat earnings in 1877). Net earnings soared from $629,536 in 1873 to $1,347,500 five years later. Finally, persistent rate skirmishes with the competing Missouri Pacific between St. Louis and Kansas City had ended when "Commodore" Cornelius Kingsland Garrison, who had won control of that road at the time of its reorganization in 1876, became in early 1877 a leading holder of StLKC&N securities. A man of considerable business acumen, Garrison knew much about finance and transportation. Earlier in his impressive career he had profitably operated one of the strongest banks in California, had been involved with the Nicaragua Steamship Company and later had initiated a steamship service between the Port of New York and Brazil. "Possessing a large fortune, his financial operations were of great variety and magnitude."[75]

It is understandable that the corporate life of the StLKC&N was not long—not because it was a sickly property, but rather because of its good financial health and strategic position. By 1879 the national economy had rebounded fully from hard times, and railroad entrepreneurs, investment bankers and other capitalists began to think in terms of "system building," namely, to fuse smaller roads into larger more efficient, profitable and competitive units. "I have long been of the opinion that sooner or later the railroads of the country would group themselves into systems," reflected Charles Elliott Perkins, vice president and general manager of the CB&Q, in 1879, "and that each system would be self-sustaining—or . . . cease to exist & be absorbed by those systems near at hand & strong enough to live alone." That would be the fate of the StLKC&N, becoming in 1879 the western portion of a promising interregional trunk line, the Wabash, St. Louis & Pacific Railway.[76]

The Jay Gould Years

GOULD

In the post–Civil War period a star appeared in the constellation of railway leaders, and by the end of the 1870s it had grown even brighter. This cosmic phenomenon was Jason "Jay" Gould (1836–1892), a brilliant and innovative rags-to-riches New York State–born capitalist who left an indelible, albeit at times controversial, imprint on the nation's transportation network. In the process, he did much to shape the modern Wabash Railroad. His early career involved the tannery trade, but Gould entered the unpredictable and cutthroat world of big-time business, becoming in his mid-twenties a Wall Street trader. Initially lacking money and connections, he survived financially through shrewd investments and learned much in the process.[1]

In 1867 Gould moved beyond the status of obscure capitalist when he became a director of the Erie Railway, a company that in

its thirty-five-year corporate life had had a checkered history. Although in 1851 this "technological marvel" of a railroad had gained positive acclaim for creating the first route between "the Ocean and the Lakes," specifically linking the Hudson River about twenty-five miles north of New York City with Lake Erie, the road's overall physical condition and revenues subsequently worsened, forcing it into bankruptcy in 1859. Within a decade after its reorganization, the Erie gained the unenviable reputation for being the "scarlet woman of Wall Street." The troubles began when several "rail rogues" entered the picture. Shrewd and accomplished, speculator Daniel Drew, "the leading brigand of the Wall Street pirates," discovered the property and adroitly manipulated its stock. Then, in 1867, a three-way battle broke out for control, with interests represented by Drew, John Eldridge of the Boston, Hartford & Erie Railroad and "Commodore" Cornelius Vanderbilt of the New

The Rogers Locomotive and Machine Works in Patterson, New Jersey, has just completed the *Col. Robert Andrews*, No. 325, of the Wabash, St. Louis & Pacific. In 1880 this handsome American engine entered service but eleven years later became scrap. (Alco Historic Photos)

York Central Railroad (NYC). Two other financiers joined the fray, the young, flamboyant trader James "Jim" Fisk and Gould, his associate. When the smoke cleared, the crafty Vanderbilt had lost. Although later negotiations among these moneymen produced a compromise agreement, the plight of the "weary Erie" worsened. Few contemporary corporations were ever more maligned.[2]

Nevertheless, Gould, the epitome of the American get-up-and-go spirit, took charge of the looted Erie in 1868 and in a short time transformed it into a better property. When he took control, "its iron was worn and its roadbed in bad order," concluded the *Railroad Gazette* in early 1871. "There is now no better track in America." Added the *Gazette,* "Then it was scarcely safe to run twenty miles an hour; now the road is as safe at forty-five miles as human precaution can make it." By the time his connections with the company ended in 1872 Gould had failed to establish it as a major inter-regional system, although he had tried mightily to accomplish this Herculean feat. Gould's years at Erie suggested that, as a railroader, he was more a builder than a wrecker.[3]

Just as the infamous "Great Erie War" haunted the Erie Railroad, it forever sullied Gould's image. He never overcame a reputation for trickery and backdoor activities. Moreover, his pivotal role in a bizarre attempt in 1869 to corner the nation's gold supply convinced onlookers that he was a financial predator. It would be newspaper publisher Joseph Pulitzer who captured what so many thought of this small, soft-spoken and shy man, when he described him as "one of the most sinister figures that have ever flitted bat-like across the vision of the American people."[4]

Gould did not fade away from the business arena after his much-publicized setbacks. Rather, he forged ahead. As he continued to reveal his talent for stock trading, Gould became involved in the affairs of several rail and nonrail corporations, most notably the Union Pacific Railroad (UP). Although the building of this long and vital segment in a transcontinental rail link had captured the imagination of the American public, the road languished, largely because of its unusual legal relationship with the federal government, the Credit Mobilier construction scandal of 1872–1873 and poor management. When Gould arrived at UP, the company hovered on the brink of bankruptcy. As a member of the road's executive committee—he preferred to operate outside the limelight—he performed his financial and managerial magic. The company modernized, built profitable extensions, developed land and mineral resources, and fought for the best rates with interchange partners. So successful was Gould that within a few years the road could afford to pay dividends, even though the nation was in the midst of a depression. Moreover, his reputation was on the mend. Observers seemed surprised that Gould had not become involved in the UP solely to manipulate its stock and came to admire his wide-ranging achievements. Just as his efforts at improving the Erie had been a rehearsal for his actions at UP, collectively they prepared him well for the Wabash and his other railroad ventures.[5]

Although Gould could take considerable pride in his six years of wrestling with the challenges at UP, he knew that he was unlikely to overcome one enormous obstacle: Washington, D.C. Because the road possessed a federal charter, it was in reality a creature of Congress and subject to the often unpredictable winds of Gilded Age politics. Gould spent an inordinate amount of time wrangling with federal officials about the UP's construction loan, land-grant matters and mail and other services to the government. Although he did not liquidate his position in the UP, he did sell a major part of his holdings in 1879, providing him with capital for other investments.[6]

Between 1879 and 1881, Gould surprised the financial world by forging an impressive railroad network that spanned much of the nation. His insatiable ambition to create *his own* railroad empire knew few bounds. One property that became the core of these emerging "Gould Roads" was the Missouri Pacific. Gould ingeniously used this carrier, acquired in 1879, as a nucleus for the development of a Southwestern combine that soon counted the International & Great Northern; Missouri, Kansas & Texas (Katy); St. Louis, Iron Mountain & Southern (Iron Mountain); and Tom Scott's moribund Texas & Pacific. Some observers believed that Gould sought "complete monopolization of local business rather than the control of through traffic." In any event the east- and west-of-Mississippi segments of the future Wabash also entered his orbit. Gould's involvement even extended to several railroads in the East, including the Central Railroad of New Jersey; the Delaware, Lackawanna & Western; and the New York & New England. It became apparent that his goal was to create a truly transcontinental system, and he was off to an impressive start with units that stretched from the Atlantic Ocean to the Gulf of Mexico and into the West. By 1880 Gould dominated more than 8,000 miles of line, an accomplishment then without equal in the annals of American railroading.[7]

It would be incorrect, however, to suggest that Gould, this man with unbridled ambition, single handily assembled the future Wabash. That honor surely must be shared with "Commodore" C. K. Garrison (see chapter 2). A seasoned businessman, Garrison possessed a flare for successful investments in transportation companies and grasped the strategic potential of both the St. Louis, Kansas City & Northern Railroad (StLKC&N)

and the Wabash Railway. His control of the Missouri Pacific gave him an opportunity to gain firsthand knowledge of regional railroad affairs. Garrison correctly recognized that the powerful "Iowa Pool," a gentlemen's agreement launched in 1870 between the Chicago & North Western (C&NW); Chicago, Burlington & Quincy (CB&Q) and Chicago, Rock Island & Pacific to stabilize rates between the Union Pacific at Council Bluffs and Chicago, might be challenged if traffic could be diverted south and east around these Chicago-Omaha trunk lines.[8]

It did not take long for Garrison to swing into action. Early in 1877, he acquired a substantial stock interest in the StLKC&N and placed his son, W. R. Garrison, vice president of the Missouri Pacific, on the road's board of directors. Then, in November 1878, the Commodore assumed control of the Wabash and in the spring of 1879 became its president. He smartly took advantage of its bargain-basement stock prices. Shares were performing poorly, affected by incessant rate wars and lackluster management. As one railroad trade journalist tersely described the road, "The Wabash has been distinguished of late years for its eagerness to get traffic. It has succeeded very well, but apparently by sacrificing its profits." It would be Garrison who became the force for completing the StLKC&N into the Omaha gateway. With that accomplished in the latter part of 1879, the Iowa Pool could be outflanked, if by indirection. Freight cars now rumbled over the StLKC&N and its controlled properties to St. Louis, where they could continue their journey to Chicago and other eastern points.[9]

Garrison, too, made the Wabash Railway an even better placed road. Angered by the Alton's recent thrust into Kansas City and a pooling agreement between the Alton and the Illinois Central (IC), and fully sensing the well-recognized position of Chicago as *the* national railroad Mecca, he decided to enter the Windy City. With control of both the StLKC&N and Missouri Pacific, an independent route to Chicago held great utility. Such a line would also add value to the existing Wabash.[10]

Garrison believed that the Wabash had two practical options for reaching Chicago. The less expensive course, albeit one fraught with potential problems, centered on hammering out some type of long-term trackage-rights arrangement with the IC, thereby creating an "independent line." The other involved snapping up an existing, though nondescript shortline and using it as a springboard to Chicago. When negotiations with the IC dragged out for months, the Garrison road proceeded to act and in May 1879 formally acquired the Chicago & Paducah Railroad (C&P). The price was reasonable: $12,000 per mile.[11]

The C&P was typical of scores of Midwestern carriers that took shape during the golden age of railroad construction. The company expected much but accomplished little. It had hoped to operate 400 or more miles but assembled fewer than 100. In June 1872, a group of largely local capitalists, led by Colonel F. E. Hinckley, received an Illinois charter for a railroad between Paducah, Kentucky, on the Ohio River, and Chicago, a line that would mostly parallel the IC. These businessmen would incorporate into their road two earlier projects. One was the Fairbury, Pontiac & Northwestern Railway Company, launched in 1867, that had built thirty-one miles of track diagonally between the LaSalle County community of Streator and Fairbury, in Livingston County, a line seemingly headed toward the upper Mississippi River rather than Lake Michigan. The other was the Bloomington & Ohio River Railroad Company, incorporated in 1869, that had partially completed thirty-four miles of line on a north-south axis between Bement, a station on the Toledo, Wabash & Western (TW&W) about sixty miles south of Fairbury, and Windsor, a village in Shelby County. Proponents of the C&P sought to forge a connecting link and expand both ends to allow them to exploit anticipated north-south freight and passenger traffic. As for the latter, "It must be remembered the growing North-west is becoming thickly populated, and that since the war the Southern Mississippi Valley has greatly increased in population," argued a company prospectus. "The desire to visit St. Paul and the Northern Lakes in summer, as well as New Orleans and the Gulf States in winter, is so general, that, with a direct, rapid, and comfortable mode of travel, such as the through palace [sleeping]-cars, by way of the Chicago and Paducah Railroad will furnish a good through passenger traffic must be assured."[12]

Although the logic for creating the C&P may have been flawed, construction crews wasted little time in shaping this pike. They first completed the Bement-Windsor portion of the former Bloomington & Ohio River and followed with the installation of the intermediate sixty-two-mile segment between the former Fairbury, Pontiac & Northwestern at Fairbury and Bement. Not long thereafter they reached Effingham, fifty-eight miles south of Bement, and built a ten-mile extension between Shumway and Altamont. But by this time the C&P had depleted its financial resources, and hard times never allowed for more trackage. In 1878 the *Railroad Gazette* called the property "one of the least productive of the newer Illinois railroads" and added that "there are but one or two tolerable towns on it from one end to the other." Although the C&P ran from nowhere to nowhere in particular, it still made some key connections: at Streator with the CB&Q; Chicago Junction, near Pontiac, with the Alton; Bement with the TW&W; Windsor with the Indianapolis & St. Louis; and Effingham with the IC.[13]

With the C&P in hand, the Wabash board on June 5, 1879, decided to build to Chicago as quickly as possible. Neither the distance nor the topography was troublesome. In fact, the "Chicago Extension" would take advantage of some grading that had been completed in the early 1870s by the ill-fated Decatur & State Line Railroad. Construction workers rapidly completed the ninety-one-mile Wabash subsidiary, the Chicago & Strawn Railway Company, between the C&P at Strawn and a junction near Chicago with the fifty-mile-long Chicago & Western Indiana Railroad (C&WI), a convenient property that supplied both trackage rights into the city and terminal facilities, including wharfs on the Chicago River. By August 1, 1880, the building process was mostly finished, and a contract had been signed with the C&WI. Then, on the morning of August 9, the first regular passenger train left 22nd Street in Chicago bound for St. Louis, and another carrier had formally joined Windy City railroading.[14]

WABASH, ST. LOUIS & PACIFIC

Enter Jay Gould. Needless to say, he had been watching with envy the creative actions of Commodore Garrison. With the transportation map of the Midwest soon to be significantly altered by new routes—StLKC&N to Omaha and Wabash to Chicago—under construction, control of these roads offered attractive opportunities for the imaginative railroader. During the early part of 1879, Gould secretly began to buy the generally depressed Wabash stock. Then the big coup occurred. Gould convinced the seventy-year-old Garrison to sell his Wabash holdings and to allow usage of the StLKC&N. Even after Garrison resigned from the Wabash presidency in April, the financial world did not fully grasp the role of Gould, who kept accumulating Wabash stock. By the time the facts were widely known, Gould was in the catbird seat. The estimated investment amounted to less than $2 million, a good price, indeed.[15]

When Gould took the throttle of the Wabash, he came together with several gifted individuals who would remain with him for years, and these men would make important contributions in shaping the Wabash. One was millionaire banker Solon Humphreys, who served on the StLKC&N board and possessed a thorough understanding of railroad finance. Another was Ossian D. (O. D.) Ashley, a talented railroad operator with a quick mind and strong will who had been deeply involved in the reorganization of the TW&W. Still another was A. L. Hopkins, correctly categorized as "a first-rate railroad man."[16]

These men and other major investors associated with the former Garrison properties agreed with Gould that a merger of the Wabash with the StLKC&N was in order. This took place officially in November 1879, with most of the financial details decided by early July. The new 1,400-mile firm became known as the Wabash, St. Louis & Pacific Railway Company (WStL&P). The "& Pacific" did not necessary mean that the company intended to push to the Pacific Ocean, but it correctly implied that it would have "& Pacific" connections. The railroad's initial president, Cyrus W. Field, the famed promoter of the first transatlantic telegraphic cable, knew the property well as a result of earlier involvement with the Wabash Railway, and he had useful business alliances. He refused a salary and agreed to serve only until an "experienced railroad leader" could be found. That took place in April 1880, when Humphreys assumed the presidency.[17]

Almost immediately, the WStL&P plunged into a period of awesome construction, purchasing and leasing. With new connections about to be completed to Omaha and Chicago, the Gould property set its sights on another major destination, Detroit, the burgeoning metropolis of Michigan. This city was attractive for more than its bustling businesses; Detroit offered important railroad links to Canada, to New York City and to New England via several possible Ontario routes, the most probable one being the independent Great Western Railway of Canada. Because Vanderbilt roads dominated Detroit traffic, Gould found that he could enlist the support of James Frederick Joy, a brilliant Detroit lawyer who earlier in his career had energized the Michigan Central Railroad and had done much to shape rail expansion in the trans-Mississippi West. Joy loved his hometown and promoted it in every possible way.[18]

As a new member of the WStL&P board of directors, Joy believed that the Gould group could crack the Vanderbilt rail empire's hold on Detroit by building a fifty-five-mile exten-

In the 1870s engineer William A. Ray and fellow crew members of the Detroit, Eel River & Illinois Railroad locomotive *Junior* pose for posterity. Interestingly, both coal and wood fill the tender of this low-horsepower American-type engine. In 1879 the Logansport, Indiana-based shortline entered the fold of the Wabash, St. Louis & Pacific under a lease arrangement. (Author's Coll.)

sion from near the eastern terminus of the WStL&P at Toledo northward through country that "is almost as level as a floor." Even though two roads, Lake Shore & Michigan Southern (LS&MS) and the Canada Southern, already linked Toledo and Detroit, another line was hardly an impossibility. In fact, discussions already had taken place between Gould operatives and representatives from Detroit, and prospects looked promising for such an undertaking. By June 1879 rumors appeared in the press that "the new road from Toledo to Detroit will at once be built for the joint use of the Wabash, Grand Trunk and Great Western, of Canada." Reports also circulated that Gould and William H. Vanderbilt would hammer out a lease agreement for use of either the LS&MS or Canada Southern trackage between the two cities. Neither of these scenarios came to pass. Instead, a new line would reach Detroit from Indiana, not Ohio.[19]

Reminiscent of other portions of the Wabash, the "Detroit Extension" was the result of a mix of existing trackage and new-line construction. The role played by Joy involved more than being a Detroit booster, because he possessed excellent business contacts, especially among English investment bankers. In 1877 this seasoned railroader had acquired for himself and a group of bondholders the bankrupt Eel River Railroad, a ninety-three-mile road that largely followed the valley of the Eel River across Indiana between Logansport, Auburn and Butler. The company had had a wearisome past, having been reorganized (with appropriate name changes) several times since its birth in 1852 as the Auburn & Eel River Valley Railroad. With Joy's assistance, the WStL&P in 1879 leased the pike for a ninety-nine-year term with a generous annual rental of $90,000. Not only did the Eel River provide a practical means of reaching Detroit, bypassing the congested Toledo ter-

minal, but its control reduced feeder traffic to the LS&MS and, more important, disrupted a route for LS&MS movements between Detroit and Indianapolis. Noted a trade reporter, "[Eel River] removes, it is claimed, a formidable rival for the Southwestern traffic." If Gould built from Butler to Detroit, he observed, "that line would give a nearly air line between St. Louis and Detroit." Yet the construction crossed an area that was hardly starved for rail transport, going "through a country already pretty well cut up with railroads."[20]

Plans for the Detroit extension moved forward as expected. Company officials organized the appropriate subsidiary firms in Indiana, Michigan and Ohio, and soon these corporate units formally became the Detroit, Butler & St. Louis Railroad (DB&StL). In a process that was typical during the great construction era, railroad representatives solicited financial support from organizations, including public bodies, and individuals most likely to benefit from this expanded rail service. In the case of the DB&StL, agents scoured on-line locales, meeting with considerable success. Major contributions included $10,000 pledged by the Detroit Board of Trade and $10,200 subscribed by twenty-four of its members. There was also direct corporate support: the Detroit Bridge & Iron Company and the Detroit Stove Company, for example, each pledged $1,000. But most backing came from private citizens of considerably lesser means. The majority was for small amounts, frequently ranging from one dollar to fifty dollars. And these numerous backers hailed from all along the projected route: 63 from Adrian, 87 from Willis Station, 204 from Mill Creek, 210 from Blakesley, 99 from Blanchards, 100 from Griffith, 103 from Holloway, 106 from Thurburs and 110 from Britton.[21]

The actual entry of the WStL&P into a growing, vibrant Detroit occurred without difficulties. Construction for this 114-mile extension began in June 1880, with completion in August 1881. The line, known as the "Detroit Division," formally opened on August 14, and the first through passenger train from St. Louis, via the Eel River and the DB&StL, steamed into Detroit's Brush Street Station over tracks of the Grand Trunk Railway. Despite this start, it took several months to fully ready the line. "For the present only two trains daily will be run over it," announced an industry observer, "as there is still a good deal of work to do in building sidings and stations."[22]

Completion of the DB&StL provided additional benefits. It offered a practical way to establish relatively direct service between Detroit and Chicago. Not long after the line opened, the company worked out an arrangement with the Baltimore & Ohio Railroad (B&O) to operate through passenger trains between the two cities via the B&O interchange at Auburn Junction, Indiana. "This line is about the same length as the Michigan Central [the principal route]," commented the trade press. Although this service would later be diverted to the Chicago & Atlantic (Erie Railroad), then in the 1890s to the Wabash's own line across northern Indiana and eventually to the Pennsylvania Railroad, the use of the Detroit Division as a link between Detroit and Chicago became a long-standing tradition. The Detroit connection also meant that the WStL&P could strengthen its traffic ties with the East. A favored interchange with the Great Western Railway of Canada allowed access to the Buffalo, New York, gateway, greatly augmenting its recently established "line of steamers" between Toledo and Buffalo.[23]

Not only did Gould considerably strengthen the WStL&P through the lease of the Eel River and construction of the DB&StL, but rapid expansion continued. This involved a plethora of mostly pur-chased and leased lines both east and west of the Mississippi River. In 1880 alone the following units entered the system: lease on July 1 of the 136-mile Quincy, Missouri & Pacific between West Quincy, Missouri, and Milan, Missouri (extended in 1881 to Trenton, Missouri); lease on October 1 of the 247-mile Toledo, Peoria & Warsaw (TP&W), which crossed Illinois between State Line, Indiana, and Warsaw with trackage rights to Burlington, Iowa; lease on October 1 of the 131-mile Missouri, Iowa & Nebraska (MI&N) between Keokuk, Iowa, and Humeston, Iowa and lease of the connecting (at Centerville, Iowa) twenty-four-mile Centerville, Moravia and Albia Railroad. In that year, too, the WStL&P picked up a minor twenty-one-mile feeder road, the Clarinda & St. Louis Railway (C&StL), which connected Clarinda, Iowa, with the Omaha line at Roseberry, Missouri, and closely paralleled a branch of the CB&Q. (A decade later the C&StL was abandoned, an unusually early casualty of over-expansion.) By spreading across southern Iowa and northern Missouri, the WStL&P directly challenged the CB&Q, which had pioneered in the area. Also in 1880, the WStL&P purchased control of the 132-mile Champaign, Havana & Western (CH&W), a property that both the CB&Q and IC badly desired. This Illinois shortline ran from Urbana westward through Lincoln to Havana, Illinois. At White Heath, a thirty-mile branch extended south to Decatur. By the end of 1880, the WStL&P owned and operated nearly 2,500 miles of line, an increase of nearly 700 miles from the previous year. The road stretched from Detroit and Toledo to Council Bluffs and Kansas City and also served the major cities of Chicago and St. Louis and their respective hinterlands.[24]

More additions came in 1881, another banner year for growth. There was construction of the Covington branch, which extended nearly fifteen miles between the Indiana communities of Attica and Covington. Built by WStL&P subsidiary Attica, Covington & Southern Railway, this appendage, located mostly on the former towpath of the Wabash & Erie Canal, handled principally agricultural traffic. Yet rumors circulated that the branch might be advanced southward, perhaps to Terre Haute, a developing regional railroad center, or more likely into the coalfields near Brazil, Indiana.[25]

And there would be another lease. Gould pushed deeper into the upper Midwest through control of the Des Moines North-Western Railroad, a three-foot-gauge line that was building toward Minnesota and Dakota Territory with the likely objective of meeting the Northern Pacific at some point. But at the time the road reached only Jefferson, Iowa, seventy miles from its terminal city, Des Moines, where it met the mainline of the C&NW. In 1882, however, the slim-gauge track was extended to Fonda, Iowa, a village on the IC's Chicago–Sioux City route, 115 miles from the state capital.[26]

It was purchase rather than construction or lease that accounted for the bulk of line acquisitions during 1881. The largest addition involved the Danville & South-western Railroad (109 miles) and the Cairo & Vincennes Railroad (C&V) (158 miles), together arcing along the southeastern part of Illinois from Cairo, at the confluence of the Ohio and Mississippi rivers, and meeting the WStL&P at Danville. Included in this nearly 300-mile-long "Cairo Division" was a ten-mile stub, officially the St. Francisville & Lawrenceville Railroad, that left the main stem at St. Francisville, Illinois, for Vincennes, Indiana. For nearly a decade, these properties had been in the hands of J. S. Morgan & Company and had proved to be a "long-term headache" financially. Humphreys, who served on the C&V board, was likely responsible for the WStL&P's involvement. The second longest purchase was a wholly Indiana-centered operation, the 161-mile Indianapolis, Peru & Chicago Railway that connected two of the three cities in its corporate name: Indianapolis and Peru. Instead of Chicago the road ran north from Peru to the Lake Michigan port community of Michigan City. The WStL&P also added two ideally placed feeders, the seventy-three-mile Peoria, Pekin & Jacksonville Railroad (PP&J), wrestled away from a sale to the Chicago, Rock Island & Pacific, and the forty-seven-mile Springfield & Northwestern Railroad. The former linked Peoria, a key interchange point and the hub of the TP&W, with Jacksonville on the old Northern Cross. Moreover, the PP&J served Havana, the western terminus of the recently acquired CH&W. The latter acquisition, the Springfield & Northwestern, had as its southern terminus Springfield and met the PP&J and CH&W to the northwest at Havana.[27]

Surely the least attractive, even foolish, purchase consummated in 1881 involved the seventy-six-mile Havana, Rantoul & Eastern Railroad (HR&E). This narrow-gauge pike extended from West Lebanon, Indiana, on the mainline of the WStL&P between Decatur and Logansport, westward to Le Roy, Illinois (it had been projected to Havana and an announced connection with the Fulton County Narrow Gauge Railroad). Why Gould showed interest in what was at best a minor agricultural line is a mystery. Perhaps he worried that during this time of a national narrow-gauge building craze an east-west network of these roads might use the HR&E as a critical link between built, under-construction and projected carriers from Ohio through Indiana to Illinois and other destinations. Yet the WStL&P publicly announced why it was supposedly acquired: "a very considerable increase of business is anticipated." Once more a spiderlike web of lines was being spun through central and eastern parts of Illinois, a state that during

Bad things can happen on a railroad, and they did on a winter day in January 1883 near West Grove, Iowa. Explained S. R. Wood, a railfan and photograph collector, in 1939: "In this wreck [on the Ottumwa branch], four of the engines had been trying to get thru the heavy snow and became stalled. Four relief engines were sent out to break thru the snow to meet them. The engineers of the relief engines agreed beforehand that the one [engineer] on the leading engine keep a sharp lookout for the stalled engines and would give one sharp toot of the whistle as a signal for all to shut off steam. On sighting the stalled train, the engineer of the second engine became excited and in violation of the agreement gave a sharp toot of his whistle right after the leading engineer had done so, thus sounding to the other two engineers like a 'toot-toot,' or come-ahead signal. The latter, then, instead of shutting off, applied more power and shoved the two leading engines into the four stalled ones." A messy wreck resulted. (Author's Coll.)

the Gilded Age encountered an explosion of rail mileage: 4,823 in 1870; 7,018 in 1880 and 9,936 in 1890.[28]

While control of the Havana, Rantoul & Eastern was small potatoes, 1881 also witnessed schemes to expand drastically the property. A case in point involved the WStL&P and the Central Railroad of New Jersey, a road in which Gould had a financial interest, entering into a contract with the sprawling Pennsylvania Railroad Company (PRR) that would permit these roads to use trackage between Red Bank, Pennsylvania, on the PRR's subsidiary Allegheny Valley Railroad, and Milton, Pennsylvania, on a connecting affiliate, the Philadelphia & Erie Railroad. "Under this arrangement the Wabash, St. Louis & Pacific Railway Company and the Central Railroad of New Jersey were to promote the construction of a road between Red Bank and Youngstown, O," noted a PRR source, "and it was expected that if these two railroads availed themselves of this trackage privilege, both the Philadelphia & Erie Railroad and the Low Grade Division of the Allegheny Valley Railroad

would be greatly benefited thereby." But this plan for an East Coast outlet for the WStL&P, which likely would have involved the Erie Railroad between Youngstown and Huntington, Indiana, or an Erie connection at Corry, Pennsylvania, directly with the Allegheny Valley, never progressed.[29]

Although by the end of 1881 WStL&P mileage had soared to 3,349, with about two-thirds east and one-third west of the Mississippi River, the rate of increase then slowed considerably. The following year this Gould property acquired the seventy-one-mile St. Louis, Jerseyville & Springfield Railroad between Bates and Grafton, Illinois; leased the Des Moines & St. Louis Railroad between Albia and Des Moines (thus connecting the Des Moines North-Western with the Centerville, Moravia & Albia); extended the Des Moines North-Western to Fonda; and installed a twelve-mile branch between Champaign and Sidney, Illinois.[30]

By 1883 the map of the WStL&P revealed a impressive 3,518-mile railroad, with mainlines that reached Chicago, Council Bluffs, Des Moines, Detroit, Kansas City, St. Louis and Toledo. With the exception of Buffalo, New York, these would be the principal terminals of the Wabash throughout its corporate life. Gould certainly understood the importance of through business, a concept that some of his contemporaries never grasped. Then there was that maze of feeder and secondary routes, most heavily concentrated in Indiana and Illinois. Perhaps the oddest part of the system was the narrow-gauge line northwest of Des Moines that stuck out like an uncrossed "T." There were also WStL&P cargo boats on Lake Erie (with a favored connection at the docks in Buffalo with the Delaware, Lackawanna & Western Railroad) and a proprietary interest in a barge line on the Mississippi River between St. Louis and New Orleans. To operate this large expanse of rail lines in 1883, the company divided the trackage into four divisions, calling them simply the Eastern, Middle, Western and Northern.[31]

Causal observers found much to like about the Wabash, St. Louis & Pacific. It was a railroad with important terminals and convenient connections. Several of its stems provided the shortest distances between major terminals; for example, the Omaha–St. Louis line was sixty miles shorter than the route of the closest competitor. Indeed, the road "forms a great national highway between the East, West, North and South, while its intimate relations with connecting lines assure its patrons the speediest and surest means of reaching any part of the country." It served not only an array of manufacturing and business enterprises but agriculturalists in a large part of the corn and hog region of the Midwest and in portions of rich winter wheat country as well.[32]

Often when consumers used the "new" railroad which was not a party to existing pooling agreements, they reaped unexpected benefits. The most striking example involved an incredibly intense battle waged between the Alton and the WStL&P for passenger business between Chicago, Kansas City and St. Louis. In the fall of 1880, not long after the Gould road entered the Windy City, it drastically slashed ticket prices to introduce itself to the traveling public and allegedly to compensate patrons who "were forced to drive a long distance to and from the 22nd Street Station." A not-so-happy Alton followed suit with cheaper tickets. It did not take long for the original fare of $7.50 to St. Louis to drop to only one dollar, with the fare to Kansas City only slightly more. Although an agreement temporarily increased rates, the conflict soon resumed, and the rate war was not finally settled until June 1882.[33]

Not everyone, however, applauded Gould's activities and accomplishments. Industry observers worried about the future of the WStL&P with its "heavy charges for interest and rentals," and there was the belief that the company lacked proper focus. "It has a small income and yet can not confine its energies to developing any one avenue of traffic, but must of necessity seek to develop them all, with the effect of producing only a very poor or indifferent result." Notwithstanding these complaints about the management of the WStL&P, the Vanderbilt-controlled roads bemoaned what had transpired in "their home territory," especially with traffic losses from Detroit and to southwestern points, and the Alton fussed about an aggressive St. Louis–Chicago competitor. But most of all, the CB&Q fumed about incursions into northern Missouri and southern Iowa. In 1880, Charles Elliott Perkins, the road's vice president and general manager, summed up the situation this way: "The Wabash is a nuisance to us all now."[34]

But what would Perkins and his board of directors do about this "nuisance?" Earlier the CB&Q had protected itself from Gould when it learned that he sought the Kansas City, St. Joseph & Council Bluffs Railroad by paying top dollar for additional stock, but it still felt the sting of the loss to Gould in 1871 of the larger Hannibal & St. Joseph Railroad (although it regained control at a fair price in 1883). Later, in 1880, when Gould revealed that extension of the MI&N westward across the southern tier of Iowa counties from Humeston to Shenandoah, on its Omaha line, was imminent, Perkins and his associates knew that they would need to be proactive. As constituted, the MI&N would not only parallel the mainline of the CB&Q across much of southern Iowa but would create a connecting artery between Omaha and Toledo with other major gateway options, both real and possible. (Acquisitions between 1880 and 1882 did just that.) The CB&Q told Humphreys that, if this construction occurred, it would build alongside the MI&N. Privately, there were acid stomachs among CB&Q leaders. On September 16, 1880, Perkins informed John Murray Forbes, his cousin and fellow board member, that "I conclude that Gould either can't or won't make peace. I don't believe he can't, and that leaves only the conclusion in my mind that he won't."[35]

On the same day as Perkins's missive to Forbes, James Joy wrote his longtime financier friend and recent partner in the Eel River purchase Elijah Smith, then involved in the affairs of the CB&Q, to explain the Gould position. "[I] am very sorry to see a fight between the two companies like these. But now I will say to you that the Chicago, Burlington & Quincy is wrong in the fight, and cannot maintain its position upon any proper principle." And he explained *why* the CB&Q was amiss in opposing the MI&N extension:

> It is now more than twenty years, probably, since Keokuk and the people of the country along the line through the southern counties of Iowa organized that road which is now creating this controversy. They undertook to

build it, and had the right to build it, and actually did build nearly a hundred miles of it. They got into difficulty and appealed to the Chicago, Burlington and Quincy to help them and take the road and extend it. Their argument with the Chicago, Burlington and Quincy was that it was through a country tributary to the Burlington and Missouri road, as it then was, and that the Chicago, Burlington and Quincy could command its business at Keokuk, and maintain rates also on both lines. The question for the Chicago, Burlington and Quincy to consider, was whether it was worth its while to take up and adopt that road, extend it as far as it saw fit, and use it to enable it both to maintain rates and also command its business. It was carefully considered and discussed when I was at the head of the Chicago, Burlington and Quincy. . . . On the fullest consideration, and after much discussion, a committee . . . recommended that the Chicago, Burlington and Quincy and the men connect with it, should not take it or adopt it.

> That was done with the full conviction derived from experience that the road would go through under some auspices. It might fail and be sold once or twice, but was sure to revive again and go on to completion was only a question of time. That was the action, then, of the Chicago, Burlington and Quincy. What right has it to complain now, when with all the aid the country can give, the Wabash now sees it may complete and obtain not only that road, but its shortest possible line to Omaha and the Pacific?[36]

Perhaps Joy's cogent arguments, which Smith surely shared with Perkins and his colleagues, may have promoted them to rethink their position. Then there was a short letter from Humphreys to Perkins written on September 13, 1880, from New York, that "we have given authority to organize a Company *in* [emphasis added] Nebraska to enable us to construct a Road in that State, which it will be most essential for us to build provided the C.B.& Q. go on building Roads making all the principal stations on our Omaha lines in Missouri and Iowa competitive." A CB&Q-inspired compromise went shortly to the WStL&P. Without doubt, the Perkins group wanted to avoid warfare and the costs of needless construction and therefore proposed that the two roads *jointly* extend the property. At an October peace conference held in New York City, which also included the UP, the parties agreed on matters of non-invasion so as to stabilize conditions both in Iowa and west of the Missouri River. As for the MI&N, it would be a cooperative venture, and soon the Humeston & Shenandoah Railroad was formed to push rails ninety-seven miles to the west from Humeston to Shenandoah. Shortly after New Year's Day in 1883, the WStL&P began running through passenger trains across southern Iowa between Chicago and Council Bluffs via the TP&W, "which is considerably shorter than the route heretofore used." As Humphreys bragged in an exaggerated fashion, "[This line creates] almost an air line from Toledo and Detroit to Council Bluffs and Omaha, connecting with the Union Pacific."[37]

The compromise of October 1880 did not mean that all was well between Perkins and Gould. There were to be incursions by the Missouri Pacific into "Burlington territory" west of the Missouri River and other bones of contention, which partially explain why in 1881–1882 the CB&Q built a heavy-duty line from central Nebraska to Denver, Colorado. As for the WStL&P, the agreement allowed it to construct "local lines in Iowa." But when Gould subsequently encouraged J. S. Clarkson and other Des Moines capitalists to build the Des Moines & St. Louis Railway, Perkins felt that the spirit if not the actual provisions of the compact had been violated.[38]

While Perkins headed a stable, prosperous railroad, although forced to be less standpat because of Jay Gould, the empire created by his nemesis showed signs of weakening by 1883. Then, in 1884, the year of a nasty bankers' panic, it seemingly crumbled. Gould had more to worry about than the WStL&P. He needed to focus on saving the three properties that by this time constituted the core of his corporate holdings: Missouri Pacific system, Manhattan Elevated Railroad in New York City and Western Union Telegraph Company. "Like many great generals, he conquered more than he had the resources to protect," explained historian Maury Klein, "and the ensuing struggles took a heavy toll on both his financial and his physical resources."[39]

BANKRUPTCY

By the spring of 1883 the perceptive and resourceful Gould, who had uncharacteristically assumed an official leadership role as president of the WStL&P, realized that trouble was brewing in his far-flung railroad empire. As he juggled a number of fire batons, Gould decided to lease the WStL&P to his Missouri Pacific affiliate, the St. Louis, Iron Mountain & Southern Railway, a decision that directors and stockholders duly endorsed. "The lease of the property . . . has been undertaken strictly for the benefit and advantage of the stockholders, and their success, which is now assured, shall be considered of great value to the company," explained a self-assured Gould to the trade press. "The fact that a very large amount of the stock [of the WStL&P] is held by the directors of the company, I myself being the largest stockholder, should be a sufficient answer to the malicious and unfounded reports recently circulated."[40]

The public response to the lease was mixed. The St. Louis press liked the announcement: "The great danger was that the

Wabash system with its 3,500 miles of road and with its valuable connections with important business points . . . would be consolidated not with a St. Louis system, managed in the interest of St. Louis and of Missouri," editorialized the *St. Louis Post Dispatch,* "but with a Chicago system, managed in the interest of Chicago." Most observers, however, believed that the lease demonstrated that Gould was up to more chicanery. Some thought it involved some cleverly devious stock-watering scheme—a common Gilded Age railroad sin. A member of the Fourth Estate suggested, tongue in cheek, that "If Mr. Jay Gould would sprinkle some of his watered stock along the line of his various railroads, fewer fields would be burned up by sparks from his engines."[41]

Although the Iron Mountain arrangement may have bolstered investor confidence in securities of the WStL&P, by spring 1884 the financial clouds had darkened. A portion of the floating debt came due on June 1, and the troubled economic condition of both the nation and the road augured poorly for payment. Rate wars devastated income. This hurt the company, which relied heavily on overhead traffic, especially from Western connections.[42]

That it was not the only railroad to encounter money strains was surely of little solace to the WStL&P. In 1884 and 1885, a number of carriers throughout the country sought bankruptcy protection. Some of the more prominent failures included the Denver & Rio Grande; Houston & Texas Central; Nickel Plate Road and New York & New England. Financial observers quickly labeled these industry troubles the "railroad panic of 1884," and for the next several years reports of negotiations and reorganizations splashed across the front pages of the nation's popular and financial press.[43]

One story that became widely reported took place in mid-May when the Iron Mountain officially notified the WStL&P that "the net earnings of the Wabash line, operated under the lease. . . , are insufficient to pay the interest and other fixed charges, and that, as the lessee company, it will no longer advance for the deficiency." Rather than wait to see what would happen with this impending financial crisis, Gould pursued an aggressive course. The response of WStL&P leadership surprised the business world and later led writers and scholars to consider the strategy a novel approach to modern business bankruptcies.[44]

Even though no creditors of the WStL&P had taken legal action to protect their investments, on May 28, 1884, Solon Humphreys, Gould's associate and a company director and former president, entered the U.S. District Court in St. Louis, and informed Judge Samuel Treat that the road verged on insolvency and asked him to place it in receivership. The company requested that Humphreys and Thomas E. Tutt, a St. Louis banker, be named coreceivers. The judge duly considered the request and in the process wisely consulted Nathaniel Shipman, a U.S. district court judge in Connecticut, and David Brewer, a senior circuit judge. Both jurists were familiar with railroad bankruptcies and knew the importance of maintaining freight and passenger operations. They agreed with Treat that the requests made by the WStL&P should be granted. Humphreys and Tutt assumed their new positions, and Gould resigned as company president.[45]

It appeared that Gould's plan to save the WStL&P from an unfriendly reorganization would work and hence save his control over this vital property. Soon after Humphreys and Tutt took charge, they issued court-approved receivers' certificates. These were used to pay maturing notes, some of which had been endorsed personally by Gould, Humphreys, Sidney Dillon and Russell Sage,

Jay Gould and his associates on the Wabash, St. Louis & Pacific successfully sold stocks and bonds to foreign investors. Amsterdam commission agents Hubrecht, Van Harencarspel and Vas Visser, for example, offered shares and bonds on the Dutch market. These men specialized in securities of American railroads, including the WStL&P (Augustus J. Veenendaal, Jr., Coll.)

thus saving these men from major losses or possible financial ruin. It became clear that the court considered the floating debt to be superior to the lien of the general mortgage bondholders. Some were shocked, most notably bondholders who lived in England and Holland.[46]

Opposition rapidly developed. Almost immediately, journalists in the United States and abroad, especially in London, where some major investors lived, blasted the "Wabash swindle." They felt that the bondholders, who thought that their investments were protected legally, would likely suffer in the forthcoming reorganization. One publication even wondered whether the federal judiciary had become part of Gould's law department. Another believed that recent events "contribute to make the history of

Wabash since Mr. Gould took it one of the most remarkable and interesting that has ever occurred in American railroading." Added the paper: "It is even phenomenal, embracing in a comparatively short period nearly every phase of kite-flying, watering, stock-jobbing, [and] bankruptcy of the company. . ., which are so frequently commented on it London and Amsterdam as being the common characteristics of American railroad management."[47]

More upsetting than the negative press coverage were subsequent legal actions. Certain bondholders of the WStL&P components east of the Mississippi River, many of whom were English investors, questioned the legitimacy of the receivership. In December 1886, they convinced Judge Walter L. Gresham of the Seventh Circuit Court in

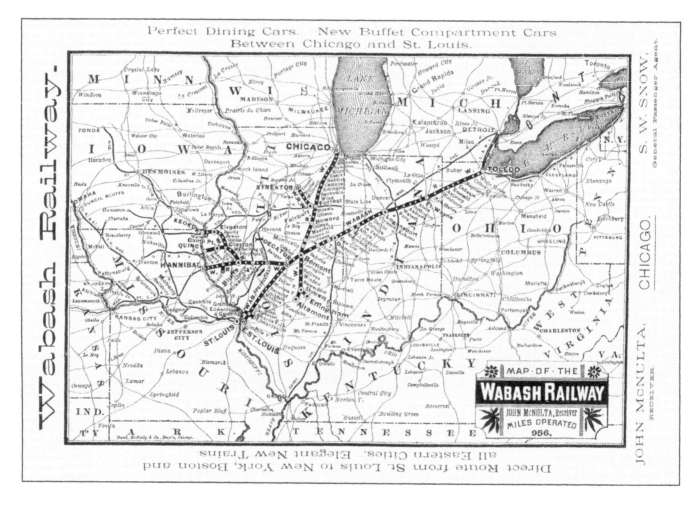

The Wabash Railway of the late 1880s, which consisted largely of former Wabash, St. Louis & Pacific lines east of the Mississippi River, issued this combination system map and promotional advertisement. (Don L. Hofsommer Coll.)

Chicago to remove coreceivers Humphreys and Tutt on the grounds that they "were not impartial parties." As Judge Gresham himself said about their actions, "The boldness of this scheme . . . by denying equal rights to all bondholders secured by the same mortgages is equaled only by its injustice." He then named Thomas M. Cooley, a distinguished member of the Michigan Supreme Court and professor of law at the University of Michigan, to be their replacement. Soon thereafter, Judges Brewer and Treat intervened and ordered Humphreys and Tutt to continue their services but to turn over to

Cooley the account books and other records that belonged to certain pieces of trackage, including the 258-mile Chicago Division. Humphreys and Tutt, furthermore, were to retain all money and rolling stock that was not part of the Cooley-protected lines. What developed then was the extraordinary separation of the lines under *two* receiverships, adding immeasurably to the complications and expenses of the bankruptcy.[48]

Meanwhile, reorganization under the general outlines envisioned by Gould and his associates continued to evolve, although the receiverships led temporarily to creation of two new railroads rather than a continuance of a single Wabash, St. Louis & Pacific. On March 1, 1887, the lines generally *west* of the Mississippi River became the Wabash Western Railway Company with O. D. Ashley as president. Initially, this property was to be known as the "Wabash, St. Louis & Western Railway"; however, a more descriptive name and one less likely to be confused with the WStL&P was chosen. The Wabash Western did not operate most of the mileage that had been acquired during the halcyon years of the early 1880s, but rather 641 miles that included trackage between St. Louis and Kansas City, Moberly and Des Moines, Brunswick and Pattonsburg, and the Columbia and Glasgow branches. It also operated an "Eastern Division," consisting of more than 350 miles. These lines consisted of the segments between Clymers, Indiana, (near Logansport) and Detroit; Attica and Covington; and Sidney and Champaign and the leased trackage via the Chicago & Atlantic (Erie) between Laketon Junction, Indiana, and Chicago. A bondholders committee, which worked with receiver Cooley (and, after he resigned to become the first chair of the newly created Interstate Commerce Commission with his successor, John McNulta), operated much of the pre-1880 WStL&P *east* of the Mississippi River and flew the corporate banner of the Wabash Railway Company. Therefore, what remained amounted to nearly 950 miles and included the trackage between Toledo and Keokuk, Iowa; Chicago and Effingham and Altamount, Illinois; Decatur and East St. Louis, Illinois; and the Fairbury, Edwardsville and Pittsfield branches. Other leased and controlled lines reverted back to their bondholders and operated either as independent shortlines or once the reorganization became finalized joined major trunk carriers. Ultimately, the WStL&P lost nearly $5 million on these forfeited affiliates.[49]

The process of restructuring caused its share of disruptions and concerns for those individuals associated with leased lines or ones that had not been fully fused into the WStL&P. The woes experienced by those who owned the leased Eel River Railroad Company in Indiana reveal the kinds of problems encountered. On September 29, 1886, Elijah Smith wrote to Humphreys and Tutt that "your Company is taking gravel from the gravel bed on the line of the Eel River Road for the purpose of graveling portions of the Wabash line other than the Eel River Road. As we are obtaining no income for the Eel River line and there is no definite proposition for the taking care of the Eel River line in the reorganization, I must protest on behalf of the stockholders of that Road against such action and request that it be discontinued at once." The receivers responded, agreeing to pay. Yet they continued to use the stone from the quarry located a few miles east of Logansport along the Eel River, and Smith once more protested, telling them that the supply was limited and demanding that they "stop taking of gravel for the use of the road of the Wabash outside of the Eel River road."[50]

The owners of the leased Eel River had more to worry about than a depleted gravel pit. The company later complained to the receivers that it had "received no rental or revenue of any kind whatever since the rental due June 1, 1884." Moreover, the firm protested that "it is made known to us that the equipment of this Company which is unusually large, and before the lease always earned considerable revenue—say about $30,000 per annum, outside of the regular operation of the Railroad, and which equipment by the terms of the lease was agreed to be kept separate and distinct, has been mingled with and so mixed up with the other equipment of the Wabash Company as not to be distinguished, and shows no revenue, while the Company is being charged as part of its operating expenses for use of cars, or a proportion of interest on car trusts, when it has more cars per mile belonging to it than any part of the Wabash Road itself."

Then there was the machinery problem. The Eel River expressed its anguish about missing machinery from its shops complex in Logansport. "The machinery of this Company has been taken from the shops . . . and carried to the shops of the Wabash Company without any consent from or accounting to this Company." The Eel River also fussed about the installation of "old and second hand" rails on its line without proper record-keeping and accounting procedures. Not surprisingly, legal threats followed, but for the most part the Eel River had to absorb its financial losses.[51]

Nonrailroaders, too, encountered problems with the bankrupt carrier. In a bizarre turn of affairs, residents of Salisbury, Missouri, located on the Moberly–Kansas City line and the terminus of the Glasgow branch, made news when they retaliated against the company for not paying back property taxes, estimated at $11,000. When their earlier complaints went unheeded, a group of public-spirited citizens decided to make known their unhappiness with this "flagrant tax-dodging." On January 4, 1886, they chained an eastbound Wabash passenger train to the tracks as it was about to leave town, with the intent of holding it hostage until the receivers paid. The irate crowd told the engineer that he could leave with the mail car but not with the remainder of the train. "Passengers were detained," reported a local newspaper, "and of course were as mad as wet hens." One angry salesman informed his firm in Kansas City "that he would return home on the next train, and cease work rather than travel through a territory only penetrated by the Wabash." A railroad representative wired the Chariton County sheriff,

asking him to release the train, and announced that the road would quickly pay its tax bill. Even though the town marshall arrested the sheriff when he sought to "free" the train "for unnecessarily drawing firearms on those who had the train," the matter was shortly resolved. Salisbury finally got its money. Thereafter, even though the company had cleared its account, many residents of the community continued to consider it a poor corporate citizen.[52]

Although the mid and late 1880s proved to be years of struggle for the receivers and others involved in the bankruptcy, the Wabash at last emerged from bankruptcy on May 15, 1889, as the Wabash *Railroad* Company and included both the Wabash Western Railway and the Wabash Railway. This became possible when the purchasing committee, headed by the indefatigable O. D. Ashley, succeeded in buying out at top dollar the interests of a minority bondholders protection committee that controlled part of the east-of-the-Mississippi trackage. The central financial features of the reorganization, which comprised thirty-eight different mortgage loans, required first-mortgage bondholders to exchange their securities, which averaged 7 percent interest, for new blanket first-mortgage bonds that paid only 5 percent interest. And second-mortgage bonds were similarly exchanged for general second-mortgage bonds that bore 5 percent interest. Fortunately for Gould, he retained control through his ties with the triumphant purchasing committee, and the railroad appeared poised to meet the challenges of the times.[53]

Although arguments have been made that the complex Wabash bankruptcy case can be regarded as the origin of modern corporation reorganizations, precedents of the important features had already been established. In his essay, "The People's Welfare and the Origins of Corporate Reorganization: The Wabash Receivership Reconsidered," economic historian Bradley Hansen has argued cogently that "three features of the Wabash receivership are said to mark it off from previous receiverships: submission of the request by the debtor rather than by a creditor; the appointment of interested parties as receivers; and its secondary focus on the protection of creditors' interests. All three were in fact common features of railroad receiverships prior to 1884 and were defended by judges as responses to the quasi-public nature of railroads." Though some aspects of the Wabash bankruptcy might smack of wrongdoing, Hansen makes it abundantly clear not only that there were a variety of significant precedents but also that judges by the 1880s nearly always agreed that their *foremost* obligation was to keep economically troubled railroads in operation, thus protecting a "public interest." That is exactly what happened with the Wabash. Although for a few years it functioned as a bifurcated carrier, freight and passenger trains nevertheless plied its steel rails, and a stronger, reorganized railroad was in the offing.[54]

THE SOUTHWEST STRIKES

While there existed a reasonably strong esprit de corps among WStL&P employees, which led to a variety of festive activities and other social interactions especially in the several "Wabash towns," this railroad family during the early 1880s grew steadily more anticompany and prone to familial bickering. Not only did Gould and then the receivers confront a multitude of financial challenges, but labor unrest arose also. The consequences were some of the most significant strikes to haunt Gilded Age America and work stoppages that the public closely associated with Gould.[55]

The key to understanding labor troubles

on the WStL&P that flared into major strikes in 1885 and again in 1886 is money. Operatives for the company and its major predecessors had received pay commensurate with those who worked for neighboring carriers in the past, but in the early 1880s, as the road's income declined, paydays were sometimes skipped. "Many were met whose average incomes was [sic] $30.00 a month and who, on this pitiful pittance, were expected to keep life in a wife and from two to five children," reported the *St. Louis Post-Dispatch* in March 1882. "This would be hard enough to do were cash paid for the labor, but the Wabash Company deliberately declines to pay the laborers their money when it is due. . . . There is no excuse for withholding from the laborer his hire, and when the Wabash Company defers the payment of wages earned in January until March, it is simply practicing upon the weakness of the poor." A tightness of funds, the company argued, explained the missed wages.[56]

Since its founding, hundreds of employees on the WStL&P had belonged to unions. Most were highly skilled workers. Engineers, for example, generally joined the Brotherhood of Locomotive Engineers, which dated nationally from 1863, and firemen enrolled in the Brotherhood of Locomotive Firemen and Enginemen, formed a decade later. Although these emerging brotherhoods would soon focus on such "bread-and-butter" issues as higher wages, shorter hours and improved working conditions, and would strike to achieve these goals, at this time they functioned largely as mutual benefit societies. Brotherhoods provided accident, death and burial insurance, and were appropriately known as "coffin clubs." Each month, a member might pay a dollar or less for this much-wanted and needed security. The brotherhoods, too, provided their members with social activities, not unlike the Patrons of Husbandry for farmers. The always popular dinners and dances gave these groups a distinctive fraternal atmosphere. Resembling nonrailroad-based organizations, the brotherhoods stressed the importance of self-help and mutual assistance, repeatedly adorning their charters, publications and social and public events with such mottoes as "Benevolence," "Charity," "Industry," and "Sobriety." They reflected the prevailing Victorian views of life and labor.[57]

Coinciding with the development of railroad brotherhoods, the WStL&P and many other carriers in the 1880s also saw the appearance of workers, usually nonoperating employees, belonging to the Knights of Labor. Organized in 1869, the Knights created America's first widespread industrial union movement. Unlike the American Federation of Labor (AFL), which began to take shape in the mid-1880s, the Knights never fully accepted the wage system and repeatedly dabbled with cooperatives or worker-owned businesses, ranging from cigar factories to coal mines. Coinciding with their somewhat collectivist attitudes, the leadership of the Knights did everything it could to avoid strikes. Also differing from the AFL, the Knights allowed semiskilled and nonskilled workers into their locals or "assemblies." At times, too, women and people of color gained membership.[58]

Led by the charismatic, albeit somewhat inept and alcoholic, Terence V. Powderly, the Grand Master Workman, in the early and mid-1880s membership in the Knights grew impressively in the Midwest. Local assemblies proliferated, primarily consisting of coal miners and railroaders who were mostly shopmen, car repairers and track workers. Although there is no way of knowing how many Knights the WStL&P employed, there were at least assemblies located in communities where there were terminals and shops facilities. As labor troubles heightened, sup-

port increased; for example, Assembly No. 93 in Moberly, Missouri, grew from 152 in 1884 to 456 a year later. And by 1886 its roster had swelled to 1,158 members.[59]

Unhappiness on the WStL&P grew prodigiously stronger, triggered on February 27, 1885, by a 10 percent wage reduction, precipitating a strike by the Knights at Moberly and among operatives in other communities, including those employed in the shops at Fort Wayne, Indiana. Backed by the brotherhoods and the unorganized generally, the work stoppage spread to other parts of the railroad and then throughout the Gould system. A typical handbill strikers distributed on the WStL&P read:

NOTICE!

To the Public and Workingmen Especially. Whereas, the Wabash employees. . . [have] scarcely made enough in the last two years to keep their family, and therefore cannot stand a further reduction. They have resolved to make a bold stand against their oppressors, and will use all lawful means to win. Therefore they beg and entreat all men of employment to stay away from the Wabash shops, repair tracks and depots all along the entire line. . . .
Committee[60]

After a short time, labor peace returned on the Gould system. The prolabor governors of Kansas and Missouri, where much of the unrest occurred, intervened as mediators and toiled mightily to resolve the dispute. Most of all, restoration of the wages that had been cut pleased workers in Moberly and elsewhere. Their average wage of $1.50 per day was reestablished. The agreement also provided that "no official shall discriminate against the Knights of Labor or question the right of the employee to belong to the Order."[61]

But the peace was short lived. When the WStL&P began to layoff shopmen who belonged to the Knights, tempers flared, and in

THE JAY GOULD YEARS   71

August another strike erupted. Because Gould was out of the country during the first work stoppage, his role in that conflict was limited, but this time he was in New York City and became actively involved. He soon stunned some in the business community by inviting to his posh Manhattan home the Knights' leadership, including Powderly. Although Gould had no plans to recognize the union as the bargaining agent for either the WStL&P or his other railroads, he was willing to talk about mutual concerns. "In the meeting with Powderly," according to Maury Klein, "Gould promised to use his influence with the Wabash and to hear any grievance arising on roads under his control." Shortly thereafter, the WStL&P ended its layoffs and Powderly called off the second strike. In the workers' view, the Knights had won and Gould had lost— David had defeated Goliath. As a result, Knight membership soared among railroaders, and overall it rose from 110,000 in July 1885 to 730,000 a year later.[62]

The Knights-inspired labor unrest, however, had not ended, and the epicenter shifted from Moberly, Missouri, and the WStL&P to Marshall, Texas, and Gould's Texas & Pacific Railway (T&P). Trouble flared up on February 19, 1886, when the T&P fired Charles Hall, a foreman in one of the car shops and local union member who held the title "Master Workman of District Assembly 101." Immediately, Martin Irons, a top-ranking official of the Knights and a man with an organizing mission, ordered members to leave their jobs. Soon this work action spread to other Gould properties, including the WStL&P. The strike shocked both Powderly and Gould, neither of whom wanted or expected the walkout. Indeed, Powderly had made it clear to everyone that "it is, or was, well known that I not only did not favor the ordering of strikes, but opposed entering upon them until the depths

of the last harbor of peaceful adjustment had been sounded." The Knights' leader assumed (incorrectly), however, that the Missouri Pacific could force the T&P to reinstate Hall and that all would be well. But the Missouri Pacific made it clear that it had absolutely no control over the T&P, including matters of personnel. Furthermore, the T&P was in bankruptcy, and power rested with the court and its receivers. Gould did not plunge into the fracas. Rather, he continued his policy of allowing chief subordinates to make decisions, including those involving labor, unless they were likely to cause some major calamity. In the case of the WStL&P, this meant that the able A. A. Talmage, vice president and general manager, would be the point man.[63]

It did not take long for the strike of 1886 to go badly for the Knights. Train brotherhoods mostly ignored the stoppage, and the Gould roads began dismissing strikers and finding permanent replacement workers. The sentiments of a Missouri newspaper editor summed up the feelings of many who lived in WStL&P communities: "Moberly has had enough." When some strikers vandalized railroad equipment and property, the public became alarmed, rightly worrying about the safety of rail travel. Violence broke out in several locales, including the sprawling yard complex in East St. Louis, Illinois. In previous conflicts, disturbances had been negligible, and that state of affairs, together with Gould as a symbol of corporate evil, "the money monarch," had produced considerable public sympathy. Indeed, strikers had successfully conveyed the notion that disorder and violence were contrary to their principles and fully distanced themselves from the widespread turbulence that had swept the B&O and other railroads during 1877.[64]

Powderly, who lacked any real control over his striking local assemblies, thought that he could bring about an acceptable settlement.

After another meeting with Gould, he mistakenly believed that their conversations had produced some scheme for direct arbitration that would allow strikers to regain their jobs, when in fact they had not. By the end of March, it was not clear whether the strike was still ongoing. Exclaimed an embittered former striker, "Martin Irons has done us more harm than a thousand Jay Goulds could." Frustrated at the lack of progress in setting issues, some members of the Knights again turned to violence. By the end of the first week of April, though, it became apparent that the strike was over. The Gould roads were in full operation, trains were running and shops "with a large force of men" were humming. The hardcore protesters, however, remained unwilling to concede defeat, and in the final major event of the conflict a riot broke out on April 9 in East St. Louis. When nervous law enforcement officers, frightened by what they considered to be a threatening mob, fired into it, six nonstriking bystanders died. The Illinois Militia soon arrived and restored order.[65]

The sensational Haymarket Square affair in Chicago quickly overshadowed the deaths in East St. Louis. On the evening of Tuesday, May 4, a bomb suddenly exploded during a public rally called by labor activists to support striking workers at the McCormick Reaper Works and to demand the eight-hour day. It was here that a variety of orators spewed forth their antibusiness and anticapitalist messages. Socialist Albert Parsons, for one, elicited from the fiery crowd this reaction to his mention of Jay Gould: "Hang him!" The subsequent explosion, which left seven police officers dead and scores injured, prompted many Americans to conclude, despite the absence of conclusive proof, that anarchists and their allies were guilty of this bloodshed. A powerful antilabor sentiment swiftly swept the nation and would remain strong for years to come.[66]

The repercussions of the labor unrest by the Knights of Labor on the Gould roads were varied, but most significantly, this conflict led to the rapid demise of this labor union. By 1890, the Knights of Labor had become only a shadow organization. Although the Knights had no direct connection with the Haymarket Square tragedy, the organization suffered, in part because of the violence associated with the union during the strike of 1886. The collapse of the Knights made possible the rising dominance of the AFL and a dramatic transformation of American unionism. With the exception of the short-lived American Railway Union in the 1890s, the AFL, with its emphasis on bread-and-butter issues for skilled workers, would for decades reign supreme among the majority of unionized blue-collar workers.

The disputes of 1885 and 1886 were costly as well. Railroad revenues declined; income for workers dropped; shippers, businesses and merchants suffered. Then there were property losses. In the 1887 report *Investigation of Labor Troubles in Missouri, Arkansas, Kansas, Texas, and Illinois*, a committee of the U.S. House of Representatives pegged the financial costs of the strikes at more than $4 million, a tidy sum for the mid-1880s.[67]

It would take months, even years, for the emotional and financial wounds of the strikes to heal. For some railroaders and their families, the suffering associated with the walkouts would be vividly recalled for generations. The overall impact on the Moberly community, a center of Knight agitation, was summed up nicely by the *Moberly Daily Monitor*:

> When the strike ended only a small proportion of the strikers were taken back, and the others had to seek work elsewhere. As work is not abundant in the country, many of these failed to find employment and have been idle for months. Many, too, have been

evicted from the houses they were renting and have found it difficult to find shelter for their families. In a large number of instances this could be accomplished only giving chattel mortgages on personal property, while the distressed men found nothing by which they could procure the necessary food and clothing for the comfort of their families.

Frequently, too, it has happened that these liens have matured without a dollar having been paid. Of course the goods are forfeited and family is left without any of the comforts of a household. Debts made previous to the strike remain unpaid and the credit of the workman is lost, and this, too, in cases where the striker has returned to work.

The evidences of distress are everywhere apparent and even the more thrifty of the workmen have found themselves greatly cramped and forced to a most rigid economy. The effects of the strike will be felt for a long time to come.[68]

In addition, the name of Jay Gould was usually not fondly remembered along the WStL&P. This seems unjust: he cannot be fairly labeled an archetypal "robber baron." Hardly an evil force in the bankruptcy or the labor disputes, Gould tried mightily to make the railroad an attractive and viable part of his massive system, spending what was available for betterments and attempting to improve the road in other ways. Examples of his efforts are numerous. For instance, in the summer of 1884 the company added the splendid equipment of the Mann Boudoir Car Company to its passenger trains between St. Louis and Chicago and St. Louis and Kansas City. A few years later a journalist said of "Mr. Gould's Wabash": "Here is a road with comparatively light passenger traffic, which goes to considerable expense for extra watchmen, flagmen and laborers; and for what? To carry passenger at one cent a mile—less than half price." And Gould's atti-

tudes toward the working man were those commonly shared by most contemporary men of business. "I have been all my life a laborer or an employee of laborers. Strikes come from various causes, but are principally brought about by the poorest and therefore the dissatisfied element. The best workers generally look forward to advancement in the ranks or to save money enough to go into business on their own account. They get better pay here than in any other country." He concluded with this widely held thought: "My idea is that if capital and labor are let alone they will mutually regulate each other."[69]

THE GRANGER CASE

While the bankruptcy and confrontations with the Knights of Labor would forever be etched in the history of Gilded Age America, another event also gave the WStL&P a measure of immortality. This road would successfully challenge the great regulatory reform triumph of the Granger movement of the previous decade. After the Granger statutes appeared, several railroads contested them in state and lower federal courts in Illinois, Iowa and Wisconsin, and in every case they met with defeat. In *Munn v. Illinois,* the U.S. Supreme Court in 1877 sustained the Granger codes, specifically allowing the Illinois Railroad and Warehouse Commission to control rates charged by quasi-public corporations that were "clothed with a public interest." Theoretically, the much-criticized "long haul—short haul" practice of rate making had ended. By the early 1880s, the Illinois commission, which sensibly had come to recognize the higher proportionate cost of a short haul for freight movement, computed rates on all shipments by utilizing five-mile units for the first 150 miles, ten-mile units for the next fifty miles and twenty-mile units for transportation that exceeded 200 miles.

Although charges for a long haul were cheaper per mile, local rates on identical shipments could not exceed through rates.[70]

Just as the initial Granger laws produced a flurry of railroad reaction, the continued implementation of the statutes caused further unhappiness among the carriers. Railroad executives were nearly unanimous in their belief that free competition based on the laws of supply and demand offered the only effective type of regulation. Nor did all shippers endorse the Granger reforms. These consumers, who were usually part of merchant-dominated pressure groups, objected to the practice of some roads recouping revenues lost on regulated local business by increasing unregulated through rates. Without question the post–Granger reform era meant that the rate-making process would be complex and contradictory. By the early 1880s, a wide range of individuals and groups concluded that only the national government could deal effectively with the "railroad problem." It would be the WStL&P that would aid efforts in 1887 to make federal intervention a reality.[71]

In 1886, the chance for solving the rate-making dilemma came before the U.S. Supreme Court in the case of *Wabash, St. Louis and Pacific Railway Company v. State of Illinois*. The receivers of the company gladly appealed a decision by Illinois regulators that involved an alleged rate discrimination against a Gilman, Illinois, shipper. Specifically, the railroad asked Isaac Bailey and F. P. Swannell to pay $65 (or twenty-five cents per hundred pounds) to transport a carload of "goods and chattels" (grain) from Gilman to New York City. On the same day, the road charged Elder & McKinney of Peoria $39 (or fifteen cents per hundred pounds) for a similar load of carload freight to the same destination. Furthermore, this car traveled eighty-six miles further than the one from Gilman. "The freight being of the same class

in both instances, and carried over the same road, except as to the difference in the distance, it is obvious that a discrimination against Bailey & Swannell was made in the charges against them, as compared with those against Elder & McKinney," argued Illinois officials, "and this is true whether we regard the charge for the whole distance from the terminal points in Illinois to New York city, or the proportionate charge for the haul within the state of Illinois."[72]

Everyone, including officers of the WStL&P, realized that at first glance a discriminatory act had occurred. In its defense, the railroad pointed out that the Peoria customer used its services more often, that the real cost was switching at the point of origin and that both shipments required essentially the same amount of time getting the car into an eastbound train. The Court, however, was unmoved by these arguments. In the view of the justices, the key issue involved interstate versus intrastate commerce. In the decision for the majority, Justice Samuel F. Miller wrote, "This court holds . . . that such a transportation is 'commerce among the states,' even as to that part of the voyage which lies within the state of Illinois, while it is not denied that there may be a transportation of goods which is begun and ended within its limits, and disconnected with any carriage outside of the state which is not commerce among the states." Miller continued, "The latter is subject to regulation by the state, and the statute of Illinois is valid, as applied to it. But the former is national in its character, and its regulation is confided to congress exclusively, by that clause of the constitution which empowers it to regulate commerce among the states."[73]

While the WStL&P and other railroads took satisfaction in the ruling of the high court, the immediate reaction of the public proved to be largely negative. Advocates of the Granger laws found the decision troubling. Even though freight rates were in decline because there was too little business for too much rail, the public generally feared that this decision would encourage additional rate gouging. "Evidently, according to Judge Miller and his assenting brethren, the railroads have the states by the throat and there is no power but congress that can loose the death-producing gripe," commented a Missouri newspaper editor. "Strangulation must follow as there is no probability that a Republican senate will weaken the power of the great corporations from which they must hereafter derive their campaign fund."[74]

Consumers, though, arguably carried the day. Even before the decision of *Wabash, St. Louis & Pacific Railroad Company v. State of Illinois* overturned *Munn v. Illinois*, U.S. Senator Shelby M. Cullom of Illinois led a popular investigation into railroad practices, especially those that seemed discriminatory. The action of the Supreme Court, the so-called Cullom Report and pressures from certain shippers and carriers led both houses of Congress to pass by large majorities an Interstate Commerce bill, which President Grover Cleveland signed on February 4, 1887. This landmark measure created the Interstate Commerce Commission (ICC), which provided the regulatory arm to ensure that railroads would establish reasonable and just rates, end discriminatory practices, refrain from using traffic pools and file rate tariffs and annual reports with the ICC. A new and better day seemingly had dawned in the often strained relationship between the public and the railroad enterprise, although the ICC did not receive the right to establish maximum rates.[75]

Jay Gould would not live to encounter the effects, both good and bad, the Interstate Commerce Act would have on the railroad industry. Suffering from incurable tuberculosis—the "white plague"—and the death in 1889 of his beloved wife of twenty-six years, Helen

"Nellie" Miller Gould, his personal life was in tatters. On December 2, 1892, only fifty-six years old, Gould passed away at his Fifth Avenue home in New York City.[76]

When they read of the death of Gould, many Americans may have believed that his premature passing was just retribution for a selfish, "public-be-damned" robber baron, but those who knew him thought different. After receiving news of Gould's death, which had occurred a few hours before the regular meeting of the Wabash Railroad board of directors, president Ashley, who recently had headed the Wabash Western and had served on the WStL&P purchasing and reorganization committee, provided this brief eulogy for his business associate:

> During the past eight or nine years it has been necessary for me to confer and advise with [Mr. Gould] frequently, and I take pleasure in stating the he has always given me an attentive hearing, even when the demand upon his time was urgent and pressing. Many complicated and vexatious questions have arisen which required the most judicious and careful treatment, and I have always found him disposed to give us the benefit of his calm and deliberate judgment. When our views were not harmonious, he has always listened to my expression of them with patience, kindness and consideration, and I am sure he was always glad to have me state them frankly and freely. I do not recall an unkind word during these years of business intercourse.[77]

The end of the Jay Gould years on the Wabash did not diminish the manifold problems the carrier would face in the next two decades. Declining rates, intense competition, labor unrest and enhanced federal regulation haunted the management of the Wabash and the leadership of the American railroad network.

The Wabash Matures

THE TURBULENT NINETIES

Following its reorganization, the Wabash Railroad Company appeared poised for a promising future. Its debt level had been significantly reduced, and it no longer faced a multitude of expensive annual lease payments. Net earnings for the fiscal year ending June 30, 1890, amounted to more than $3.6 million, reflecting both its positive financial restructuring and the beneficial results of a good mix of local and overhead traffic. The ledger books, albeit briefly, got better. As the firm reported two years later, "The gross earnings per mile are higher for 1892 than for any year since 1880 and the net larger than any since 1887 and 1890." The company, too, had a strong management team that included president O. D. Ashley, vice president James F. How and general manager Charles M. Hays. And there re-mained a significant Gould connection. Even before the passing of Jay Gould, his eldest son, the affable and gregarious George Jay Gould, assumed a seat on the company's board of directors, joining such seasoned railroad financiers as Sidney Dillon, James Joy and Russell Sage.[1]

Although during the early 1890s the Wabash encountered some economic bumps, its owners and managers possessed the wherewithal to make additions that they considered essential. Their expectation was to provide an even stronger foundation for profits. While the railroad map of the Midwest had for the most part become stable after an orgy of track laying in the late 1870s and 1880s, there would still be some important pieces of trackage that would be added after 1890, although most involved cut-offs and feeder or tap lines, this being especially true in the central and eastern Midwest.[2]

The premier "Wabash town" was Decatur, Illinois, and the company fittingly erected a major building that accommodated travelers and divisional officers and their staffs. In this ca. 1905 postcard view an electric streetcar of the Decatur Railway & Light Company stands at the station. (Author's Coll.)

WABASH RAILROAD STATION
DECATUR, ILLINOIS

The first mileage increase of note, modest though it was, came about under the banner of the Peru & Detroit Railway (P&D). The Wabash did not like the track configuration in Logansport, Indiana. It needed to cross lines controlled by the Pennsylvania Railroad (PRR) in order to link its own route with the leased Eel River Railroad, so it began to explore possibilities for a better, direct tie between the two carriers, reviewing the possibility of connections between Peru and Chili, Peru and Mexico, Peru and Pettysville and Wabash and Laketon (now Ijamsville). In February 1890, it became publicly known that the first of the four proposed routes, the 9.6-mile line between Peru and Chili, would be selected. In March 1889, friendly business interests in Peru, led by promoter Charles H. Brownell, had organized the P&D to build the connector. Part of the strategy of these small-time entrepreneurs involved having the Wabash consolidate its regional maintenance and repair operations at Peru by relocating the Eel River facility from Logansport. Thus, with a combination of local and Wabash financing, the $120,000 link quickly took shape, and on November 30, 1890, the first official train steamed over the P&D. That same month the railroad was leased to the Wabash for ninety-nine years, with the latter agreeing to operate and maintain the property and to offset rental charges by paying interest on the first mortgage bonds that it already owned. Therefore, no money changed hands between the Wabash and the P&D. Shortly thereafter the Wabash closed the Logansport shops and purchased real estate in Peru between Broadway and Grant streets. (It had refused free land at the east end of town, preferring to be closer to the business district.) "It brings to this city not less than 500 active men with their families, including the train men from the Detroit Railroad," crowed a local newspaper. Brownell, who

served as president of the P&D, and his associates, of course, delighted in what had occurred in their hometown.[3]

With the P&D in its orbit, the Wabash directed its principal freight and passenger traffic over the new road. Mainline trains avoided the twenty-one miles on the Eel River Railroad between Logansport and Chili; this segment saw only the two local passenger trains that the Wabash initially dispatched and a minimal number of freight runs. Because there were no communities of consequence along this section of the Eel River, the public suffered little.[4]

In a classic case of town rivalry, residents of Logansport may have cared little about construction of the P&D cutoff, but they did not take kindly to the loss of *their* shops to neighboring Peru with the accompanying drop in the railroad payroll. It was no surprise, therefore, that Logansport interests sought redress from the courts. Their plan to regain the repair facilities was to seek receivership for the Eel River, believing that reorganization would end the ninety-nine-year lease to the Wabash. More than businessmen and lawyers became involved; local editors joined the fray. Soon a journalistic war of sorts erupted. At one point the *Peru Journal* charged that "people of the old, dead town of Logansport are low, mean and envious and their remarks are idiotic." A Logansport paper proclaimed that "POUTING PERU. DRINKS MISSISSINEWA WATER AND REFUSES TO BE COMFORTED." Even though the war of words calmed down, the legal conflict lingered for years. Toward the end of the 1890s, a state court annulled the Wabash lease and appointed a receiver for the Eel River. The Wabash would not accept this verdict and appealed to the Indiana Supreme Court. Three years later, the high court sustained the decision of the lower court.[5]

It appeared that Wabash was about to lose a portion of its vital Detroit line. Therefore, at the turn of the twentieth century, the company wisely decided to tie the Toledo line at New Haven, near Fort Wayne, directly with the Detroit trackage at Butler, Indiana. A local newspaper, however, thought that this rumored construction was "probably a bluff," for it believed that "the Wabash Company could better afford to buy out the original stockholders of the Eel River Road, than to build a new line." But it did not. In February 1902, the first train ran over this twenty-seven-mile connection, which the Wabash built through its paper affiliate, the Fort Wayne & Detroit Railroad. The P&D became excess mileage, although between 1902 and 1906 the Wabash converted that portion of the road between Peru Junction and Peru into a second mainline. In 1907, when the Wabash no longer needed the surplus trackage, it sold 7.33 miles of the P&D to an emerging traction project. Soon this segment became an electrified part of the Winona Interurban Railway that would shortly link Peru with Goshen, becoming a strategic part of Indiana's sprawling network of traction lines. The Eel River, on the other hand, attempted to rebuild itself and in the process restarted the Logansport shops, but for justifiable economic reasons it soon sold out to the PRR. The former shortline, reorganized in 1901 as the Logansport & Toledo Railroad, subsequently served as a modest appendage of that immense system.[6]

The early part of the 1890s saw another Wabash project in the Hoosier State, construction of a major line across the northern tier of counties. What the Wabash wanted was its own direct access to Chicago from Detroit and Toledo. At the time the company possessed trackage rights to the Windy City over the Chicago & Atlantic Railway (C&A), an affiliate of the Erie, from Laketon Junction, Indiana, to Hammond and then used the Chicago & Western Indiana Railroad to complete its entry into Chicago. The

lease with the C&A, scheduled to expire on June 30, 1892, required the Wabash to pay an annual basic charge of $90,000. The company also shared the cost of station and track maintenance, adding thousands of dollars more to the arrangement. This agreement, moreover, precluded the Wabash from handling any local business along the C&A.[7]

Wabash management knew that it could do better. Perhaps in an effort to avoid incurring the wrath of neighboring carriers, the road made it clear that it was only attempting to upgrade a current traffic pattern. "It may be said that the number of railroads now existing in the United States is more than enough to do the business of the country," remarked a company official. "On the other hand, the facilities possessed by existing railroads in the way of terminals, second tracks and means of handling business effectively are, to a large extent, inadequate. These facilities must be improved by direct betterments of the lines now in existence, but in some cases also by supplying unconstructed links, the effect of which will not be to open new lines of travel, but to avoid the expensive parts of existing routes."[8]

In the latter part of 1891, work began on the Wabash's "unconstructed links." Survey and property acquisitions for the Montpelier & Chicago Rail Road, which the project was briefly called, proceeded with dispatch. By the early part of the following year, the general contract was let on this 150-mile Chicago-Detroit "airline," and soon thirty-three subcontractors began their labors. Gangs of Italian, African American and local workers appeared at the construction sites. Their efforts were greatly facilitated by the sparse patterns of settlement, largely level topography and few major streams. Further aiding the endeavor were sections of already graded rights-of-way, including a lengthy stretch immediately west of Montpelier,

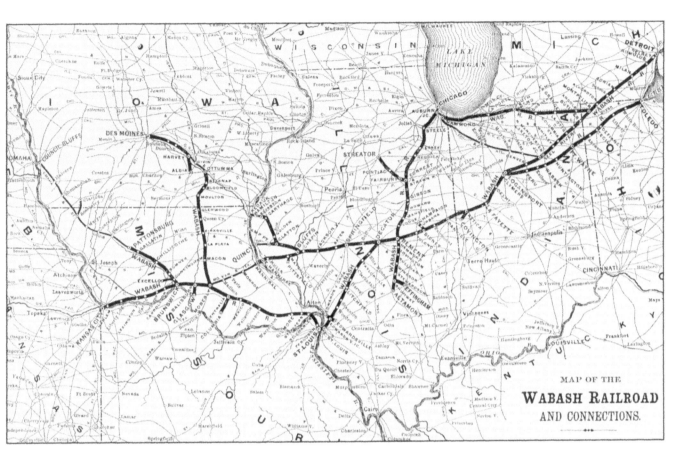

MAP OF THE

WABASH RAILROAD

AND CONNECTIONS.

Ohio. About twenty years earlier, the ill-fated Chicago & Canada Southern Railroad (C&CS), which sought to create a low-grade line between Detroit and Chicago, had done some construction before the depression of the 1870s forced a cessation of work. Although hard times explain why the C&CS ended its building, the company had encountered a nasty obstacle that temporarily delayed the Wabash push across Indiana, an enormous sinkhole near Westville in LaPorte County. "The contractors for the Wabash extension have struck a sink hole . . . into which 3,000 car loads of dirt have been dumped without appreciable effect," came a report in the spring of 1892. "It is the same hole which stalled the old Canada Southern

builders after 50,000 yards of dirt had been dumped therein, besides all the brush and rubbish that could be scrapped up." Unlike the cash-starved predecessor, the Wabash finally established a stable grade over the massive hole.[9]

Local residents, too, delighted in the prospects of having the iron horse. Although deeply disappointed when the C&CS had failed, they knew that the Wabash would at last answer their prayers for fast, dependable and convenient transportation. Residents of Wakarusa became so excited that in October 1892 they celebrated when crews, using a modern Harris track-laying machine, arrived in their community from the East. They could not wait for the first

This ca. 1890 map of the Wabash Railroad reveals a system that had largely been completed. The new "Montpelier and Chicago" line is shown as being under construction. Yet there are several missing links, including the "air-line" extension between the Iowa communities of Moulton and Albia. (Author's Coll.)

regularly scheduled passenger train. The citizens fed 300 workers, and "an entire steer and 150 loaves of bread were consumed." And more than 2,000 people turned out for the entertainment, which included music provided by the Wakarusa Cornet Band and a popular hometown singing quartette.[10]

Management seemed pleased with its big $3 million construction project. In late November 1892, forty miles of the eastern portion of the line officially opened between Montpelier and Wolcottville in LaGrange County. With much fanfare the company announced proudly that "the New Chicago-Detroit Line of the Wabash Railroad WILL BE OPEN FOR BUSINESS ABOUT MARCH 1ST, 1893," although the first through passenger train over the extension did not arrive in Chicago until the morning of April 21, 1893.[11]

Officials had reason to be gratified. The addition was "first-class in all respects," sporting modern steel rails spiked to solid oak ties and "with no grade over 26 feet to the mile" and "particularly free from curves." Furthermore, the extension gave the Wabash the shortest route between Chicago and Detroit, fulfilling the construction objective. Its length was 271 miles, or twenty-five miles shorter than the previously leased line. Moreover, distances between these cities for its well-established rivals Chicago & Grand Trunk and Michigan Central were 319 and 285.5 miles, respectively. Even though the extension missed every county seat and place of importance (much to the unhappiness of residents of Goshen whose thriving community the line avoided by only a few miles), there was the realistic hope that the "country traversed is a rich agricultural district and will, within a few years, contribute a valuable local traffic to the company." This would generally be true, and in 1899 by building a five-mile branch north from Helmer, Indiana, it served exclusively a large cement works at Stroh.[12]

The only fly in the ointment came with some unfavorable area and regional newspaper coverage that related to a land deal involving company officials. A Hudson, Indiana, editor alleged that Wabash "insiders," through their newly launched Indiana Improvement Company, had speculated in real estate at a southern Steuben County town site that became "Ashley," the location of a small shops complex. Troubled by this allegation, president Ashley investigated and in June 1893 reported to the board of directors that nothing untoward had transpired. "A year or more since some of the officers of the Company asked me in St. Louis if I saw any objection to their taking an interest in a land company which proposed to buy where the round house and repair shops were to be located," explained Ashley. "To this I replied that I saw no objection, provided the Railroad Company should have the first chance of any land purchased, at its actual costs, but that this must be fully understood in advance." Continued the Wabash executive, "A purchase by the Improvement Company was accordingly made near and adjoining . . . Hudson, and of the land purchased the Wabash selected 80 or 100 acres and paid for the same at cost, the Improvement Company also giving the right of way through their land." Ashley, however, ignored the obvious matter of insider knowledge of the company's plans for support facilities along the Montpelier-Chicago line.[13]

During the investigation, Ashley made the wise decision to meet with residents of Hudson. Perhaps the real motivation behind charges of ethical wrongdoing involved location of the local depot. It was to be in the adjoining Ashley, which Hudsontonians thought to be inconvenient for their shipping and travel needs. Ashley lent a sympathetic ear to their concerns and agreed to "the removal of the depot 300 or 400 feet nearer Hudson [to be called "Ashley-Hudson"], so as to be about midway between it and the new town." The tempest in the teapot ended, although at the public gathering Ashley had residents sign a paper that "expressed themselves entirely satisfied with the new arrangement."[14]

About the time of the Hudson brouhaha, a severe panic struck Wall Street, quickly making a shambles of the American economy. In the immediate aftermath of the May 1893 disaster, a host of banks and businesses collapsed, estimated at more than 15,000 by the close of the year. During the summer, twelve of the largest ore steamers on the Great Lakes never left their home ports. And it did not take long before various railroads entered bankruptcy. Victims of this economic calamity included such major carriers as the Atchison, Topeka & Santa Fe, Baltimore & Ohio, Erie and Union Pacific. By the end of what were to be five troubled years, about one-third of the nation's railroad network fell under court protection.[15]

Although the Wabash weathered the economic storm, it felt the sting of hard times. Not surprisingly, its net earnings declined or remained flat. In 1893 the figure stood at $3,412,80, but a year later sank to $2,721,068. Net earnings for 1895 stood at $3,038,809 and in 1896 increased to $3,564,538, but in 1897 earnings dropped slightly, to $3,547,628. Soon after the panic hit, officials took a cautious approach to spending. "[I]t has been the policy of the Wabash management," revealed the company during the summer of 1893, "to limit betterment expenditures to the means available for such purposes." For the duration of these hard times, there would be virtually no new lines, depots, repair facilities and the like or large purchases or upgrading of rolling stock or other major rehabilitations. To be certain, the overall good condition and range of the property made this a practical economy. Fortunately, during the summer and early fall of 1893 the Wabash and

several other Midwestern roads benefited from travelers drawn to the enormously popular World's Columbian Exposition in Chicago. But, as Ashley observed, "The gain in passenger traffic stimulated by the World's Fair in Chicago having, to some extent, offset the decrease in freight, . . . it would be imprudent to count upon any exemption from troubles which are so general and far reaching."[16]

As part of its response to the depression, the Wabash liquidated unwanted assets and made other financial adjustments. In September 1895, for example, it sold to co-owner Chicago, Burlington & Quincy Railroad its interest in the Humeston & Shenandoah Railroad. This transaction brought $450,000 in cash into company coffers. Paralleling other businesses, management reduced "unnecessary operations," including closing many country stations at night and annulling some regularly scheduled trains. Hundreds of mostly blue-collar employees were furloughed. The railroad also slashed wages. Beginning April 1, 1894, all engineers, firemen, brakemen and conductors took a 10 percent reduction, which remained in effect until 1896. Other employees found their paychecks similarly reduced. Though unpopular with workers, especially locomotive engineers, this cut was hardly as painful as it might appear. The national economy suffered from acute deflation, and therefore the magnitude of this reduction did not significantly decrease an individual's buying power.[17]

Although the Wabash stayed out of bankruptcy court and tightened its belt considerably, it could not avoid one of the nastiest labor disputes of the decade, the Pullman Strike of 1894. Not long before workers at George Mortimer Pullman's Palace Car Company struck to protest drastic wage cuts (in some cases slashed 50 percent), high rents for company-owned housing and layoffs,

Eugene V. Debs, the charismatic former national officer of the Brotherhood of Locomotive Firemen and Enginemen, launched the American Railway Union (ARU) in Chicago. This industrial organization, which was opened to all white railroad workers below the rank of division superintendent, quickly displaced the scattered remnants of the Knights of Labor and challenged the powers of the established craft brotherhoods.[18]

The initial months of the ARU revealed a workingman's organization with potential. In April 1894, Debs and his associates called a strike against the Great Northern Railway (GN) because employees believed that the company prospered at a time when it cut wages. After eighteen days, during which time most of the road's operations were shut down, Debs and James J. Hill, president of the GN, submitted the dispute to arbitration. Three nonrailroad businessmen, who included milling magnate Charles Pillsbury, decided largely in favor of the ARU. The walkout ended happily for workers but also for Hill, who did not relish a labor war.[19]

Heartened by the success of the ARU against the GN, disgruntled workers at the vast freight and passenger car building and repair complex in the company town of Pullman, Illinois, located on the far South Side of Chicago, turned to Debs and his union in the belief that they could help them to improve their lot. (They were eligible to join the ARU because the Pullman Company operated a shortline railroad near the factory.) As a result, Pullman employees flocked to the ARU at a time when membership among railroad workers, especially in the Midwest, also greatly increased. It would be the discontented at Pullman who fervently believed that management and Pullman himself had ignored their demands. This sparked the strike that would bear the firm's name. The company continually objected to *any* form of collective bargaining,

preferring to discuss matters of wages, rents and the like on an individual basis. Moreover, Pullman, observed a biographer, "had no conception of the true state of affairs in his shops, nor of the injustices being heaped upon his employees." The dismissal of three operatives, probably because of their activities on a workers' grievance committee, led to a walkout at the Pullman plant on May 11, 1894.[20]

Pullman operatives would not be disappointed with Debs and his ARU. After a series of discussions with Pullman workers and company representatives, the union announced on June 22 that its members would not handle Pullman cars as of midday on June 26 unless the firm squarely addressed employee complaints. Although Pullman officials expressed concern about an impending boycott, they received backing from the powerful General Managers Association of Chicago (GMA), which consisted of prominent railroad officials, including representatives from the Wabash. George Pullman and the GMA strongly agreed that the ARU should be crushed and responded accordingly.[21]

The boycott of Pullman cars began as threatened. Within a few days more than 150,000 men voluntarily abandoned their posts and "never before had there been such a strike in the United States." Pullman and the GMA did their best to resist. Although confrontations between workers and managers occurred widely, much of the unrest centered in Illinois. The state, of course, was home to Pullman's principal plant and was nation's greatest rail hub. Sporadic confrontations erupted early on, and disorder increased on July 5, 1894, when Chicago-area strikers snarled service on the Chicago, Rock Island & Pacific, torched nearly fifty cars that belonged to the Illinois Central and attacked railroad equipment in the vast stockyards. The following day witnessed even more destruction. Rioters destroyed nearly $350,000 of railroad property, this time equipment belonging to the PRR taking the brunt of the strikers' anger. With the aid of local law enforcement officers, federal marshals and state and federal troops, along with court injunctions, Pullman and the GMA by July 13 broke the strike and trains moved without interference. Debs had been arrested and jailed, and the "Debs Rebellion" was summarily crushed. The ARU stood in shambles, and soon many of its members found themselves permanently blacklisted by much of the railroad industry.[22]

While labor unrest in greater Chicago garnered most of the national press coverage, communities with Wabash facilities, too, experienced troubles. The work stoppage frankly surprised company leaders. "[The strike] seemed the more inexplicable for the reason that it is very generally understood that Wabash trainmen have had less cause for complaint than those on almost any other railroad in the West," related management to investors. "Many of them had served the Company for periods aggregating in some cases twenty-five to thirty years. Their grievances or complaints . . . had always received the willing consideration of the subordinate and general officers." Even organized labor appeared taken aback by what happened. Much to the chagrin of the leadership of the Brotherhood of Locomotive Engineers, which along with the other operating brotherhoods opposed the boycott, about 400 of the 438 engineers on the Wabash joined the spreading walkout. A similar percentage of firemen also left their posts.[23]

Unlike the Great Southwest strikes of the mid-1880s, ARU activities did not center in Moberly, Missouri, but rather in Decatur, Illinois, site of a large shops complex and bustling hub of the road's east-of-the-Mississippi train operations. At the time of the Pullman unrest, the Wabash employed more

than 700 men in this strategic rail town and contributed approximately $50,000 in monthly payrolls to the local economy. Because of layoffs and wage reductions, Wabash workers, particularly in Decatur, seemed inclined to embrace the ARU.[24]

On June 30, the work stoppage became a reality in Decatur. By early evening, regularly scheduled train service had ceased and the local yards assumed the appearance of a "deserted race track." The following day, a Sunday, large crowds, estimated at nearly 5,000 and some dressed in their best clothes, gathered at the depot and in the yards. They came largely out of curiosity. All was peaceful, and the only reported problem, according to a local observer, was that some women's "dainty gowns and white kid shoes . . . suffered in the cinders."[25]

The holiday atmosphere in Decatur, however, quickly ended. Instigated by Wabash officials, a telegram signed by "500 Sufferers," who allegedly had been stranded at the Decatur depot, was sent to Governor John Peter Altgeld. The message demanded that he bring about the end to their entrapment. Somewhat surprisingly, this friend of labor, who had courageously pardoned some of the Haymarket rioters, took the request seriously. The governor contacted the Macon County sheriff, who apparently was close to the Wabash, and learned that he and his deputies were concerned about protecting public safety. Troubled by situation, Altgeld responded by dispatching state militia to make certain that "all trains unlawfully held are released at once." About the same time, Altgeld also sent troops to other railroad centers in the state, including Illinois Central facilities at Cairo. Decaturites thought that Altgeld had overreacted. After all, there had been no violence in Decatur or Macon County.[26]

There was also no real animosity on the part of Decatur residents toward the 600 or so Wabash employees who joined the Debs crusade. Indeed, the community over-whelmingly supported the strike, giving credence to the notion that labor disputes are more likely to be endorsed in places where citizens know the strikers and their families rather than in major metropolitan centers, where such interpersonal relationships are less common or nonexistent. The ill will expressed by Decaturites centered on the scores of strikebreakers the Wabash brought to town, men often recruited in Eastern cities by agents of the GMA. For example, barbers, who were concentrated in the neighborhood around Union Depot, refused to serve the "new men."[27]

Real violence never came to Decatur. Said one striking Wabash engineer, "We want to win but we want to do so as honest men and to sustain our reputation as law-abiding citizens." The presence of state troops, too, arguably gave potential troublemakers pause. Yet, on July 9 a few days before the national strike collapsed, an engineer was slightly injured by an object thrown into his cab as his locomotive neared a city street crossing.[28]

Labor peace was fully restored in Decatur and throughout the Wabash by July 11. Late that day and the next, some strikers in Decatur asked for reinstatement. The rather abrupt end of worker solidarity demoralized those less anxious to abandon the cause. On July 12, the company proclaimed that operations were "in apple pie order."[29]

The impact of the Pullman strike was considerable. Hundreds of Wabash workers never regained their jobs. Management punished the strikers, often telling former ARU members that it would be "useless and a waste of time" to seek their old assignments. The railroad, however, did reinstate many nonactivists. For instance, the foreman at the Decatur carshops rehired 140 of the 200 strikers. These men may not have been truly supportive of the ARU, but more likely they possessed badly needed skills. Trackmen, on

the other hand, who could easily be replaced, especially during a time of severe depression, were "out for good." For some time individuals who joined the ranks as strikebreakers felt the animosity of employees who had gone out but had been rehired. Unpleasant memories and deeply held grudges faded slowly.[30]

The railroad also suffered. "The strike of employees during the first half of . . . July, 1894, during which time the operations of the road were almost entirely suspended, were only reduced by the wages forfeited by the striking force," wrote Ashley. "It is roughly estimated that a net loss of from $300,000 to $400,000 resulted." Property damages, however, were modest, limited to about $25,000. And, too, some public ill will developed against the road. Class tensions rose during the depression, and much anti-capitalist, antirailroad sentiment flared up during and after the Pullman affair. Regardless of whether they were prolabor, patrons did not care for disrupted service and added travel expenses. When a minister from Kirksville, Missouri, became stranded in Moberly on his way home from St. Louis, he was "compelled to come around via Hannibal at considerable cost and delay." He apparently thought much less of the Wabash and took no solace that similar problems confronted travelers in Decatur, Montpelier and Springfield.[31]

THE NEW CENTURY

Fortunately for everyone involved with the Pullman strike, and for those who suffered the hard times spawned by the Panic of 1893, a major upturn in the economy occurred toward the end of the decade. Prosperity, though, failed to return with any degree of permanence, and in 1907 there would be a sudden downward slippage, a brief but sobering "bankers panic."

In the interim, however, a feeling of optimism spread throughout America, and leaders of the Wabash Railroad were hardly immune. Net income figures, which jumped from $3,742.975 in 1897 to $5,146,256 in 1901, made for happy souls in the general offices in St. Louis.[32]

With revenues increasing, management decided to make the improvements that it had judiciously postponed. Even before the depression had fully lifted, the Wabash in 1897 took advantage of bargain-basement prices and purchased 15,000 tons of eighty-pound steel rails, which it immediately installed on some of its most heavily used lines. The same year president Ashley happily told stockholders that "the repairs in every department have been completely and thoroughly maintained [and that] the rolling stock has also been increased by the purchase of 500 box cars of modern stock." Betterments, too, included installation of automatic couplers and air brakes on hundreds of pieces of older freight equipment that lacked them, a process that shops personnel completed by 1899. Although officials wanted up-to-date cars, the federal government in 1893 had passed the Safety Appliance Act that called for elimination of dangerous link-and-pin couplers and hand brakes (by 1890 most passenger cars had Westinghouse-type air brakes). Of course, in this age of regulation the Wabash had to make positive responses, and in this case the price tag amounted to about eighty dollars per car.[33]

At the turn of the twentieth century, the Wabash embarked on what might be considered part of the "second building of American railroads." This involved such betterments as double tracking much of its busiest lines, easing grades, bridge renewals, replacement of scores of wooden trestles with solid embankments, new or replacement interlocking plants at busy junctions and crossovers, improved signaling devices and in certain urban areas grade and street separations. At the end of 1899, for example, Joseph Ramsey, Jr., vice president and general manager, told Ashley of the great need to double track the line between the Sangamon River bridge near Decatur and Bement and to reduce grades between Taylorville and Bement. "The construction of the double track is work the importance of which has been fully understood by yourself and the other Directors . . . for several years, and the increased traffic has made it now almost an absolute necessity," explained Ramsey. "The reduction of the grades referred to will enable us to increase our freight train loads between the coal fields and Chicago from 25 to 35 percent over the present load. The Boody Hill grade [near Boody, Illinois] is 41 feet to the mile and is the ruling grade between the coal fields and Decatur. With this grade reduced and the Cerro Gordo grade [near Cerro Gordo, Illinois] also reduced, there would be no heavy grades from the coal fields to Bement." Within a few years this double tracking and grade reductions along with additional improvements on the heaviest used segments would either be planned, begun or completed.[34]

Wabash management also embarked on replacement or expansion of a variety of facilities. Although civic critics believed that the company should have taken on even more of these improvements, much was accomplished. In late 1905, the Wabash gained praise for the opening of its new freight terminals in St. Louis. The massive 300,000–square foot structures, located between Franklin Avenue and Biddle Street, offered customers "the most extensive facilities of their kind in St. Louis." The local press lauded the Wabash. "St. Louis now becomes the terminus of the system for freight as well as passengers and shipments from all points on the Wabash, east as well as west, are billed direct through to St. Louis and delivered in the very heart of the business section." About a year later the Wabash received acclaim for the completion of a new shops complex at Decatur. Even more so than the St. Louis freight terminals, this construction was utterly immense. The *Railroad Gazette* offered this brief description: "The plant includes a car shop, 88 ft. x 464 ft.; blacksmith and machine shop, 80 ft. x 294 ft.; storehouse with two story office building at one end, 40 ft. x 464 ft.; wood mill, 80 ft. x 238 ft.; tin, cabinet, upholstering, glazing and electrical shop, 40 ft. x 350 ft; power house, 60 ft. x 108 ft., besides a dry kiln, dry lumber sheds, iron, coal, coke and other material sheds and racks, and a laboratory building." The list of betterments involved much more, including a new 796-foot brick outbound freight house near the Loop District in Chicago.[35]

During these go-go years the Wabash once again sought to expand. The principal spark that ignited this policy was George Gould. Spoiled and impulsive, he unfortunately lacked the quick and penetrating intellect and the general business acumen of his late father. The rationale for creating this "bigger Wabash system" involved more than the obvious objectives of increasing line haulage and strengthening connections. As the depression faded Gould seriously contemplated massive enlargements to the network of lines his father had earlier assembled, and he would take direct action after the turn of the century in an effort to create a transcontinental Gould system. Part of this emerging strategy involved extending the Wabash to the Buffalo gateway and to forge direct links with the Delaware, Lackawanna & Western; Erie; Lehigh Valley and New York Central System to New York City, Boston and other East Coast destinations.[36]

What became known as the Buffalo Division began to evolve in 1897. Rather than building through a rail-rich section of south-ern Ontario, the Wabash decided to seek trackage rights between Detroit and Buffalo. The company hammered out a lease agreement with the Grand Trunk Railway of Canada to use nearly 230 miles of its partially double-tracked Southern Division between Windsor, Ontario, and Suspension Bridge, New York, via Glencoe, St. Thomas and Welland, and then another twenty-ones miles of the Erie into Buffalo from Suspension Bridge and Black Rock. Also involved in the negotiations were discussions with the Lehigh Valley to use terminal trackage in the Buffalo area. The strategy, however, would face a bottleneck of sorts—namely, car floats would be needed to cross the Detroit River between Detroit and Windsor. Finally, on January 24, 1898, long-term contracts were signed and the "Buffalo Extension" became reality, creating the longest mileage arrangement among North American railroads.[37]

By March 1898 Wabash equipment, with its own crews, began running into and out of Buffalo. Passenger trains terminated at the conveniently located Erie station, and freights mostly used Lehigh Valley facilities. The largest amount of cargo came from or was destined for Chicago and traveled over the recently opened trans-Indiana extension. Soon, too, the southern Ontario city of St. Thomas became a Wabash town, site of the division's headquarters. Management then and in the future knew that the lease scheme had been a wise course of action. "The results of the operation of the Buffalo Division for the first week," reported Ramsey to Ashley, "settle beyond question the success of that extension, and while we may (and probably will) have weeks during the year which will not reach $27,000 earnings, I am convinced that the average gross earnings of that division per week for the year around will exceed that amount." Ramsey would be correct.[38]

The only pronounced downside to the

new Buffalo service involved a shortage of rolling stock. In that respect, some progress soon occurred. By the end of 1899, the Wabash had acquired sixty-five new locomotives, additional freight equipment—mostly boxcars—and cabooses. Ramsey nevertheless complained privately to Ashley and the board of directors that there is "the general impression that the Wabash was well equipped, but this is not correct." Statistically, the figures bore him out. The Wabash had only 5.8 cars per mile of railroad. By contrast, the Illinois Central claimed 9.0, the Chicago & Eastern Illinois, 14.5, the PRR, 20.0, and the Baltimore & Ohio, 22.0. This shortfall meant higher equipment rentals and difficulties at times serving customers, remaining as one of the company's most nagging problems.[39]

Part of the Wabash improvements to the eastern port of its system involved a better connection with the Chicago line at Montpelier from Toledo. As Ashley succinctly explained to the trade press, "Will open up a short and direct line between Toledo and Chicago, with advantages which are obvious." In March 1901 the company organized the Toledo & Chicago Railroad Company and issued $3 million in new securities to pay for a fifty-seven-mile extension westward from Maumee (Toledo) to Montpelier through the prosperous Ohio agricultural towns on Delta, Wauseon and West Unity. Construction crews easily completed the extension that crossed a nearly level countryside and service began without any complications.[40]

After the depression ended, the Wabash also made some important line changes west of the Mississippi River. A notable improvement involved gaining better access to Des Moines. During the feverish expansion of the Wabash, St. Louis & Pacific (WStL&P) under Jay Gould, the Iowa capital was reached through an affiliate, the Des Moines & St. Louis Railroad (DM&StL). Between May 1881

and August 1882 this carrier constructed a sixty-eight-mile line between Des Moines and Albia, where it met the Centerville, Moravia & Albia Railroad (CM&A). By using that controlled shortline and a twenty-one-mile portion of the leased Missouri, Iowa & Nebraska (MI&N) to Glenwood Junction, Missouri, and a connection with the old North Missouri, a route was forged between Des Moines and St. Louis. But with the subsequent bankruptcy and reorganization, the CM&A and MI&N were lost. The results were twofold: the Wabash used its own doglegged line to Ottumwa, Iowa, and there gained trackage rights over the Chicago, Rock Island & Pacific Railroad (Rock Island) to Evans (near Oskaloosa) and from there to Harvey, forty-four miles south of Des Moines, where it met the DM&StL. In February 1886 the DM&StL, which was then owned by a bondholders committee of the WStL&P, ended freight and passenger service on the twenty-four-mile segment between Harvey and Albia and for all practical purposes abandoned the trackage. Fortunately for the public, a largely parallel, heavy-duty branch of the Chicago, Burlington & Quincy (CB&Q) operated between Albia and Des Moines.[41]

By the late 1890s the Des Moines service demanded attention. The route via Ottumwa and Harvey was considerably longer and more circuitous than the earlier service through Albia. Then there were their annual rental charges for thirty-eight miles of two Rock Island branch lines. Moreover, the Wabash had only limited access to a rapidly expanding soft-coal mining industry in southern Iowa with its scores of semipermanent camps, especially in the vicinity of Albia and Centerville. It was also apparent that the company's interest in the Des Moines Union Railway, a well-positioned terminal and switching road, which dated from mid-1880s, was not being fully exploited.[42]

To upgrade significantly its route to Des

Moines, management knew that it would surely need to build northwesterly from Moulton, Iowa, where the Ottumwa line veered sharply to the east, to Albia. As part of the larger improvement plan, the out-of-service Albia-to-Harvey segment would be completely rebuilt. But how would the Wabash bridge the approximately thirty miles between Moulton and Albia? There was no doubt about the section between Moulton and Moravia, a thriving farming community in Appanoose County that abutted the Monroe County line: an "air-line" could be extended without too much trouble across that somewhat hilly terrain.[43]

But from Moravia to Albia there were two viable options. The first involved using portions of an abandoned CB&Q branch line. It had been installed in 1880 by an affiliate at a time when the parent road constructed nearly 300 miles of feeder lines in southern Iowa to protect its traffic base from would-be competitors. The other possibility would be to purchase the old CM&A, which the WStL&P had earlier used as the link between the MI&N and the DM&StL. That 24.4-mile road remained in operation as the reorganized Albia & Centerville Railway (A&C), which was owned by Russell Sage and Centerville businessman and later governor Francis M. Drake and leased to the Iowa Central Railway with which it connected in Albia.[44]

In November 1898, Ramsey inspected the A&C and sent a detailed report to Ashley. He noted that "the entire line, with the exception of a few points on curves and in cuts is what we call 'a mud ballasted' road; that is surfaced with and filled in with surface soil or earth. It is fairly well drained and it rode quite well as a speed of from thirty five to forty miles an hour." The freight business was largely coal from on-line mines, and the "passenger traffic is light and nearly all secured to and from Centerville, which is the

County seat." If the A&C could be acquired for no more than $10,000 per mile, he recommended its purchase, estimating that between Moravia and Albia, "it will cost from $1,500 to $2,000 per mile to ballast and put the track on the A&C Road in good condition." And Ramsey made a positive assessment of the abandoned CB&Q grade, lauding its generally attractive curvature and gradients and concluding that "it will cost us to build our road between Moravia and Albia on the old grade between $11,000 and $12,000 per mile."[45]

The Wabash rapidly pushed ahead with the task of creating its own line between Moberly and Des Moines. Because the company could not work out a satisfactory purchase price for the A&C (the Wabash refused a lease), it decided to take advantage of the less expensive, though still satisfactory, abandoned CB&Q right-of-way. Yet it chose only the seven miles between Moravia and the mining camp of Selection, concluding that it would be better to build from that point into Albia. The Board then organized the Moulton, Albia & Des Moines Railroad to complete this project. As the Wabash and most carriers had customarily done with extensions, it accepted the first-mortgage bonds of the affiliate (and in some cases stock as well) in exchange for the funds required for construction.[46]

By late spring 1899 hundreds of workers with their mule-drawn scrapers and other equipment swarmed along the Moulton-Albia-Harvey route. In November, the Albia *Friday Union* could report that "a Wabash engine and coach passed over the Wabash from Moulton to Harvey and return, on Wednesday forenoon [November 22]. Officers of the Wabash were in the coach, and inspected the new track." Almost immediately, regular freight and passenger service began, and by December the interchange of goods and travelers in Albia with the Iowa

Not long after the Wabash upgraded its route between Albia and Des Moines, Iowa, a section gang, based in Lovilia, accommodated a local photographer. This image is unusual in that the names of these often anonymous maintenance-of-way employees are identified: "Bill Fulk, boss, Bill Luman, Scot Hetherington, Ling Luman, Arthur Langdon." (Author's Coll.)

Central had become regularized.[47]

Just as the Wabash got its Des Moines route in proper order, it moved to do the same for its Omaha line. But unlike the former, the Omaha route did not involve any construction. Rather, the Wabash in 1901 worked out a purchase agreement with the bondholders of the Omaha & St. Louis Railroad (see chapter 2), whose property extended nearly 145 miles between Pattonsburg, Missouri, and Council Bluffs, Iowa. The transaction cost the Wabash about $3.5 million. Two years later, the Wabash merged the thirty-eight-mile Brunswick & Chillicothe Railroad, which constituted the southern portion of the Omaha line, into its corporate structure.[48]

Although not involving a purchase, Wabash management wisely eyed the seventy-mile line of the Missouri-Kansas-Texas Railway (Katy) between Hannibal and Moberly. This "Hannibal Cut-off Route" allowed the Wabash to avoid the congestion of St. Louis with its tonnage between Des Moines, Kansas City and Omaha and Chicago, Detroit and Toledo. Although the predecessor Toledo, Wabash & Western had briefly controlled the Hannibal & Central Missouri, builder of the line (see chapter 1), in late 1897 the Wabash secured joint trackage rights with a twenty-one-year lease agreement with the Katy. The arrangement worked so well that, in 1906, the Wabash renegotiated the contract for a ninety-nine-year period on a basis of an annual payment of $500 per mile and interest on improvements that

In 1912 a Wabash passenger train rumbles over the lightly-built Excelsior Springs branch. The absence of a turntable at Excelsior Springs likely explains why the locomotive is running backwards. Although a hazardous operating practice, the low speed lessened the possibility for derailment. (Author's Coll.)

the Katy promised would "put the road in first-class order." Wabash officials worried about not being able in the future to reach such a favorable deal. "There is a liability of a change in ownership [and] . . . we know the contract could not be extended on anything like these terms."[49]

There would also be some additional increases to mileage west of the Mississippi River. In 1901, the Wabash purchased the nine-mile Kansas City, Excelsior Springs & Northern Railway that connected with its

Kansas City mainline at Excelsior Springs Junction, Missouri. In 1893 this "lightly" built pike had opened as the Excelsior Springs Railroad to serve health spas in Excelsior Springs. But during the depression the railroad failed, and for a nominal amount the Wabash acquired the reorganized company. Management believed that it could tap a considerable local passenger market, mainly visitors from Kansas City who wished "to take the waters" at this popular resort community. Initially, the company succeeded. In 1903, for example, it sold 110,000 round-trip tickets from Kansas City to Excelsior Springs. The Wabash also built several industrial spurs, mostly along the Moberly to Des Moines line to reach coal mines. Resembling similar trackage elsewhere, they usually operated for only a few years and were then retired.[50]

Although construction of the Excelsior Springs Railroad represented work of promoters who were unattached to the Wabash, like some others in the Midwest, the company did its best to nurture independent steam shortlines to provide feeder traffic. Success varied. The greatest number of schemes occurred along the Omaha line, with three feeder routes in Iowa ultimately being completed. The first was the 8.7-mile Tabor & Northern Railway, which opened in 1889 between a connection at Malvern, southwesterly to the college community of Tabor. In 1912, local interests, encouraged by the Wabash, constructed the 17.5-mile Iowa & Southwestern Railroad between the Wabash at Blanchard, near the Missouri state line, through College Springs to Clarinda, seat of Page County. According to one commentator, the more than 4,000 residents of Clarinda had "always felt that their city was handicapped materially by the fact that they had no road competing with the Burlington and that an irreparable mistake had been made when the old Clarinda and

St. Louis line was allowed to go under in 1890." Indeed, the St. Louis, Kansas City & Northern had aided the ill-fated Clarinda & St. Louis (see chapter 3). About the time the first train steamed over the rails of the Iowa & Southwestern, another independent feeder opened to benefit the "inland" community of Treynor in eastern Pottawattamie County. The twelve-mile Iowa & Omaha Short Line Railroad reached the Wabash at Neoga, a depotless station about five miles from Council Bluffs, and the Wabash accommodated the road by granting it trackage rights into Council Bluffs.[51]

The development of all-weather roads and more dependable automobiles and trucks doomed these shortlines, which had filled the last nooks and crannies of the Midwestern railroad map. In 1916, the Iowa & Southwestern and Iowa & Omaha Short Line both quit, although the Tabor & Northern limped along until 1934. It was surely fortunate for investors that another Wabash-backed carrier along its Omaha route, the Red Oak & Northwestern Railroad, never opened. Yet it did become more than a paper proposition. In 1912, a consultant reported that "the grading for this [fourteen-mile] line is being done and the ties are on the ground" between Imogene and Red Oak, the seat of Montgomery County.[52]

With the exception of the Tabor & Northern, this shortline strategy at best provided modest amounts of traffic for only a brief period. Nevertheless, the company might have been wise to have granted direct financial assistance to business interests in the Marion County, Iowa, town of Pella. This vigorous community of nearly 3,000 mostly Dutch Americans expressed interest in constructing a four-mile road to the Des Moines line "from the center of the town to a connection with the Wabash at Howell." Situated on a secondary line of the Rock Island, Pella promised good traffic opportunities. If this tiny affiliate were to have been built, there was scant likelihood that the Rock Island would have retaliated against the Wabash.[53]

The new post-1897 prosperity caused the Wabash to consider obtaining additional smaller roads. In 1898, officials gave serious thought to acquisition of the St. Louis, Kansas City & Colorado Railroad (StLKC&C). This road operated approximately sixty miles of line from St. Louis westward to Union, Missouri. Not long after the Wabash rejected this purchase, the Rock Island acquired the company and by the early years of the twentieth century had extended the trackage from Union to Kansas City, making it a competitor for trans-Missouri freight shipments.[54]

Acquisition of the StLKC&C might have been a good decision, but the Wabash was discerning enough not to acquire or even assist financially the St. Joseph Valley Railway. This rather unusual Indiana carrier, which sported both electric (St. Joseph Valley Traction Company) and steam-powered divisions, ran largely parallel to the Montpelier-Chicago line between Elkhart and Angola, a distance of sixty miles. The Wabash was intrigued that this property "will afford a good means of access to Elkhart, . . . , and considerable business from the excellent agricultural section which it traverses." But the road was poorly built, suffered from inadequate rolling stock and needed to be extended eastward, ideally to Montpelier. Moreover, the Wabash would have to negotiate with Herbert Bucklen, the eccentric Arnica Salve founder, who owned the bonds and nearly all of the stock.[55]

Although during the early part of the twentieth century the Wabash did not find itself the owner of an electric interurban, this new, alternative form of intercity transport became popular in every state that it served. By 1915 Ohio, Indiana and Illinois became the heartland for what many optimistic investors initially thought would be the transportation wave of the future; the three states collectively claimed more than 6,000 miles of electric interurban track. Some carriers, including the mighty PRR, were openly hostile to these "juice" roads, fearing that they would seriously damage passenger revenues and in a few cases freight income. The PRR fought traction projects tooth and nail. At times it bought out their franchises, sent crews to prevent the physical crossing of its lines and entered into lengthy and expensive litigation. PRR officials believed that this fresh technology heralded the coming of the age of competition, an assessment that proved to be correct.[56]

The Wabash, on the other hand, usually showed a willingness to work with interurbans. The motivation clearly involved enhancing its revenue stream. "Business is business," retorted Joseph Ramsey when asked about the road's closeness to an interurban. On the basis of commentaries made by the executives and members of its board of directors, the Wabash considered some interurbans to be friendly feeders rather than hostile competitors. For years the Wabash enjoyed good terms with the Iowa Southern Utilities Company (ISU) (née Centerville, Albia & Southern Railway), the electrified successor to the A&C. This interurban handled Wabash passengers who boarded ISU cars at Albia and Moravia and provided a connection for carload freight, mostly outbound coal and inbound merchandise. In a similar case, the Wabash developed amicable ties with the Kansas City, Clay County & St. Joseph Railway (KCCC&StJ). Constructed late in the interurban era, in 1913 the company opened a twenty-eight-mile line between Kansas City and Excelsior Springs and a fifty-one-mile one between Kansas City and St. Joseph, Missouri. Even though the former trackage

immediately slashed passenger business on the Excelsior Springs branch just as it did on the mainline of the Chicago, Milwaukee & St. Paul between Kansas City and Excelsior Springs, the Wabash nevertheless worked in harmony with the KCCC&StJ for movement of freight and passengers, largely to St. Joseph via Kansas City. Another steam railroad, the Chicago Great Western, which developed strong ties with several Midwestern interurbans, however, generated a more extensive carload freight business with the KCCC&StJ. The Wabash also found the Toledo & Western Railway (T&W), which operated between Toledo and Adrian, Michigan, and Pioneer, Ohio, to be a useful interchange partner, especially for carload freight shipments. In fact, in 1924 the Wabash and the Willys-Overland Company, an automobile manufacturer, jointly purchased the interurban, with the Wabash investing $200,000. Traffic, mostly Willys-Overland shipments, moved over T&W rails between Fitch yard in Toledo and the Wabash interchange at Adrian.[57]

Even though the Wabash was hardly enthusiastic about the development of the 400-mile "McKinley Lines," the Illinois Traction System, one of the largest and most powerful Midwestern interurbans, which by 1907 served such cities on the Wabash as Danville, Decatur and Springfield, officials did not retaliate, and they mostly had a good relationship with the road. For example, in 1906 the Wabash agreed to assist the traction company with its overhead crossing of Wabash rails at Bement, selling the necessary real estate at a reasonable price and making other adjustments.[58]

Additional examples exist of a "friendly" Wabash. The company allowed the little Keokuk Electric Company, a seven-mile interurban that connected Keokuk with Hamilton and Warsaw, Illinois, to operate over its Mississippi River bridge. This was a rare accommodation by a steam road. The Wabash also cooperated with the Lafayette & Logansport Traction Company, a future component of the Fort Wayne & Wabash Valley Traction Company, when in 1907 it was building between the two Indiana communities in its corporate name. The Wabash adjusted its bridges in Delphi and Logansport to provide for safe overhead crossings, a construction policy that benefited both carriers.[59]

Still, there were instances when the Wabash found these upstart interurbans a general nuisance. Although the company did not seek to destroy them, it did get involved in a few brief, though unsuccessful, passenger rate wars. In 1903, for example, it sparred with the new interurbans in the Wabash valley when it matched their fares before deciding that it was a foolhardy policy. "These [traction] roads are designed to serve the local traveler who goes but a short distance, usually the farmer destined for the market town," reflected a realistic president Ramsey in 1904. "With their numerous trips and willingness to stop almost anyway to accommodate the public, it does not make financial sense for our railroad to compete for this type of customer."[60]

PITTSBURGH

While patrons of the Wabash surely found local improvements of note, whether a new line, replacement depot or renewed livestock pens, the most significant betterment was undeniably an extension to Pittsburgh, Pennsylvania, a teeming city of 325,000. At the time of its construction and opening, the project received national attention, being considered by pundits to be the "most exciting event in the history of the Wabash." But when the extension failed to produce the anticipated financial results, its leaders received sharp criticisms for their poor planning and shortsightedness. When

in 1911 the Wabash again entered bankruptcy, observers commonly blamed the "Pittsburgh folly" or "Gould's final folly" for the road's collapse.[61]

By the dawn of the twentieth century, Pittsburgh had developed into the greatest manufacturing center in America. At the heart of its economic life was the gigantic iron and steel industry that Andrew Carnegie, more than anyone, had done so much to create. His sprawling Homestead mills epitomized the city's production might. This "iron and steel workshop of the world" generated a staggering amount of freight traffic, estimated by the U.S. Census Bureau to be more than three times the tonnage officially reported by any other city on the globe. It was greater than the combined totals of Chicago, New York and Philadelphia. But other manufacturers also flourished in the aptly named "Smoky City," making for a vast array in the goods generated. The Pittsburgh Chamber of Commerce noted that the railroad freight business consisted principally of "iron, steel, pig iron, bridge and structural shapes, sheet metal, plate glass, window glass, tumblers, table ware, electric machinery, iron and steel tubes, armor plate, tin plate, air brakes and other railway safety appliances, locomotives, steel cars, fire brick and the raw materials that these product makers required, including coal, coke and limestone." By good fortune large quantities of the essential ingredients for manufacturing these products were located in areas surrounding the city. It was the center of approximately 100,000 square miles of soft-coal reserves; all of Great Britain possessed only 11,000 square miles. Pittsburgh was a railroader's dream place, a modern "Pot O'Gold."[62]

Two individuals played pivotal roles in the Wabash quest for the rich traffic of Pittsburgh and beyond, George Gould and Joseph Ramsey. Gould had a vision. Like his father, he thought in terms of assembling a true transcontinental railroad system. But Jay Gould died before he could bring about such a triumph, and only C. P. Huntington and Tom Scott had ever seriously attempted to create a transcontinental network. Gould inherited control of the International & Great Northern, Missouri Pacific, St. Louis Southwestern, Texas & Pacific and the Wabash, and with this empire the thirty-seven-year-old railroad magnate possessed the core for a transcontinental. Gould trains operated on more than 10,000 miles of line extending from El Paso, Texas, to Buffalo, New York. Disappointed that he failed to gain an interest in the Southern Pacific when in 1901 E. H. Harriman of the Union Pacific acquired that western giant, Gould took control of the Denver & Rio Grande and the Rio Grande Western. He proceeded to fuse them into the Denver & Rio Grande Western, thus giving his far-flung system access to Salt Lake City and Ogden, Utah, suitable jumping-off places for a route to the Pacific. Gould would soon begin to construct the Western Pacific from Salt Lake City to Oakland, California.[63]

Expansion in the West did not mean that Gould was not looking east. In the late 1890s, he had toyed with the idea of reaching the Atlantic seaboard through control of the Lake Erie & Western; Buffalo, Rochester & Pittsburgh; and the Reading. Perhaps the Wheeling & Lake Erie Railroad (W&LE) would be part of this strategy of moving eastward from Toledo. But at the turn of twentieth century, his attention was on Pittsburgh as the intermediate objective.[64]

It would be the creative mind of Ramsey that would influence Gould's specific thinking about railroads in this region. Born in the South Hills of Pittsburgh on April 17, 1850, Ramsey received solid training in civil engineering from Western University (University of Pittsburgh) and at age nineteen be-

gan his career in railroading. After service with a variety of roads, including the PRR, in 1895 Ramsey joined the Wabash as general manager and vice president. In June 1901, he accepted the presidency. This accomplished railroader, who was smart and resourceful, not only possessed excellent organizational skills but always had a good eye for details, as revealed in a stream of reports he provided Ashley and the board of directors while serving as general manager.[65]

A native Pittsburgher and former employee of the PRR, Ramsey intimately understood his hometown's industrial potential and the local railroad situation. For some time shippers had been unhappy with the PRR's almost monopolistic presence in the city. The company allegedly charged high rates, and its service was less than adequate, verging at times on the awful. It was Ramsey who convinced Gould that Pittsburgh should be part of the eastward expansion of the Wabash.[66]

Ramsey also believed that a practical line into Pittsburgh was possible. Even though conventional wisdom held that every available route had been taken, he knew well the lay of the land and the possibilities of modern engineering and construction. In fact, in the early 1880s Ramsey had conducted an engineering survey into the city for a route, a line that two decades later the Wabash would closely follow. Of course, Ramsey shared these insights with George Gould.[67]

With Gould's backing, in 1900 Ramsey started the process of reconnoitering the greater Pittsburgh region to pinpoint the line. He was ever mindful of an entrance that would have minimal gradients and few curves. Because he wanted to run the road into the heart of the city, Ramsey needed a feasible way to bridge the mighty Monongahela River. In each case, he felt confident that he could accomplish these objectives. The diligent labors of Ramsey and his staff, including his accomplished chief engineer, James W. Patterson, quickly paid a big reward when they learned that a moribund traction company, the Pittsburgh & Mansfield Railroad (P&M), had earlier received federal approval to construct such a vital downtown span. Although the firm's permit had expired, Ramsey was able to get its authorization quietly renewed in a routine Congressional measure. Amid these maneuvers, the Wabash gained control of the P&M and with it the legal authority to cross a navigable stream. Other preparations occurred, including incorporation of three affiliates—Pittsburgh, Carnegie & Western; Cross Creek; and Pittsburgh, Toledo & Western—to build segments of the route in Pennsylvania, West Virginia and Ohio, respectively.[68]

An essential part of the march to Pittsburgh became the creation of a business structure that could manage this multimillion-dollar undertaking. On February 1, 1901, the Pittsburgh-Toledo Syndicate (the "Syndicate") came into being. The corporation quickly raised $20 million of construction capital, with $5 million coming directly from Gould and an equally impressive amount from James Hazen Hyde, flamboyant head of the Equitable Life Assurance Society of the United States. The Syndicate's coffers filled because a few days after its creation Gould and Andrew Carnegie worked out an agreement highlighted by the Carnegie Steel Company promise to send 25 percent of its traffic over Gould's roads. Moreover, there were hints that Carnegie might increase that commitment. The agreed-to amount was hardly insignificant; in 1900 the enterprise had shipped about 80 million tons of freight. Carnegie also endorsed a connection between his Union Railroad, which linked East Pittsburgh with the Homestead mills, and the Pittsburgh, Carnegie & Western, the soon-to-be-built Syndicate line into Pittsburgh.[69]

There is no doubt that Carnegie badly wanted a dependable, low-cost transportation alternative to the PRR, and he correctly saw the Wabash project to be that option. The steel king was especially annoyed at the PRR—and in particular its president, Alexander J. Cassatt—for recently ending rebates to large shippers and for creating "a community of interest" with the New York Central System to do the same, making it virtually impossible for Carnegie to use his long-employed divide-and-conquer strategy.[70]

News of the plans of Ramsey and Gould, which they wanted kept secret, nevertheless reached PRR headquarters in Philadelphia. The railroad had an array of informants, mostly company employees, who repeatedly sent reports of varying quality to lower-level officials, who directed some or all of them to Cassatt's office. When the top brass of the PRR learned of Wabash doings in greater Pittsburgh, they apparently did not immediately show alarm. The powerful men thought that an "invasion" of their most lucrative territory was unlikely because of the long distance to the closest connection with the Wabash, the Toledo area of northwestern Ohio. With the great density of railroads in the Buckeye State, the cost of building a transstate road to reach the Ohio River and beyond might not be financially feasible and could take years to complete.[71]

But by April 1901, Cassatt and his associates became increasingly worried about the Wabash. They were dismayed when the Syndicate sought to take hold of the W&LE. This 430-mile single-track carrier connected Toledo with Wheeling, West Virginia, and operated several important branches, including lines to Cleveland and Zanesville. Because these routes resembled a crude cross on the railway map of Ohio, the public often referred to this predominantly coal- and ore-carrying company as the Iron Cross Route. The W&LE also owned a stub that ran along the west bank of the Ohio River between Warrenton and Steubenville, Ohio, the end of which was only about sixty miles from Pittsburgh. In a frantic bid to prevent a Gould takeover of the W&LE, the PRR bought as many shares as possible, yet fell short of the amount needed for control. By this time, the Syndicate had a majority stock interest, thanks in part to a well-positioned ally, Myron T. Herrick, who soon would become governor of Ohio and wielded considerable political power because of his close connections with President William McKinley. This powerful Cleveland banker had invested in the Syndicate and earlier had been the W&LE receiver. A month later, Ramsey assumed the presidency of the Iron Cross Route.[72]

It appeared that Ramsey and Gould were about to pull off one of the great coups in modern railroad history, breaking the PRR's grip on Pittsburgh. A multitude of major problems, however, developed. Carnegie sold his steel holdings to J. P. Morgan, Sr., the king of American high finance, not long after making the traffic accord with Gould. It became unclear initially what the successor United States Steel Corporation would do about the agreement, although eventually this Morgan-controlled behemoth would renege. Likely, too, Wabash interests woefully underestimated the response of the PRR. In August 1901, Russell Sage stated that he did not believe that the extension would annoy the PRR and admitted, "We could not afford to antagonize [the] Pennsylvania—it is too great a property." But the Wabash did. The "Standard Railroad of the World" possessed enormous resources and under Cassatt was not opposed to using an iron fist, something that labor organizers already knew and traction executives throughout its territory were quickly learning. For example, Pittsburgh politicians loyal to the PRR stymied construction efforts. The project needed a bridge-enabling ordinance to enter

the city legally, and it also required permission to build along a downtown street to a proposed depot site, but the Common and Select Council bodies refused to consider these measures. Local lawmakers seemed to be up to more mischief, suggesting that the Wabash pay an expensive open-ended franchise fee and that it not be allowed to use bituminous coal–burning locomotives in the city. Other railroads faced neither requirement. The PRR also bought up real estate to prevent or delay the building process and pressured the Pittsburgh & Lake Erie Railroad (P&LE), an affiliate of the New York Central, to resist the Wabash as well. And Cassatt sent a special message of sorts to Gould. In 1901, a dispute erupted between the PRR and Gould's Western Union Telegraph Company that led the feisty PRR chief executive to "descend to about the level of primitive man." With no settlement in sight, in May 1903 Cassatt finally dispatched crews to demolish 60,000 telegraph poles, with their huge forest masts, and to remove 1,500 miles of wire from along the PRR's rights-of-way. Eventually the courts sanctioned this wanton destruction, and the PRR turned to the Western Union's chief rival, Postal Telegraph Company, for replacement service. When a Pittsburgh cartoonist had Cassatt saying to Gould, "Stay West Young Man," he meant it.[73]

Even though the Wabash lacked the necessary ordinances from the city of Pittsburgh, it pushed ahead with its costly and difficult project. Ramsey continually expressed his optimism. In the latter part of 1901, he told the financial community that "the Pittsburgh extension will be completed in about a year and a half, and it will be of great benefit to the Wabash company." That timetable seemed to be wishful thinking. The "shortest grade regardless of topography" philosophy meant major, if not at times monumental, grading, bridge building and tunneling. In the downtown area alone the railroad needed to bridge the Monongahela and bore 3,342 feet through Mt. Washington and nearly a mile through a rocky barrier at Greentree. (The latter became more time-consuming and expensive when an old coal mine caved in under the tunnel floor.) Thousands of men and machines labored on a variety of challenging, even dangerous, assignments. Some of them proved deadly. The worst single tragedy occurred when the north structure of the half-mile cantilever bridge over the Monongahela collapsed, killing ten workers. An outbreak of smallpox also left a death toll among construction gangs and seriously impaired others.[74]

In time, tensions with Pittsburgh's city hall and Philadelphia eased. Widespread public anger over the poor service and continued arrogance of the PRR, stirred up by Charles Rook, editor and publisher of the *Pittsburgh Dispatch,* did much to force enactment on February 3, 1903, of the necessary municipal statutes. When Cassatt realized that the Wabash could not be blocked from the city, the PRR relented. His next strategy, it appeared, was to invest heavily to strengthen service, especially for freight customers in the Pittsburgh district. Between 1902 and 1909, the company—even under the relatively cautious leadership of James McCrea, who succeeded Cassatt after his sudden death in 1906—had spent more than $25 million on local improvements, including $3.6 million for the Brilliant cutoff that sped freight movements in the region. By embracing "the best defense is a good offensive philosophy," the PRR improved its overall public image. Moreover, Cassatt, who was both a superb civil engineer and a talented businessman, also may have concluded that the Gould project was doomed because of high construction costs and questionable potential for heavy freight volume.[75]

The Pittsburgh project required more

than building 59.9 miles of "twin ribbons of steel winding over the hills and valleys, burrowing deep through the solid rock of Mt. Washington and riding high over the blue Monongahela into the Golden Triangle." It involved construction of freight and passenger yards, interchange spurs and sidings, repair shops and other support facilities, the most massive of which was the ten-story flat iron–shaped depot, or "headhouse." Erected at the intersection of Ferry and Liberty streets in the Lower Triangle, or Point District, this building was conveniently situated to the city's business district and close to three of its major streetcar lines. Designed in the neobaroque style by St. Louis architect Theodore C. Link—whose earlier works had included Monticello Seminary in Godfrey, Illinois, St. Louis Union Station in St. Louis, and the Wabash Employe's Hospital Association main building in Decatur, Illinois—the steel and concrete structure's 124,000 square feet offered ample waiting room, office and shop space. It became an instant landmark with its fancy dome, large clock and decorative marble, tile and glass mosaic work. Ramsey correctly predicted that the depot would be "creditable to the road and an ornament to the town." A massive 415-foot balloon-style steel train shed, four-story brick freight house and power plant also made up the station complex, estimated to have cost about $1,250,000.[76]

In the summer of 1904 the Wabash proudly introduced its Pittsburgh extension to the traveling public. In a full-page advertisement in the *Official Railway Guide,* for example, the company proclaimed: "OPENING OF PITTSBURG LINE JULY 2, 1904." The copy added that "The Wabash Pittsburg Terminal Railway, between Jewett, Ohio, and Pittsburg, Pa., is now completed and open for business, thus forming a most excellent modernly constructed through line, in connection with the Wheeling & Lake Erie

If there ever was an American railroad station that was a "white elephant," the cavernous passenger-office building erected by the Wabash Pittsburgh Terminal Company in Pittsburgh, Pennsylvania, surely wins. The volume of anticipated train traffic never materialized on the costly extension. Even before the Wabash lost control of its WPT affiliate, there were few daily arrivals and departures. (Author's Coll.)

THE WABASH MATURES 99

and Wabash Main Lines, from Pittsburg, Pa., to Chicago, St. Louis and the West." Although there was no ceremonial driving of a gold or silver spike or formal orations, crowds of well-wishers gathered to observe the first outbound train, pulled by a high-stepping Atlantic-type (4-4-2) locomotive, which departed in the late afternoon on the second for St. Louis. A brass band appeared at the station and played an appropriate tune for this "New World's Fair Line from Pittsburg," the lively "Meet Me in St. Louie, Louie, Meet Me at the Fair." This rousing music delighted the assembled and surely would have pleased every Wabash employee at this triumphal moment.[77]

Less popularized, but enormously important, were efforts to bolster freight revenue. Agents worked hard to generate as much business as possible. To aid their cause, the Wabash acquired $14 million of the capital stock of the Pittsburgh Terminal Railroad & Coal Company, which became a steady shipper of local coal, and spent $12 million to take charge of a strategic thirty-six-mile industrial pike, the West Side Belt Railroad, and its considerable coal properties. The belt road's terminals in Pittsburgh and Clariton provided "nearly all the important establishments in the Pittsburg district." Yet it took time before this investment and other traffic arrangements built up much freight traffic. It was not until June 1906 that the Wabash received its first trainload of steel from the former Carnegie mills and delivered its first shipment of iron ore from Lake Erie. It took until February 1907 before a traffic agreement was worked out with the P&LE so that it might use "that company's spur tracks to various manufacturing works." Tonnage soared initially: 346,735 in 1905; 2,084,432 in 1906 and 3,004,791 in 1907, but dropped sharply in 1908 to 2,247,964 tons. "The Pittsburgh Terminal is now earning $25,000 per mile

and the Wheeling & Lake Erie $17,000 per mile," opined an optimistic Ramsey about freight operations in 1907. "These are splendid earnings. . . . Both roads have all the business now they can handle."[78]

In May 1904, the Wabash created a special corporate structure for its Pittsburgh operations. The company united holdings of the Syndicate and construction railroad affiliates Pittsburgh, Carnegie & Western; Cross Creek; and Pittsburgh, Toledo & Western into the Wabash Pittsburgh Terminal Railway Company (WPT). As part of this restructuring, WPT took control of the W&LE through ownership of 51.73 percent of its capital stock. The Wabash owned all of the equity of the WPT and as much of the debt as would be needed to control the corporation if a bankruptcy were ever to occur. Those bonds, most of which were a second mortgage, were offered for sale to traditional buyers of such securities, including life insurance companies and savings and loan associations. Foreign investors, particularly from Holland, also acquired them, mainly because they were discounted and hence relatively inexpensive. These actions collectively were designed to underwrite the incredibly costly endeavors of the WPT, which ultimately approached $45 million.[79]

The PRR watched closely the affairs of the WPT and the Wabash. Written reports, newspaper clippings and the like continued to flow from the field to company offices in Pittsburgh and Philadelphia. Station agents, freight representatives, division superintendents and the PRR's "various friends" told of Wabash plans to build lines into the coalfields of Ohio and West Virginia, to acquire small regional roads and shortlines and to strengthen in various ways its position in the PRR domain. At best, most were rumors; neither the Wabash, W&LE, nor WPT built as reported, although occasionally the W&LE explored possible additions, including the Pittsburgh, Lisbon & Western Railroad and the Salem (Ohio) Railroad, both of which served the Columbiana County, Ohio, area. And, not surprisingly, betterments were made, usually involving installation of passing tracks or industrial sidings or spurs.[80]

Just a few days after the first passenger train left the Pittsburgh passenger terminal, the general superintendent of the PRR described for the general manager a trip that he made with another official on July 8 from Toledo to Pittsburgh. The report would hardly trouble any officer of the PRR.

We had intended to leave Toledo [Union Station] on train No. 2, due to leave there at 8:22 A.M. When the time came for this train to depart, it was marked up "On Time," but was later changed to "Two Hours Late." We then left on the local accommodation train due to leave Toledo at 9:00 A.M., arriving at Pittsburgh at 6:30 P.M.

This train left Toledo on time, the only passengers on it for Pittsburgh being Mr. Trimble and myself. The train was delayed by reason of the parlor car on the rear end having hot box, and lost some twenty minutes on this account. The car was set off. The train also lost forty minutes on account of express and station work, and arrived at Navarre [Ohio] one hour late. At this point the fast train, No. 2, was reported only ten minutes behind, and we got off the accommodation and boarded the through train.

The accommodation train seemed to do a very fair local business and had a very comfortable parlor car on it; the fare is 25 cents over any portion of the road. The parlor car had a buffet, which aimed to serve a broiler lunch. The lunch was very poor indeed, the meat being tainted; the porter informed me it was the only steak he had on the train.

Train No. 2, the fast train, is scheduled to leave St. Louis at 8:30 P.M., Toledo at 8:22 A.M. and to arrive at Pittsburgh 3:45 P.M., stopping

at several of the principal points. The running time is very fast. Yesterday, this train left Toledo 2 hrs. 40 mins. late, with a combined car, reclining chair car, a sleeper for Pittsburgh, sleeper for Wheeling and a dining car, the dining car to be attached to westbound train No. 15 at the meeting point. We arrived at Pittsburgh 4 hrs. 25 mins. late. . . .

From Toledo to Norwalk, the road has 85 lb. rail, good ties, and some little ballast. It rides very comfortably at present, excepting through the large towns. In all the large towns, not only is the alignment bad, but the line and surface is in bad shape, and none of the fast trains can pass through these towns with comfort at a high rate of speed. From Norwalk to Navarre, the track is not in as good shape. There seems to be considerable 70 lb. rail in the track, there is very little ballast, and evidences of pumping [of mud] were noted at many points. On this portion of the road, fast speed could not be made comfortably.

From Navarre to the top of the hill, east of where the W.&L.E. crosses under the Pan Handle [PRR], the track is better, and 50 miles per hour can be made with comfort and safety. From the top of the hill to Warrenton the track is not so good. The track on the river bank, from Warrenton to Mingo Junction, is in very bad shape and is not safe for fast speed.

From Mingo to Pittsburgh, the rail appears to be 90 lb.; the ties are apparently eight feet in length and six inches in width. There is some gravel ballast in the track, some broken sandstone, and some rip-rap; in many places the bank is settling under the track and the elevation of the curves is very bad. In one place we noted that the cement wall holding the large fill had been pulled out of line; in other places the cement work appeared to be cracking, and in a number of places there were slips and slides.

The Pullman cars were not the best cars

built and were manned by entirely new porters and conductors.

On No. 2, after Mr. Trimble and I got on, I ascertained from the conductor of the Pullman car that there were no passengers in the Wheeling sleeper at all, and five in the Pittsburgh sleeper. Two of these were Mr. Trimble and myself; the other three were returning officials of Allegheny City, who had been furnished "dead-head" transportation. Later, one other man boarded the train. He was a railroad man. . . .

There were probably twelve passengers in the coaches. Some of them appeared to be railroad men, and three of them had come through from St. Louis.

The westbound trains which we passed were all very lightly loaded. Especially was this the case with the train which left Pittsburgh at 7:30. This train had one Chicago and two St. Louis sleepers. So far as I could see, the Chicago sleeper was empty, and there were not more than three or four passengers in both St. Louis sleepers.

Before a very fast schedule can be safely maintained over the W.&L.E.R.R., longer sidings will have to be constructed and the line through the towns upgraded.

After the Wabash Pittsburgh Terminal is completed from Mingo to Pittsburgh, I should think there would be no difficulty in maintaining a high rate of speed, as there are practically no road crossings and the line is fairly good, although abounding in tunnels and bridges.

I should think, with a little dissemination of the facts with regard to the time the Wabash is making, it would not be a difficult thing for our Passenger Department to hold our own in the travel both to St. Louis and Toledo.[81]

Although the Wabash made improvements on the Pittsburgh extension and the WPT possessed a line that was superior to the paralleling St. Louis main stem of the PRR,

the early, lackluster assessment of its passenger service by the PRR official would mostly hold true. Business failed to develop as expected. By 1906, the peak year for service, the company operated only four daily through trains to and from Pittsburgh and two daily local or commuter runs between the terminal and either Pryor, Pennsylvania, or Mingo, Ohio. They hardly taxed the capacity of the WPT's physical plant. Never did the Wabash take sizable numbers of riders away from PRR trains bound to or from Chicago, St. Louis or Toledo. Within a few years a magazine writer penned a poignant piece, "Palace Depot for Two Trains A Day," in which he sadly noted that the "magnificent depot of cut stone, marble, and bronze, costing one million dollars, is being used for a service of only two trains a day." Its waiting room usually remained quiet. "At times not a soul is visible, save a blue-garbed janitor or two, who step about noiselessly and with a constrained air as if the solemnity and quietness of the place laid a spell on them." Further east on Liberty Street, however, stood Pittsburgh's Union Station "where no less than 225 trains each way enter and depart from a great Union Station that bustles with life, noise, and gaiety." Yet both facilities represented similar investments.[82]

Before it became apparent to Pittsburghers and others that the Wabash terminal might be fairly called "Ramsey's million-dollar blunder," the Gould-Ramsey duo decided to make the Steel City more than the Pennsylvania state end point of the Wabash System. They had their eyes on Baltimore, Maryland, as a suitable East Coast terminus. Although this major seaport had the rail services of the PRR and the Baltimore & Ohio, which recently had entered the PRR's orbit, another carrier, the Western Maryland Railroad (WM), in which the city of Baltimore held a substantial interest, also served the metropolis. The WM was not a gigantic road, possessing slightly more than 250 miles of single-line track. Yet it stretched from Baltimore westward toward the Pittsburgh area with its mainline running to Hagerstown, Maryland, and it operated appendages, including several into southeastern Pennsylvania.[83]

Although in February 1902, Ramsey told the *Wall Street Journal* that the "Wabash is not at the present time seeking a seaboard route at all," a few months later the Wabash officially took action to do just that. On May 7, 1902, its involvement with the WM formally began. On that date, the Baltimore City Council authorized sale of the municipality's interests in the road to the "Fuller Syndicate," which included Gould, Ramsey, Myron Herrick and several of the their investor colleagues. The deal involved a cash payment of more than $8.7 million and a commitment for construction of a modern port facility in Baltimore. Residents liked the prospects of an independent Wabash in their midst, which they felt would "yield to Baltimore a splendid opportunity to regain her lost commercial prestige."[84]

Named for E. L. Fuller, wealthy head of the International Salt Company, this syndicate, with the WM in its pocket, planned to link the property with the Pittsburgh extension. Specifically, a line would leave the new construction in western Pennsylvania at Patterson's Mills, running via Waynesburg, to a connection at Montrose, West Virginia, with another Syndicate-controlled road, the coal-carrying West Virginia Central & Pittsburgh Railway. That carrier's tracks wound northeastward to Cumberland, Maryland. The Syndicate would extend the WM to that historic Maryland canal town from Cherry Run, Maryland, a distance of about sixty miles through the valley of the Potomac River. The route to tidewater was hardly an airline and necessitated some heavy construction, including five tunnels. Moreover, the WM itself was no

speedway; its mainline "with its present heavy grades and light rails, is wholly inadequate to handle the freight from Pittsburg."[85]

It did not take long before the Syndicate initiated work on its new acquisition. In addition to "betterments and improvements" on the existing lines and construction of the Port Covington harbor facility, it expended resources on building the line between Cherry Run and Cumberland, not an easy construction task. Finally, in February 1906, at a cost of about $7 million, the extension opened. Freight service began in March, and passenger service followed in June. By this time, the WM had officially absorbed the West Virginia Central & Pittsburgh, making it a 540-mile road (through ownership and lease).[86]

The Wabash never tied its Pittsburgh extension via Waynesburg and Montrose to the burgeoning WM. Rather, the Steel City later would be reached by the "Cumberland Extension," an eighty-six-mile line linking Cumberland with the P&LE at Connellsville, Pennsylvania, completed in August 1912. This was a wise choice of routing. By connecting with the P&LE, the WM enjoyed the shortest line between Baltimore and Pittsburgh and the lowest grade across the Allegheny Mountains. Thus, the WM had expanded far beyond its original geographic niche, becoming an important coal originator and a significant link in east-west merchandise traffic. But by 1912 both the WPT and the WM were in the hands of court-appointed receivers, and Gould's dream of creating a gigantic traffic combination from the Atlantic to the Pacific had been shattered forever by a series of financial reversals.[87]

BANKRUPTCY

By early 1905, trouble had begun for the Wabash system. The practical Ramsey began to quarrel openly with the self-absorbed Gould. For some time, Ramsey had been annoyed by Gould's general inattention to the problems that confronted both the Wabash and the WPT. As early as December 1903, in a lengthy report to Gould and the board of directors, Ramsey blasted his superiors for not responding to his urgent requests for more rolling stock. "The traffic requirements of the Wabash road are today beyond our ability to supply equipment to move and we are forced to decline daily good paying traffic on account of shortage of equipment and motive power, and this condition has been existing for some time."[88]

Although Gould surely recognized the merits of Ramsey's concerns, he blocked Ramsey's specific requests. Gould was not anxious to pay for betterments, be it for rolling stock, track work or the like. Instead, he preferred to use profits from the Wabash and his other properties for expansion and for his own pleasures, which ranged from polo ponies to keeping a mistress in New York City. Gould drained what should have been solid, profit-making carriers by practicing the fine art of "skinning the road."[89]

The crown prince of the Goulds was radically different from his famed father, and these traits hurt his far-flung railroad empire. "Exactly in contradiction to the father George was mercurial in temperament, hasty and uncertain in his judgments, careless and nearsighted in his calculations, extravagant and self-indulgent in business as in personal habits," observed journalist Ernest Howard. All who knew Gould realized, too, that he was extremely jealous of delegating his official power, the impact of which was made worse by his frequent travels abroad. His late father, however, had relied heavily on competent managers and allowed them to do what needed to be done, including when he was in Europe or elsewhere.[90]

In April 1905, these tensions between Ramsey and Gould became public news when Ramsey resigned as president of the WPT. The press speculated why this event had happened. One associate believed that managing the Pittsburgh extension was too much for anyone. "I think that Mr. Ramsey resigned simply because . . . the load he was carrying in operation of the main system and building into Pittsburg was too great." Although the pressures of the WPT were undoubtedly a factor, the reason also involved his deteriorating relations with Gould. A Ramsey friend speculated that "Mr. Ramsey has resigned because he wanted to be the actual president . . . and not a mere clerk for Mr. Gould. Mr. Gould was continually interfering with Mr. Ramsey in the conduct of his business, frequently going over head and doing things which Mr. Ramsey felt to be a humiliation for a man in his position, and consequently he had to get out." Muckraker Burton J. Hendrick would later write: "Gould, from the first, manifested the family characteristic of looking upon the Gould railroads as family perquisites. 'Ramsey, can't I run my own property as I want to?' he once testily remarked to the president of the Wabash, who had entered a protest against certain of his acts." Ramsey himself told the financial press that "I resigned the presidency of the Wabash Pittsburgh Terminal Company because I did not find myself in close harmony or accord with the policies that controlled." Ramsey refused to suffer fools and egomaniacs, including even a rich and powerful one.[91]

Although no longer president of the Wabash subsidiary WPT, Ramsey remained at the throttle of the Wabash. He apparently intended to stay on as long as possible if he could purge himself of the troublesome Gould. Ramsey hoped that he could have sympathetic men placed on the board of directors and that he could then do what be believed essential for making the Wabash a profitable and dynamic property. In his efforts to become the "real" president,

In the early twentieth century, travelers along the Wabash surely admired the architecturally pleasing depots in the Illinois cities of Quincy and Springfield. The Quincy scene from ca. 1908 highlights the passenger depot that on two sides prominently feature the WABASH name. In the left background stands the company's freight office. The ca. 1910 view of the Springfield station reveals both an attractive structure and the small "shack" used by the road crossing guard who protected traffic on Washington Street. (Author's Coll.)

Wabash Station, Quincy, Ill.

Wabash Railroad Depot. Springfield, Ill.

Ramsey issued a circular in September 1905 to "Debenture and Stock holders of the Wabash Railroad Company," in which he asked for their support. "Under this statement of the results of my administration, I feel that I am entitled to ask you to honor me with your proxies, for use at the annual election of directors."[92]

Ramsey's strong personality, combined with this proxy ploy, were too much for Gould. The proxy fight fizzled, and at the board meeting held on October 2, 1905, members, with only Ramsey objecting, passed a resolution stating in part: "That in view of existing conditions, . . . that [Ramsey] be, and is hereby, relieved from the powers and duties of that office." Ramsey departed an angry man, and he never regained momentum to his career. Shortly after leaving the Wabash, he took the presidency of the New York, Pittsburgh & Chicago Railroad, a projected line designed to compete with the PRR. Later he helped to create a none-too-successful Ohio shortline, the Lorain, Ashland & Southern Railroad, popularly known as the "Ramsey Road," which he headed until his death in 1916. Before its abandonment in the early 1930s, this property fell into the hands of the PRR and Erie.[93]

Gould surely needed Ramsey at both the WPT and the Wabash. He was an individual of undeniable talents. Ramsey's performance impressed financial analysts. Not long after his ouster, a writer for *Moody's* noted that "under his administration the earnings [of the Wabash] per mile rose from $6,600 to $9,900, a gain of 50% in a highly competitive territory." Company officials also respected and generally liked their departed boss. During the Ramsey-Gould bout, morale among executives plummeted, especially at a time when resources were thin and economic clouds loomed on the horizon. "We required a strong captain at the

helm," reported a disgruntled Wabash official, "and now he is gone."[94]

Gould, however, fortuitously found a competent replacement for Ramsey. The newest president of the Wabash and WPT was Frederick A. Delano. Born in Hong Kong in 1863 to a wealthy family of China traders, Delano received an outstanding education, graduating in 1885 from Harvard College. He immediately launched his railroading career in the engineering department of the CB&Q and rapidly moved up the rungs of the corporate ladder. By 1905, he served as that road's general manager at Chicago.[95]

Much like his predecessor, but with a more pliable personality, Delano knew how to attend to problems. But insufficient resources prevented him from making the improvements he thought necessary. At this time, Gould was not only involved with the Fuller Syndicate but was also heavily committed to financing the western-most unit of his transcontinental railway network, the Western Pacific Railroad, that shortly would link the Denver & Rio Grande Western at Salt Lake City with San Francisco Bay. The financial situation for the WPT and the Wabash became acute when the Panic of 1907 struck, briefly interrupting the unrivaled prosperity that the nation had enjoyed for much of a decade. Neither additional borrowing nor Gould's family fortune could prevent the failure of the WPT and W&LE in 1908 and the subsequent tumbling into receivership of his various and highly leveraged railroads. The Wabash fell victim to bankruptcy in 1911. The panic dealt the Gould empire a blow from which it never recovered, and George Gould saw his father's railroad legacy slip away.[96]

In 1908 the financial woes of the WPT and its affiliate W&LE came to a head. On New Year's Day, the WPT was unable to pay interest due on more than $30 million of

In 1909, in addition to the financial woes that plagued the Wabash, the company experienced a disastrous wreck near Glenwood, Missouri. On Sunday, August 28, 1909, passenger train No. 51, crowded with excursionists going to an old settlers reunion at Greenwood, collided with an extra freight train, killing two persons and injuring about twenty others. A Kirksville, Missouri, reporter described what happened: "The crew of the freight claim that . . . as No. 51 does not run on Sunday, they supposed that they had a clear track, the collision occurring on a curve and the timber being dense prevented the crews of both trains from observing their danger until it was too late. When it was seen that a crash was inevitable the engineers and firemen of both trains jumped and the fireman of the freight was caught beneath the wreckage and his life was instantly crushed out." (James Holzmeier Coll.)

first mortgage bonds. A few months earlier, however, the WPT had loaned the W&LE $300,000, which hardly helped a road that faced some hefty obligations—for example, owing nearly $500,000 to the Wabash for car and locomotive rentals. The W&LE showed signs of becoming a transportation slum. It had about a quarter of its car fleet "bad ordered" and urgently needed a wide range of physical improvements. Moreover, in August 1908 the company faced payments of principal and interest on its three-year 5 percent notes. Furthermore, the general physical condition of the WPT was steadily declining, even though it was a new railroad. Its eighteen double-track tunnels, especially, required constant attention, and its car fleet remained inadequate.[97]

By midyear the financial house of cards collapsed. On May 29, the WPT was declared insolvent. As expected, its two court-appointed receivers were close to Gould:

Pittsburgh banker Francis H. Skelding, a director of the West Side Belt Railroad, and Henry W. McMaster, WPT general superintendent. On June 8, the W&LE experienced a similar fate. B. A. Worthington, an experienced railroader who Delano had earlier named to manage the W&LE, assumed his role as receiver.[98]

The Wabash initially absorbed the economic shock waves caused by the panic, but its corporate health steadily deteriorated. By mid-1911, the picture looked bleak. Although the company lost $159,259 for the 1908–1909 fiscal year and earned $545,718 for 1909–1910, the figures for 1910–1911 revealed a lost of $403,421 and much more red ink was anticipated. According to Delano, the company suffered on various fronts, including higher wage costs, more expensive fuel bills, less competitive freight and passenger service because of deferred maintenance on rolling stock and track and "very high" equipment rentals. The latter for fiscal 1911 alone amounted to a whopping $1,021,000. But the financial mess caused by the financial failures of the WPT and W&LE, most of all, explains the financial crisis. Since 1904 the Wabash had issued more than $41.5 million of bonds, with all but $2 million going into refunding operations or being pledged as collateral for money raised to help out either the WPT or W&LE. Too few dollars then were left for maintaining and upgrading the Wabash. Its annual fixed interest charges soared from $3,114,000 for fiscal year 1904 to $4.8 million on the eve of its bankruptcy. This financial chemistry proved destructive, forcing the Wabash into bankruptcy on December 26, 1911.[99]

The Wabash began 1912 in the hands of U.S. District Court for the Eastern District of Missouri. Fortunately, Delano, who continued as president, won appointment as one of the three receivers. He was joined by company vice president Edward B. Pryor and St. Louis businessman William K. Bixby. With Gould's influence waning, Delano had more power to shape what most observers believed would be a resurgent railroad.[100]

Could the Wabash have been spared financial disaster had the Pittsburgh Extension and other projects not been undertaken? There is no denying that the financial commitments made to the push eastward led ultimately to receivership and reorganization. Yet the Wabash seems partially to have been a victim of bad timing. If the WPT and W&LE projects had been completed and a route to the tidewater opened as the nineteenth century closed, the scenario might have been vastly different. If traffic promised by Carnegie had fully materialized early on, business would have boomed rapidly, creating an environment attractive to investors who would be forthcoming to help rehabilitate the W&LE, to modernize and expand motive power and

car fleets of the Wabash and its subsidiaries and to make other revenue-enhancing improvements. If Gould had allowed Ramsey more freedom in his actions and had been more willing to reinvest in his railroads, the financial situation would have been strengthened. These "what ifs" simply did not happen.[101]

It became easy for critics to poke fun at what Gould and Ramsey had accomplished. "Such a jumble of viaducts, tunnels, bridges, cuts, fills, arches, trestles, and culverts civilization had never before seen," were the not-so-flattering words of one faultfinder. But to break the monopoly of the PRR, these undertakings became essential. Although the Pittsburgh freight and passenger terminals seemed a colossal waste of precious funds and detractors liked to stress their white elephant qualities, these facilities were built with a view to handling transcontinental business. And Gould and Ramsey *did* succeed in their building efforts; John Rehor, historian of the Nickel Plate Road, is correct when he concluded that "the 59.9-mile Pittsburgh Extension was one of the boldest and most interesting railroad construction projects ever undertaken and completed in the eastern United States."[102]

It appears that the essential point of the Pittsburgh Extension is frequently missed. When such expansion worked well, as it did with new-line construction between Toledo and Chicago or the lease of trackage between Detroit and Buffalo, critics kept silent. Even though the WPT and W&LE ventures failed, the quest for Pittsburgh was hardly lunacy. "There is no doubt that the extension into Pittsburg was necessary for the Gould system, if it intended that the system should keep its proper place in the general transportation scheme of the eastern states," observed a railroad analyst in 1904. "Before the purchase of the Wheeling & Lake Erie, the Wabash was completely shut out of the entire district which produces possibly the richest and most lucrative railroad tonnage that is produced anywhere in the United States." A good idea does not always turn out well.[103]

Although the troubled Pittsburgh extension became reality and continued to operate after 1916 as the independent Pittsburgh & West Virginia Railway, the greater Pittsburgh area still lacked wholly adequate railroad service. Editorialized the *Railway Age* in 1918: "Today even the Pennsylvania Railroad directors would acknowledge that Pittsburgh needs more railroad facilities. The Pittsburgh district shippers gained only a fraction of what they would have, had the [WPT] . . . been carried out successfully, but still they gained something."[104]

Even with bankruptcy and the lingering Pittsburgh problems, the Wabash had matured into an important interregional carrier. While shedding itself of the WPT and W&LE, it remained a wholly viable property with entry into some of America's most active rail gateways. In 1912 a Chicago railroad expert thought much of the property. "The System not only serves to connect Chicago, St. Louis, Kansas City, Omaha, Detroit and Toledo—six of the most thriving cities of the United States—cities that are destined to become much larger and much more important than they are at present— but also passes through and serves numerous important and rapidly growing manufacturing cities and towns." The Wabash was a road with weaknesses but hardly a carrier with a fatally flawed assortment of lines.[105]

"Follow the Flag"

SYMBOL AND SONG

For nearly nine decades, the Wabash affected countless people in a myriad of ways, doing so in two distinct fashions. The first included the public's contact with its trains, personnel and overall presence in community life. The other covered the multitude of experiences involving thousands of men and women who worked for the company. For a vast number of midcontinent residents, the Wabash was *their* railroad, the "Good Ole Wabash."[1]

Americans have long associated a distinctive flag logo with the Wabash. Yet it took a decade or so for this enduring hallmark to evolve. Most roads commonly selected a circle, diamond, rectangle, square or shield, and in 1884 the company placed the Wabash name in a rectangle directly in the forward glare of a locomotive headlight, an eye-catching technique that some nonrailroad firms also used. Usually THE GREAT WABASH ROUTE phrase accompanied this artwork, which the railroad duly registered with the U.S. Patent Office. But in 1886 the

In the early 1900s a not-so-glamorous two-car local or commuter train leaves Dearborn Station in Chicago with American-type locomotive No. 569 for power. This engine joined the roster in 1899 and for the next thirty-four years continued to be a workhorse. (Wabash Railroad Historical Society)

The cover of the June 1, 1891, Wabash Railroad public timetable features this romanticized young man steadfastly carrying the Wabash banner. At this time the company promoted itself as "The Banner Route." (Author's Coll.)

SUMMER EDITION.—WEST BOUND.
JUNE, 1891.

The Banner Route

H. B. McCLELLAN, General Eastern Agent,
402 Broadway, NEW YORK.
J. D. McBEATH, New England Passenger Agent,
290 Washington Street, BOSTON, MASS.

railroad abandoned the trademark design of the rectangle for a flag or banner. "The brass hats thought they could make a better impression with the banner qualities of their railroad if they put it on a flag," observed railroad writer G. H. Burck in the early 1930s. "They were right, for it is often referred to as the banner railroad." Indeed, the

Wabash briefly advertised itself as "the Banner Line of the Central States," and for several years in the 1890s "the Banner Route."[2]

Although the Wabash was not the only railroad that employed a flag motif, its specific format was undeniably unique. The company opted for THE WABASH LINE (later shortened to WABASH) in gold (or white) characters positioned on a blue (occasionally black) square centered on a red flag. Initially, though, the banner also included a locomotive with WABASH in the direct beam of the headlight, a carryover from the earlier rectangular emblem. "Some thoughtful and enthusiastic official, who has succeeded in keeping his identify secret, conceived the idea that the Wabash should come out of the shadow of the night into the full light of day—that there was too much locomotive and too much headlight and not enough 'Wabash' in the banner," recalled the road's general solicitor in 1921, "and so the locomotive with its flaming headlight was consigned to the scrap-heap and the banner took the form as you see it today." Fittingly, the flag, attached to a decorative staff, appeared to be flapping in a gentle breeze.[3]

About 1912 another important emblem change took place. From then until 1964, when the railroad itself became a "fallen flag" carrier, the words "Follow the Flag" (always placed in quotation marks) became part of the core logo. Most everyone who considered these advertising words likely concluded that they meant the obvious: ship and travel via the Wabash Railroad. In the 1920s, one official saw a simple, logical connection to the phrase's origins: "[With] many thousand enthusiastic employees singing the praises of the Banner Route . . . [they] should naturally adopt the slogan 'Follow the Flag.'" Yet employees and others with an intimate knowledge of the carrier believed that the phrase had a historic association with the special pay cars used to distribute cash wages, a practice that the Wabash ended in 1905. Although exact details are sketchy, the phrase may actually date back to the days of the North Missouri Railroad. "An engine carrying what was known as a pay flag went over the road just the day ahead of the pay car . . . [for] the purpose of letting all employees know the pay car would come the next day," explained a company writer. "From the fact that the pay followed the flag, came the coining of the remark, 'follow the flag.'"[4]

Just as the genesis of "Follow the Flag" is shrouded in a misty past, so, too, are the origins of one of the most famous of all railroad ballads, "The Wabash Cannonball." This hobo classic ranks with "The Wreck of the Old 97," "The Orange Blossom Special," and "The City of New Orleans" in its popular recognition as a great American "railroad song." Many individuals have been able to place the Wabash name in a railroad context because of their familiarity with "The Wabash Cannonball," which appeared in sheet music in 1904 and later in recorded form. Its catchy melody is easily recognized and has found varied uses, even as a campaign song for Henry Howell, Jr., in his 1973 bid for the governorship of Virginia.[5]

This well-known traditional folk song, however, has limited ties to the Wabash Railroad. Although the most widely sung lyrics refer to some cities that the Wabash served, including Chicago, Kansas City and St. Louis, the road never reached Ashtabula, Ohio, Birmingham, Alabama, or St. Paul, Minnesota, which are also mentioned. Still, the Wabash and its predecessors operated *Cannon Ball* name trains. In July 1885 the Wabash, St. Louis & Pacific advertised its "Cannon Ball Train" between Chicago and Kansas City via Hannibal and Moberly, which may have inspired the song. A few years later, the Wabash Western briefly dispatched the *Omaha Cannon Ball*, a passenger

By the time the Wabash distributed its public timetable of December 9, 1906, it had firmly established usage of the modern Wabash banner logo. For a number of years before World War I, the company made much of Niagara Falls as a tourist destination and frequently featured views of this popular natural attraction. (Author's Coll.)

train between St. Louis and Omaha that connected with the Union Pacific's *Flyer* at Council Bluffs. Over the years, some loyal Wabash employees made certain that the words made sense in a Wabash context; the train served the "right" cities, including Fort Wayne, Decatur and Peru. On February 26,

1950, the Wabash Railroad, wishing to exploit the name recognition of this mythical train that seemingly ran everywhere, reintroduced the *Cannon Ball*. This time, however, the *Cannon Ball* passenger train operated between St. Louis and Detroit and actually outlasted the Wabash itself, disappearing on April 30, 1971, nearly seven years after the Norfolk & Western Railway (N&W) took control of the Wabash.[6]

RIDING THE WABASH

Even though the Wabash did not operate America's most prestigious passenger trains, it ran several first-class services that became heavily patronized. By the early years of the twentieth century, the *Continental Limited* and the *Banner Blue Limited* were surely its best known and most popular. The former, which first entered Wabash timetables in 1898, traveled between Kansas City and Buffalo, via St. Louis and Detroit. But shortly thereafter the company dispatched two *Continental Limited*s, one running between St. Louis and Buffalo and the other between Chicago and Buffalo, consolidating its elegant Wagner Palace Car Company equipment at Detroit. Initially the consist contained a sleeper and coach that continued to New York City over the rails of the Delaware, Lackawanna & Western Railroad and a sleeper to Boston by way of the West Shore and the Fitchburg Division of the Boston & Maine railroads. Shortly after making its debut, the *Continental Limited* won the attention of the press. "On Tuesday, June 7, [1898] the new fast train . . . the Continental Limited, No. 5, ran from Tilton, Ill., to Granite City [Illinois], 176.6 miles in 182 minutes, being an average speed of 58.22 mph," reported the *Railroad Gazette*. "Stops were made at Tolono, Decatur and Litchfield. . . . The cars are new and have wide vestibules. Some of them were built at the Toledo shops of the Wabash."[7]

Speed remained an important part of the *Continental Limited* operation. When neighboring carriers bragged of "ballast scorching," the Wabash won similar attention. In 1902, the *St. Louis Republic* noted that the *Continental Limited* had sprinted "from Staunton to Carpenter, [Illinois] 10.2 miles, the time was seven minutes or at the rate of 87.42 mph," and on the same trip it had made the longer run from Decatur to Granite City in only 101 minutes, exceeding sixty miles per hour. The office car of president Joseph Ramsey, which was attached to the train, surely explains the impressive speed of this particular run. Even when the *Continental Limited* carried no company brass, every effort was made to meet the schedule and to "run hot" if delays occurred. In the 1950s, Charles E. Fisher, founder of the Railway & Locomotive Historical Society, recalled his encounter in the spring of 1913 with the *Continental Limited* when he was "railfanning" while a student at the University of Michigan. "I had not bothered with lunch and when the 'Continental Limited' pulled into Ft. Wayne, half an hour late, there was one cold and hungry young man waiting for the train. As soon as we started, I headed for the cafe coach and I had the best beefsteak dinner, or so it seemed to me, I ever had for $1.25. I missed nothing. After dinner, I went up to the smoker and that Baldwin ten-wheeler talked all the way to Detroit. We made only one stop—Milan, Mich., and that engineer picked up those 30 minutes. It was dark so I could not actually see the speed but that engineer did a fine job with that ten-wheeler and those four steel cars and it was worth it to ride right behind him." Fisher also remembered that "the road had just been freshly ballasted with that orange colored gravel and I wish you could have seen the sides of those coaches when I got out at Detroit." Speed, of course, meant on-time schedules and occasionally equipment that required extensive cleaning.[8]

Whereas residents along the route of the *Continental Limited* may have been able to set their timepieces on its comings and goings, the Wabash operated an even better train beginning in 1904. In an effort to succeed in a competitive market and to take advantage of a throng of fairgoers expected to visit the Louisiana Purchase Exposition in St. Louis that year, the company introduced the *Banner Blue Limited* between Chicago and St. Louis to augment its other through trains. Pullman provided two costly train sets—each consisting of a combination baggage car and smoker, combination coach and chair car, combination dining and buffet car and combination parlor and observation car—that were both handsome and fully state of the art. "They are painted in royal blue, with gold decorations," announced the *Official Railway Guide*. "The interior finish is African mahogany inlaid with holly, and the entire train is brilliantly lighted by electricity, so arranged that each passenger may control

Early in the twentieth century Wabash passengers might take a name train like the *Banner Limited* that operated between Chicago and St. Louis. In what was presumably a publicity photograph, riders in March 1912 crowd the observation platform next to passenger locomotive No. 614, a 4-4-2 or Atlantic, built by Brooks in 1903. (Wabash Railroad Historical Society Coll.)

Dinner in the diner was always a treat for railroad passengers, and often the highlight of a rail journey. This unidentified view of an accommodating Wabash dining car staff dates from ca. 1910. (Author's Coll.)

These expenditures on new name trains were hardly surprising. Officials believed that, to generate additional revenues, they needed to upgrade and expand passenger service, and statistics bore them out: passenger earnings rose handsomely from $3,995,102 in 1899 to $8,917,829 in 1905. Management also accepted the idea that a marquee value existed in providing high quality trains. The hope, even expectation, was that if satisfied passengers had freight to ship, they would insist that it would also go over the Wabash. "That Illinois hog farmer who has taken our Banner Limited will want his livestock to have the same fine ride," declared a traffic official in 1915.[10]

Yet the majority of Wabash passenger trains, which resembled those on other roads, were hardly luxurious. Less-modern equipment made up some long-distance trains, and usually even older rolling stock comprised main- and branch-line locals. A typical non-named train of the period included an American-type (4-4-0) locomotive, a combination baggage, express and mail car and two or three wooden coaches. With speeds hardly comparable to the limiteds, these trains chugged along at thirty to forty miles per hour. According to various state railroad commission reports, the Wabash happily avoided serious confrontations with the traveling public over matters of on-time performance, cleanliness and safety of its trains.[11]

The Wabash also provided limited commuter operations for the suburbanites of Chicago and St. Louis. Compared to most of the railroads that dispatched commuter trains in the greater Chicago area, the Wabash offered only modest service. Still, it was practical for residents of such Chicago neighborhoods and suburban villages as Ashburn, Chandler, Landers, Oak Lawn, Orland Park, Palos Springs and Worth to commute during the workweek to the Loop and other city destinations. Not only did long-

the lights of the seat which he occupies. Two electric fans are in each car." Seconding these comments were the observations made by a Wabash trainman: "[T]hey sure were beautiful trains to look at. The cars were all painted a royal blue with gold gilt letterings and trimmings, and the interior of the dining and observation cars were the last word in trimming and fixtures." The seven-hour trip with limited stops meant that the Wabash could compete with the premier passenger train between Chicago and St. Louis, the *Alton Limited,* operated by the Chicago & Alton. "The Only Way Route" of the Alton became less so.[9]

distance locals call at all or some of these stations along the twenty-four-mile route south of Dearborn Station, but several commuter runs also plied the rails between Orland and Chicago. In 1904, for example, there were six trains each way that were solely for commuters.[12]

Beginning in the 1870s, the company provided suburban trains over the twenty-three miles of line between St. Charles and St. Louis. In October 1890, this service included three daily-except-Sunday runs between St. Charles, Bridgeton and Ferguson. At Ferguson, these trains either continued to the Vine Street Station in St. Louis via Woodland, Jennings and Baden or to St. Louis Union Depot via Rosedale and Forest Park.[13]

One of these commuter trains, No. 52, became a cherished local institution. Known as the "Comm," six days a week it left St. Charles at 6:41 A.M. and arrived in downtown St. Louis (not Union Station but at the foot of Washington Avenue) sixty-one minutes later after having made eighteen stops. Usually the Comm consisted of two vintage coaches, by custom one for passengers boarding in St. Charles and the other for Ferguson patrons. Explained veteran conductor, Jack Plackmeyer, to a *St. Louis Globe-Democrat* feature writer in 1930, "Quite a bit of jealousy between them folks [Fergusonites] and the St. Charlesans. Good natured, of course. Hasn't been a fight on the train in thirty years to my knowledge. Plenty of arguments. Red hot ones on everything from Hornsby's batting average to companionate marriages, but all in fun. The Ferguson folks claim that St. Charles is 'Little Germany' and insist that every St. Charlesan has sauerkraut for breakfast. The St. Charles folks come right back by claiming that every Fergusonite must live on a side hill where the doors swing shut by force of gravity. They insist that never in sixty years has a man or woman from out that

way ever closed a door behind him." Concluded the *Globe-Democrat* journalist, "The 'Comm' carries a happy family. On it several generations in the same family have ridden to their labors. On it there are romances and forensic declamation, gay badinage and genuine sorrow for a fellow commuter in trouble. They play cards and read and josh. They smile with Jack and have no fault to find. The 'Comm' is a tradition as old as the Wabash Railway itself."[14]

As with every passenger-carrying railroad, the Wabash hosted seemingly countless special runs and excursions. The agent at Sidney, Illinois, recalled that, following the opening in 1923 of Memorial Stadium at the University of Illinois, the company sent up the Champaign branch "five or six specials from St. Louis, Detroit, Indianapolis, and possibly Springfield." In 1922, a Moberly newspaper reported that a special six-car train would travel through the community from St. Louis to Kansas City, transporting the troupe and equipment of "The Passing Show," a theatrical company. Much earlier in 1886 another Moberly newspaper noted that an excursion train would leave the local station at 5:00 A.M. to handle a party of African Americans to Ottumwa, Iowa, so that it might attend "a grand entertainment given by the Ottumwa colored folks." And for years the Wabash operated special trains or added cars to its regularly scheduled runs to bring students to and from "College Town U.S.A," Columbia, Missouri, home of the University of Missouri and two small women's schools, Christian College (today's Columbia College) and Stephens College. The community's other railroad, the Missouri-Kansas-Texas (Katy), provided similar service.[15]

At times a trip on the Wabash involved something special or out of the ordinary. Although since the Civil War the road had avoided train robberies, there were hundreds of accidents. Wabash trains were no different from those of any other carrier in that they hit livestock, trespassers and vehicles. And the company had trains that occasionally "went into the ditch" or derailed. The latter, even of a minor nature, was certain to receive coverage in local newspapers. If human carnage occurred, the wreck nearly always grabbed the attention of the regional or national media.[16]

Although all accidents had unusual, if not unique, characteristics, the head-on collision in September 1904 near Bement, Illinois, between a fast mail train and the *Continental Limited* was typical of such tragic events of the era. Though no one died because the locomotive engineer on the eastbound *Limited* misread a train order, injuries were widespread and property damage was considerable. Twenty-five years later, a brakeman on the mail train vividly recalled the event:

> Now I remember at the time they hit, I was walking through one of the cars toward the head end, and when the crash came, I went sailing over the backs of the seats and piled up with a lot of the passengers in the front end of the car, and the crashing, grinding sound of iron and wood, and the terrific roaring noise made by the escaping steam from the two demolished engines, mingling with the screams and cries of the frightened and injured passengers, sure was something awful.
>
> Now after I got myself untangled from the struggling mass of people on the car floor, I run back to the other end of the car and tried to open the doors so that we could get out, but as the car was sort of twisted out of shape, the doors were jammed in such a manner that we could not get them open, so we got the people out through the broken windows, and when I got out I could see them carrying injured people out of all of the cars on both trains.[17]

Just as everyone who was aboard the ill-fated trains near Bement surely remembered the nightmarish aspect of this "corn-field meet," probably every passenger who was aboard a Wabash train at 2:00 P.M. on September 19, 1901, would also recall an unscheduled stop. Throughout the system, the company honored the assassinated William McKinley on the day of his funeral in Canton, Ohio. Trainmaster J. A. Heether, for one, sent to "All Trains and All Engines" operating on his Moberly-based division the following order: "'God's will not ours be done.' All trains and Engines will stop for five minutes at two o'clock P.M. Sept 19th out of respect to memory of President McKinley."[18]

FAIRS

Before the demise of passenger service, America's railroads did much to promote travel to fairs and special celebrations of all types. The Wabash was no exception. Though the Miami County Fair held in Peru, Indiana, may not have necessitated an extra train, fairgoers probably noticed an additional coach or two on local passenger trains during this popular annual August event. When it came to large fairs or expositions, the Wabash not only added equipment or even extra trains but actively promoted the events. The passenger department distributed a variety of literature to stimulate travel to the World's Columbian Exposition held in Chicago in 1893. One descriptive folder advised prospective visitors on when to make their trip: "'Go early and avoid the rush' is a good motto to adopt. The Exposition opened May 1st and will not close until October 30th, 1893. During the first months of the Exhibition everything is fresh and in perfect order. . . ." And to encourage patronage of Wabash trains the text writer added: "An excellent plan would be to arrange for a

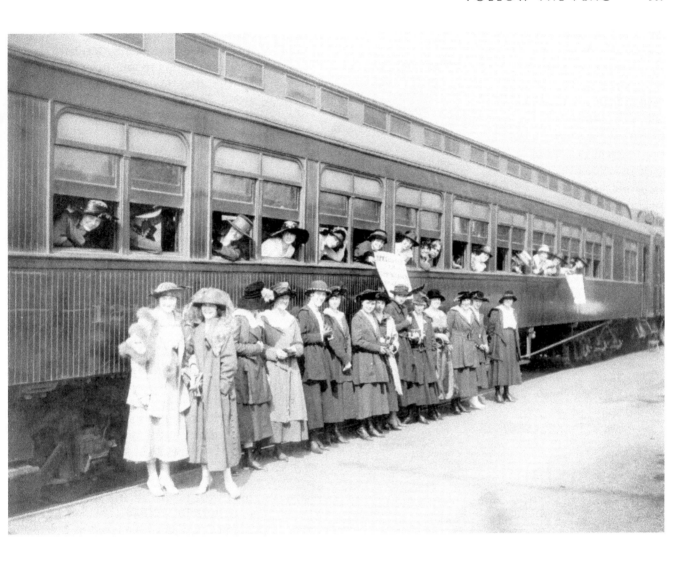

summer's outing, going first to Chicago, then visiting the Great West, the Rocky Mountains, etc., returning via St. Louis and the Wabash for another look at the World's Fair in the fall, and witnessing in St. Louis the superb Autumn Carnival of the Veiled Prophet, the great St. Louis Fair and Exposition, and the grand nightly illuminations of miles and miles of streets which have made the Mound City famous the world over." For those passengers who went only to the

"Great White City," they likely toured the Transportation Building, which featured a variety of exhibits including "the sedan chair, the elephant howdah, carts, wagons and stage-coaches from every land, . . . and the modern locomotive, dining car and palace car such as the Wabash uses."[19]

Beginning with the Chicago World's Fair, the Wabash became a contributor to three major international expositions of the era. In May 1891 the board of directors voted to

In about 1920 a group of Stephens College students await departure of their train to Columbia, Missouri, home of this two-year all-female institution. Scores of students selected Stephens in part because of the convenience of Wabash passenger service. (Wabash Railroad Historical Society)

The Wabash passenger department made much of the Columbian Exposition held in Chicago in 1893. The company did its best to capitalize on fair traffic, which was especially important since the country was rapidly sinking into a depression in the wake of the Wall Street panic of May 1893. The railroad distributed thousands of brochures that sought to entice visitors to the exposition and hence riders to its trains. (Author's Coll.)

ment for all roads, including the Wabash. The company significantly increased its passenger business to and from Chicago by transporting thousands who made up the nearly 27.5 million fairgoers. These travelers left with the feeling that they had visited one of the great cities of the world, a wonder of the modern age, and they surely realized that the Wabash was a proper way to continue their contracts with this vibrant and fascinating metropolis.[20]

The next gala fair that drew major involvement of the Wabash was the Pan-American Exposition, held in Buffalo in 1901. Conceived by civic boosters in 1899 to "promote commercial and social interests among the States and countries of the Western Hemisphere," the Exposition's organizers sought financial backing from corporations, including railroads. At first the Wabash avoided making a financial commitment, which annoyed general manager Ramsey. As he wrote in June 1900 to president O. D. Ashley, "I am of the opinion that the Wabash should subscribe about $20,000. Our interest in the passenger traffic of Buffalo is fully as great as that of the Grand Trunk." (That Canadian carrier already had donated $25,000.) Ramsey's insistence, coupled with news that the Wabash was the *only* Buffalo railroad that had not contributed, prompted the board of directors in July 1900 to commit $15,000.[21]

As with the Chicago World's Fair, the Wabash enthusiastically promoted the Pan-American Exposition. The company extensively advertised the event in its public timetables, bought newspaper space in the important cities along its routes and distributed special promotional folders. Although it is not clear what positive impact the exposition had on passenger revenues, it surely was far less than that of the Chicago event. Approximately eight million visitors, less than a third of the Chicago attendance, entered the

make a payment of $4,000 to the fair board, a small amount when compared to the support provided by several of the large Chicago-based carriers, particularly the $150,000 the Illinois Central contributed. This financial commitment to this celebration of the four hundredth anniversary of Christopher Columbus's voyage to the New World, of course, proved to be a good invest-

gates at Buffalo between its opening and closing dates, May 1 to November 1, 1901.[22]

Chicago and Buffalo were rehearsals of sorts for the Wabash's greatest involvement with such events. Unlike either of the previous two fairs, this time the Wabash gave generously to make the Louisiana Purchase Exposition (LPE) in St. Louis, the celebration of the centenary of the Louisiana Purchase from France, one the greatest and most successful fairs in American history. Yet the company did more than contribute $65,000 to the LPE's general fund. It assisted in a variety of additional ways. For the opening day of the Pan-American Exposition, for example, the Wabash dispatched a special Pullman train to Buffalo to allow LPE dignitaries, including LPE president David R. Francis, to examine the grounds and to discuss matters with Buffalo civic leaders and fair officials. The railroad paid all expenses, and as Ramsey told Francis, "The sleeping cars which will be used in the train will be held in Buffalo until the return trip, so that the guests need not arrange for checking of baggage while in Buffalo nor for hotel accommodations." As the LPE began construction of the massive complex of buildings and public spaces at Forest Park, the Wabash authorized the expenditure of $250,000 to connect its tracks with the fair site, install a small yard and erect a temporary station "of an appropriate style and size." The company also built a strategic coach-storage facility in the Page Avenue neighborhood, providing a convenient connection with the belt line of the Terminal Railroad Association of St. Louis (TRRA) to Merchants Bridge, which spanned the Mississippi River north of the Eads Bridge. And complementing this improvement, the TRRA, near its Page Avenue junction with the Wabash, established a coach-holding yard at Pastime Park. Unquestionably, the Wabash was going to make the most of its superb location to the grounds,

something that no other passenger road could claim.[23]

This enthusiastic commitment to the LPE did not mean that relations between the railroad and the fair company were always cordial. In 1902 a nasty dispute erupted between the LPE and the Wabash over the use of a parcel of real estate, "the Catlin Tract," located on the north side of the grounds near De Baliviere Avenue. The railroad leased the land for its use, but the LPE also had its eyes on it, in response to which Ramsey told Francis that the chair of the committee on grounds and building had earlier indicated that the LPE was not interested in the tract. Then, in September 1902, LPE employees under the cover of darkness began sewer construction beneath the street at the Wabash crossing, the harbinger of other improvements. The Wabash soon learned of this unexpected activity, which it believed would interfere with its own development work, and "came on the scene and attempted to interfere." Railroad employees did interfere, dumping old freight-car wheel trucks into the excavations. The LPE remained undaunted. With St. Louis police protection, laborers resumed their digging, and again the Wabash sought to block construction. This time officers of the law arrested "a wagon load of Wabash employees," and the sewer work temporarily continued. Undeterred, the railroad won a court injunction and the fighting ceased. It would take nearly nine months before both parties reached a mutually acceptable agreement, with the Wabash finally getting the track access that it wanted.[24]

Once the LPE opened on April 30, 1904, the Wabash enjoyed a major presence. Both before and during the fair, the company promoted it heavily, including extensive magazine advertisements in such widely read national publications as *McClure's*. The May 1904 full-page announcement of its services

The Wabash became a vital part of the 1904 Louisiana Purchase Exposition by bringing thousands of riders to St. Louis. The company's handsome, temporary depot near the grounds nicely complemented the style of other fair buildings. (Author's Coll.)

contained the heading: "THE ONLY LINE TO MAIN ENTRANCE OF WORLD'S FAIR." Visitors found that the Wabash's convenient shuttle trains between Union Station and its World Fair Station left every few minutes and cost only a dime. They were delighted to discover that, as advertised, the Wabash terminus was immediately across the street from the main entrance to the 1,300-acre fairgrounds and the "district of concessions for amusements" commonly called the "Pike." Although the star attraction of the massive transportation building was the functioning locomotive testing plant of the Pennsylvania Railroad (PRR), which would spend nearly $175,000 to show that it "has always blazed the way in railroad progress," the Wabash, together with the Alton; Atchison, Topeka & Santa Fe (Santa Fe); Baltimore & Ohio (B&O); New York Central & Hudson River; Katy; Missouri Pacific; Mobile & Ohio and Union Pacific, "all had notable installations of improved rolling stock and equipment, automatic brakes, signals, terminals, interlocking switching systems, etc., showing marked progress in all lines since the World's Fair at Chicago." Fairgoers who entered the sprawling Palace of Transportation soon realized that the Wabash was a railroad of considerable stature.[25]

Support for the LPE was rewarding. The Wabash received a heavy volume of business, second only to the PRR, between April 30 and December 1, 1904, when nearly 20 million visitors entered the grounds. And it did its best to meet the crush of riders. "Now the Wabash sure did wheel their fast freights over the road, for the World's Fair was going on in St. Louis at that time," remarked a "boomer" trainman hired to handle the extra passenger traffic, "and they had to get their freight trains over the road and keep them out of the way of the passenger trains, for there were fifteen regular first class time-card passenger trains each direction every twenty-four hours, between Decatur and St. Louis, and some of these trains run in two and three sections." The financial returns were impressive; gross revenues attributed to the extra traffic approached $2.5 million. Although difficult to gauge, the goodwill generated by the road, which diligently attempted to provide the best of everything, appeared to have been considerable. President Ramsey believed that "people who went to the fair for the first time on our railroad will want to make additional trips. . . . We have received so many words of praise from the traveling public."[26]

HELPING FARMERS

The same spirit of providing outstanding service to visitors of the World's Fair in St. Louis was mirrored in the Wabash's commitment to assist its agricultural neighbors. Although the ultimate objective was to bolster income, the company sincerely attempted to be a good friend to every farmer throughout its extensive agricultural territory.

The railroad assisting the farmer was hardly unique. Most carriers serving predominantly rural regions promoted better agriculture, whether giants Great Northern and Union Pacific or the much smaller Georgia & Florida and Missouri & North Arkansas. Their expenditures for implementing a variety of programs were based on the expectation that such dollars spent would generate additional traffic through agricultural diversification and the wider application of modern farming methods. The thinking and actions of the Wabash were no different.[27]

As did other roads, the Wabash worked cooperatively with land-grant or agricultural colleges, including Purdue University, the University of Illinois and the University of Missouri, and with state and federal government agencies to achieve its objectives. One activity took place in 1911. That spring, the railroad teamed up with the College of Agriculture at the University of Missouri and the Missouri State Board of Agriculture, pioneers in this type of educational outreach, to send a "special lecture train" on a three-day, twenty-two-station whirlwind tour of the state. Consisting of several baggage and passenger cars and staffed by university and state personnel, including the dynamic and resourceful Professor F. B. Mumford, the train made scheduled stops in communities both large and small on the Des Moines, Omaha and St. Louis–Kansas City lines. Exhibits and lectures occurred on such diverse topics as "corn improvement," "feeding the dairy cow" and "the College of Agriculture." The company made its intent clear: "The Wabash Railroad believes that the results of investigations made by the College of Agriculture if applied by the farmers in their territory would increase yields, enlarge the profits and ultimately result in a fuller, better, and happier life."[28]

The Wabash did more than dispatch agricultural demonstration trains. In 1911, the company donated $1,000 to the newly formed National Soil Fertility League. The goal of this organization was to improve the overall quality of soil by showing farmers how to apply fertilizers and other enhancements scientifically. A decade later, the Wabash agreed to provide the University of Missouri College of Agriculture a $100

Management of the Wabash Railway sprang into action for the highly popular world's fairs held in Chicago in 1933 and New York City in 1939. Each time the company printed special folders to bolster travel. (Author's Coll.)

scholarship to one student from each of the eighteen Missouri counties that it served. This financial aid would assist these young men and women who attended an agricultural short course on the Columbia campus. In 1929, the company spent $6,200 for an exhibit at the National Dairy Show, held in St. Louis. But this investment, which mostly went for the construction of a cottage and barn, would be partially amortized. "The buildings are portable and can be used at other dairy shows, fairs, etc.," and they were.[29]

On the eve of the Great Depression, the Wabash briefly operated an agricultural development department. At the recommendation of its director, the company spent more than $7,000 to reconstruct an out-of-service parlor car for public meetings and lectures. One accomplishment of the department involved promotion of egg production. In addition to the refurbished parlor car, the road's Decatur shops remodeled a surplus piece of equipment as the "Wabash Poultry Pay Car." The concept was to offer active and potential poultry raisers "profit building ideas." Typically, such prearranged meetings included presentations by extension specialists and a variety of displays. In addition to items placed in the railway car, the department paid a local lumberyard to erect at trackside a model brooder house and engaged a hardware store to install a modern brooder stove. Later, the poultry special returned to show off the young chicks and still another visit occurred, "featuring on that occasion the feeding and housing of the flocks for winter egg production." While the Wabash did not expect to transport many shipments of eggs, it anticipated an increase in the transport of chicken feed and other supplies to these hopefully successful poultry producers.[30]

HAPPY WORKERS

The Wabash did not ignore the happiness of its employees. Since the emergence of the railway brotherhoods in the latter quarter of the nineteenth century, hundreds of workers gathered regularly for pleasurable social affairs, especially evening dinner dances. Management commonly endorsed such activities, at times providing a special train or

As part of an outreach program to the agricultural community, the Wabash built this popular Wisconsin-style barn as a centerpiece for its exhibit at the 1929 National Dairy Show in St. Louis. (Western Historical Manuscript Coll.)

A longtime fixture in the lives of Wabash employees was the Railroad YMCA located in Moberly, Missouri, which appears in this ca. 1910 photograph. The services provided in this facility made the working careers of hundreds of men easier and more enjoyable. (Wabash Memorial Hospital Association Coll.)

coaches and sleeping cars for divisional, state or regional brotherhood events. It also backed a variety of groups that would similarly bolster morale and ideally create a contented "Wabash family." In the mid-1890s, for instance, perhaps as a response to the bitterness caused by the Pullman strike, management encouraged workers to join the Railroad Library Club. Apparently, it paid for the books and these volumes of largely popular literature were placed in offices throughout the system. Shortly after the turn of the twentieth century, the library club disappeared, likely eclipsed by the developing reading rooms found in all the buildings of the Railroad Young Men's Christian Association (Ys) and the rapidly expanding public library movement.[31]

The Railroad Division of the Young Men's Christian Association became a favored Wabash cause. The company sought in the Ys an acceptable substitute for the ubiquitous saloon and boarding house. The latter, in fact, frequently offered more than a bed and meals. Alcoholic beverages, including hard liquors, were readily available. Even though the railroad sought to control the

negative effect of intoxicants through rigid enforcement of an antidrinking code in its *Rules of the Transportation Department,* which nearly all steam and electric interurban railroads imposed on their employees, it held to the idea that if the off-work environment could be positively altered, so too could workers' behavior. Moreover, the Railroad Y, usually located near the station or terminal, provided members with convenient, clean, low-cost sleeping accommodations and economical yet wholesome and hearty food. These Ys also offered railroaders opportunities to spend their leisure time constructively, including card rooms (gambling was strictly forbidden), reading areas and occasionally indoor bowling alleys and "splash" or swimming pools.[32]

By the 1910s, the railroad Y movement, which began in 1872 in Cleveland, Ohio, operated nearly 180 hotels nationwide, having a major presence along the Wabash. Employees found these facilities in such Wabash centers as Buffalo, Chicago, Decatur, Des Moines, Detroit, Fort Wayne, Kansas City, Moberly, Montpelier, Omaha, Peru, St. Louis, Springfield and Toledo. The Y charged a modest membership fee for its railroader clientele, and they received privileges at any location, once having paid their annual dues.[33]

The "Gould roads" had a large number of railroad Ys, in part because of Helen Gould, the eldest daughter of Jay Gould. "Miss Helen," as she was affectionately known by railroaders on the Wabash and affiliated roads, selected traditional Ys and railroad Ys as a major part of her extensive philanthropy. Although her charities ranged from Berea College in Berea, Kentucky, a self-help college for impoverished Appalachian youth, to the Crusade Against Mormonism, which focused on ending polygamy among members of the Church of Jesus Christ of Latter-Day Saints, she became strongly, even emotionally, attached to the Ys.[34]

Because of her continuous generosity, Wabash employees repeatedly honored Miss Helen. On March 13, 1912, for example, the Railroad Y in Peru organized an extensive one-day reception for her:

6:43 A.M.—Miss Gould and party will arrive at Wabash station.

10:00 A.M.—Automobile ride to places of interest in the city.

12:15 P.M.—Shop Meeting at Wabash Shops, attended by Miss Gould. . . .

3:00 P.M.—Visit to Wabash Hospital.

3:30 P.M.—Inspection of [Y] Association Building.

4:00 to 5:00 P.M.—Reception to the Ladies of Peru at the Association Building.

Evening program:—Music by Orchestra, Prayer, Address of Welcome, Response, Short Addresses by Visiting and Local Railroad Officials, Reception for Miss Gould.

11:10 P.M.—Departure by Miss Gould and party for the West.

Reports indicated that Miss Helen loved this long day spent among "her Wabash family and close friends."[35]

Although railroad Ys dotted the Wabash corridor, another facility designed for worker happiness was physically singular in nature. This was the Wabash Club, launched in 1911 and located in Ferguson, Missouri, about a dozen miles northwest of downtown St. Louis. At their first formal meeting, Club members adopted an elaborate constitution and bylaws that included a statement of intent that pleased most everyone: "The purpose is to cultivate and foster good-fellowship among the officers and employees of the Wabash Railway Company, and to discuss, formulate and execute plans which shall have in view the mutual benefit of the members and the Company." The organization, not surprisingly, received the strong support of president Frederick Delano and his fellow executives. They considered it to be an inexpensive but wholly acceptable alternative to what would have been for employees something much more meaningful, namely, a company pension system. Unlike the PRR and Chicago & North Western and some other major carriers, the Wabash lagged badly behind with a pension scheme.[36]

The centerpiece of the Wabash Club quickly became its twenty-acre club site. Situated a few blocks north of the Ferguson station near the corner of January Avenue and Florissant Road, the grounds included an attractive arts-and-crafts-style story-and-a-half wooden clubhouse with full basement and spacious veranda, a seven-acre spring-fed lake for boating, fishing and swimming, a small brick bathhouse and tennis and handball courts. And here on August 10, 1912, the Club held its first annual picnic: "There was an attendance of over 500. The members of the Club with their families and friends frolicked from noon until midnight on this occasion. There were 100-yard dashes for men and boys, short dashes for women and girls. Boating, bathing, fishing, tennis, quoits and other athletic events, including fat men's race, lean men's race; swimming and tub races; music and dancing. Chicken dinner, country style, was served on the grounds." Although a majority of active Club participants lived and worked in the greater St. Louis area, members hailed from all parts of the railroad. The organization also held meetings in non–St. Louis venues, usually division points. Speeches by officials, music by worker glee clubs and small bands, dancing and other forms of entertainment became standard fare both on and off the Ferguson grounds. There was agreement that "good fellowship is the medium through which officers and employees meet on a place of equality."[37]

The Wabash Club thrived. For decades 1,500 or more families paid their dues and helped to make the organization a success. There really became an institutionalized "Wabash family." Yet not every worker type was represented. Most notably, employees of color and their families apparently did not belong, although the constitution did not specifically prevent them from joining. If African Americans were involved with a railroad-related organization, it was likely one created for Pullman workers. In terminal cities along the Wabash, there were units of the Pullman Porters Benefit Association, and they sponsored events similar to the Club's activities.[38]

The company itself played an important role in making the Wabash Railroad Club a flourishing organization. The railroad provided no direct financing, but it leased the Ferguson property to the group "at a nominal yearly rental" and helped in other ways. Although the Club's operating budget depended upon modest annual membership fees, it relied heavy on advertising sold in its yearly hardcover *Souvenir Book,* a publication designed "to keep . . . [members] in a bit closer touch with the pulse of the organization." Railroad suppliers constituted a majority of these ad-takers, and at times company officials encouraged the firms to buy space. In May 1922, C. H. Stinson, a Wabash official, implied to the vice president of the St. Louis–based T. J. Moss Tie Company, a major provider of cross ties and bridge timbers, that it would be smart to patronize the *Souvenir Book.* The same month, the financial secretary of the Wabash Club also contacted T. J. Moss and informed its president about a forthcoming Club-sponsored dance and closed with these words: "I take the liberty of sending you herewith six tickets and shall appreciate, on behalf of the Club re-

mittance to cover. Am sure you will enjoy the affair if you attend."[39]

In time, interest in the Club among employees waned. Moreover, this type of quasi-corporate paternalism had mostly run its course in the railroad industry, although it lingered longer among some carriers. In late 1947, the Wabash sold the real estate and its structures to the city of Ferguson for $40,000 (it was valued at $100,000 in 1930), and soon the municipality opened the facility to the public. It remains as the January-Wabash Park.[40]

Wabash employees participated in other railroad-related clubs and activities, though without direct sponsorship of the company. In the 1930s, for example, workers in the Decatur roundhouse supported the Wabash Roundhouse Good Fellowship Club. An annual highlight involved a riverboat excursion on the Mississippi from St. Louis. Workers also organized baseball clubs. Even though the company did not underwrite "industrial baseball" as did some other roads, including the New York Central and Missouri Pacific, playing ball became a popular diversion for hundreds of Wabash men.[41]

HEALTHY WORKERS

The men and women of the Wabash, however, never really tired of another institution designed for their interests, the Wabash Employes' Hospital Association (WEHA). By the 1890s the company had become widely recognized in the railroad industry for its network of health-care facilities. And the medical program proved durable, continuing to operate even after the N&W assumed control in 1964.[42]

Before the Wabash, St. Louis & Pacific created its hospital department on June 1, 1884, the company and its assorted predecessors relied on local physicians to treat workers and passengers who sustained injuries. These men of medicine were compensated for their services on a case-by-case basis. In the late 1870s, however, the railroad started to pay retainers to a select number of reputable on-line physicians and surgeons who could handle its medical needs. This change reduced the possibilities for medical quackery and physicians bilking the company and resulted in better quality control.[43]

Despite this effort, the Wabash was not on the vanguard of such efforts to add medical personnel. As early as 1834, the B&O employed a physician, an action that may have been inspired by the common naval practice of carrying a ship's surgeon. Just as vessels journeyed far from medical assistance, at times carriers served areas that were nearly as remote as the high seas. And in the mid-1840s, the Rhine Railway, in Holland, hired doctors to attend to the medical needs of its employees and their families. By the post–Civil War years, most railroads had or would start some sort of regularized medical system. After all, the number of accidents increased as trackage greatly expanded, freight and passenger traffic burgeoned and train speeds soared. Moreover, officials realized that medical assistance was humane, lessened the likelihood of costly lawsuits and engendered goodwill among workers and patrons. Although common law gave little incentive for carriers to reduce the numbers of injured, most of all trespassers, who were usually hoboes, the Wabash would give any accident victim medical attention.[44]

Even prior to the establishment of the Hospital Department, the Wabash gained national attention in railroad and medical circles for creating the first systemwide professional association of railway surgeons. In late 1881 and early 1882, Dr. J. T. Woods, "a good organizer and an inventive genius in the preparation of appliances for the relief of the injured," spearheaded this movement. A former Union Army brigade surgeon, this distinguished man of medicine from Toledo, Ohio, who had recently become the largely full-time chief surgeon of the Wabash, called together other company-retained surgeons. At a gathering in Decatur on January 25, 1882, Woods told them that "prior to any organization, if such step be deemed best, I desire to call your attention to the fact, as a formal meeting of railroad surgeons, this is the first that has ever occurred. Whatever the result, we are, so far as I know, in the matter pioneers." Woods and twenty-two associates agreed to form what they called the Wabash Surgical Association. Within a decade or so surgeons on the B&O, Erie, Santa Fe, Southern and additional roads emulated the Wabash with similar professional groups.[45]

Subsequently renamed the Surgical Association of the Wabash Railway and later the Wabash Surgical Society, this organization remained active until World War II. On the eve of that conflict, it suspended its annual meetings for "duration of the emergency." The group, however, never resumed its activities, a casualty of competing specialized professional organizations and expanded access to medical information.[46]

Before the Wabash Surgical Association dissolved, its members developed a strong esprit de corps and heard an array of practical medical papers. At times these presentations were published and disseminated to everyone involved with medicine on the Wabash and also made available to other railway surgeons. At the annual meeting in 1884, Dr. C. V. Rockwell of Taylorville, Illinois, reviewed his work on the "the Induction of Rapid Anesthesia in Railway Injuries," four years later Dr. C. B. Powell of Albia, Iowa, "read an excellent paper on shock from injury" and in 1907 Dr. H. C. Fairbrother of East St. Louis, Illinois, suggested what first-aid paraphernalia should be available in a freight caboose.[47]

Whereas the Wabash led the way with a professional association of surgeons, it followed other railroads in development of a hospital system. In 1869, for example, the Central Pacific opened a temporary hospital in Sacramento, California, and a year later constructed a replacement facility with space for 125 patients. In 1882, the founder of the Wabash Surgical Association, Dr. Woods, urged that the company launch its own hospitals. Although management endorsed his proposal, workers objected. "The leaders were especially against [it], wouldn't have it in any way; while they didn't suggest anything to take its place, they wouldn't have any blankety-blank hospital or any doctors for that matter." Resistance among employees subsequently weakened, likely because of several well-received hospitals opened by other Gould roads, most notably the Missouri Pacific.[48]

The Wabash opted for what might best be described as a mutual benefit association, which other roads, including the B&O and PRR, also found attractive. Although the company underwrote the hospital buildings and some related expenses, employees paid much of the costs for their medical care. Those who joined—the program was not mandatory on the Wabash—were assessed a reasonable monthly fee, based on income, with a track laborer contributing somewhat less than half of what a locomotive engineer paid. In the 1890s, these charges ranged from thirty-five to fifty cents and in the 1950s from three to five dollars.[49]

With a modest bureaucracy in place, the Wabash rapidly implemented its medical program. The railroad purchased four large houses that could easily be modified for hospital use, and by 1886 these facilities were operating in Danville, Illinois; Kansas City; Peru, Indiana; and Springfield, Illinois. In Peru, the company bought in April 1885 the "comparatively new residence" of S. W.

Ream, "on the bluff north of the boulevard between Grant and Union streets," and had it enlarged and improved, including updated and expanded plumbing and sewage systems. By late August, the *Miami County Sentinel* reported that "the Wabash hospital is in running order and has a few patients. The physician in charge, Dr. [E. B.] North, stands high in his profession, and has an able corps of assistants. The hospital is a credit alike to the Wabash road and the city." Added the Peru newspaper, "A. W. Quackenbush, superintendent of the shops here, takes commendable interest in it, and, as in everything else, sees that the highest standard of excellence is maintained."[50]

In what might seem to be an unusual arrangement, the Wabash early on engaged several Roman Catholic nursing orders to help staff its hospitals. The nuns received a modest monthly stipend along with room and board and a chapel for prayers, vespers and masses. These women of the cloth considered healing the sick as their godly mission. One nun, who worked in a Wabash facility, commented, "Many are the souls who could tell of spiritual as well as bodily wounds healed in our railroad hospitals." Wabash employees did not object to their presence, even though the vast majority adhered to Protestant faiths, mostly mainstream denominations, never particularly friendly toward Roman Catholics. The nuns developed a strong presence among railroad personnel, particularly those in train service and office positions. Until December 1, 1926, some nuns continued their nursing work with the Wabash. The last to participate, members of the Sisters of the Third Order of St. Francis, headquartered in Springfield, Illinois, ended their services because of a shortage of nurses at their own hospitals.[51]

In the 1890s, the hospital system underwent several major changes. On March 1, 1895, at the instance of the general solicitor, the company dissolved the hospital department and replaced it with the Wabash Employes' Hospital Association. The reasons did not involve the railroad's unhappiness with these medical centers, but rather its concerns about bookkeeping and legal liabilities. Although still associated with the Wabash, the former hospital department became a wholly separate worker-controlled organization. Even though the twelve-member board of directors of the WEHA included the railroad's general manager, general solicitor and auditor, its remaining nine members came from the ranks of employees, with representation for engineers, firemen, conductors, switchmen, telegraphers and agents, mechanical and car department personnel, clerks, maintenance of way workers and "an employe from Outside Agencies and other employees not represented in the above classification."[52]

Locations and buildings also changed considerably. In 1891, the company closed the Kansas City facility, which consisted of a former private dwelling with an addition built in 1888, and sold the Third and Campbell streets property to the Hospital Department of the Kansas City, Fort Scott & Gulf Railroad. The Kansas City staff and clientele were sent to Moberly, where the Wabash had erected a specially designed hospital structure. Residents of Moberly donated the land at 415 Woodland Street, and the railroad paid approximately $40,000 for construction and furnishings. A few years before the relocation, the railroad shut down the small hospital on Wayne Street in Danville and disposed of this former residence. The loss of the Cairo lines, which joined the mainline at Danville, and the facility's modest size mostly explain this closure. The patients who had used Danville traveled to either Peru or Springfield. In 1895, because of "inadequate accommodations" at Peru, the WEHA built what the railroad trade press called "one of the completest and best equipped railway hospital buildings in the country." This $35,000 structure, located on a hill north of the Wabash station, featured two main levels. "The ground floor has eight wards, besides the operating room and pharmacy, as well as dining room, kitchen, smoking and reading rooms, toilets, etc. On the second floor are four wards, with the house surgeon's room, chapel, sisters' bedroom and ample toilet accommodations and bath rooms." Its full basement contained a forty-five-horsepower boiler, laundry rooms and storage for supplies. And a much-discussed feature was the heating system. "The furnace is regulated automatically," reported the *Peru Republican*. "A dial in the surgeon's office is set for any temperature desired and by a system of weights and pulleys the supply of gas to the furnace is regulated so that the same temperature is kept at all times."[53]

As the new century dawned, the WEHA proudly boosted modern hospitals in Moberly and Peru, and soon there would be another. The association wisely decided to close its modest Springfield facility on South Sixth Street and relocate to Decatur, the "hub city" of the Wabash. At a cost of $55,000, the "finest hospital in Illinois" opened its forty-five beds at the corner of Herkimer and Warren streets (later 360 East Grand Avenue) on October 7, 1903. To meet the costs of this smart, modern facility, the railroad donated to the WEHA the price of the land and income received from the sale of the Springfield property, which the local Catholic diocese then acquired. Periodically, the association made changes to its three facilities. A notable one occurred in 1925, when at a cost of $160,000 the WEHA expanded the Decatur hospital, enlarging its capacity to eighty-five beds.[54]

Use of the Wabash hospital facilities was heavy. Between June 1, 1884, and December 31, 1885, the system counted 1,151 surgeries

A ca. 1905 picture postcard labeled "RR Hospital, Peru, Ind." shows this handsome and functional facility of the Wabash Employe's Hospital Association. When this replacement hospital opened in 1895, the railroad trade press described it as "one of the completest and best equipped railway hospital buildings in the country." (Author's Coll.)

and 8,385 medical cases. During the calendar year 1927, the comparable figures were 19,526 and 48,777. As with most railroad-related hospitals, the Wabash treated only employees and not members of their immediate families. There was also a firm policy of not attending to certain medical conditions. "Under no circumstance will treatment be given alcoholic or venereal diseases or their after-effects, chronic diseases arising before the entering the Company's services, injuries received in fights, brawls or any other disability arising from vicious acts." The WEHA, however, did treat some non-Wabash personnel. A financial arrangement was made with both the Chesapeake & Ohio and Lake Erie & Western (Nickel Plate) to handle their area surgical and medical cases at the Peru hospital.[55]

Virtually every Wabash employee belonged to the WEHA. Even during hard times, when hundreds of men were furloughed or worked only intermittently, they usually paid their dues. To assist them during the Great Depression of the 1930s, the WEHA reduced their monthly fees to $1.25. Support also came from some workers who normally shunned medical attention. By the 1920s there were sizable congregations of Christian Scientists with active Wabash members in Decatur, Moberly and Peru and in other cities along the railroad. Although these followers of Mary Baker Eddy, the Discoverer and Founder of Christian Science, fervently believed that disease is "mortal error," records indicate that some Scientists submitted to having a broken bone set or some other "mechanical" procedure. Indeed, for decades the most common hospital cases involved "bone surgery" and "contusions."[56]

Some members of the public also received attention at Wabash hospitals. Nearly all of these patients were admitted as result of train wrecks or right-of-way accidents. One case involved what was arguably the deadliest mishap in the history of the railroad, when perhaps 100 or so passengers and crew members perished on November 27, 1901, in the aftermath of the collision, derailment and burning of the westbound *Continental Limited* near Sand Creek, Michigan. The company speedily dispatched a relief train from Detroit with thirty-three doctors that arrived at the wreck site about three hours after the accident. The most severely injured were then sent by special train to the Peru hospital. "A caboose was coupled on to the train at Sand Creek, and the hospital train started on a wild, weird journey of 150 miles," reported the *Detroit Evening News*. "Probably 100 mutilated people aboard—most of them Italians who could not speak a word of English and all were begging for assistance. The engineer and fireman realized the terrible responsibility that rested on them, and that a quick journey might mean a good deal to many." Once the train reached Peru, ambulances and other conveyances transported these accident victims to the nearby hospital, where the medical staff provided excellent care. Two months later, only ten remained hospitalized, but "none of them is bedfast." Subsequently, all were released and sent on their way at company expense, mostly to Kansas City.[57]

In addition to the hospital network, the railroad after the late 1880s had maintained a number of dispensaries throughout the system. By the early twentieth century, even minor Wabash terminals such as Bluffs, Illinois, Moulton, Iowa, and Stanberry, Missouri, had these small clinics and pharmacies, which the district surgeon supervised. They were active places. In 1927, for example, the number of medical and surgical cases treated at Bluffs totaled 1,494; Moulton, 1,940; and Stanberry, 655. The number of prescriptions filled reached 1,120 at Bluffs, 1,520 at Moulton and 927 at Stanberry. Because many of the cases involved eye injuries, large dispensaries, like those in Buffalo, Chicago, Kansas City and St. Louis, had an oculist or consulting oculists.[58]

By 1960, the costs of operating the three hospitals increased as the number of paying members decreased. This constituted a major change in the operations of the WEHA, which historically had almost always generated modest annual surpluses rather than deficits. The WEHA continued to update equipment, meeting the more stringent requirements demanded for professional and state hospital certifications. In 1957, for example, the organization spent $123,000 on betterments at Moberly. But concerns about the future viability of its three hospitals prompted the WEHA to engage an Indianapolis-based consulting firm, the Russell M. Tolley Association, to study its operations. Significantly, the recommendations made by Tolley led to the closure of the Moberly hospital, which officially shut its doors on February 1, 1961. Peru was not far behind, ending its operations three years

later. As with the shutdown at Moberly, there was much sadness. Evelyn Gilbert, a former nurse, remembered the day the Peru hospital closed: "It was terrible. I was sick to my stomach."[59]

Yet the Decatur hospital remained in operation. Members felt mildly optimistic about its future, especially when in 1967 the WEHA underwrote a third-floor addition that provided a new surgical suite. But the ax fell on the last of the Wabash hospitals. Shortly before its closure on September 9, 1972, the WEHA explained that the facility "was weakened with the curtailment of all passenger service to Decatur and the drastic cuts in number of employees made by the

In 1904 medical personnel and onlookers gather at an entrance to the Wabash Employe's Hospital Association building at Decatur, Illinois, as this medical facility admitted an injured individual. The photo caption reads: "Receiving wounded at Decatur from Litchfield, Ill. wreck." (Wabash Memorial Hospital Association Coll.)

[N&W] railroad." Objections, however, took place. Commented Charles Gallagher, a locomotive engineer and official of the Brotherhood of Locomotive Engineers, "All I've heard is why we should get rid of the hospital—never how we can keep it." And he added, "The N&W has done nothing to help this association. They have only been taking away."[60]

Even with its hospitals gone, the WEHA survived. Reconstituted as the Wabash Memorial Hospital Association (WMHA), it continues in Decatur. Initially, the WMHA used facilities at the local St. Mary's hospital but later constructed its own freestanding building at 1501 North Water Street. Its function as a primary care outpatient clinic remains important in the lives of thousands of retired Wabash personnel and active employees of the Norfolk Southern Railway, successor to the N&W, and now includes their families. By the last quarter of the twentieth century, the railroad hospital phenomenon had ended, although several WMHA-like railroad organizations existed to serve thousands of eligible clients.[61]

The Wabash realized that preventive measures were also necessary for the well-being of employees and passengers. Even though the company could not claim to be the instigator of the railroad "safety-first" crusade (the Chicago & North Western likely deserves that honor), it was one of the first supporters of such efforts. Resembling the North Western and other safety-first leaders, including the Chicago, Rock Island & Pacific and Union Pacific, the road employed special safety meetings and rallies and printed statements under the "SAFETY ALWAYS" banner. Soon, too, "SAFETY ALWAYS" became emblazoned on the company's operating timetables. Resembling the North Western model, the Wabash also used elected safety committees. These localized and coordinated bodies appeared throughout the system and were particularly active in shop and terminal facilities. At times, committee representatives spoke to family members as well. The standard message, outlined as early as June 8, 1912, about two years after Ralph C. Richards began his widely recognized work on the North Western, was that "the Safety movement is to develop in each employee a sense of personal responsibility, not alone in taking measures for his own safety, but for that of his fellow employees as well." A combination of education and moral suasion together with safer equipment, block signals and such legislative mandates as the Hours of Service Act, or the "sixteen-hour law," which Congress passed in 1907, led to a noticeable reduction in the number of accidents in the workplace, especially the always-dangerous car and locomotive shops where workers encountered an environment of flying sparks, sharp pieces of metal, toxic chemicals and other hazards.[62]

The Wabash evolved into a good railroad and a decent place to work. It may not have been the "Standard Railway of the World" or the "Greatest Railroad in the World," the haughty claims made for years by the PRR and New York Central railroads, but its proud motto of "Follow the Flag" was understood and honored by thousands.

Reorganization, War, Boom and Bust

WABASH RAILWAY

The financial carnage caused by George Gould's foray into Pittsburgh, which had triggered bankruptcy in December 1911, led to a lengthy court-supervised reorganization of the Wabash. On October 22, 1915, the reconstituted carrier, the Wabash *Railway* Company, officially received its papers of incorporation from the state of Indiana. Most signs suggested that this former Gould-family property possessed a bright future, so much so that in September 1916, Dow, Jones & Company declared that "management is fast putting the new Wabash Railway in the big railroad league." After all, the St. Louis–based road served a multistate territory that continued to grow and prosper, and it linked a host of strategic rail gateways, ranging from Kansas City and Omaha on the west to Buffalo and Toledo on the east. Although hardly a railroad behemoth like the Chicago & North Western (C&NW), Pennsylvania (PRR) or Southern Pacific, the Wabash operated 2,033 miles of mainline track and 321 miles of second mainline track and traversed another 476 miles under trackage-rights agreements, making it one of the larger and better situated "Class I" (more than $1 million in operating revenues) roads in America's heartland.[1]

The nearly four years that passed between bankruptcy and reorganization were not easy for the receivers of the Wabash Railroad, Frederick Delano and William Bixby. They served as coreceivers and, until company vice president Edward B. Pryor replaced them in 1914 in an amicable change of command, struggled to finance much-needed betterments and craft an acceptable plan of reorganization.[2]

The Wabash passenger department immodestly referred to its "new" *Banner Blue Limited* as "The Train of Trains." Even with this hyperbole, the Chicago–St. Louis name train did indeed offer amenities to the traveler, including fine meals in the dining car. (Author's Coll.)

Delano and Bixby initially thought that it would not take long to straighten out the affairs of the railroad. Their plan was to sell the customary court-approved "receivers certificates," expecting that they could generate enough to cover property improvements, new equipment and assorted other expenditures, including bond interest and equipment trust payments. When they first offered $10 million of the certificates in February 1912, they encountered a favorable market. They were able to sell notes that bore an acceptable interest rate of 5 percent a year with a seller's premium of 0.25 percent. Later that year, in May, another $1.5 million were sold under similar conditions, as were $2.5 million worth of certificates in August. All of these obligations matured on or before August 1, 1913. By the summer of 1913, however, financial conditions had changed markedly. The best terms the receivers could secure for these $14 million of certificates were 6 percent and a commission of 1.75 percent, which meant an annual rate of 7.75 percent. Because of pressing financial needs to cover certain bond and equipment trust obligations, the receivers sold another $1 million of certificates at the same costly rate. Because these certificates came due in the summer of 1914, at a time when the Great War had erupted in Europe, receiver Pryor "found it absolutely impossible to sell a new issue with which to pay off those maturing." The federal court intervened, authorizing him to offer holders of the maturing certificates new ones that paid 6 percent with a bonus of 1 percent of their face value. Fortunately for the railroad, there were takers.[3]

Not only did the down markets hinder reorganization efforts, but regulatory demands also caused problems. During the first decade of the twentieth century, the regulatory powers of the Interstate Commerce Commission (ICC) had greatly increased, the direct result of the great national house-cleaning known as the progressive movement, which pitted consumers against corporations. The overall ramifications of greater federal control were not good for the Wabash. The Hepburn Act of 1906 made the ICC the most powerful government regulatory agency at the time, empowering it to set rates based upon complaints from shippers. Much stronger still was the Mann-Elkins Act, passed four years later, which restored the validity of the long-and-short haul clause of the Interstate Commerce Act of 1887, and required proposed rate increases to be sanctioned by the ICC before going into effect. Mann-Elkins became the first federal statute that established de facto price ceilings on a single industry during peacetime, and it came in the midst of a long-term upward trend in prices. This was surely "enterprise denied," the conclusion aptly reached by business historian Albro Martin. These regulatory conditions squeezed the Wabash and other carriers, making it much more difficult for them to receive needed rate hikes; hence, they suffered financially. Furthermore, the trend toward restrictive control worried the industry. "It will be a sorry day for the Republic," remarked president Delano in 1913, "when regulation is carried to such an extreme that the owners of the railways are unwilling any longer to accept the responsibilities of management."[4]

Even the U.S. Supreme Court hurt the company's bottom line during the receivership. As of July 1, 1913, the high court mandated railroads operating in Missouri, one of the major states served by the Wabash, to honor a progressive-inspired state statute that reduced freight and passenger rates. The impact was immediate. In the case of passenger revenues, as of June 30, 1914, the railroad had handled 111,094 more riders than during the previous annual period. "If the Wabash had been permitted to charge the rates which were in effect prior to July 1, 1913," noted receiver Pryor, "its revenues would have been $348,477.62 more than they were, every cent of which would have been net revenue, as the operating expenses were not affected in the least."[5]

Notwithstanding these financial challenges, the Wabash made considerable strides in improving its physical plant and general operations. To expand capacity, the company added additional miles of double track, with the greatest concentration in Illinois. Much of the rail that work gangs installed was heavy, high-strength steel, weighing 90 or 100 pounds to the yard. Systemwide track signaling was also upgraded. In 1912 and 1913, for example, the company placed automatic block signals on its mainline trackage through Indiana. This had been required by the state railroad commission, and the company did not protest, realizing the obvious benefits for faster and safer train operations. Moreover, receivers did not overlook motive power and rolling stock needs, making expenditures that totaled more than $3.5 million. In 1912–1913, the road took delivery of seventy-nine locomotives, which included sixteen 4-6-2 Pacifics for passenger service (the last new passenger steam engines that would be purchased) and sixty-three 2-8-2 Mikados for freight assignments. The company needed freight equipment most of all. For years it was plagued with a high debit balance that resulted from foreign car hires, which in 1913 amounted to $1,083,000. By 1915, however, these expenditures, although remaining considerable, began to move downward as hundreds of new freight cars entered revenue service. "Proud as punch" with its replacement rolling stock, the railroad chiefly capitalized on the public relations value of the passenger equipment that it had acquired. In 1914 the passenger department took out newspaper and magazine advertisements that ex-

tolled the road's growing fleet of "INDESTRUCTIBLE! Wabash Steel Trains." The copywriter pointed out that "on the frame of the 68-ton steel [passenger] car is riveted the solid steel side plates, steel roof and steel floor, forming a car of *indestructible strength*." Less striking, but still of considerable importance, the company in 1914 relocated its general offices in downtown St. Louis from cramped quarters in a commercial structure at Seventh and Chestnut streets to the nearby Railway Exchange Building, the growing home for regional railroads.[6]

While these improvements were making the Wabash a stronger railroad physically, the financial problems of the reorganization process were also being solved. In ongoing meetings, which were usually attended by the receivers, representatives from the banking house of Kuhn, Loeb & Company and members of three vitally affected committees, two representing the first refunding and extension mortgage bondholders and the other the stockholders, the parties at last reached a mutually acceptable agreement, which they signed on April 28, 1915. The reorganization plan, which the court ultimately approved, contained a variety of significant features. Undisturbed would be $62,302,000 of underlying bonds on which interest had been paid during the receivership and $2,541,000 of equipment obligations. Both actions were typical of railroad reorganizations. The company would issue large blocks of both preferred and common stock and a modest amount of short-term notes, totaling $139,960,000. Although capitalization would be $205,118,000 (compared to $222,319,377 for the old company), fixed interest charges would be appreciably reduced, amounting annually to $3,183,915, or some $2.6 million less than previous obligations. Stockholders in the old Wabash had the option of paying a $30 cash assessment for each share owned, but most refused and their equity was largely wiped out. Because the Equitable Trust Company of New York, a major investor in the bankrupt Wabash, had acquired for $18 million the property at the customary bankruptcy sale, funds raised through the new restructuring, which totaled about $27 million, paid off the Equitable investment and provided necessary working capital.[7]

The Wabash Railway Company made its debut at a time when the railroad industry was at the zenith of its physical might and overall importance. In 1916, national mileage peaked at 254,251, which was the same year that electric interurban mileage reached its highest figure, 15,580 miles. Though the automobile, motorbus and truck could be found on America's streets and roads, their impact on intercity passenger and freight traffic was minimal. Still, advocates of internal-combustion vehicles expected much of this new technology. The "Railway Age" had fully blossomed. Because production of industrial goods dominated America's economic life, railroads enjoyed a special status—they made business happen.[8]

Despite the favorable economic climate, the first eighteen months of the Wabash Railway's existence came at a time of growing concerns and uncertainties. Even the most profitable railroads, including great monarchs like the C&NW, Great Northern, New York Central (NYC), PRR and Union Pacific, lacked the ability to expend much of their declining profits into needed betterments. Fresh capital for such improvements was also in short supply, because investors feared the impact of the ICC's new rate-making powers. Most carriers, including the Wabash, required upgraded facilities, ranging from better classification yards to modern signaling systems, and more equipment, especially locomotives. Moreover, everyone worried about the domestic impact of a war-

torn Europe. Prospects of a possible nationwide strike by the "Big Four" operating brotherhoods (engineers, firemen, conductors and trainmen) in the summer of 1916, which came at a time when tonnage surged because of the European war, promoted passage of the Adamson Act. This historic measure made the eight-hour day "the basis for reckoning a day's wage" for train crews, giving railroad labor one of its sweetest victories. Although initially managements refused to obey this law, in March 1917 the U.S. Supreme Court, in a five-to-four decision, upheld its constitutionality. As a result, federal authorities had become deeply involved not only in rate making as result of the earlier Hepburn and Mann-Elkins statutes, but in wage making as well. "The government had taken over both sides of the ledger, income and expenses," noted historian Maury Klein, "and the mechanisms for regulating one were in no way coordinated with those for adjusting the other." Finally, in April 1917, President Woodrow Wilson, who the previous year had run successfully for reelection on the slogan "He kept us out of war," won Congressional approval to take the nation into the conflict. Not since the Civil War did military involvement have such a pronounced impact on America's railroads.[9]

The Wabash reorganization of 1915 led to a new leadership team that would have to use every resource of the company to meet the challenges of the World War I era. A key individual was Edward Francis Kearney, who assumed the presidency. His appointment probably surprised no one; in the closing days of the receivership, he had joined Pryor as coreceiver. Although a popular and "honorable" individual who understood railroad operations, Kearney lacked a distinguished railroad career. Prior to joining the Wabash around 1910, he had entered railway service in 1882 at age seventeen as a telegraph operator for the PRR. After more than two decades with the company, Kearney became involved with its terminal operations in St. Louis, and by 1905 he had become superintendent of terminals for the Missouri Pacific.[10]

The power behind the throne actually belonged to William H. Williams ("Billy" to his closest friends), who chaired the board of directors. A rather cold and aloof man, he was known as a "plugger," one who pushed ahead with a strong will and an inbred passion for dominance. A native of Athens, Ohio, and educated in public and private schools in Toledo and Beaver Falls, Pennsylvania, Williams, like Kearney, at an early age joined the PRR. In 1890, when only sixteen, the mathematically gifted Williams became a cashier in the freight station in Toledo. Later he held a variety of white-collar positions with the PRR; Columbus, Hocking Valley & Toledo; and Pittsburgh & Lake Erie. In 1901 Williams took a major step up the corporate ladder when he moved to the Baltimore & Ohio (B&O) as assistant secretary and assistant to the general manager, a position he held for three years. He then joined the St. Louis–San Francisco (Frisco)–Chicago & Eastern Illinois as superintendent of transportation but left after a year for a two-year stint in Pittsburgh as a statistician for several business organizations, including the chamber of commerce. In 1907 Williams's career turned dramatically upward when Leonor F. Loree, the new president of the Delaware & Hudson Company (D&H) and "one of the greatest railroad men of all time," invited Williams to become his assistant. (The two had likely met when both were involved with the PRR.) A few months later, Williams became third vice president of the D&H. It would be his connections with the hulking, but brilliant, Loree and also Kuhn, Loeb & Company, named in 1912 by a Congressional probe (the Pujo Committee) as part of the infamous "money trust," that resulted in

his elevation to board chair at the Wabash.[11]

The Kearney-Williams team got off to a decent start. As best it could, management continued to upgrade the physical plant. Each of the road's operating divisions—Decatur, Detroit, Moberly, Peru, Springfield and Western (excluding the leased Buffalo Division)—received important betterments, including extensive tie and rail renewals. Better rolling stock remained a priority. In 1917 the company took delivery of twenty-five Santa Fe–type (2-10-2) locomotives and immediately placed them in service between St. Louis and Chicago, largely to increase freight tonnage capacity over a troublesome four-mile grade. Despite these expenditures, the company did not engage in spendthrift tendencies with its purchases. For example, in 1916, to improve further its locomotive fleet, shopmen in Decatur converted a number of Prairie-type engines (2-6-2) into more suitable Pacifics (4-6-2). "The design was good and the lightweight J-2's [Pacifics] performed well in both passenger and freight service for over thirty years." With a greater ability to handle "first-class" traffic, especially meat and perishables, operating revenues spiked up from $30,687,318 in 1915 to $37,721,104 for 1916 and reached $40,471,999 the following year. Once more, the Wabash became a dividend-paying railroad.[12]

FEDERALIZATION

Most railroads during the immediate pre-war period did not experience financial improvements, in part because of the impact of progressive-inspired regulations that continued under the Wilson Administration. But the coming of America's involvement in the Great War served only to worsen the situation from management's perspective. At noon on December 28, 1917, the Wabash and all other Class I steam railroads, a few strategic electric interurbans and certain steamship lines came under the control of the United States Railroad Administration (USRA). Uncle Sam "federalized" nearly all of the nation's carriers, managing their operations yet allowing owners to retrain their equity and debt holdings. Under the Federal Control Act, passed on March 21, 1918, railroads regulated by USRA were entitled to financial compensation that "would not be more than the average net operating income for the three years ending June 30, 1917," and the assurance that the government would maintain them "in substantially as good repair and in substantially as complete equipment as it was at the beginning of the Federal control."[13]

The inability of America's railroads to respond adequately to wartime traffic demands largely explains this dramatic and historic action. Months before the declaration of war, a severe freight car shortage had developed. As of November 1, 1916, a shortfall of more than 100,000 cars plagued the nation. Equipment was needed everywhere, especially to handle an array of cargoes bound ultimately for British and French ports. The bottleneck arose at the principal terminals along the Eastern seaboard, which lacked sufficient capacity to manage the increase in business. The emergency grew because of a lack of merchant ships caused by frequent German submarine attacks. When Eastern carriers insisted that they would not return these cars, once emptied, until they were reloaded for domestic destinations, the crisis mounted: by fall of 1917 the shortage approached 160,000 cars, and even more pieces of freight equipment were stuck on sidings and at yards at or near Eastern ports. Shortly after America's entry into war, railroad executives, spearheaded by the creative Daniel Willard, president of the B&O, attempted to solve the car shortage problem, but their special advisory body, the Railroads' War Board, failed to end the logistical

nightmare. It had hoped that "essential" shipments could be prioritized, but the "preference" tagging system employed was "utterly lacking in coordination." Scores of railroads would not cooperate fully; old rivalries, jealousies and suspicions remained strong. Also, no company wanted to lose revenues. In the absence of voluntarism, the federal government intervened.[14]

The USRA, which became one of the most powerful federal agencies ever established, immediately went to work to unsnarl port congestion and to ease the shortage of freight equipment. Led by director general William Gibbs McAdoo, President Wilson's able secretary of the treasury and son-in-law, and staffed largely by competent railroad men, the agency soon made its presence felt. Although the internal operating organizations of individual carriers remained mostly intact, the USRA did much to coordinate service, reducing traffic on the most congested lines and increasing it on those that operated below capacity. The agency issued directives to eliminate duplicate services, to consolidate facilities and to reduce indirect shipping. McAdoo and his successor, Walker D. Hines, who took charge in January 1919, when McAdoo retired to private life, also worked hard to bring about standardization in repair and maintenance work and new equipment. As for the latter, the USRA created five standard freight-car designs that resulted in the construction of approximately 100,000 pieces of much-needed equipment and twelve standard designs that led to production of more than 5,000 versatile steam locomotives. Standardization, McAdoo and Hines believed, was essential for truly unified operations, although not all railroad leaders agreed. Significantly, too, the USRA brought about sizeable wage increases for workers, responding to a growing labor shortage and wartime inflation, while there would be only modest freight-rate hikes.[15]

As with most other Class I carriers, the Wabash struggled during the twenty-six months of federalization. Although management understood the need to coordinate and consolidate railroad activities, there were negative effects. In February 1919, chairman Williams objected to the diversion from Wabash rails of the large volume of "pass-over traffic," especially eastbound meat shipments from the Chicago packing district that for years had moved over the "north branch" to Montpelier, Ohio. Four months later, the board of directors complained that since the beginning of federal control the company had lost approximately $1 million of passenger business between Chicago and New York, via Buffalo. The USRA canceled three trains in each direction and left only a single train, "which makes all the stops and gives inferior service as compared with competing lines." The board also noted that the state of its rolling stock was uncertain, with "those [cars] that have been returned indicate that the condition. . . is below normal." The body grumbled, too, about the overall condition of its major corridors: "The track is not in as good condition as formerly, largely because the Administration did not put in a reasonable amount of ties last year, and has not thus far made up the deficiency." The explanation was that by the end of 1919 "there will be at least 350,000 ties below normal."[16]

The period of federalization was not entirely bad for the Wabash. Most notably, the company benefited from the availability of high-quality and well-engineered USRA standardized equipment. In 1918, the railroad took delivery of 2,800 forty-ton steel underframe double-sheathed boxcars and 1,000 all-steel "self-cleaning" fifty-five-ton hopper cars. It also acquired twenty-five of the most popular USRA locomotives, the "light" Mikados. Although most of this power, which was built by either American Locomotive or Baldwin, remained in service until the early 1950s, the Wabash in late 1919 sold five of these USRA locomotives to the Pere Marquette Railroad. "We have an ample supply of locomotives at hand," noted the superintendent of motive power.[17]

No different from other railroads, the Wabash willingly supported the war effort. Early on, it made various financial contributions. In August 1917, for example, the board of directors authorized a donation of $1,000 for maintenance of the St. Louis Home Guard Regiment, "organized for the protection of St. Louis citizens and property on account of Militia being mobilized into Federal Service." And it invested heavily in the patriotic yet safe American war bonds, for instance purchasing $500,000 of the Fourth Liberty Loan issue.[18]

The majority of employees likewise showed their loyalty to the cause. Hundreds of young men rallied to the colors by enlisting or entered military service because of the draft. Some belonged to state national guard units that the Department of the Army activated during the early months of the conflict. Still, railroad labor in the Midwest, most notably among locals in Missouri, "had an antimilitaristic bias" and favored a noninterventionist foreign policy. Moreover, some employees of German heritage, including many from heavily German St. Louis, were not thrilled with American efforts to whip the "Huns." But in no way did their feelings interfere with Wabash operations.[19]

Because of labor shortages and with higher wage rates the Wabash changed its hiring patterns. Although historically the Wabash had employed only a few people of color, mostly men on track gangs, it turned for the first time to black women. During the war, the company employed several dozen African American women as freight handlers. Other roads also engaged a small number of black women as common laborers, often as coach cleaners and engine wipers. White women also found limited employment on the Wabash and most other carriers. When peace returned, however, white males replaced these women, regardless of their color.[20]

Even though the war in Europe officially ended on November 11, 1918, the USRA continued to operate and in the process would lose a billion dollars. It would not be until March 1, 1920, that federalization finally terminated. Yet the Wabash and other roads would battle for years with the federal bureaucracy over the issue of "fair compensation." Even though the company could do nothing about higher wages, increased fuel costs and other factors that characterized conditions during federal control, it could object to the standard annual rate of return that the government set at $5,826,810. The railroad argued that this compensation was unreasonably low; it should amount to at least $8,681,000. Finally, on April 22, 1922, the federal government recognized the validity of much of the Wabash claims. Still, World War I had come at a price.[21]

In the midst of federalization, the Wabash experienced a major leadership change. On March 10, 1919, president Edward Kearney, "after having taken to his bed" a few days earlier died from complications of pneumonia. The board of directors did not immediately name a successor. Instead, W. H. Williams, the board chair, assumed Kearney's presidential responsibilities until early 1920. In a bizarre turn of events, the railroad's general solicitor, James L. Minnis, who for some time had shown an abiding dislike of Williams, Winslow S. Pierce, a member of the board's executive committee who earlier had headed the reorganization committee, and several other high-ranking company personnel, decided that he would take over Kearney's duties. Minnis moved into the president's office in the Railway Exchange Building and signed official papers. In a June 1919 letter to Otto H. Kuhn, Minnis blasted Williams, in particular claiming that he was greedy and not focusing on his duties at the Wabash. "The fact that Mr.[L. F.] Loree occupies positions in numerous companies and receives large salaries from many of them is not only a scandal among Railroad Administration people at Washington but it is a scandal among railroad people generally who universally, so far as I know, condemn it in unsparing terms. Mr. Williams is his understudy and he is drawing salaries from a number of companies, which is a scandal of smaller proportion, but it is well known at Washington and will, no doubt, be very influential against the Claim of the Wabash for just compensation. These men cannot do justice to the corporations of which they are officers." Concluded Minnis: "The affairs of railroad companies are important and require time, study, and patience. A man [Williams] who jumps from limb to limb and skips about is of no value to a large corporation. His activities result in confusion and disorder among people who work." Though Kahn's specific reply is not known, the powerful financier did not abandon his support of Williams. Instead, after a short time Minnis resigned, clearing the way for the board to appoint a successor to Kearney.[22]

The board selected an accomplished railroader, James E. Taussig, as the next president of the Wabash Railway. Born on May 4, 1865, to a well-to-do St. Louis family with business ties to the Eads Bridge, the young Taussig received his education abroad, attending private schools in London, Brussels and Darmstadt, Germany. At age seventeen he returned home to clerk in the freight and yard offices of the St. Louis Bridge & Tunnel Railroad. The peripatetic Taussig soon took similar white-collar positions with a number of carriers, including the Fort Scott, Wichita & Western; New York, Providence & Boston;

Wheeling & Lake Erie (W&LE) and the Texas & Pacific. In August 1915, he became assistant to the president of Wabash and not long thereafter vice president in charge of operations. During the USRA period, Taussig served as the federal manager of the Wabash and also for the St. Louis–based Toledo, St. Louis & Western Railroad (TStL&W). Though well educated and knowledgeable about railroading, he never became a popular executive. Recalled one employee, he was a "stiff shirt, society man."[23]

SHOPMEN'S STRIKE

Fortunately Taussig and Williams worked well in tandem, even though their jobs as president and chairman of the board of directors became quite difficult. In the immediate postwar period, they faced several tough challenges, including the shopmen's strike of 1922, arguably the bitterest labor dispute that the Wabash and many other Class I railroads experienced in the twentieth century.

It is not surprising that Wabash shopmen became heavily involved in the labor unrest of the early 1920s. There had been a longstanding tradition that sanctified direct job actions, whether the active role played by the Knights of Labor during the southwestern strikes of the mid-1880s or the role of the American Railway Union in the Pullman conflict of 1894. Furthermore, before World War I some Wabash shopmen (mostly in Moberly) belonged to an "outlaw" industrial union, the American Federation of Railway Workers, and a few joined the "Wobblies," the militant Industrial Workers of the World (IWW) led by syndicalist "Big Bill" Haywood, the charismatic one-eyed former cowboy and deep-rock miner.[24]

Even though the individual motivations for the over 400,000 railroad shopmen associated with the Railway Employees' Department (RED) of the American Federation of Labor (AFL) varied, those who left their jobs on July 1, 1922, unanimously agreed that their economic position had deteriorated substantially from what they had experienced during the war years. Employed mostly in hundreds of car and locomotive repair facilities, these workers had found the Wilson administration mostly supportive. Because some Wilsonians believed that trade unionism and collective bargaining would reduce class conflict, they not only backed the Adamson Act but also encouraged creation within the USRA of the Board of Railroad Wages and Working Conditions during federalization. This body endorsed the eight-hour day, time-and-a-half pay for overtime work and stringent seniority rules and in time authorized a substantial pay hike. Once peace returned, it was understandable that shopmen overwhelmingly sought continued government operations. These workers also applauded the Plumb Plan, formulated in 1918 by railroad labor attorney Glenn E. Plumb, which called for public ownership of the railroads but with operations by a private corporation controlled by a fifteen-member board, representing equally government, labor and management. Other than among railroad workers, few supporters of the Plumb Plan emerged.[25]

Although shopmen benefited under federalization, they became uneasy with the passage of the Transportation Act of 1920 (or Esch-Cummins Act), which President Wilson signed on February 28, the day before federal control ended. This landmark measure covered a multitude of matters, but its major features provided the ICC with increased control over railroad financial issues, mergers and efforts by carriers to earn a "fair rate of return" on their investments. Indeed, the law ostensibly altered the ICC's traditional mission from being a negative force into a more positive role. From labor's perspective the law's provisions creating the Railroad Labor Board (RLB) and boards of adjustment were the most threatening. Although decisions made by the RLB would *not* be legally binding, what bothered railroad labor, including shopmen, was its makeup. The nine-member board would have three representatives each from government, labor and the public. If a probusiness national administration took power (which happened with election of Warren G. Harding in November 1920), the RLB would surely fall into the hands of "heartless and greedy Wall Street capitalists."[26]

In the early 1920s, railroad executives, who nearly universally felt the pain of a national recession, increased automobile and truck usage and other income-reducing forces, did their best to capitalize on the national shift in political power. Soon the RLB became friendly (some would say too friendly) toward the carriers. In June 1921, it recommended that wages be cut by an average of 12.5 percent. Not long thereafter, the RLB further angered shopmen when it endorsed reductions for overtime income and the growing industry practice of basing compensation on piecework rather than the more lucrative and more equitable wage basis. The RLB also abrogated the shopcrafts' national agreement, ratified in 1919, that had standardized wages and work rules industry-wide that mostly favored labor.[27]

Although strikes were threatened, the frustrated railroad workers for a while remained at their jobs. Their behavior likely stemmed from several factors: union organizational problems; a continued drop, especially between May 1921 and January 1922, in the overall cost of living; and the sluggish economy brought on by the postwar recession. But by June 1922 members of the shopcrafts became more alarmed about their situation. They shuddered at the decision of the RLB, announced on June 6, recommend-ing a wage reduction of seven cents per hour to become effective on July 1, 1922. (The RLB had not, however, suggested wage reductions for the more conservative "Big Four" operating brotherhoods.) Because the industry, including the Wabash, planned to follow the RLB guidelines, a strike now seemed likely. At its national convention, held in late April, the Railway Employees' Department, an umbrella organization of the AFL shopcraft unions, decided to put the issue to a vote. During the balloting, which began on June 8, one Wabash shopman expressed to the labor leadership in Chicago the widely felt sentiments of his coworkers: "The Boys here are determined to fight on the three issues [wages, overtime and piecework] and we do not expect to have the strike postponed or declared off on account of some big money judge issuing an injunction."[28]

It seemed to shopmen that they were on an employment roller coaster. On the Wabash, scores of shopmen had only just returned to work. Because of the sluggish economy, in 1921 the company had furloughed hundreds of men systemwide and in the latter part of December had temporarily closed its shops in Moberly, affecting more than 900 men. By April 1922, employment returned to more normal levels, including the workforce at its largest maintenance facilities in Decatur and Moberly. Soon these men would face a showdown with the company and the industry.[29]

The fateful day in the lives of thousands of Wabash employees and their families came on Saturday, July 1, 1922. F. R. Lee, chairman of the Federated Shop Crafts on the Wabash, ordered all members to stop work at 10:00 A.M. In his announcement, he warned everyone to be peaceful and expressed his hope that "some honorable way out of the difficulty would yet be found." At Moberly, approximately 1,500 blacksmiths, boilermakers, car repairers, machinists, pipe fitters and other workers laid down their tools. "There were a few sufficiently well satisfied with the decision to give a cheer or so, but the great body of men, realizing the gravity of the situation, made no demonstration." By the end of the day, of the 3,000 or so shopmen on the Wabash, 2,750 had struck, some 92 percent of the workforce. Yet a number of roads, including the Chesapeake & Ohio (C&O), Chicago & Alton, C&NW, Chicago Great Western, Denver & Rio Grande Western, Minneapolis & St. Louis, and Seaboard Air Line (SAL), had even higher percentages, and a few saw the entire workforce depart.[30]

Residents of "Wabash towns" also commonly supported chairman Lee. This was particularly true in Moberly, where citizens depended more on the company's payroll than did those in the twin shoptown of Decatur. Moberly had already been suffering, and it involved more than the earlier layoffs in the shops. "Moberly this year has been affected with smallpox, a coal strike and a bad bank failure," noted the editor of the *Moberly Evening Democrat*. Yet expressing perennial Midwestern boosterism, he added, "But in the face of it all [Moberly] has kept on her onward course in business and material progress. Let us be optimistic though the heavens fall." It was doubtful whether most of the nearly 15,000 residents would fully agree.[31]

Wabash management immediately responded to the walkout with directness and force. At various facilities, including the shops complexes in Decatur and Moberly, the railroad erected protective fences and posted armed guards. To keep its rolling stock in proper repair, the company soon hired an army of strikebreakers, who ranged from inexperienced hoboes to skilled union men who had struck against other roads but sought to take advantage of the moment. Strikers objected strenuously, however, to the use of "scabs" of any type. Much of the

strategy of the Railway Employees' Department for winning a favorable settlement involved having extensive breakdowns of motive power and equipment, forcing carriers to make concessions because of sharp revenue losses and adverse public opinion.[32]

Although strikers on the Wabash publicly proclaimed their intentions to remain peaceful, they took an activist stand against any strikebreakers or perceived strikebreakers. During the first week of the walkout, a "mob of more than 200" gathered in the early hours of the morning at the Decatur station and threatened bodily harm to fifteen men who came from Chicago to take employment in the local shops. Two days later, in Moberly, "a very large crowd" of strikers met train No. 28 from Kansas City, which carried an extra coach containing twenty-seven men "who shopmen here took to be strikebreakers." These passengers said, however, that the Wabash had hired them to be guards in Fort Wayne. The strikers swarmed around the train, and when they discovered the end doors locked, they took three of the men out through a window. They then broke into the car and marched the "guards" with their suitcases to city hall. In an upstairs room, the strikers searched their luggage and soon decided that they should leave town, believing that they planned "to scab." "The 27 men were sent out of here in a one-coach special at 11:10 last night," reported the *Sunday Morning Democrat*. "A committee of six shopmen accompanied them back to Kansas City."[33]

The same day that the Moberly strikers removed from their midst men whom they considered to be threatening, the Wabash gave shopmen an opportunity to return, although there would be no concessions to their demands. "This is to notify such employees who are now out on strike that any of them who report for work on or before the morning of July 10th, 1922, will retain their rank and seniority," announced president Taussig. Then he warned: "After that date they will be considered out of service, with *No Seniority Rights or Privileges.*" And he meant what he said; he wanted total surrender. Somewhat earlier the RLB had supported the Taussig position, concluding that the strikers had voluntarily left the service of their employers, thus surrendering their seniority rights and therefore could be permanently replaced.[34]

The railroad industry and the federal government embraced Taussig's stand, especially when the Wabash on July 14 became the first railroad in the Midwest to win a federal court restraining order against the striking shopmen, forbidding them from interfering with its property. The company also sought to recover $1.5 million for damages "already inflicted and which may grow out of the strike." PRR vice president in charge of operations General William W. Atterbury and U.S. Attorney General Harry M. Daugherty, most of all, spearheaded the movement to end the strike and to destroy RED. They hated unions and any individuals and groups that they perceived to be radicals or "Bolsheviks." (The RED acronym, to Atterbury, Daugherty and others seemed wholly appropriate, certainly in the wake of the frightening "Red Scare" of 1919–1920.) The PRR, for example, recruited strikebreakers heavily, found "thugs" for guards and sent some of its own loyal shopmen to assist coal carriers in the central Appalachian fields in maintaining their locomotives and hopper cars and to alleviate some of the negative effects of a simultaneous national coal miners strike. In late July, much to the delight of conservatives, the antilabor James Wilkerson joined the U.S. District Court of Illinois, and shortly thereafter the new jurist "handed down one of the most sweeping federal injunctions in U.S. history," which he based on the Sherman Antitrust Act of 1890. His

edict restrained strikers and their union leaders from "hindering or obstructing in any way said railway companies" in inspecting or repairing their rolling stock. Moreover, strikers were enjoined from asking anyone to quit work, "in any manner by letters, printed or other circulars, telegrams, telephones, word of mouth, oral persuasion, or suggestion." Also RED officials were told not to issue instructions to their members.[35]

Even though the Wilkerson injunction provided the Association of Railroad Executives— railroad management—with a legal and psychological victory, the strike showed few signs of ending. The resolve of most shopmen, certainly those on the Wabash, remained strong. In August, one Wabash employee, probably with time on his hands, penned a short poem to explain the "activities of the pickets on the Wabash, Moberly, Mo."

> *Along the Picket Line*
>
> In days gone by, when you and I
> Had very little sense;
> The place they used for pickets then
> Was in the building of a fence.
> But time has changed, in many lines.
> Our youth has fled away,
> So I want to call your attention
> To the use of Pickets today.
>
> If you want to know the reason,
> And will listen to my gab,
> These pickets are all watching
> To muzzle the Wabash scab.
> There are pickets who are busy,
> They have many, many functions;
> There are pickets who are humpback
> From carrying around injunctions.[36]

There emerged a glimmer of hope for Wabash strikers and their compatriots when it became apparent that few of the major railroad executives were as stridently antilabor as General Atterbury. Willard of the B&O, who had from the start of the walkout embraced a conciliatory approach and would settle shortly with his shopmen, was encouraged by Secretary of Commerce Herbert Hoover to mediate the dispute. Unlike Daugherty, at least two members of the Harding Administration, Hoover and Secretary of Labor James Davis, took a more reasonable stance toward the strikers. In September, at Willard's suggestion, the presidents of the NYC and SAL joined him in reaching an agreement with Bert Jewell, head of RED. A realist, Jewell believed that a massive defeat seemed probable and wished to avoid violating the powerful federal court injunction. He correctly sensed that the general mood of the country was antistrike, although in many railroad communities strikers received considerable support. This "Willard-Jewell Treaty" essentially called for a return to the status quo as of June 30; thus, the strike period would essentially become an unpaid vacation. Other railroads, including most of the smaller carriers, joined the agreement, but a number of major lines, including the Burlington, Illinois Central, PRR and Wabash, continued to take a hard-line position, hoping to destroy or greatly diminish the power of the shopcraft unions.[37]

As the shopmen's job action began to collapse by early fall, strikers on the Wabash became more worried, even downhearted. Their spirits had already been dampened at Moberly by the actions of Arthur M. Hyde, the conservative Republican governor of Missouri. Convinced that peace must be maintained at all cost, in late July Hyde ordered 300 National Guard soldiers, eighteen officers and a flatcar carrying machine guns sent to the "Magic City." "The governor had been informed there were 150 armed [Wabash] guards here," reported a local newspaper, "and that there was danger of trouble between the guards and the strikers." In a letter to the governor, a striker cogently argued that "there has been no disturbance

here at any time, and there was no necessity of sending troops and putting more burdens on the taxpayers of Missouri." Local law enforcement officers and most Moberlyans agreed. Even though a majority of strikebreakers lacked the necessary skills, shop facilities throughout the railroad were in operation. And when RED representatives tried to reopen talks in mid-September, the company flatly refused. Moreover, strikers and their families began to suffer. Although friendly merchants extended credit, some by September and October withdrew their support or severely limited what items might be obtained on a promise of future payment.[38]

Desperate men do desperate things, and the strikers were no exception. A few of them lashed out against their perceived enemies. In Moberly, some nonstrikers, including several foremen, had their houses splashed with yellow paint and marked with the word "SCAB" on the front and sides. In Decatur, paving bricks were thrown through windows of strike opponents, promoting Henry H. Bolz, editor of the *Decatur Herald,* to exclaim: "Ye Gods, and this in Decatur!"[39]

By November the strike on the Wabash had mostly run its course. Although the Ladies' Auxiliary of the Federated Shop Crafts arranged fundraisers, including dances and socials, and union functionary F. R. Lee visited Wabash communities to provide words of encouragement, an array of strikebreakers had been joined by a substantial number of strikers who crossed picket lines in the shops. As early as mid-October, thirty former roundhouse mechanics and car inspectors, representing about half of the local RED membership, had returned to duty at Peru. About the same time, the *Decatur Herald* reported that the company workforce in that city totaled 278 in the roundhouse as opposed to the prestrike number of only 207; in the car department, 498 versus 505; and in the locomotive department, 370 compared to 768. A few days later, the Moberly press announced a similar set of figures for the hometown shops: roundhouse, 280 (207 prestrike), car department 508 (505) and locomotive shops 374 (768). Perhaps because of the skills required, the Wabash had more difficulties finding replacement workers in its locomotive facilities, and strikers who wished to return could find jobs. Conditions became so peaceful that in November Governor Hyde reduced the number of National Guardsmen to fifty and then recalled these remaining citizen-soldiers. The Wabash also reduced the size of its guard force, and colorful characters like "Blackie" Keller and "Two Gun" Murphy left its employ.[40]

Those strikers who rejoined the Wabash paid a high price. Not only had they lost wages for four, five or more months and had become debt-ridden, but also they had surrendered their seniority rights and likely their own specific shop assignments. A seniority list, published in 1935 for the pattern department in the Decatur car shops, listed the status of its six active employees, although it did not note specific job tasks:

Name	Occupation	Seniority Date
V. Ballington	Pattern Foreman	Jan. 4, 1912
M. R. Smith	Pattern Maker	Sept. 23, 1922
Keven Smith	Pattern Maker	Oct. 11, 1922
W. D. Leber	Pattern Maker	Oct. 25, 1922
C. J. Skelly	Pattern Maker	Oct. 30, 1922[41]

The Wabash likewise found the strike disruptive and expensive. During the first months of the walkout, it had to annul scores of freight and passenger movements, largely because of a lack of operable equipment. On July 11, for example, the company canceled fifty-four trains. In February 1923,

management revealed to federal authorities that it had employed nearly 12,000 men to keep the vacancies of 3,401 strikers filled, because of the high turnover rate, and hired 680 "special guards" to protect its property. The expenses of transportation and housing for these strikebreakers and security personnel amounted to $100,508. The railroad also paid bonuses of $179,621 to white-collar personnel who oversaw shop-related activities. The final costs, the company announced, totaled $1,296,278.[42]

By the early months of 1923, Wabash shop operations ran smoothly, but the "Wabash family" was hardly back together. The Wabash Club, which never had a large number of shop employees as members, may have provided some healing as did the generally good economic times that by the mid-1920s had returned for wage earners in the Midwest. Morale on the job may also have been improved by the absence of a considerable number of former strikers, including the most militant, who never returned. Although hardly a fair assessment, management believed them to be "hard-line" troublemakers and gloated that they "are no longer in our midst to sow any seeds of disharmony." There was an involuntary diaspora of sorts, with scores of former shopmen seeking work elsewhere. Most drifted into the bustling factory cities of the North; Chicago, Detroit and Milwaukee became popular destinations. A few years after the strike, a former employee wrote sadly to Jack Conroy, a carman who also left Moberly and in time became a prominent radical writer, that "the railroad strike [had] scattered the old bunch from Moberly, Mo." Beyond question, painful memories of the walkout lasted for years. Often craft, kinship and community ties had been damaged or destroyed. In the minds of many workers and nonworkers alike the Wabash management gained a reputation for being antilabor and uncaring about its employees, a view that would linger for some time. "The strike marked many a man and when he thought about the Wabash he would remember that strike back in '22 and all that lost prized seniority and money."[43]

The shopmen's strike continued to haunt some businessmen. As late as 1941, W. N. Jennings, head of the Central Coal & Supply Company in Moberly, informed PRR executives in Philadelphia, who had just established stock control over the so-to-be launched Wabash *Railroad* Company, that "the new merchants of Moberly would like to receive a pardon and be known as a friend of the Pennsylvania Railroad Company." The reason was the 1922 strike. "The town merchants of that day allowed the strikers to put cards in their windows expressing sympathy for the strikers. Naturally, this offended the Wabash officials. . . . These merchants are also gone, but some of the older Wabash officials have not forgotten. If possible, we would like to start with a clean slate and cooperate in every way possible with the Pennsylvania Railroad Company." For decades, the legacy of the strike permeated life in the shoptowns of the Wabash.[44]

ANN ARBOR

Beyond its labor provisions a major feature of the Transportation Act of 1920 involved a proposed cartelization of the railroad industry. The measure directed the ICC to prepare consolidation plans whereby strong and weak carriers would be merged, albeit on a voluntary basis. The congressional architects believed that this recasting would best serve the public interest; the older notion of forced competition seemed wholly passé in the modern postwar period. The law also contained an elaborate, though controversial, plan for equalizing earnings between the powerful and the not-so-powerful. In the

"recapture of excess earnings" clause, half of the earnings of carriers over 6 percent of their value, which the Valuation Act of 1913 had supposedly determined, were to be earmarked for a fund administrated by the ICC. The proceeds would be made available to struggling companies for debt restructuring and capital improvements. The other half would become a "rainy-day" fund that would cover bond interest, rents and dividends when earnings dropped below the 6 percent mark.[45]

In following the dictates of the 1920 act, the ICC prepared a set of consolidation plans. Rather than turning the project over to staff members, the ICC engaged William Z. Ripley, an expert on railroad finance at Harvard University, to oversee the crafting of this plan for a limited number of systems. Ripley and his colleagues worked with dispatch, and on August 3, 1921, their proposal was made public. Of the major Class I carriers, the Wabash would experience an unusual fate: Ripley proposed to *split* the railroad into two parts, reminiscent of what befell the Wabash, St. Louis & Pacific in the wake of the bankruptcy of 1884. The eighteen-system scheme placed Wabash lines east of the Mississippi River in "System No. 4—Erie," which included the Erie; D&H, Delaware, Lackawanna & Western (DL&W); Bessemer & Lake Erie and several smaller roads. Trackage west of the Mississippi would join "System No. 13—Union Pacific–North Western." Needless to say, neither the Wabash management nor its owners were keen on dismemberment and soon united with other railroads to object to various aspects of the Ripley proposals. One argument used by the company was noted by Williams in a letter to Albert Erskine, president of the Studebaker Corporation: "[The proposal] thus destroys the advantages shippers secure from the present short route of the Wabash." The ICC itself, moreover, was not certain that it was feasible to work out a limited number of systems to which *all* the railroads would voluntarily agree. It held public hearings on consolidation plans for much of the remainder of the decade before finally releasing its own version on December 9, 1929.[46]

This "final" consolidation arrangement represented a compromise based upon suggestions made by railroad executives, ICC commissioners and other interested parties. This time the Wabash would not be split at the Mississippi. Instead, among the twenty-one units proposed, it became a principal component of "System No. 7—Wabash-Seaboard," parts of which somewhat resembled George Gould's earlier concept. The ICC paired the Wabash with the Lehigh Valley (LV), Norfolk & Western, Pittsburgh & West Virginia (successor to the Wabash Pittsburgh Terminal), Western Maryland and W&LE and, of course, the sprawling SAL. System No. 7 would also contain a collection of mostly anemic Southern shortlines and would have trackage rights over portions of the Grand Trunk, PRR and Reading railroads. "It would run from Omaha to Miami via Buffalo," observed historian Richard Saunders, "and did not appear to have much geographic cohesion (except that, in an odd way, it resembled the later CSX and Norfolk Southern systems)." Or as a Cleveland railroad expert described System No. 7, "Drunks holding each other up."[47]

While the ICC developed guidelines for railroad consolidation during the 1920s, the Wabash formulated its own plans for expansion. One involved acquiring control of the Ann Arbor Railroad Company. This 294-mile largely "bridge line" ran diagonally across Michigan's lower peninsula from Toledo to Frankfort on the eastern shores of Lake Michigan. It crossed through rich farmlands, desolate wetlands and cut-over lumber sections, pine forests and scores of small communities with such enchanting names as

Azalia, Beulah, Lulu, North Star, Temperance and Urania. This modest interstate carrier surprisingly lacked branch lines; it was all stem. The Ann Arbor, or "Annie" as the road was affectionately known, also owned all of the capital stock of the Ann Arbor Boat Company, which by the mid-1920s operated a fleet of five car ferries from its docks at Elberta, a short distance from Frankfort, to rail connections at Manistique and Menominee, Michigan, and Kewaunee and Manitowoc, Wisconsin. The Ann Arbor, too, had stock control of a thirty-eight-mile shortline, the Manistique & Lake Superior Railroad. This former privately held Upper Peninsula logging road, which the Ann Arbor had owned since 1911, offered interchanges with both the Duluth, South Shore & Atlantic and Minneapolis, St. Paul & Sault Ste. Marie (Soo Line) railroads and served some continuing lumber businesses and other customers.[48]

The man who had shaped the Ann Arbor was the colorful James Mitchell Ashley. A former five-term Republican congressman from Ohio and territorial governor of Montana who previously had worked as a newspaper editor and attorney, Ashley was a tall, corpulent man whose "abundant white hair was worn long, down nearly to his coat collar in the style affected by Henry Ward Beecher." After he retired from politics, he decided to take part in the railroad-building boom of the Gilded Age. "I got out of a job in politics, came back to Toledo," explained Ashley to his chief engineer in the early 1890s, "and having no business to get back into and very little money, I decided to build a railroad."[49]

The core of the future Ann Arbor covered the trackage between Toledo and Ann Arbor, Michigan. In 1876, Ashley acquired the assets of two ill-fated ventures, the State Line Railroad and the Toledo, Ann Arbor and Northern Railroad, and united them under the corporate banner of the Toledo & Ann

Arbor Railroad. This company succeeded in linking its namesake cities.[50]

In the halcyon years of the 1880s, Ashley expanded his modestly profitable road. By launching or winning control of several firms, he realized his overall goal of extending his rail line into the northern portions of the lower peninsula, terminating at South Frankfort (renamed Elberta in 1911), a good harbor, second only to Grand Traverse Bay in the region. On September 21, 1895, the Ann Arbor, successor to the Toledo, Ann Arbor and North Michigan Railway (TAA&NM), came into being.[51]

There is no question that Ashley knew how to leverage his assets and to exert the proper pressure to assemble his road. He and his two sons owned the construction company that built much of the property, and the family firm gladly accepted the railroad's debt and equity. It sold the bonds for whatever they would bring to cover construction costs and kept the stock. The latter gave the Ashleys voting control over the railroad and the possibility of future earnings. In order to generate additional funds and contain costs as the rails crawled northwestward, the governor's elder son, James ("J. M. A. Junior") Ashley, took the lead. "He had been the man out at the front on all of the construction periods, highly successful at wheedling bond issues out of townships and villages and getting right of way agreements, or if unable to settle the right of way, in getting grading and tracklaying done without it." These actions prompted a former general superintendent of the company to write, in 1936, "The building of the Ann Arbor Railroad had as much of the romantic element about it as any business in Michigan excepting the clearing of the great pine forests and the automobile industry."[52]

The Ashleys had the good sense to exploit the excellent harbor near Frankfort. About 1890 the railroad contracted for the construction of two car ferries that were designed to carry twenty-four thirty-foot freight cars on their own wheels. In late 1892 the company placed in operation *Car Ferry No. 1,* the first revenue-carrying vessel to move regularly scheduled tonnage across Lake Michigan, and shortly thereafter it introduced *Car Ferry No. 2.* With these boats in translake service, the Ashley road offered faster and more economical freight service to and from destinations west of Lake Michigan than either the all-land rail route via the Chicago bottleneck or what competing break-bulk freighters could provide. The "floating bridge" concept would be a long-lasting Ashley legacy.[53]

The final decade of the nineteenth century would be times of great change for the Ashley road. The devastating depression of the mid-1890s, which came in the aftermath of the Panic of 1893, threw the TAA&NM into receivership. In the subsequent reorganization, the Ashleys lost control, although for years James Ashley's younger son, Henry W. "Harry" Ashley, served as general manager. Wellington R. Burt, a lumber baron from Saginaw, Michigan, took charge along with Eastern investors. During the four years of receivership and the several decades afterward, the property became greatly improved, including line relocations, better track structure and modern rolling stock.[54]

The improvements between 1890 and 1905 were impressive. One railroader, who initially traveled over the then 282-mile TAA&NM in 1890, commented that "My first trip, a rear platform inspection all the way, convinced me that I was on a 'jerkwater' railroad. It was a single-track line, laid with 56-pound rail on ties that were 90% hemlock with no ballast anywhere on the line except over a few 'sinkholes' where cinder ballast had been used, probably not over two or three miles in all." But fifteen years later a PRR superintendent crossed 270 miles

(Toledo to Thompsonville, Michigan) of the 292-mile stem and made these remarks: "The track rides very well, except in a few places. So far as I was able to determine, the greater portion of the road has been relaid in the past few years with 70 lb. rail. The road is pretty well ballasted with gravel. . . . The bridges have been strengthened so that they can run on freight trains an engine heavier than a class 'R.'" This observer was impressed not only with the through traffic but also with the considerable volume of on-line car loadings. "I found a very heavy [sugar] beet business," were one of his positive observations.[55]

A few years before the PRR official journeyed over the Ann Arbor, the Wabash became interested in the railroad. Although the company made no efforts to buy the line from the Wellington Burt group, a syndicate, some of whose members "are very close to the Wabash," acquired the property. An industrial analyst concluded that "there is no doubt that the operation of the road will be friendly to the Wabash." Indeed, the "Gould crowd" was involved, seeing that the Ann Arbor meshed with the Wabash's plans to reach Pittsburgh and beyond, anticipating that iron ore and other products from Minnesota, Michigan and Wisconsin would travel eastbound to Toledo and then to Pittsburgh area mills over the W&LE and the Wabash Pittsburgh Terminal and that shipments of steel and other manufactured products would follow the same route westbound.[56]

The attractiveness of the Ann Arbor grew for the Wabash. By the early 1920s, the Ann Arbor had significantly increased its freight traffic across Lake Michigan because of the dependable all-season service that a modern all-steel ferry fleet provided. For the fiscal year ended June 30, 1913, the road had transported 10,870 cars westbound by water and 19,908 loads eastbound; the comparable figures for 1923 were 19,442 westbound and

30,034 eastbound. The Wabash already obtained some of this long-haul business, receiving it either at its connections with the Ann Arbor in Toledo via the Toledo Belt Railway or at Milan, Michigan, thirty-seven miles west of Detroit. Though a preponderance of Ann Arbor traffic was eastbound, dominated by timber products, the Wabash believed that it could sizably boost the westbound volume, especially with the burgeoning numbers of motor vehicles produced in Detroit and Toledo and destined for markets in the northwest. Moreover, even a doubling of westbound traffic could be accomplished without any increase in the number of locomotives or crews required to handle it. And these cars would not be delayed by the congestion caused by the Chicago gateway, which resulted in considerably increased transit time. The estimated savings for a movement between Detroit and St. Paul, Minnesota, via the Ann Arbor, for example, as compared with the a route through Chicago, was three days. The Ann Arbor also had other assets, the most alluring were its substantial real-estate holdings in Toledo, which promised attractive sites for industrial development.[57]

Although the Pittsburgh troubles, bankruptcy, reorganization and war prevented any further involvement between 1905 and 1920, by the early 1920s an energized Wabash could seriously consider acquisition of the Ann Arbor. On May 19, 1925, the Wabash entered into a contract with a New York City brokerage house to acquire about one-third of the Michigan road's preferred and common stock. Funds available in the company treasury financed this transaction, estimated at more than $1.27 million. This arrangement, too, granted the Wabash an option, which it utilized, to purchase additional shares of Ann Arbor preferred and common, providing the former with more than 54 percent of the latter's securities. And the Wabash kept buying; by 1930 it owned 99.43 percent of Ann Arbor's stock.[58]

As required by federal regulatory statutes, the Wabash needed approval for its investment plans. In fall 1925, the ICC conducted the requisite hearings and released its decision on November 2. Because there were no public or industry objections, the ICC gave the stock control proposal its blessings. Still, there was a caveat of sorts. The commissioners noted in their official statement that "nothing in this report or in the order to be entered herein is to be construed as waiving or limiting our right to make disposition of the Ann Arbor under our final consolidation plan." Yet Commissioner Joseph B. Eastman, who joined his colleagues to endorse the stock purchase but was always an independent voice, candidly admitted, "It is quite true that we can give the Ann Arbor such place in our final consolidation plan as may please our fancy. But as a practical matter, once the Wabash acquires a majority of the stock of the Ann Arbor, any separation of that road from the Wabash in the final consolidation plan will be a wholly empty gesture, unless the Wabash consents to separation or the power of eminent domain is used to pry the two roads apart."[59]

Once the Wabash took stock control, both roads benefited as expected. They reaped the rewards of aggressive traffic solicitation; freight representatives found that they could successfully promote the advantages of new and improved routings. Furthermore, this corporate arrangement helped to tap the considerable business generated by a booming automobile industry based in Detroit. Tonnage and revenues increased as follows: in 1925, when the Ann Arbor was still independent, the Wabash interchanged 116,970 tons, which produced for it a net income of $168,775, but four years later the former reached 333,000 tons and the latter $594,000.[60]

In the midst of these prosperous and optimistic times, the Ann Arbor would proudly display its new company logo, a smart blue burgee. This swallow-tailed marine flag complemented nicely the decades-old Wabash banner, becoming a visual reminder that a close relationship existed between these two Midwestern carriers.[61]

THE FIFTH SYSTEM

Inspired by a major spike upward in net railway operating income ($8,941,275 in 1923 and $12,252,515 in 1925), easy bank credit and the ongoing work by the ICC to consolidate the multiplicity of separate railroads into large, balanced systems, the Wabash, under the generalship of board chairman Williams, became deeply involved in rail unification proposals. Williams remained close to Leonor Loree, so Wabash plans became intertwined with those of Loree and his D&H. Williams, in fact, concurrently held a vice president's title on the D&H, publicly affirming this connection, and he encouraged Loree to use D&H's large earnings to make substantial investments in Wabash securities.[62]

In the decade following the Transportation Act of 1920, prospects for regrouping eastern railroads seemed unending. By 1924 the aggressive and talented Van Sweringen brothers (O. P. and M. J.—always in that order—or simply the Vans), Cleveland real-estate developers turned big-time railroad entrepreneurs, had emerged as a dynamic force in regional railroading. On the eve of World War I they had acquired the strategic Nickel Plate Road (New York, Chicago & St. Louis) and had made it into a money-making bridge carrier. In 1923 the Vans garnered industry-wide attention when the reclusive bachelors won ICC approval to merge the relatively weak Lake Erie & Western (popularly known as "Leave Early & Walk") and the somewhat more profitable TStL&W, the "Clover Leaf Route," into their core road, scoring the only significant ICC-approved merger of the decade. The commission subsequently wished to maintain the status quo until it had completed its planning procedures, which would surely resolve the growing railroad consolidation muddle. It would not take long for the brothers, who dreamed of becoming railroad titans, to use holding companies, thus skirting ICC authority, to assemble control over some major roads, including the C&O, Erie, Pere Marquette and W&LE. What they achieved was essentially a "fourth" railroad system in the East, joining the already established B&O, NYC and PRR.[63]

As the activities of the Van Sweringens became clear to Eastern railroad executives, they reacted with proposals of their own. The most powerful road in the East, the PRR, responded by suggesting a "Fifth System," believing that it could control what happened to the remaining "unallocated" carriers, including the independent D&H. If a friendly, though maverick Loree could use his firm's ample treasury to assemble a new combine, then the PRR, which was not really interested in expansion, might well protect its connections and markets allied with a new Eastern rail giant. Unless the probusiness Congress intervened, which seemed unlikely, the ICC lacked real clout with its consolidation plans. And these were proposals that had not yet been finalized. Therefore, the PRR and its rivals believed that they could present to the commissioners with a fait accompli.[64]

The ambitious Loree rose to the challenge. Working with Williams, these men had their eyes on a system that in addition to the D&H and Wabash would include the Buffalo, Rochester & Pittsburgh (BR&P); LV; Pittsburgh & West Virginia and Western Maryland. This assemblage of roads would create a somewhat circuitous truckline,

stretching from Kansas City to New York City and would serve most of the nation's leading industrial centers, including thriving Pittsburgh, and some of the better bituminous coalfields.[65]

If the Loree-Williams Fifth System were to become reality, a top priority involved control of the LV. This nearly 1,500-mile-long New York–to-Buffalo coal and fast merchandise carrier offered the critical link between the D&H and Wabash and gave entree to the greater New York City area. A prosperous company with its common stock widely scattered, its securities would have to be purchased on the open market at relatively high prices. Loree began quietly buying LV stock in 1924, and by 1927 the D&H held about a quarter of its shares. In early 1926 the Wabash started its own acquisition of LV common stock and within a year or so had accumulated 258,929 shares or about a 20 percent interest. The cost neared $24 million for this key interchange partner at the Buffalo gateway.[66]

Plans for a Fifth System moved ahead. In 1925, the D&H negotiated an option to lease the BR&P on a long-term basis. This road, which owned 368 miles of track and operated another 218 miles under lease or trackage-rights agreements, served the cities of its corporate name and several productive coalfields. Moreover, Loree appeared poised to revive the dormant charter of the New York, Pittsburgh & Chicago Railroad that called for construction of a low-grade freight line across much of Pennsylvania, extending from the LV at Easton to the Pittsburgh gateway. Although this particular scheme quickly fizzled, hardly a disappointment to the PRR, in mid-1925 the D&H applied to the ICC for permission to build a comparable line as a key component of these grand plans.[67]

Although the PRR, now headed by the iron-fisted General Atterbury, provided modest support to Loree and Williams, major reversals followed. The ICC not only rejected the idea of new construction in Pennsylvania, but refused to honor the D&H lease of the BR&P. In fact, the B&O and NYC soon took possession of the property. Moreover, the Vans became instrumental in taking over the W&LE, considered a vital part of the Fifth System. Loree, too, found the management of the LV hostile to his designs, and in early 1928 LV officials showed their independence by barely winning a hotly contested proxy fight with Loree and Williams for control of the board. Seeing his plans turn to dross, Loree sold the D&H's stock holdings in the LV (and also in the Wabash) to the Pennsylvania Company, the holding company affiliate of the PRR. He had initially asked $85 million but received $62.5 million, making a tidy profit of $21 million for the D&H. Though badly disappointed that he had failed to fashion a larger railroad system, Loree disposed of these securities near the top of the bull market, thus enabling the D&H to weather the economic storms that followed the stock market crash of October 1929.[68]

Why did the Pennsylvania pay handsomely for the Lehigh Valley and Wabash securities? The PRR had long coveted the LV because of its traffic base and strategic location. The LV handled considerable merchandise and coal tonnage and possessed much better entrances to Buffalo and New York City than did the PRR. There was also some thick icing on the cake: LV paid substantial annual dividends. The PRR did not buy the Wabash common for its dividends, but, according to one financial analyst, "It got the Wabash out of the way as the possible backbone of a rival trunk line."[69]

But had the PRR successfully rid itself of a possible Wabash "nuisance?" W. H. Williams remained imbued with the notion of having his road become a core unit in a major grouping of Eastern railroads. In a widely re-

ported speech, on October 15, 1929, only a few months before the ICC issued its final report on suggested rail unifications, Williams told a meeting of the Associated Traffic Clubs of America, in St. Louis, that the Wabash board of directors "at an early stage of the consolidation discussions . . . determined that public interest required the utilization of its extensive properties as part of an independent system serving the industrial and agricultural areas between the Missouri and Mississippi rivers and the Atlantic seaboard." In fact, the Wabash had acquired its substantial stake in the LV as a first step. Even though the sale of LV and Wabash stock in 1928 by the D&H had given the PRR a substantial position in both the LV and the Wabash, Williams contended that his road remained an independent player. "I do . . . deem it my duty publicly to state that our own consolidation plans were developed and matured long before these stock transactions; that our program has been carried forward without consultation with, and without the knowledge of any other railway interest, and that our plans contemplate a system which shall be independent of and definitely competitive with all other systems." Still, Williams admitted that "it would be an idle pretense if I should ignore the 48% ownership of Wabash stock by interests affiliated with Pennsylvania Railroad. I shall not ignore this situation, nor will I permit it to be a handicap upon the freedom of my expressions."[70]

Three months before his St. Louis presentation, the Wabash executive had done more than express his continuing interest in a fifth independent Eastern trunk line. The company had formally applied to the ICC to unify more than 7,000 miles of railroad. Its specific plan contemplated control of eight roads, either under lease or by stock purchase; joint control in another; one-sixth interest in four others; and one-seventh interest in and joint use of another and various trackage-rights agreements. In addition to the Wabash, the principal components would be the Akron, Canton & Youngstown; Chicago & Illinois Midland; Lehigh & New England; LV; Pittsburgh & West Virginia; Toledo, Peoria & Western; Western Maryland; and W&LE. It was not a foolish assemblage, yet it would be one that would have difficulty competing with the NYC and PRR especially and perhaps even with the B&O and the properties controlled by the Vans.[71]

The major powers within the industry in the East showed no enthusiasm for the Williams plan. Also, they did not care for Williams's willingness to back "System No. 7" (Wabash-SAL) outlined in the final ICC report. In fact, they worked against creating a "Fifth system" of *any* type, although they had little to fear. The advent of the Great Depression dramatically altered the financial and political picture of all the Eastern carriers. Railroad executives soon focused their attention on remaining solvent and in some cases how they might shape a bankruptcy reorganization. In the harsh economic conditions of the day, however, unification could mean all-important savings as money became tight. The dollar amount might be considerable, ranging from reduced costs that could be anticipated from administrative consolidations to line downgrades or even partial abandonments and sales.[72]

The long-lasting fallout for the Wabash in the consolidation frenzy of the 1920s involved its financial relationship with the PRR. In 1930 the ICC challenged these newly established ties, ordering the Pennsylvania Company to divest itself of its LV and Wabash holdings. The commission considered these two railroads collectively to be direct competitors of the PRR and thus contended that the investments violated the 1914 Clayton Antitrust Act. Moreover, the ICC recently had endorsed "System No. 7,"

which meant a LV and Wabash independent of the PRR. General Atterbury and his associates argued, however, that the PRR was not attempting any "restraint of trade." Rather, these stock purchases "amounted to an investment for the best interests of the road" and came at a time when the Eastern rail consolidation alignments were in flux and the final ICC plan had not been circulated.[73]

Although penalized by the ICC, the PRR found relief in the federal courts. When the lower courts concluded that the Pennsylvania Company had legally acquired the LV and Wabash stock "for investment purposes, and not to lessen competition," the PRR was relieved. Yet the federal government challenged the decision rendered by the Third Circuit Court of Appeals, and the case made its way to the U.S. Supreme Court. On March 19, 1934, a divided court voted four to four, thus allowing the lower court verdict to stand. The *St. Louis Star-Times*, which despised what the PRR holding company had done, concluded that "the Wabash has been inside the Pennsylvania's stomach for so many years that it ought to be pretty thoroughly digested by this time." In reality, though, the Wabash remained largely independent of the "Standard Railway of the World," but the presence of its principal shareholder could not be overlooked.[74]

BUILDING A BETTER WABASH

It was mostly the "roaring '20s" for the Wabash Railway. Admittedly, the postwar recession had produced grave times, but it was a short-lived downturn, and the worst effects of the shopmen's strike lasted only briefly. By 1923 financial conditions improved for both the nation and the railroad industry, and this prosperity continued throughout the remainder of the decade. The Wabash took great pride in reporting that it had experienced "the largest single day's movement of freight on record in its 88 years' history, on Friday, August 20 [1926] when 11,334 carloads were moved." Two years later the company recorded its heaviest volume of freight business ever, generating 5.5 billion revenue ton miles as compared with 5.4 billion in 1926, the previous record. Earnings generally reflected these impressive freight-hauling accomplishments. Between 1921 and 1929 net railway income remained strong, averaging more than $9 million annually.[75]

To keep up with traffic demands and growing competition, particularly from the increasingly common automobile, bus and truck, the Wabash spent heavily on a range of improvements to its physical plant during the 1920s. As it had done in the past and would continue to do in the future, during the decade millions of dollars went into the track structure, with heavier (often 110 pound) rails, hardwood ties and crushed-rock (and sometimes burnt clay) ballast. A number of passing tracks were lengthened and industrial sidings installed. Better bridges likewise became a priority. The most impressive new structure opened on January 31, 1927, an $850,000 double-track steel and concrete structure near Decatur measuring 1,062 feet in length and standing sixty-nine feet above the Sangamon River. The company also continued to place automatic block signals on its main stems. In 1923 and 1924, for example, such betterments appeared on the Kansas City line between Birmingham and Harlem, Missouri.[76]

One type of improvement, which the Wabash underwrote, came from frequent public and political pressures, namely, urban grade separations. As the automobile gained enormous popularity after World War I, city streets, whether in Chicago, Detroit or St. Louis, became congested. Motorists did not like to be stopped on major thoroughfares by passing trains. Railroads—among them the

Wabash—realized the benefits of grade separations to include matters of safety, efficiency and cost savings with the elimination of crossing guards and gates. But these improvements were almost always expensive, time-consuming and disruptive of train movements. Not surprisingly, carriers balked at times at making such capital commitments.[77]

The Wabash encountered its biggest grade separation headache in St. Louis. For fourteen years, railroad officials and city leaders wrangled over how busy Delmar Avenue should be crossed. The railroad wished to have the track on an embankment and the street run underneath while the city wanted the tracks depressed. Both, however, agreed that this was "the most dangerous and objectionable grade crossing in the city of St. Louis." The nastiness of the dispute, which had entered the courts, became so great that the company published a short pamphlet that pleaded its case. "The Wabash Railway is now and always has been ready and willing to compromise the Delmar Grade Separation Controversy with the City of St. Louis," emphasized president Taussig. At long last, in January 1926, an accord was struck. Once a mutually acceptable settlement had been reached, construction began on what would be a viaduct *over* the Wabash tracks. The railroad paid 60 percent of the $500,000 price tag.[78]

The community was overjoyed when the span officially opened on June 18, 1928. "Ten thousand persons marched over the western rise of the Delmar viaduct above the Wabash Railroad tracks," reported the *St. Louis Star*. "They were preceded by a brass band, and street cars moved slowly in their midst. They headed east on the wide paving of the brilliantly lighted span to a point 100 feet from the east end of the viaduct at Hamilton avenue, where spectators were assembled before a flag decorated wooden platform." An array of speeches followed as did a festive street carnival. Surely Wabash executives were relieved that the project had been completed and warmly received by the local citizenry.[79]

Bridge and grade separation projects were not the only part of constructing a better Wabash. The decade witnessed completion of a number of important structures, some of which had been in the planning stages for years, though others were not. When, on February 26, 1924, flames destroyed the massive coach shop and stores department buildings in Decatur, causing an estimated $750,000 in damages, the company faced a major rebuilding project. But it responded rapidly to this costly and disruptive conflagration. "To prepare plans and estimates for new buildings, remove the debris from the site of a disastrous fire, salvage all usable material and then erect a new brick and steel passenger car repair and paint shop on the location of the old buildings, in a period of *156* days, is an engineering accomplishment worthy of more than passing notice," exclaimed *Railway Review*. The replacement structures were large and state of the art.[80]

More bad luck struck the Wabash complex in Decatur. On May 9, 1927, a tornado slammed into the relatively new locomotive shops, inflicting heavy damage. Yet by the end of the year repairs and new construction had been completed, creating a highly functional facility. Workers installed a new transverse shop in the middle of the old longitudinal plant, ensuring "the most advantageous use of both the new and old portions of the shop." Fortunately, the company was able to use more than 80 percent of the original structure.[81]

To increase shipper satisfaction and bolster freight revenues, the Wabash paid attention to commodity-service facilities. In 1928, it opened a modern brick and concrete fruit and vegetable house in St. Louis between Carr Street and Franklin Avenue, highlighted by a three-story unit on the northern end that contained various support functions, including a large auction room. A year later, the Wabash became a partner with the PRR and Pere Marquette in the construction of a $5 million union produce terminal in Detroit that covered a twenty-six-acre site along West Fort Street near the downtown commercial center. It, too, offered produce brokers an even more spacious auction auditorium. The Wabash also either rehabilitated or acquired terminal grain elevators in Chicago, Council Bluffs and North Kansas City. In July 1925, for example, the Wabash Elevator Company, a wholly owned subsidiary, purchased the Rialto Elevator "of the most modern type of construction," located on the Calumet River in Chicago.[82]

The Wabash took pride in all of its brick and mortar betterments during the 1920s, but the crown jewel was surely Delmar Station (originally called Delmar Boulevard Station) in western St. Louis. Early in 1928, the company approved plans to erect a reinforced concrete depot in "modern Roman style" at 6001 Delmar Boulevard, close to the newly opened Delmar Viaduct. Officials wanted an attractive and highly functional suburban station that could serve passengers "from this high class residential district and surrounding suburbs." The company most of all had the business traveler in mind. Those who were going to Chicago, Detroit, Kansas City or other destinations usually would not have to journey into the heart of St. Louis. Moreover, they could arrive from their out-of-town destinations twenty minutes or so before their trains terminated at Union Station. On overnight trains, the company would set out a Pullman car on one of the convenient sidetracks at the station, allowing patrons to board and retire long before the scheduled departure time. And every traveler benefited from a facility being situated on important streetcar and bus lines and offering excellent taxi and parking accommodations.[83]

It took about eighteen months to complete the station. "The doors of the New Delmar Boulevard Station were opened to an expectant St. Louis public on the morning of the first day of August [1929]," announced the proud editor of the *Wabash News,* a short-lived company magazine. He reported that the access to station platforms "is by means of enclosed stairways and by passenger elevator. Stairways are well lighted and equipped with bronze safety treads and brass hand rails." Everyone seemed impressed. "I was in St. Louis yesterday [October 3, 1929] and looked over this station which cost approximately $350,000.00," reported James M. Symes, an official of the PRR, to a fellow executive. "I will say that it is about as nice a small station as any I have ever seen and compares favorably to our station at Euclid Ave., Cleveland, O."[84]

Even though the Great Depression loomed in the near future, the investment in the Delmar Station paid off handsomely. During the first month of operation, according to one industry source, "they have doubled their Chicago–St. Louis travel which they attribute to the opening of this new station." Although not all Wabash trains served this "West End District" facility, every train bound to and from Des Moines, Kansas City, Omaha and the Twin Cities did, and others that stopped used Merchants Bridge via Terminal Railroad Association of St. Louis trackage rather than the downtown Eads Bridge.[85]

The 1920s were the heyday of the long-distance passenger train, and the Wabash did its best to meet competition. In September 1925, the company introduced the "new" *Banner Blue Limited* between St. Louis and Chicago, which it immodestly dubbed the "Train of Trains" with the "World's Finest Railroad Equipment." It sped between

The Wabash took considerable pride in the opening of its suburban station on Delmar Boulevard in St. Louis in August 1929. This facility attracted additional patronage, especially from business travelers who lived in western St. Louis or in St. Louis County. "It sure was a beautiful and highly functional depot," remembered longtime Delmar agent Ollie (O. K.) Blackburn. (Author's Coll.)

its urban terminals in only 6½ hours, and the exterior of the entire consist was richly enameled in "deep Banner blue and striped and lettered in gold," giving it a most attractive appearance. But the Wabash did not ignore its other major runs. In early December 1927, the company took out print and radio advertisements to ballyhoo its "New Standard of Wabash Service," announcing that "effective December 11th, the most complete transportation service in its 90 years of serving the traveling public" would begin. It made much of forty-four new passenger cars, shortened running times and other

In March 1925 a Wabash Railway cameraman took this "staged" photograph of the "old" *Banner Limited* at the station in Decatur, Illinois. In the 1920s travelers usually wore their Sunday best clothing and hoped that coal dust would not soil their garments. (Wabash Railroad Historical Society Coll.)

improvements to its overall operations. Most every name train would be affected, including the *Detroit Special, Midnight Limited, Omaha Limited* and *Pacific Coast Limited.* "A steady program of improvement begun in 1925 is being pushed forward without interruption," reported *Omar D. Gray's Sturgeon Leader* in January 1928. This small-town Missouri newspaper made much of improvements for non-Pullman travelers who were likely readers of this story. "Letters have come in from all over the country from railroad officials as well as from individual pas-

sengers commenting on the seats in the chair cars which were designed by a group of surgeons for the comfort of passengers. The care and painstaking effort given by the Wabash to provide the most comfortable and convenient equipment has been met with an immediate favorable response from the traveling public."[86]

The Wabash received more well-deserved kudos for a new train, the *Central States Limited,* which it introduced in June 1929. The company wished to establish fast, luxury service that no other road could offer directly between Detroit and Kansas City, a distance of 715 miles. By using the Moberly-Hannibal-Decatur line, this name train allowed travelers to avoid a change of trains in St. Louis or a change of trains and likely of stations in Chicago. The scheduling adopted called for a noon arrival in the Motor City, which "permits a half day for business in Detroit," and its 5:45 P.M. arrival in Kansas City allowed for easily making a number of connections to the West. No one would quarrel with the Wabash's contention that it possessed the shortest and most direct route between these two rapidly growing urban centers. Unfortunately for passengers who found the *Central States Limited* pleasant and convenient, it became an early casualty of the Great Depression, making its final runs in early 1932.[87]

With a bevy of fine, modern passenger trains, the Wabash passenger department did its utmost to promote usage. Even in the wake of the October 1929 crash, the railroad spent heavily on promoting summer trips, especially those to Chicago, Detroit, and points in Michigan and Wisconsin. "Wabash passenger department representatives who are listed on the last page of this folder, will gladly and courteously give you at their offices, expert travel information to fit your time and purse," announced one lavishly illustrated brochure. "Or if you prefer, will arrange for a personal talk in your home, or office. Of course there is no obligation." More than ever, prospective vacationers were courted heavily.[88]

Following the end of federalization, the Wabash also sought to bolster its overall freight operations. Improvements to track structure, support facilities and the like contributed to a better, more dependable freight sector. Management wished to build upon an enviable reputation for fast freight service. The road received from its principal interchange partners at Buffalo—the DL&W

and LV—a large tonnage of manufacturers' and miscellaneous freight for westbound shipment. It gained even more interchange traffic from connections in Kansas City and St. Louis, especially from the Missouri Pacific, in fresh fruits and perishables, along with sizeable quantities of packing house products that originated in Kansas City and Omaha. Accordingly, it needed to wheel these cargoes as quickly as possible. In this regard, Wabash management and employees adopted the slogan, "Fast freight means just what it says on the Wabash."[89]

The Wabash benefited from new and better-designed locomotives. In the mid-twenties, the company acquired from the Schenectady works of the American Locomotive Company several large orders that in 1923 totaled thirty K3 Mikados (2-8-2) and two years later forty-five K4s and K5s. Five of the engines received in 1925 (numbers 2600–2604) were three-cylinder, rather than the standard two-cylinder, types. During the spring of 1925 the company assigned these three-cylinder machines to handle early evening "red ball" merchandise trains from St. Louis to Chicago that needed to make morning deliveries. They met their schedules and generally performed well. "The three-cylinder class K-5 engine handled time freight trains averaging 8.1 per cent heavier than the trains handled by the class K-3 two-cylinder engine of similar proportions during the corresponding period of previous year, and at a coal consumption of 4.2 per cent less on the ton-mile basis," reported W. A. Pownall, the mechanical engineer in Decatur. "The average train for the three-cylinder class K-5 was 55 cars, as compared with 45 cars for the class K-3. And when compared with the 2-10-2 locomotives, which had arrived in 1917, the three-cylinder engine fuel performance was 16.96 per cent better."[90]

About the same time as the Wabash introduced its three-cylinder engines, it started to equip its freight locomotives with Worthington feed-water heaters (some already sported Schmidt superheaters). This add-on equipment saved from 10 to 15 percent on fuel costs and recovered about 15 percent of the feed water from the exhaust steam. Such an improvement helped to make possible a fast freight run from Kansas City to Delray (Detroit), a distance of 712 miles, in the actual running time of thirty-four hours and ten minutes.[91]

Furthermore, the Wabash received high marks for its locomotive maintenance. Fading anticompany feelings spawned by the shopmen's strike, the upgraded engine facility in Decatur and scores of replacement engines help to explain why in 1928 the ICC's Bureau of Locomotive Inspection gave the road its best rating. Among carriers that owned 150 or more locomotives, only 6 percent of Wabash fleet had major defects in 1927, and inspectors had to order only two locomotives be taken out of service for major repairs.[92]

Because the Wabash annually handled about one-half million tons of less-than-carload (LCL) shipments, it sought to speed up delivery time, especially at its big city terminals. Dependable and more powerful locomotives were not enough. The improvement of service to company patrons in Chicago, for example, captured the attention of the commercial and trade press. On March 1, 1927, the railroad became the first in the Windy City to dispatch a fleet of motor trucks and trailers to provide same day service to customers. Formerly, it often took from twenty-four to seventy-two hours to transfer this LCL freight via conventional "trap cars" from the receiving depot on 49th Street to its downtown freight station on Polk Street.[93]

Although acquisition of two small railroads in Indiana may not have enhanced the overall quality of freight operations, Wabash involvement pleased shippers who "could more intimately experience its legendary red carpet service." In 1926, the company took stock control of the "New Jersey," the eleven-mile New Jersey, Indiana & Illinois Railroad (NJI&I). This oddly named carrier had been built early in the twentieth century by the Singer Manufacturing Company in South Bend and apparently drew its name from states where the firm operated plants. The road served several industries in South Bend, including the sprawling Studebaker wagon and later automobile complex, and connected at Pine, Indiana, with the Chicago-Montpelier line. A much smaller property and generator of many fewer carloads of freight was the Lake Erie & Fort Wayne Railroad (LE&FtW). Opened in 1904 by the Fort Wayne Rolling Mill Company, this two-mile terminal road, which the Wabash acquired in April 1929, offered access to this manufacturing plant and several smaller shippers. Neither the NYC nor the Nickel Plate was pleased with this Wabash acquisition, although the ICC gave its approval. The Wabash decided to operate both the NJI&I and LE&FtW as separate corporate entities, largely for legal and tax purposes.[94]

Although not involving a purchase, the Wabash cemented its usage of what it rightly had come to consider an absolutely vital segment of its system, the approximately seventy-mile line between Hannibal and Moberly. The line was owned by the Missouri, Kansas & Texas Railroad, but the Wabash had leased the trackage since the late nineteenth century. In April 1923, the two roads signed a ninety-nine-year lease agreement. For an annual rental of $120,000, the Wabash received an exclusive right of usage. It also gained an option to purchase the line at any time during the term of the lease for $2.4 million.[95]

BANKRUPTCY AGAIN

In the late 1920s few if anyone associated with the Wabash anticipated a forthcoming financial crisis. The company's balance sheets looked solid. Net income for 1928 stood at $11,950,039, although it would plummet dramatically within three years. Even though the stock market faltered badly in October 1929, an immediate panic did not ensue. On New Year's Day, 1930, Andrew Mellon, a prominent Pittsburgh banker and Secretary of the Treasury, declared, "I see nothing in the situation that warrants pessimism." Secretary of Commerce Robert Lamont concurred, predicting "for the long run" a continuance of progress and prosperity. President Herbert Hoover, moreover, repeatedly uttered reassuring statements about America's economic future.[96]

As the decade of the 1930s dawned, W. H. Williams continued to envision the Wabash as the core for a major railroad system in the East. "The Wabash has negotiations in progress with a view of acquiring railroads allocated to it under official railroad consolidation plan of the Interstate Commerce Commission," reported the *Wall Street Journal* in February 1930. In April, the board of directors approved an application seeking ICC permission to purchase the capital stock of the W&LE. History seemed about to be repeated. Because of the strong opposition from the Nickel Plate, part of the Van Sweringen megasystem network, the Wabash in June withdrew its application.[97]

About the time the Wabash considered acquisition of the W&LE, it issued $15 million of bonds through its longtime banker Kuhn, Loeb & Company. Management wished to retire certain notes, reimburse its treasury for some previous capital expenditures and provide for future betterments. Part of the money realized from this bond sale underwrote the cost of a major increase in the road's motive power. Between January 1930 and January 1931, the road took delivery of twenty-five Mountain (4-8-2) and twenty-five Northern (4-8-4) engines from the Baldwin Locomotive Works. Both the Mountains and Northerns commonly replaced Mikados in mainline service. The latter initially mostly found assignments wheeling tonnage over the 272-mile stretch between Decatur and Montpelier. But later in 1931, Walter S. Franklin, a member of the executive committee, told fellow members of the board of directors that acquisition of these locomotives had been foolish. "They really replaced power which would have been satisfactory for some years to come."[98]

As the dark clouds of depression loomed, the board of directors squandered some of its financial resources. At a meeting held on March 14, 1930, the body unanimously approved granting a bonus of $100,000 to board chair Williams, for "conducting and directing measures involved in the undertaking of this Company to preserve the integrity of its property and to advance its prestige, its importance and its usefulness in the transportation field." A month later, the board raised Williams's annual compensation from $60,000 to $140,000, which was second in the railroad industry to General Atterbury of the PRR, who in June 1929 began receiving a salary of $150,000 per year. These financial windfalls for Williams would later be examined by the ICC and a Congressional committee.[99]

Williams did not falter in his efforts to make the Wabash as efficient and profitable as possible. A two-day meeting of officials held in April 1931 at the St. Louis headquarters produced a confidential 345-page transcript of proceedings in which management painstakingly explored ways to improve maintenance, operations and service. Williams repeatedly urged everyone to consider new courses of action and always to try harder. "Now see what contribution you can make. . . . I say now and I said to you before, I do not want you to get the impression that we are pessimistic. We are not. We recognize we are in a situation that requires a lot of hard work; we recognize the inefficiency of the past, we recognize that many men on this property would have a different view had there been proper instruction in the past. I am interested in what step[s] you are going to take and what your performance is to be in the future. I am merely interested in the facts as to that performance, and not in your good intentions."[100]

Irrespective of any accomplishments derived from such an exhaustive executive retreat, in the latter half of 1931 the Wabash began to experience a substantial decline in revenues, especially freight, as factories, mines and other enterprises contracted their operations. At the meeting of the executive committee held on September 2, 1931, Williams announced that, "due to the continued depression in business and consequent falling off in revenues of the Company, every possible effort is being made to reduce expenses, and that to date such reductions have amounted to $170,358 per month, or $2,044,296 per year."[101]

Economizing, however, could not save the Wabash. By the end of 1931 the railroad would be operating in the red, posting a net income loss of $7,050,746. "Traffic just went to hell," and this was especially true for shipments of automobiles and trucks, iron and steel and soft coal. When the T. J. Moss Tie Company of St. Louis demanded $49,651 on overdue accounts, the road could not pay. The tie firm understandably turned to the courts for relief, charging that the "Wabash is completely insolvent." Interestingly, Nat S. Brown, general counsel for the Wabash, prepared the bill of complaint, realizing that the Moss claim was only the tip of a financially troubled iceberg and

wishing to steer the bankruptcy in the best possible fashion. The railroad lacked money to pay about $4.7 million in ordinary current operating bills and faced default on $616,000 of principal, plus interest, due on some equipment trust certificates.[102]

In some respects, the Wabash went down fighting. The last best hope involved a substantial loan from the PRR. Although General Atterbury and his board publicly deplored "the necessity of any railroad receivership," they rejected the request. "In view of its large investment in the Wabash Railway Company the Pennsylvania feels that it should not add to the investment it has already made." Surely, the reasoning involved the financial woes then facing the PRR. During the Great Depression, the company barely managed to escape bankruptcy, and it saw its common stock plunge from $110 to $6.50 a share between 1929 and 1932. Perhaps an earlier confidential report to Atterbury may have had some impact. An unidentified investigator thought little of the Wabash, contending that parts of the railroad have "very light traffic," that it was too dependent on bridge business and that it was "not well entrenched in either Kansas City or Omaha." This report closed with these cutting remarks: "A careful analysis of the Wabash leads one to doubt its place in any transportation system and raises the question as to just why it was built."[103]

The black day for the Wabash came on December 1, 1931, when the U. S. District Court for the Eastern District of Missouri in St. Louis declared the company insolvent. Once again court-appointed receivers would be at the throttle of the bankrupt carrier. Neither James Taussig nor W. H. Williams, however, would participate in the forthcoming process of reorganization. On September 9, 1931, Taussig retired. At age sixty-six, he wished "to devote his time to personal affairs." Williams then took over the presidency, but he remained as board chair. About five weeks later, on October 14, Williams suffered a massive heart attack and died in his St. Louis hotel room. He was only fifty-seven years old. Pressures of the Wabash job and his recent ouster by the Van Sweringen interests from the boards of both the Missouri Pacific and Texas & Pacific railroads had placed him under enormous strain.[104]

Not long after Williams's passing, the board of directors named Walter S. Franklin president. He was picked as the result of deliberation between the board's executive committee and top officials of the PRR. Because the PRR was the largest stockholder of Wabash securities, the board thought that the PRR needed to be consulted. "The Pennsylvania people were very cooperative," recalled coreceiver Frank Nicodemus in 1939. "They said they would look over their organization and perhaps later look outside of their own organization and make a suggestion." The Wabash, however, already had its eyes on Franklin. "They [PRR] took [Franklin's candidacy] under advisement," remembered Arthur K. Atkinson, Wabash treasurer, "and finally agreed that he could take this place."[105]

The newest president of the Wabash hailed from the East. He was born in Ashland, Maryland, on May 24, 1884, and received his collegiate education at Harvard College, graduating in the class of 1906. Not long after he received his sheepskin, Franklin joined the PRR as a clerk in its transportation department. Except for World War I, when he had charge of moving troops through England and a brief stint heading a New York commercial trading firm, he worked for the PRR. By 1929 he had become the capable general superintendent of the company's Northwestern Region, headquartered in Chicago, and not long thereafter he accepted the presidency of the Detroit, Toledo & Ironton Railroad, a firm that the PRR had recently acquired from auto mogul Henry Ford.[106]

This "Pennsylvania man" was joined by his coreceiver, Frank C. Nicodemus, Jr., assistant general counsel of the Wabash. Nicodemus also came from Maryland, a native of Baltimore, where he was born on December 11, 1881. After graduating from the University of Maryland law school in 1901, he joined the legal department of the Western Maryland Railway and later became associated with the New York City law firm of Pierce & Greer. The senior partner, Winslow S. Pierce, served on the Wabash board of directors, and it was through him that Nicodemous became part of the road's legal staff.[107]

In slightly more than sixteen years, the Wabash Railway had come full circle. The new corporation, full of hope and promise, had failed during the early years of the Great Depression. It won the inglorious distinction of being the first major steam road in the Midwest and one of the first nationally to enter bankruptcy during these years of struggle. (Somewhat earlier, the SAL and Florida East Coast Railway had faltered as well.) Williams deserves some blame. Perhaps if he had been more cautious, especially with activities associated with the Fifth System, the Wabash would have not slipped so quickly into receivership. Yet forces well beyond the control of any railway executive worked against maintaining corporate solvency. A number of giants, including the C&NW and Rock Island, also would seek court protection, and holding-company empires likewise collapsed, best illustrated by the Van Sweringens' Alleghany Corporation. The financial statistics were exceptionally grim: in 1932 railroads posted a revenue decline of 22 percent from the previous year and a 45 percent drop from 1929. Everyone, including Franklin and Nicodemus, hoped that the morrow would bring a better day and that the Wabash could become a solvent, even robust, property.

Depression, Rebirth and World War II

HARD TIMES

The crushing national depression of the 1930s posed some of the greatest challenges in Wabash history. Management already had dealt with the early plunge into bankruptcy, and after December 1931, it had to accept control by a federal court. The wishes of U.S. District Court Judge Charles B. Davis required satisfaction. Although receivership offered financial protection from creditors, coreceivers Walter Franklin and Frank Nicodemus needed to achieve a workable reorganization, one they hoped would not take too long or be too acrimonious. To execute a corporate restructuring, the men faced the daunting task of placing the company in good financial order. Throughout these hard times, two objectives would remain foremost on their agenda: cost reduction and enhanced earnings.

Just as major leadership changes occurred on the eve of bankruptcy, they also took place early on in the court-managed receivership. On October 19, 1933, Franklin resigned as coreceiver to rejoin the Pennsylvania Railroad (PRR) as its vice president in charge of traffic. A month later, however, the Interstate Commerce Commission (ICC), at the insistence of the Wabash board of directors, authorized him to serve as Wabash president and also as a director. The board believed his service to be invaluable. (Soon thereafter Franklin severed his ties with the company and the coreceivers absorbed his duties.) Norman B. Pitcairn succeeded Franklin. Born

During the Great Depression the Wabash did its best to promote itself. A major attraction of "Railroad Week" in Decatur, Illinois, held in June 1935, was display of the mighty 4-8-4 Northern-type locomotive No. 2907. This Class 0-1 freight locomotive was built in October 1930 by the Baldwin Locomotive Company, and officials wanted visitors to know that it cost a whopping $111,683. It was, however, a sound and long-lasting investment; this engine remained on the property until January 1956. (Author's Coll.)

on November 8, 1881, in Harrisburg, Pennsylvania, he attended Princeton University, graduating in 1903 with a degree in civil engineering. As was typical of engineers who entered railroading, Pitcairn started at the bottom as a rodman for the PRR. By 1931, he had advanced to general superintendent of the Eastern Ohio Division, and when Franklin later that year stepped down as president of the Pennroad-controlled Detroit, Toledo & Ironton, Pitcairn took his place. Franklin nominated Pitcairn for the receiver's position, and it was endorsed by representatives of both the Stockholders Protective Committee, which had been formed following the bankruptcy, and the Reconstruction Finance Corporation (RFC), the federal agency designed to provide financial relief to businesses, especially railroads.[1]

When it came to slashing costs, the court and coreceivers immediately turned to wage reductions. The coreceivers themselves received annual compensation that was in line with most other railroad executives. Instead of the outlandish salary paid W. H. Williams, each realized a monthly check of $1,700, although the Wabash originally gave Franklin $3,000 a month. Beginning January 26, 1932, shopmen, excluding laborers, took a 15 percent wage cut. This came in the wake of major layoffs, and for several months all of the car and locomotive departments had been operated part-time. Subsequently, the railroad industry and the brotherhoods agreed to a *temporary* 10 percent wage reduction. This cut would be restored gradually: 2.5 percent on July 1, 1934; 2.5 percent on January 1, 1935; and the remaining 5 percent on April 1, 1935. Coming at a time of massive, widespread unemployment and modest deflation, grumbling about these wage reductions was modest.[2]

Not all workers applauded the Wabash's response to the depression crisis. Some Wabash shopmen complained when man-

agement decided that everyone would work only on a *full-time* basis, leading to the furloughing of many of their colleagues. In April 1932, this policy had been implemented for the nonlocomotive workforce, but not until May 1934 did it cover those in the locomotive departments. Before full-time work became universal, employees labored for twelve to fourteen days each month rather than the customary twenty-six days. The company sought to spread employment, however, for train crews, including yardmen and switchmen. After all, the quest for economies had led to reduced service; no divisions or lines were immune. In October 1933, at the request of the labor brotherhoods, monthly mileage for passenger trainmen was capped at 5,500 miles and for freight crews at 3,500. Yard employees and switchmen faced a limit of 208 hours per month. Clerks, too, shared the available workload with a commensurate reduction in wages. Rather than the standard six-day, 44.5-hour week, on April, 1, 1933, they began a five-day, forty-hour-week schedule. But in mid-1933 management decided that it must cut the clerical force. Even by spreading duties, the staff was found to be "too large for work on hand." Moreover, much to the unhappiness of many, the company mandated that all remaining clerks return to a full-time basis. While generating substantial payroll savings, these policies caused significant job losses. In Moberly, for example, by 1934 only thirty-eight clerks remained. In 1929, by contrast, there had been 120. The laid-off clerks would be only part of more than 2,500 Wabash employees, or about a quarter of the workforce, who found themselves victims of the Great Depression.[3]

As American businesses scrambled to reduce costs through restructuring, the Wabash decided to streamline as well. In January 1932, the company consolidated five of its operating divisions into three.

Specifically, the Detroit and Peru divisions were merged into a new unit based at Montpelier. The Decatur Division absorbed the Springfield Division, and the Moberly and Western divisions were combined at Moberly. The various terminal divisions, however, were not affected. The company did not reveal the amount of savings realized, but obviously it needed fewer supervisory and clerical personnel. That same month it accomplished a savings of $300,000 annually by reducing staff and finding smaller, less expensive rental space for its office operations in the financial district of New York City. Then on September 1, 1934, the road centralized all of its accounting offices in Decatur, closing down similar operations in Chicago, Moberly, Montpelier and St. Louis.[4]

Although some economies realized during receivership were transitory, others produced permanent savings. Line abandonments and cooperative trackage agreements meant both short- and long-term financial gains. Since its reorganization in the late 1880s, the Wabash, unlike some Midwestern carriers, had not been burdened with excessive numbers of "branches and twigs." It was largely main stems, and where there were appendages, they frequently generated respectable volumes of traffic. The Columbia, Ottumwa and Streator lines, for example, were continual moneymakers. But competition from motor vehicles, operating over a steadily improving network of primary and secondary public roads, doomed the weakest branches. Livestock, for instance, loaded at a branch-line station could travel to local or terminal markets by truck faster and usually cheaper than by rail. These livestock shippers had options. In hard times, gypsy truckers eagerly sold their transportation services at extremely low rates, and some stock raisers acquired their own trucks, whether new or used, and others shared vehicles and services with neighbors.[5]

Wabash management quickly started the process of pruning its branches. Although at times regulatory permission took longer than expected, during the 1930s the company successfully eliminated several money-losing lines. These included the fifteen-mile Covington branch from Attica to Covington, Indiana; a six-mile segment of the Quincy line between Clayton and Camp Point, Illinois; the ten-mile Excelsior Springs appendage from Excelsior Springs Junction to Excelsior Springs, Missouri; and a whittling away of the Bement-Effingham-Altamont trackage. As for the latter, the company initially retired the 9.48 miles between Shumway and Altamont, a quintessential twig, and then turned to the sixteen miles between Stewardson and Effingham. In this longest removal to date, the Wabash could cogently make its case for abandonment. Because the section had become "freight only," poky way-freights generated less and less income. Freight revenues in 1930 stood at $4,440.44, slipping to $3,725.97 in 1933 and then a year later declining to $2,302.14. Moreover, the track structure had deteriorated badly, about half of the cross-ties were untreated, ballast consisted of only cinders and dirt and the timber bridges were full of rot. The rails themselves, all laid prior to 1891, were light, weighing either fifty-six, fifty-nine or sixty-three pounds to the yard. Then in 1938 the Wabash won permission to retire another twenty-four miles of the former Effingham line between Sullivan and Stewardson. It also pushed to abandon the 15.37-mile Salisbury-Glasgow branch, but that request hit regulatory snags. It would not be until February 25, 1942, that that service ended and the rails, ties and other salvageable materials were removed.[6]

Even on a profitable line Wabash management might realize much-needed savings. Although over the years the company developed coordinated trackage arrangements with other carriers, including the Illinois Terminal Railroad and the Nickel Plate Road, the change of note during the Great Depression involved approximately twenty miles of the Moberly–Des Moines line. During World War I, the United States Railroad Administration (USRA) ordered the Wabash and the Chicago, Burlington & Quincy (CB&Q) to share trackage between Albia, Iowa—located on the CB&Q mainline between Chicago and Denver—and Tracy, Iowa, approximately twenty miles north on the heavy-duty Des Moines branch of the CB&Q. The Wabash closely paralleled the CB&Q trackage between Albia and Tracy, and each road served the communities of Lovilia, Hamilton and Bussey. Under the USRA edict, trains of both roads traveled over the CB&Q between Albia and the Monroe County–Marion County line north of Lovilia (eleven miles) and the Wabash from the county line through Hamilton and Bussey to Tracy (eight miles). But after federalization ended, the CB&Q and Wabash returned to their former routes. Because both carriers sought economies during hard times, they later agreed to return to the single-line arrangement of the USRA era. In late 1933 an understanding was reached, and by December 17, 1935, the necessary physical connections had been made and the savings begun, estimated at approximately $11,000 annually. Both companies, too, scrapped most of their own redundant trackage and station structures, including the Wabash depot in Lovilia and the CB&Q depot in Bussey.[7]

The Wabash also employed the concept of coordination for one of its major passenger operations. From the opening of the Chicago-Montpelier trackage in the 1890s, several daily trains operated over this 272-mile route between Chicago and Detroit. The arrangement generally worked well, although this Indiana trackage, except for the South Bend connection, lacked any centers

of population. The company, however, could continue to compete for the more lucrative long-distance business between the Windy and Motor cities by using the high-speed, multitrack line of the PRR between Chicago and Fort Wayne. Because both railroads wished to reduce costs and enjoyed a close relationship, they quickly reached an agreement. Effective April 2, 1933, the Wabash ended its last through passenger train, reducing service across northern Indiana to a daily local (and then only a mixed train) and substituted jointly operated trains with the PRR between the two terminals. This arrangement saved the Wabash more than 40,000 passenger-train miles monthly, and through patrons benefited as well. The Wabash now could offer much faster schedules with three well-equipped and convenient daily trains, which ran in the morning, afternoon and evening. Although the new routing was twenty-two miles longer, these Wabash-PRR trains competed effectively with the best service offered by the Michigan Central, even with its crack *Twilight Limited*. The only losers were South Bend passengers. Before the Wabash-PRR joint agreement, they had access to sleeping-car service that operated over the Wabash subsidiary New Jersey, Indiana and Illinois (NJI&I) via the Pine, Indiana, connection with the Chicago-Montpelier line.[8]

Not every effort to develop a money-saving cooperative program worked as intended. In the mid-1930s a proposal by the RFC that the Wabash locomotive facility in Decatur become the "Consolidated General Locomotive Shop" in Illinois for the Alton, Chicago & Eastern Illinois (C&EI), Chicago & Illinois Midland (C&IM), Illinois Terminal (IT) and Wabash died, even though a series of meetings and reports mostly favored the concept. If implemented, the Alton would have closed its locomotive facility in Bloomington, the C&EI would have done the same in

Danville, the C&IM in Taylorville, and the IT in Decatur. The old competitive rivalries between the roads and the immediate costs of relocation likely explain why the plan never became more than a good idea.[9]

Understandably, the coreceivers carefully reviewed matters of equipment. In December 1932 Franklin reported to the board that more than 4,000 pieces of rolling stock (mostly freight cars) needed to be retired and "should not be given repairs under any conditions." This scrutiny continued. In another instance, management in the late 1930s informed the board that "a recent inspection of the existing rolling stock . . . develops that a total of 37 units, consisting of 11 locomotives and 26 units of work equipment, are worn out and unfit for further service, that the 11 locomotives are from 27 to 33 years old, and that on account of age and generally worn out condition, the expense for repairs to machinery and boilers, ranging from $7,000 to $12,000 per engine, is not justified in view of the service that would be obtained from this class of power." Scrap-metal dealers, and at times company employees, cut up this unwanted equipment; the housecleaning was ongoing and exhaustive.[10]

An important consequence of the close attention the Wabash paid to its equipment was that it reduced significantly the age of its freight-car fleet. By 1935, only 4 percent of its cars were more than twenty-five years old; only five other Class I railroads could make a similar claim. Furthermore, the Wabash held the lowest ranking for roads having cars more than twenty-years old; the figure stood at a mere 3.1 percent. Because car loadings remained weak during much of the Great Depression, the company did not face expensive car rentals. When, at the end of the decade, the economy turned upward, it purchased, leased or built additional freight equipment.[11]

During the 1930s the Wabash employed an imaginative and economic way to dispose of some of its derelict freight equipment. At the Decatur shops employees were told that they could have any parts, including lumber, if they provided the "sweat equity" to scrap these cars. "In the spring of 1934, three other fellows and I took on the job of dismantling old Wabash . . . wooden box cars, which were available to any employee desiring to do so on their own time," recalled one worker. "There being four of us, we each got a fourth of the car, taking turns with the metal roof and the doors, if they were any good." This ambitious individual used his share of the salvageable materials to build a three-room house in the north end of Decatur. He also obtained a locomotive cab and converted it into his garage. "It was off of an old switcher that was being scrapped. I put doors on it; had it for quite awhile."[12]

The Wabash liquidated other assets, too. It began in earnest to seek regulatory permission to suspend agency service in little-used rural stations. Once the states agreed, these surplus depot buildings were frequently sold, with some finding adaptive uses as houses, garages, barns and small commercial businesses, and at times removed from trackside. In 1936, the foremost property sale occurred when the railroad transferred ownership of its Rialto Elevator, located at 104th Street and Commercial Avenue in Chicago, to the Star Grain Company, a division of the Washburn-Crosby Company. The selling price was $700,000, although eleven years earlier the Wabash had acquired the facility for $650,000 and had spent more than that amount to expand storage capacity from 1 million to 2.6 million bushels. The company needed this money and expected to have Star Grain as a customer.[13]

With the coming of the New Deal in March 1933, the Franklin D. Roosevelt administration continued the Reconstruction

Finance Corporation. Launched in December 1931 by a reluctant Herbert Hoover, this agency loaned money to banks, insurance companies and railroads in need of liquidity. Determined to rid the nation of hard times, New Dealers increased the presence of the RFC in the business sector. Although the Wabash coreceivers and board members held strong, conservative Republican Party views, they hardly shunned the prospects for long-scale financial assistance from the federal government, even if it might come from liberal Democrats. Business for the Wabash at one point in 1933 was about one-fifth of what it had been in the late 1920s. Other pragmatic railroad executives took a similar approach. After all, the industry was in economic shambles. By 1933 receivers or trustees operated 41,698 miles of bankrupt lines, a total that in 1939 peaked at 77,013 miles.[14]

The Wabash ably tapped federal assis-tance. Shortly after the RFC opened for business, the company sought a substantial loan. On February 10, 1932, the ICC approved a request for $7,173,800 from the railroad division of the RFC to meet maturing equipment trusts and to pay other pressing obligations. Judge Davis then authorized the railroad to issue as security the same amount in receivers certificates. By 1935 the Wabash had received loans from the RFC of nearly $16 million.[15]

The company also received aid from the Public Works Administration (PWA). Begun during the frantic first 100 days of the New Deal, this relief and recovery agency was designed to boost employment and to stimulate the economy by increasing demand for durable goods. As with RFC funding, the ICC and Judge Davis needed to be involved, and both readily agreed to authorize the issuance of $1,481,000 in receivers certificates

During the 1930s the Wabash replaced some of its motive power, resulting in surplus steamers either being sold or scrapped. This October 2, 1938, view of the shops in Decatur, Illinois, reveals a large number of locomotives on the "dead line." The photograph also conveys the sprawling nature of this major Wabash installation. (Author's Coll.)

as collateral for a like amount of federal loans. This PWA money paid for 10,000 tons of heavy steel rail and 3,000 tons of metal fastenings and subsidized the cost for repairing and modernizing about 1,500 pieces of rolling stock. Once funding became available, track improvements were launched in the spring of 1934 on main stems in Illinois, Indiana and Missouri, and about the same time the car work kept scores of employees busy in Decatur and Moberly.[16]

The Wabash also used the PWA to help finance one of its largest betterment projects of the century, a replacement bridge over the Missouri River at St. Charles. The existing spans, which at various times had been updated since their completion in 1871, had become wholly inadequate for faster, longer and heavier trains. In 1929 civil engineers started to survey an appropriate site for the replacement structure, and they recommended a location that was about one-half mile downstream (north) of the existing bridge. Following approval by the board and the Army Corps of Engineers, construction of the supporting piers started in October 1930. Graders also began to shape the necessary line-relocation between Robertson, a station near St. Louis Municipal Airport, and the east approach. But in November 1931, long before workers could finish the bridge or relocate the tracks, hard times halted the project.[17]

Once the Wabash had responded to its immediate postbankruptcy problems, it renewed construction of the Missouri River span. In December 1934, the railroad organized the Wabash–St. Charles Bridge Company to facilitate the project. A combination of railroad funds ($932,996.20) and bonds ($2,350,000) sold to the PWA, provided financing. When the first train, a fifty-six-car Moberly-bound freight, rumbled over the structure on October 13, 1936, it signaled that at last this modern and massive steel and concrete bridge had been completed. The statistics were impressive: the four-span cantilever-type bridge measured approximately 1,700 feet in length and rested on five main piers, the largest being 156 feet in depth from track level to bed rock; the bridge contained 8,800 tons of high-test steel and 26,300 cubic yards of concrete and masonry. Nearly seven miles of new roadbed and track were constructed between Robertson and a point west of St. Charles along with a replacement passenger depot in St. Charles. This capital improvement provided an estimated 1.5 million man-hours of employment for workers who lived in the St. Louis area, exactly what the PWA had in mind.[18]

Management publicized its new St. Charles bridge. Although somewhat moderated by New Deal programs, the Great Depression remained, and the mood of the country lacked the optimism that had characterized the previous decade. Nevertheless, the building and opening of the Missouri River span provided much-appreciated positive news and spotlighted a "progressive Wabash." The big day for celebrating this construction feat came on October 29, 1936. A special thirteen-car train, with approximately 400 dignitaries, left Union Station in St. Louis for the official dedication ceremonies held at the new St. Charles depot. "The guests were royally entertained," reported a St. Charles newspaper. "In the way of refreshments nothing was missing." Everyone received an attractively printed souvenir booklet that reviewed the history of the St. Charles area and its bridges. Wabash officials must have been pleased; coverage was extensive, including feature stories, often with photographs, in newspapers, magazines and engineering and railroad trade publications.[19]

Just as the St. Charles bridge enhanced efficiency and surely boosted morale among Wabash personnel, more than a year earlier another improvement had a similar impact.

Wishing to keep up with rail passenger competition and to regain business lost to highway travel between Chicago and St. Louis, the company responded by offering fast, deluxe air-conditioned service. Although it would not introduce internal-combustion "streamliners" as did the CB&Q and Union Pacific, it followed the model set in the Midwest by the Chicago & North Western Railway (C&NW). In January 1935 that road inaugurated its *400* trains between Chicago, Milwaukee and the Twin Cities, scoring a considerable public-relations victory with these conventional steam-powered consists that covered the roughly 400 miles in about ten hours. In early June 1935, the Wabash placed its daylight *Banner Blue* trains on a five-and-a-half-hour schedule, a reduction of one hour, thus offering C&NW-like mile-a-minute service. Wabash rivals Alton, C&EI and Illinois Central moved quickly to provide similar equipment on speeded-up schedules.[20]

The Wabash prepared carefully for the debut of the new *Banner Blue*. From the 4-6-2 locomotives to observations cars, the train sets were placed in tip-top mechanical order and highly polished and enameled in the color appropriately known as "Banner Blue." Maintenance-of-way employees made improvements to long stretches of track for the trains to handle the anticipated high speeds and to provide passenger comfort. The company temporarily increased the size of its section gangs by about 140 men and lengthened their workweek from five to six days. Always mindful of publicity, members of the passenger traffic department worked closely with journalists about the forthcoming inaugural runs and made plans for special departure and arrival ceremonies at Dearborn Station, including the appearance of Frankie Masters, "the popular band maestro."[21]

Most residents along the Chicago–St. Louis route knew that the new *Banner Blue* trains would make their maiden trips on June 3, and thousands saw the show. "Circus day crowds turned out Sunday to watch the Wabash Banner Blue trains race by on their speeded-up schedules," reported the *Decatur Review*. "At Decatur, the only stop on the run between [suburban stations] Englewood and Delmar, such a crowd greeted the arrival of the first Banner from the south that police were required to keep back the crowds." All went well for passengers, watchers and the Wabash; the northbound *Banner Blue* arrived at Dearborn Station three minutes early, and the southbound train steamed into St. Louis Union Station two minutes ahead of schedule.[22]

In terms of publicity, the inaugural runs of the "blue streaks" were a smashing success. Wrote a delighted L. W. Bade, assistant passenger traffic manager, to his boss, H. W. Watts: "Mr. Philip Hampson of the Chicago Tribune, a personal friend of mine, was on hand to cover the situation [arrival of the *Banner Blue* in Chicago], and while he explained it would be a hard job, due to the fact that all the railroads were demanding the same attention, the Wabash was the only line that was successful in having a picture appear in the Chicago Tribune. The same applied to the [Chicago] Herald and Examiner."[23]

The Wabash worked hard to continue the high quality of *Banner Blue* service, the company's signature passenger train. Speeds were maintained and equipment upgraded when financially possible. In early 1937, the company added attractive combination dining–tap room cars to the consists. "The car is divided into 2 sections by an aluminum screen partition," noted *Railway Age*, "and seats 24 in the dining room and 12 in the tap room." Even with keen competition from the three other roads linking Chicago and St. Louis, patronage on the *Banner Blue* remained high, although the Alton's streamlined *Abraham Lincoln* surely

After the early 1930s the Wabash experienced a close corporate relationship with the Pennsylvania Railroad and also worked cooperatively with this powerful Eastern trunk road to generate passenger traffic between Chicago and Detroit. The joint *Detroit Arrow* became a competitive train in this market and important to each road. A folder, dated September 24, 1939, promotes this "fast" intercity service. (Author's Coll.)

FROM THE HEART OF CHICAGO

The DETROIT ARROW

4¾ HOURS

TO THE HEART OF DETROIT

Two other fast trains daily ★ ★ ★

All trains air-conditioned

PENNSYLVANIA RAILROAD
WABASH RAILWAY

won the honor for best overall train between these two urban centers.[24]

Introduction of the refurbished *Banner Blue* did not mean that the Wabash ignored other trains and lines. Service on the joint Chicago–Detroit route with the PRR remained competitive with equipment and timetable improvements. Moreover, since 1932 the Wabash had been adding air conditioning to certain trains. By 1935, it offered patrons "only pure filtered air, with all dirt, dust, cinders and smoke removed" on all cars between Chicago and St. Louis and on major runs between St. Louis–Des Moines,

St. Louis–Kansas City and St. Louis–Omaha. On September 25, 1938, the company introduced a new Chicago to St. Louis passenger train, the *Blue Bird,* which replaced the *St. Louis Special.* "Recent trends in train travel between St. Louis and Chicago have indicated a strong public approval of late afternoon departures from both cities," ran the Wabash newspaper announcement. "To meet this requirement, and to keep pace with the times, the Wabash has now made it possible for their patrons to complete the business day in St. Louis and yet reach Chicago that same evening." As with the revamped *Banner Blue,* this train was both visually and physically attractive. "The Blue Bird is a train of exquisite beauty—blue and gold outside and luxury and comfort inside. One of the smartest and most modern of all standard trains." All would surely agree. Another appealing feature was the "tasty, home-cooked economical meals served in spacious, attractive cars."[25]

No different than other major railroads during the Great Depression, the Wabash achieved modest success in bolstering its passenger revenues by slashing passenger fares and doing what it could to promote travel. On December 1, 1933, for example, the company and other members of the Western Passenger Association made dramatic rate reductions: chair coach tickets dropped from 3.6 cents to two cents per mile, and Pullman rates fell from 3.6 to three cents per mile and the surcharge for Pullman fares was eliminated. Similarly, the railroad offered a plethora of special travel bargains. For central Missouri teachers, the Wabash in November 1933 announced that they could travel from Moberly to the state teachers convention in St. Louis and return for only four dollars. Later that same month, the railroad offered a $2.65 round-trip ticket between Moberly and Kansas City for football fans to attend the Thanksgiving Day gridiron match between archrivals University of Missouri and University of Kansas. As in the past, there would be inexpensive rates both by coach and sleeper to the principal fairs of the 1930s, including the Century of Progress, in Chicago (1933–1934); the Great Lakes Exposition, in Cleveland (1936–1937); the World's Fair, in New York (1939–1940); and the Golden Gate Exposition, in San Francisco (1939–1940). At times, fares fell to unbelievably low levels. In September 1933, the company charged only $6.50 for a special two-day round-trip in its "big, roomy reclining chair cars" between Moberly and Niagara Falls, a distance of nearly 900 miles.[26]

Even with bargain-basement prices for Wabash passenger trains, thousands decided to travel without tickets. The number of hoboes who hitched rides, usually on freight trains, reached the highest level since the cataclysmic depression of the 1890s. At the depths of the Great Depression, in 1932 and 1933, there were hundreds of thousands of men (and some women and children, too) in search of elusive jobs. "Hobo jungles" in terminal areas and at junction points were particularly active, especially before the New Deal relief programs became fully operational. With some frequency, on-line newspapers reported the arrests (usually for vagrancy, trespass or petty theft), injuries or occasional deaths of these unwanted passengers.[27]

Nearly every homeowner along the Wabash likely had hobo visitors during the Great Depression. But differing from common railroad policy, these "knights of the road" might be treated with kindness and respect. "When the [Wabash] trains would stop in Wakarusa or Wyatt, the hobos would leave the train and begin to walk looking for food or work (or both)," related a former resident of rural Wakarusa, Indiana. "Sometimes they would stop at our farm. Dad and Mom never turned any away. Dad (and Mom) would put them to work; e.g., cutting,

splitting and piling firewood, cutting weeds, etc. Mom would give them a good meal and pack for them eggs, bread, sometimes meat, and fresh vegetables from our large garden. They then went on their way."[28]

The most spectacular and newsworthy hobo episode on the Wabash occurred in May 1932. During that month, thousands of World War I veterans marched on Washington, D.C., to demand passage in the U.S. Senate of the Patman Bill, which promised payment of a bonus to these former servicemen. One sizeable contingent of this "bonus army" that came mostly from Oregon concluded that the only way that it could participate in this "petition in boots" was to hop a series of freight trains. When the determined men reached Council Bluffs, Iowa, they decided to "commandeer" a Wabash freight bound for Luther yard in St. Louis and forced the crew to add five empty boxcars. Though hardly pleased, Wabash officials allowed these bonus marchers to proceed. "How can you arrest 500 men? And after all, why should we discriminate against veterans?" Once the protestors arrived in St. Louis, they proceeded eastward to the nation's capital on a Baltimore & Ohio freight train in a vain effort to win their much-needed bonus money.[29]

The Wabash did not ignore ways to improve freight service, the meat-and-potatoes of its business. Just as with its passenger trains, the company, with regulatory approval, reduced freight charges. In early 1934, for example, it drastically cut rates on less-than-carload (LCL) shipments between Kansas City and St. Louis. Management cogently argued before the state commerce commission that it was losing considerable LCL traffic to trucking companies that connected these two Missouri cities and that the firms were skimming off the cream of its high-profit merchandise business. Efforts were also made to enhance freight operations. In spring 1934, the Wabash, working with the Canadian National, launched fast freight service to New England by way of Detroit and Windsor, which gave third-morning delivery of shipments from Chicago and St. Louis and fourth-morning delivery from Kansas City and Omaha. At the same time, it sped up connections with the Minneapolis & St. Louis (M&StL) at Albia, designed in part to get more interchange business for Kansas City and the Kansas City gateway that the M&StL customarily gave to the Atchison, Topeka & Santa Fe at Nemo (near Monmouth), Illinois.[30]

Although the Wabash did not establish "piggyback" freight service—hauling loaded truck trailers on flatcars—like the financially strapped Chicago Great Western and the New York, New Haven & Hartford successfully did in the 1930s, it showed a willingness to innovate with intermodal shipments. In 1934, the Wabash and the Delaware, Lackawanna & Western, working with Acme Fast Freight, Inc., a major freight-forwarder, experimented with containerization. The American Car & Foundry Company constructed two prototype shockproof flatcars that each held two specially designed containers for either carload or LCL shipments. The design permitted transfer of these containers between flatcars and trucks without the use of a crane. An especially designed tractor-trailer was also part of this creative railroad-highway arrangement. Even though the concept and equipment were generally sound, regulatory problems, most of all, prevented a form of containerization that eventually became popular. The same story happened to other contemporary container experiments, including the "magic box" used for a few months in the early 1930s by the C&NW for transporting LCL goods between Chicago and Milwaukee.[31]

The ability to be frugal, hardworking and creative had limitations. The Great Depression struck at a time when nature ran through one of its most brutal cycles. The worst drought of the twentieth century struck much of the Midwest and nearly all of the Great Plains. Agriculturalists, important shippers on the Wabash, saw their crops wither in the fields, their livestock die from lack of water and eerily biblical plagues of insects ravage anything that survived the intense summer heat. The troubles began in 1934. "During the growing season, March to May [1934] the states served by the Wabash suffered greatly from drought conditions, the rainfall ranging from 37% of normal in Iowa to 62% of normal in Michigan," reported the company in 1935. "The lack of moisture continued through June and July with abnormally high temperatures, greatly reducing production of farm products in this territory." Conditions in 1935, unfortunately, failed to improve much, and 1936 would be the worst year of the "dirty thirties."[32]

The Wabash could not do much to combat the lack of rain and extreme heat, but it did respond. For one, the company reduced charges for the transportation of animal feed and distressed livestock. And it attempted to conserve water as best as possible, most of all in drought-ravaged Moberly. When Rothwell Park Lake dropped to alarmingly low levels in the summer of 1934, the division superintendent instructed train crews to have their locomotives take on water at other locations, if possible. This sagacious policy immediately saved about 300,000 gallons daily. But the situation at the lake worsened, and the city of Moberly, even though it had a contract to provide water to the railroad, cut off the supply, forcing a daily water train to operate to and from Brunswick, Missouri, where this precious liquid was pumped from the Grand River into a string of tank cars. In time, repeated rains and a new reservoir ended the water crisis in Moberly.[33]

WHEELER INVESTIGATION

Protected by the bankruptcy court, helped by money-saving and revenue-generating responses, and assisted by various amounts of federal aid, the Wabash Railway showed considerable aplomb during the worst economic downswing of the twentieth century. The company's operating income generally mirrored the national gyrations during this time of severe economic stress.

1929: $63,796,583	1934: $33,569,925
1930: $52,247,176	1935 $41,492,890
1931: $41,525,531	1936: $46,428,262
1932: $32,466,114	1937: $46,133,734
1933: $31,691,927	1938: $40,472,327[34]

Reflecting the larger economic picture, the roughest years for the American economy occurred immediately before the New Deal brought about increased consumer confidence and spending. But then the upward figures reversed in the midst of the severe and unexpected "Roosevelt Recession" of 1937–1938, the worst decline since 1933. Between October 1937 and May 1938, durable goods output sank by more than half, industrial production dropped by approximately one-third and business profits plummeted by about three-quarters. Not surprisingly, many Americans, especially those on the political right and left, believed that hard times would never end.[35]

With the economy still in distress, considerable antibusiness feelings existed on both Main Street and on Pennsylvania Avenue in Washington, D.C. Although Roosevelt had "saved" American capitalism, strong sentiments prevailed within the New Deal camp to bring about meaningful reforms in addition to obvious needs for relief and recovery. Significant legislative triumphs followed. Chief among these new regulatory safeguards was the Securities and Exchange Act of 1934, which added the Securities Exchange Commission to the galaxy of federal agencies, and later the Public Utilities Holding Company Act of 1935, which required all public-utility holding companies to register and file specific information on their corporate organizations. Despite these changes, some liberal reformers believed that even more regulation was essential; the nationalization of basic industries might even become a goal.[36]

Spearheading the drive to rein in big business was a longtime crusader against large corporate interests, Burton K. Wheeler, a Democratic U.S. Senator from Montana. The running mate of presidential hopeful Robert M. La Follette, Sr., on the insurgent Progressive Party ticket of 1924, Wheeler espoused the "common man" views of the once-dominant William Jennings Bryan wing of his party. Wheeler resented "big biz" and defended what he thought were the aspirations of small agriculturalists and entrepreneurs. One means of obtaining his kind of America was through enforcement and the enhancement of antitrust codes. Although the "New Freedom" program of the first Wilson administration promoted business competition, mostly through preventative rather than punitive antitrust policies, serious weaknesses, Wheeler believed, still remained. Moreover, the Montana progressive was not opposed to outright government ownership.[37]

Wall Street did not care for the combative and acerbic Wheeler, but he became a darling to countless workers, farmers, independent business people and self-employed professionals. In Congress he was respected, even greatly admired, as one of the valiant old crusaders for progressivism and consumer rights. Included among his devotees was the junior U.S. Senator from Missouri,

U.S. Senator Harry S Truman of Missouri, a protégé of Senator Burton K. Wheeler of Montana, did much to make the "Wheeler Committee" probe of railroad finance a national sensation, much to the chagrin of Wabash management. In 1940 Senator Truman stands for a photographer at Washington Union Station in Washington, D.C. Soon he would win a bitter political contest for renomination to the Senate, aided considerably by Wabash union members throughout the state. (Harry S Truman Library)

Harry S Truman, who had long embraced a Bryanesque worldview. During Roosevelt's second term, it would be the combination of Wheeler and Truman on the Senate commerce committee that would undertake an extensive probe of the financial workings of the railroad industry.[38]

The Wheeler investigation had a prearranged agenda. An underlying belief existed that the problems that had befallen railroads beginning with the Florida East Coast, Seaboard Air Line and Wabash bankruptcies were attributable to the cupidity of corporate executives and their boards of directors and the machinations of Wall Street speculators and financiers. If these evils could be fully exposed, then corrective regulation would prevent such shortcomings in the future. Early on, Wheeler extolled the merits of more stringent rules for investments made by railroads and their subsidiaries. "Honest" investors, especially those from rural and small-town America, could rest assured that their assets would be fully protected.[39]

The primary target of the Wheeler investigation became the sprawling railroad domain assembled in the 1920s by O. P. and M. J. Van Sweringen and especially the workings of their Cleveland-based holding company, the Alleghany Corporation. By the time the probe began, shortly after the 1936 general elections, however, both brothers had died. Even so, the committee explored a variety of dimensions of the Van Sweringens' once mighty and by then largely collapsed business empire. Special attention was given to the roles played by leading investment firms involved with the brothers, particularly J. P. Morgan & Company and Kuhn, Loeb & Company. The Wheeler body also grilled members of some of the major old-line Wall Street law firms. Wheeler and Truman thought that they would be able to reveal extensive fraud and

illegalities committed repeatedly by these financiers and their lawyers.[40]

The Wabash did not escape scrutiny. There were several matters that interested the Wheeler Committee. One involved its acquisition in 1926 and 1927 of Lehigh Valley (LV) stock, then valued at $23 million, but by 1937 practically worthless. Wheeler charged that the balance sheets that were submitted to the ICC and the New York Stock Exchange did not disclose these acquisitions. Furthermore, the senator objected strenuously to the revealed practice of Williams pledging the credit of the Wabash for these stock purchases. "There is nothing in the Transportation Act, and nothing indicated by that act, that could in the slightest degree as it seems to me authorize the board of directors of a railroad company to give carte blanche to the president of the railroad to go out and buy stocks of another railroad, do it secretly, to any extent practically that he might desire." Despite this rhetorical outburst, Wheeler knew this was a common practice.[41]

Nor did Wheeler or his associates favor the practice of the Wabash carrying on its books as current assets unpaid dividends from the Ann Arbor and the NJI&I. At the end of 1930, the Ann Arbor declared a dividend of more than $1 million and the NJI&I voted $165,000 in dividends on its common stock. In the latter case, this amount represented more than four times what the railroad had earned during the calendar year. Moreover, in 1930 the Wabash with income of $3,781,000 (less the $1 million of Ann Arbor dividends, which "was so much moonshine"), paid a dividend of $3.7 million, with the PRR collecting approximately $1.5 million. These practices incorrectly suggested that the overall financial health of the Wabash was much better than it really was, "hoodwinking" causal, and even seasoned, investors. "[Although the Wabash] was on the brink of financial collapse," according to the investigation transcript, "it continued to paint on its books and in its published statements a rosy picture of corporate health." At best, the Wabash employed the bookkeeping of hope.[42]

Just as the ICC earlier had indicated its unhappiness with the handsome bonus and the 133 percent salary raise given Williams in 1930, so, too, did the Wheeler Committee raise this matter, exploring these reckless acts of compensation with considerable gusto. Again, the official suggestion was that another misrepresentation had occurred. In the minds of the investigators these payments indicated to outsiders that they were undoubtedly coming from a company that was financially robust and hardly likely to fail.[43]

As with the probe of the Alleghany Corporation and other railroads, Senators Wheeler and Truman expressed concern about investors who had acquired relatively expensive Wabash securities before the bankruptcy only to see their investments shrink markedly in value. In 1931, company bonds, which sold at highs of between $90 and $105, during the next two years fell to lows of between $2 and $43. Stocks followed a similar precipitous decline: highs in 1931 ranged from $26 to $51, only to stand in 1933 at a dollar or less. Once more the message from the committee was clear: if the railroad had been less than straightforward about the true state of its finances in 1930 and 1931, it was doubtlessly guilty of victimizing an unsuspecting investing public. Yet the historic ups and downs of American capitalism seemed not to affect their thinking.[44]

After more than a year of public testimony and behind-the-scenes investigations, the Wheeler probe petered out in March 1938. Several committee recommendations would eventually be incorporated into the Transportation Act of 1940 (Wheeler-Lea Act), but the Wabash paid no type of penalty, except for some short-term negative

press coverage. The most scathing report about the company appeared in the ultraliberal *New Republic* magazine, which, fortunately for the Wabash's image, had only limited circulation in the Midwest.[45]

At times Senators Wheeler and Truman made mountains out of molehills. The extraordinary compensation to Williams, for instance, while foolish in hindsight, was the prerogative of the board of directors and entirely legal. Admittedly, several major carriers had been poorly managed in the 1920s, and it was undeniable that millions of dollars had been misused on ill-advised buyouts and takeovers. Still, it was hardly a crime to have failed to anticipate the Great Depression. Moreover, the Transportation Act of 1920 had urged voluntary consolidations, and carriers such as the Delaware & Hudson, PRR and Wabash wanted to make certain that they were protected and had the most advantageous corporate partners. "In truth, Truman and Wheeler had uncovered little in the way of criminal activity and had carefully skirted the difficult, politically unrewarding task of addressing the more fundamental problems of the nation's rail system," concluded Truman scholar Alonzo L. Hamby. "In the course of the exercise, they may have libeled a few targets just as surely as Joe [Senator Joseph] McCarthy would libel another type of scapegoat a decade-and-a-half later."[46]

REORGANIZATION

Those observers who early on believed that the Wabash Railway could be speedily reorganized were badly mistaken. They failed to anticipate a host of internal and external problems, and a replacement corporation would not make its debut for more than a decade. Part of the delay involved the federal bankruptcy code. The Wabash sought court protection more than a year *before*

Congress significantly altered the law. The modified measure ended the practice of having a court-appointed receiver or receivers who ultimately sold the property, usually to a group of bondholders. Under Section 77 of the Federal Bankruptcy Act of 1933, a protected carrier operated under the aegis of one or more trustees that the federal court and the ICC carefully supervised. Therefore, for the first time regulators played an active and positive role. "In the entire history of the ICC probably nothing that the Commission undertook has met with such general approval as its behavior in reorganization of bankrupt carriers of the 1930s," opined transportation economist George W. Hilton. "The Commission helped bring about the reorganizations quickly and typically with conservatism concerning the railroad's future [earnings] prospects." Although his conclusions fit a number of carriers, including the C&NW, Erie and Monon, they, of course, did not directly affect the earliest casualties of hard times. Nevertheless, the ICC remained a player in these reorganizations, including that of the Wabash.[47]

Wabash coreceivers Franklin and Nicodemus and then Nicodemus and Pitcairn pushed foreword their reorganization plans. As the Wheeler investigation suggested, the PRR closely monitored what was happening. After all, it felt compelled to protect its sizable stock position in the Wabash. That in itself helps to explain why there was not an early agreement among groups representing debt and equity owners.[48]

In time, this slowness annoyed the federal court. On April 19, 1937, Judge Davis directed the security holders, through their respective representatives, to formulate and within sixty days provide a plan of reorganization, but he granted them a thirty-day grace period. (Davis subsequently extended the due date until July 12.) Finally, two days late, on July 14, 1937, Nicodemus and Pit-cairn, who had been working with investor groups, filed the basic documents. That same day, Davis directed them to proceed with the plan and to organize a new company. On October 2, 1937, the receivers, for tax purposes, incorporated in Ohio the Wabash *Railroad* Company.[49]

As everyone expected, the core of the July 1937 plan for reorganization called for a sizeable reduction in capitalization. The current level of $318,930,000 would be slashed to $187,439,000, with the expectation that the replacement company could handily manage interest payments, even if operating income slumped. A significant feature of the proposal called for an assessment of $7 a share on the three classes of existing stock, preferred A, preferred B and common. In return equity holders would receive $7 par value of new income 4.5 percent bonds, and one share, a half share and one-third share, respectively, of new common. The plan also called for the absorption of the Ann Arbor, which would become another "fallen flag" railroad. From the perspective of the PRR, the proposal would come at a price, costing its subsidiary, the Pennsylvania Company, which held the Wabash securities, approximately $4,730,600 to meet the assessment. Specifically, the Pennsylvania Company owned 312,900 shares of Wabash preferred A and 362,900 shares of its common.[50]

But the July 1937 plan was hardly carved in stone. On January 14, 1938, the receivers gave Judge Davis a modified proposal. Some adjustments to the overall capitalization were made, and it was decided for financial reasons that the Ann Arbor would remain a wholly-owned subsidiary. Then on March 16, the Wabash *Railroad* Company applied to the ICC for authority to issue the new securities and otherwise to carry into effect the provisions of the plan. The recession, which continued to plague the nation, however, resulted in a major earnings slump.

"Owing to changed conditions," the receivers decided to again revise their reorganization plan. They therefore asked the ICC for dismissal of their proposal, and on October 22, 1938, their request was granted "without prejudice."[51]

It would be more than a year before the reorganization advanced significantly. Additional negotiations took place between various financial interests, including the PRR. On July 3, 1940, another version went to Judge Davis. After more fine-tuning, the plan proceeded to the ICC, where public hearings were held on December 16–17, 1940. The proposal was modified further to meet certain objections, and the so-called final plan, dated March 15, 1941, went back to the ICC and hearings resumed on April 11.[52]

The major rub in this deliberative process involved the PRR. The company told the ICC that it "cannot support the plan since . . . [it] does not recognize adequately the existing value in the common and preferred stock owned by it and other stockholders." The PRR argued that the strong upturn in the national economy, spawned by the outbreak of World War II in September 1939, had altered the picture. The Wabash, of course, benefited from the heightened industrial activities. Even though the PRR expressed publicly its willingness to compromise, it became apparent that it would accept an impasse before permitting its financial interests to be severely damaged. The specific suggestions that the PRR had in mind for revision, however, did not please the principal bondholders. "From the information at hand, it would appear that the plan as proposed does not have sufficient support from all classes of creditors and stockholders to warrant the belief that the present plan can be consummated," lamented Oliver Sweet, ICC finance director, in mid-February 1941. "Nearly two months have elapsed since the hearing was adjourned and we are anxious to dispose of the application without unnecessary delay."[53]

Shortly before the ICC restarted its hearings on the nearly decade-long reorganization process, the PRR made its position clear. The railroad (along with the Pennsylvania Company) asked authority to purchase all of the common stock issued or such number of shares as would give it at least half of the total capital stock. In no way did the PRR want to lose control of what it considered to be a strategic and ever-more-valuable property.[54]

The PRR was not the only railroad that thought the Wabash of great worth. Shortly after the PRR made its application to the ICC for control, the New York Central (NYC) and its subsidiary Pittsburgh & Lake Erie raised objections. Their representatives contended that, "if the present application were granted, there would be created a Pennsylvania Railroad system of such overwhelming size and power as to overshadow all other railroad systems in Eastern territory." The NYC worried not only about direct control of the Wabash but also about the stock holdings of both the PRR and Wabash in the LV and the domination by the Wabash of the Ann Arbor. Moreover, the NYC did not care for the substantial holdings that the PRR held in the Boston & Maine; New York, New Haven & Hartford (New Haven); Norfolk & Western and several other carriers.[55]

Fortunately for Wabash reorganization prospects, the NYC and PRR did not come to blows. Opposition from the NYC "vanished into thin air" when formal hearings began at the ICC on June 12, 1941. The major compromise that attorneys from the contending carriers worked out involved the PRR placing its New Haven and LV holdings in a trust arrangement and "shares of stock of the Lehigh Valley owned by the Wabash which will become part of the assets of the reorganized Wabash upon consummation of the re-

While bankers, officials, regulators and others hammered out the Wabash reorganization, the company continued to upgrade its operations. This included keeping locomotive engineers properly trained. This 1939 photograph shows an "Engineers' School of Instruction Car" that traveled throughout the system. (Western Historical Manuscript Coll.)

organization are [to be] placed under a trust agreement." In practice, a trustee would vote these securities completely free from the influence of the PRR. Such roads as the NYC also approved the condition made by the ICC that the PRR maintain joint rates, joint routes, interchange points and "channels of trade through gateways of the Wabash" that had existed prior to PRR control.[56]

On August 7, 1941, good news for the Wabash and also for the PRR came from the ICC. It tentatively approved a plan of reorga-

nization for the Wabash and at the same time authorized the PRR to acquire stock control of the reorganized company. By this time, the reorganization proposal called for capitalization of $192,647,795 with fixed charges of $2,558,418, a realistic proposition. As for PRR domination of the Wabash, the ICC commented: "The lines of the Wabash are naturally complementary to those of the Pennsylvania and together form a direct route from Kansas City to the Eastern seaboard, avoiding the congested terminal areas of St. Louis and Chicago." Added the commission, "Such a route under a coordinated arrangement is of particular importance at the present time. The control sought also will be desirable from the standpoint of an amalgamation of weak to strong roads."[57]

The PRR would bring about this control through a complicated stock-purchase scheme. Because the reorganization plan did not entitle Wabash stockholders to new securities, the entire stock of the new company, which amounted to 598,186 shares, would be deposited in an escrow account with the Bank of Manhattan in New York

City. Those debt holders eligible for this stock would withdraw their allowed number. Then all remaining securities would be subject to sale at $12.75 a share to holders of the preferred A and common stock, in that order of priority. The PRR did not have to fret about not obtaining control under this scheme: "Large holders of refunding and general mortgage bonds, to whom the stock will go, have signified their intention of selling their stock to the Pennsylvania." When finally tabulated, the cost of the Wabash securities to the PRR reached approximately $6 million, which in itself was a reasonable

On December 1, 1941, the Wabash Railway Company was sold to the Wabash Railroad Company in a largely ceremonial event at the Wabash Fruit Auction House, located at Second and Carr streets in St. Louis. Several Wabash officials occupy the front row: (left to right) Norman B. Pitcairn, coreceiver; Tom K. Smith, one of the four reorganization managers; Frank C. Nicodemus, Jr., coreceiver; and Arthur K. Atkinson, secretary to the reorganization managers and treasurer for the receivers. (Western Historical Manuscript Coll.)

amount for protecting a prebankruptcy investment of more than $60 million.[58]

In September 1941, the final roadblock in this tortuous process of reorganization was overcome. Judge Davis endorsed what the ICC had approved. Participation by the PRR, he argued, was an integral part of the "plan underlying the plan" of reorganization. And Judge Davis seemed satisfied with the chain of events. The reduction of capitalization and fixed costs pleased him, and the process, albeit slow, had worked out well. "It was an evolution of negotiations carried on over a period of four years by representatives of all classes of security holders." Later, on December 15, 1941, Judge Davis approved the final sale of the bankrupt property to its new owners that followed the ritualized selling of the property to the reorganization managers on December 1. Then at the stroke of midnight, January 1, 1942, the Wabash Railroad Company joined the corporate world.[59]

A new Wabash required a new president. The first annual meeting of the company brought the unanimous election of Norman Pitcairn, who since 1933 had served as co-receiver. Unlike the Williams's salary fiasco, Pitcairn would receive an annual compensation of $50,000, comparable to what other Class I railroad chief executives earned. His colleague, Frank Nicodemus, who had been coreceiver from the start of the bankruptcy, gladly assumed the position of general counsel. Yet, unlike Nicodemous, Pitcairn was not generally well liked by his subordinates. They considered him to be "stern" and complained that "he would always lord it over the Wabash men that he was from the Pennsy." Nevertheless, the mood at the Wabash was universally bullish. In addition to a favorable restructuring, net income for the first quarter of 1942 reached $1,067,006 as compared to $477,491 for the same quarter in 1941. Wartime traffic augured well for the "good ole Wabash."[60]

WORLD WAR II

In the first months of 1942 the Pitcairn management team had no way of knowing how world turmoil would tax the Wabash. But following the surprise Japanese attack on Pearl Harbor on December 7, 1941, and the rapid declaration of war against Japan, Germany and Italy, the United States expanded its military forces, industrial production and everything else that would help to ensure total victory for the Allies over their aggressive and vicious enemies. Railroads would play a pivotal role in winning World War II, and the Wabash would be an important cog in the wartime transportation machine. "Keeping 'em rolling for Victory" became the universal slogan.

Just as in World War I, this grave emergency meant that selfish, competitive objectives had to be subordinated to the national interest. Also paralleling the earlier conflict, the federal government became intimately involved in wartime railroading. Although federalization had taken place in 1917, railroads during World War II remained in private hands. Despite this difference, the Office of Defense Transportation (ODT), headed by ICC Chairman Joseph B. Eastman, closely supervised railroad operations. A host of ODT "service orders," which required the heavier loading of equipment, conservation of rolling stock and limitations on civilian travel, contributed to the efficient movement of military personnel, material and supplies around the country and in much greater volume and with less confusion than during the Great War. Fighting enemies on two fronts, necessitating use of both Atlantic and Pacific ports, helped with the flow of freight and passenger equipment.[61]

The work of the ODT and the unstinting cooperation of carriers, shippers and the armed services allowed records to be set in transportation of goods and people. Freight traffic, measured in ton-miles, skyrocketed from 373 billion in 1940 to 737 billion in 1944, a figure that would not be equaled until 1966. Passenger volume, expressed in revenue passenger miles, soared from 23 billion to 95 billion, a peak figure that would never again be equaled and was almost twice the total of the previous record set in 1920. Moreover, railroads transported 83 percent of the increase in *all* traffic between 1941 and 1944, and they moved 91 percent of all military freight and 98 percent of all military personnel.[62]

Like nearly every Class I carrier, the Wabash experienced an unprecedented increase in its freight and passenger business. Revenue freight climbed from 21,992,696 tons in 1941 to 31,817,862 tons in 1943 and stood at 29,502,898 tons in 1945. The number of passengers carried in 1941 totaled 803,094 and peaked three years later, at 2,326,194. The last year of the war, 1945, would be the second busiest ever, with 2,169,025 passengers. Not only did military travelers take Wabash trains, but so did civilians. These passengers, many of whom had forgotten about railroad timetables and their local depots, returned in droves because of severe rationing of gasoline, tires, batteries and other products necessary for maintaining and operating automobiles and commercial buses. Moreover, Uncle Sam demanded a mandatory highway speed limit of thirty-five miles per hour. It quickly became clear that the nation could not afford to build a war economy on top of a consumer economy.[63]

Passenger services provided by scores of daily Wabash trains marked the years of the war for many riders, especially those in uniform. For the rest of their lives, they remembered these travel experiences and the events associated with them. "I enlisted in the W.A.A.C. [Women's Army Auxiliary Corps] and was sworn in on July 13, 1943," recalled St. Louis resident Rose Roelke in 1985. "I was

then called to active duty on Aug. 18, 1943. Between the time I enlisted and the date of active duty, the W.A.A.C. was changed to the W.A.C. [Women's Army Corps] so we all had to be sworn in again. They had a special swearing in ceremony for our group at the [St. Louis] Union Station before we left for Basic Training at Fort Des Moines, Iowa. This was done on the evening of Aug. 17, 1943 before we boarded the regular overnight Wabash train [to Des Moines]."[64]

When hostilities ended in August 1945, Staff Sergeant Robert Williams was stationed in the Philippines. His fondest dream was to return home by Christmas Eve to Decatur, Illinois, 6,000 miles away. It would be a challenge but there was hope, for by December he was on American soil. Then luckily, late in the afternoon of December 24, the army finally mustered him out at Jefferson Barracks south of St. Louis. By the time his bus arrived at Union Station, Williams knew that it was too late to catch the *Detroit Limited,* No. 2 or "Big Two" as it was frequently called. Because he was familiar with *The Midnight,* he realized that that train could deliver him to Decatur early on Christmas morning, the best that he could expect. But when Williams finally reached the busy ticket window with his military travel voucher, the agent informed him that No. 2 had not yet departed, likely held for connecting passengers and mail. He was overjoyed; he would be home in time for the cherished family gift-giving on Christmas Eve. After Williams disembarked at his hometown station, he had these lasting thoughts: "Number Two would soon head out and disappear into the darkness of East Decatur yard. It had 375 miles to go, and its marker lights would fade this night as it bore other passengers to happy reunions like the one it had made possible for me. Those marker lights would never fade from my memory, though."[65]

On July 7, 1946, John F. Humiston, an award-winning photographer of Midwestern railroads, caught troop train Extra No. 7441 speeding over the Grand Trunk Western crossing at Ashburn, Illinois. The flapping white flags on the locomotive attest to its "extra" status. (John F. Humiston photograph)

The Wabash family enthusiastically embraced the war effort. Pearl Harbor stunned Americans, and it created a unity that had been lacking for years, even during World War I. Management urged every employee to buy war bonds, and thousands complied. When 100 percent of the switchmen on the Moberly Division made such a commitment, it publicized their patriotic achievement. The board of directors also invested, purchasing hundreds of thousands of dollars of these securities. Beginning in 1942, the Wabash acquired Canadian war bonds, subscribing $50,000 for the Dominion of Canada Third Victory Loan; $50,000 for the Fourth Victory Loan and $50,000 for the Fifth Victory Loan. Similarly, the board do-

nated generously to the National Red Cross War Fund and to the National War Fund, Inc., which supported the United Service Organizations (USO). In large Wabash stations and terminals, the USO provided assistance to traveling military personnel and their families. The railroad also gave to local patriotic causes. In November 1943, for example, it added $500 to the Randolph County (Moberly) War Chest Fund.[66]

The Wabash responded to the war in other ways. Throughout the conflict it took out public-spirited advertisements in on-line daily newspapers declaring: "SERVICE FOR VICTORY KNOWS NO SUNSET ON THE WABASH. Sunset means the dawn of day for many a Wabash train crew, for Wabash Service for Victory goes 'round the clock. Every few minutes, a Wabash train starts its swift journey—carrying troops or civilians in comfort and safety or delivering essential materials where and when they're needed. Every Wabash employee puts his best efforts into Service for Victory." And more modest activities also encouraged patriotism. One took place in Moberly in 1944 when railroad workers proudly installed a wooden sign near the station that proclaimed that Lt. General Omar N. Bradley (a former short-term employee who admitted that he "held only two jobs: Wabash and U.S. Army") was a local boy. Wabash families, with company backing, also pitched in on the home front, ranging from collecting scrap metal and milkweed pods (for life preservers) along rights-of-way to providing refreshments and good cheer for troops at various station stops.[67]

The Wabash received considerable attention and praise for its military railway-training program. In early 1943 the federal government requested that company personnel assist hundreds of soldiers who needed to learn about a variety of railroad operations. Officials made available experienced employees and arranged accommodations for the men in uniform. By 1945, approximately 500 military personnel had received this practical instruction. The program apparently worked well. In September 1944, the commanding officer of the 741st Railway Operating Battalion told Pitcairn that "the successful completion of this training is in a great measure due to the splendid cooperation received from officers and employees of the Wabash Railroad Company." Management beamed. "The Wabash officers and employees have deemed it not only a duty but a privilege to make this further contribution to the war effort."[68]

Although the war greatly complicated domestic transportation, the Wabash coped mightily with the challenges created by global conflict. Personnel, particularly the most skilled, were in short supply as the draft and enlistments drained the workforce, especially in the shops and terminals, station service and track maintenance. As of March 1, 1946, 2,916 employees had entered the armed forces; a significant number for a company that had an average workforce of about 12,000. Thirty-one of these men made the supreme sacrifice for their country. Fortunately for the railroad, some veteran employees decided not to retire and served "for the duration." Management sought to find replacements, placing such newspaper advertisements as this one: "Wanted—Males—Railroad carpenters, carpenter helpers, extra gang laborers, machinists, boilermakers, telegraph operators. Steady Work, good pay." High school–age youth, ineligible for the draft, were eagerly sought for a variety of tasks. Unlike some Midwestern carriers, the Wabash did not turn extensively to what it considered to be nontraditional workers, including women, people of color and Hispanics.[69]

The Wabash also confronted material shortages, government bureaucracy, the surge in traffic and higher taxes. One illustration involved the sale to subsidiary Ann Arbor in July 1942 of two miles of ninety-pound relay rail to replace worn-out eighty-five-pound rail near Lulu, Michigan. To complete this transaction, the War Production Board (WPB), which had assumed control of all second-hand rail, needed to give its approval. Ultimately the director of industry operations of the WPB agreed, but with the stipulation that the Ann Arbor make available "90% of the rail released" to other potential users and again with WPB sanction.[70]

Getting the "tonnage over the road" became a top priority. One response came in mid-1943 when management decided to convert its five, three-cylinder Mikado (2-8-2) freight locomotives into two-cylinder Hudsons (4-6-4). The nontraditional design had not worked especially well for freight handling. "They were not adaptable to heavy freight service at the speeds now required." Nevertheless, the Wabash could not ignore this potentially beneficial power. "In order to expedite the movement of troop trains and other heavy passenger trains due to increased transportation of army and navy personnel traveling in the line of duty or on furlough or leave," explained Pitcairn to the board, "this Company is converting five Mikado freight locomotives into passenger locomotives, at an estimated cost of $177,105." Employees at the Decatur shops worked with dispatch, and by September 1943 the first of these "P-1" class engines entered revenue service. About the same time, the company also spent nearly $100,000 to install thirty-five miles of manual block-remote control signals between Decatur (Mercer Street) and Springfield (Starnes Street) and made other signaling (including centralized traffic control) and track improvements "to insure the safe and speedy operation of trains [carrying] . . . troops and war materials."[71]

During the war, employees were mindful of security and safety. In the early months, workers were told to watch for acts of possible terrorism, and throughout the war years management stressed "SAFETY ALWAYS," emphasizing that being alert for danger was a patriotic service. Nevertheless, in August 1942 one of the worst accidents in memory took place about a mile and a half west of Warrenton, Missouri. A maintenance-of-way crew, consisting of a white foreman and nine African American laborers, was working on the roadbed with air compressors and apparently did not hear an approaching passenger train, which was running about forty minutes late. "The train, rounding a bend, smashed into the section gang, hurling bodies and equipment along the right of way," reported the *St. Louis Post-Dispatch*. "Nine of the men were killed [instantly and] one lived about 20 minutes."[72]

The horrendous accident near Warrenton shocked the Wabash family, yet the railroad pushed ahead with its business. Officials in

On May 14, 1944, during the busiest year of the war, railfan Robert J. Foster found a 4-6-4 Hudson in St. Louis, Missouri. Three months earlier Decatur shop workers had rebuilt No. 2602, a 2-8-2 Mikado, into this Class P-1 locomotive. No. 702's snappy smoke lifters are apparent. (Author's Coll.)

The gawky Motor No. 4001 is caught by an unknown photographer on an unknown date. The motor train is probably standing in the Springfield, Illinois, station on its run from Hannibal, Missouri, to Decatur, Illinois. (Gary Roe Coll.)

St. Louis continually worried about equipment to meet wartime needs. Although the company could rebuild steam engines, it could not expect to begin replacing its existing fleet of motive power with the newly introduced and widely acclaimed diesel-electric locomotives. Major dieselization would have to wait until after V-E and V-J days. Before Pearl Harbor, the company had acquired a few diesel-electric switch engines, and management was pleased with their performance. The earliest arrivals came in 1939 and were assigned to yard operations in Chicago, Moberly and St. Thomas, Ontario. One was No. 51, a forty-four-ton 350-horsepower product from General Electric (GE). This siderod switcher, which acquired the affectionate name of "Tillie the Toiler," performed so well that it remained on the ros-

ter for twenty-two years. Also purchased in 1939 was a 600-horsepower switcher from the American Locomotive Company (Alco), No. 100, that shunted cars until its retirement in 1966. The Wabash also acquired three more 600-horsepower switchers (Nos. 101, 102 and 103), built by Electro-Motive Corporation rather than by Alco or GE. They stayed active until the early 1960s. An additional twenty-three diesels, all switchers, were purchased from several different manufacturers between 1940 and 1945, and they had long, productive lives.[73]

The diesels, which appeared in various yards during the war era, were not the first internal-combustion equipment owned by the Wabash. Since 1926 it had operated two gasoline-electric passenger units (called "motors" by Wabash personnel), built by Electro-

Motive Corporation. Traditionally these "doodle bugs" had been assigned to main or secondary mainline service, including the runs between Brunswick and Maryville, Missouri, and Decatur and Hannibal. Although the company saved on crew costs (there was no fireman), breakdown rates by these motors were annoyingly high, and at times they struggled to pull more than a single heavyweight coach. By the outbreak of the war, this equipment might rest on sidetracks, but because of wartime scarcities, the Wabash creatively recycled one of them. In 1943, the Decatur shops converted No. 4000, which had been out of regular service since 1939, into a maintenance-of-way "family car" to house section laborers and their families. This type of rolling stock was needed in "the smaller towns along the line where neither housing facilities nor labor are available due to present conditions."[74]

During World War II the Wabash continued its efforts to amputate money-losing appendages. Although the demand for railroad freight services had spiked upward, other carriers might serve customers. Truck service was an option, but fuel, tires and parts were rationed or difficult, if not impossible, to obtain. During 1942, the company finally got the right to scrap the fifteen-mile Glasgow branch, and its rails and fastenings "would be made into armaments." In July 1942, it sought to abandon the remaining portion of the old Altamont-Effingham branch, the twenty-three miles between Bement and Sullivan, Illinois. "The revenue is very light and is not sufficient to justify its continued operation." But howls from shippers and regulatory restraints halted abandonment, and this trackage remained in operation for years. A similar problem occurred with the 4.83-mile Stroh branch in Indiana. When the cement plant in Stroh closed in October 1941, car loadings plummeted from 1,191 to 132 for the first six months of 1942. The

company sought permission to abandon, but it would not be until March 1945 that work crews could dismantle this stub on the Chicago-Montpelier line. In the Stroh case, retention of rail service was considered vital for most of the war.[75]

During World War II, the Wabash finally took total possession of the 69.75-mile Hannibal-Moberly line. Under terms of the lease negotiated in 1922 with the Missouri-Kansas-Texas (Katy), the Wabash had the option of outright purchase for $2.4 million. (The Katy stopped running its trains over the trackage in 1923.) In 1943, the Wabash exercised its contractual prerogative and on December 23, 1944, received the deed. "This line is an important link in the Wabash System for which there appears to be no satisfactory alternative route," an understatement, indeed, that Pitcairn told board members. David P. Morgan, editor of *Trains*, a few years later called the move "indubitably the best bargain Wabash ever closed."[76]

Although the World War II era created enormous traffic for the Wabash and America's railroads, there were managerial concerns. Rail workers nationally grew restive because of the effects of a growing and widespread wage-price squeeze, and in early 1943 they demanded substantial pay increases. A settlement was not forthcoming, and the brotherhoods threatened to strike. The Roosevelt Administration intervened and briefly nationalized (in name only) the carriers, forcing workers to remain at their jobs. The federal government rightly argued that "continuous operation of some transportation systems was threatened by strikes," something that the war effort could not tolerate. In January 1944, a wage settlement was reached and labor peace returned. This accord increased operating costs for carriers and ironically came at a time when the ICC steadfastly blocked any freight-rate hikes, fearing that they would fuel the fires of inflation.[77]

At the end of World War II, No. 670, a high-stepping 4-6-2 Pacific, heads a passenger train out of Fort Street Union Station in Detroit. This magnificent piece of motive power, built by Baldwin in 1912, saw decades of assignments on the Wabash, finally being scrapped in 1953. (Author's Coll.)

Still, the bottom line for the Wabash looked acceptable, though earnings reflected wages increases, freight-rate controls and other increased costs. In 1942 the company posted a net income of $6,826,791, which in 1943 rose to $8,758,574, although a year later it dropped to $6,518,154 and slid again in 1945 to $5,966,722. Reflecting the black ink on the ledger sheets, the Wabash began paying dividends on its stock: $4.50 on preferred and $1.00 on common stock. The dollar rate for the latter remained until 1947, when it was doubled.[78]

The new Pitcairn administration appeared to function well, which was certainly the feeling among board members. "That the contrast between our very fine Directors' meetings of today and those in earlier administrations is most striking," reflected Allen P. Green, founder and president of the A. P. Green Fire Brick Company in Mexico, Missouri, in 1943. "In the past the trend of meetings was formal and the information as to the condition of the property, its operating results and other factors was at times meager; that today the Board through the written record in the individual Directors' books not only of the agenda of the meeting and the pertinent facts of the railroad's condition and operation is fully informed and is put in possession of valuable and illuminating data; that as the meeting progresses the officers meticulously explain and give the background of the matters presented for action by the Board."[79]

With total victory over the Axis powers by August 1945, America found strength in the hope that this time a better world would emerge from the battlefields. The Wabash Railroad also appeared poised for a bright future. The feeling of honesty, cooperation and confidence implied in the commentary of veteran board member Green would continue. There would be a "New Wabash."

The New Wabash

POSTWAR REVIVAL

As the national economy moved steadily from the production of guns to that of butter, a spirit of optimism flourished on the Wabash Railroad. The pent-up demand for consumer goods, scarce or unobtainable during the war, stimulated manufacturing, especially in the smokestack factory centers of the Midwest. The recently launched administration of Norman Pitcairn expected that the company would easily adjust to a peacetime environment. In March 1947, Pitcairn reported to stockholders that, in the latter part of 1945 and throughout 1946, hundreds of employees who had served in the armed forces or had taken special wartime assignments had returned to their former posts and "the transition to a peacetime basis is being accomplished rapidly." Investors likewise felt encouraged. Knowledgeable observers thought that Pitcairn possessed good business instincts and that he had a "controlling grasp of affairs." The reduction of the outstanding debt by more than $30 million, or approximately 30 percent, between January 1942 and December 1946 rightly impressed securities analysts.[1]

On the first day of service for the *City of Kansas City,* the dining car staff assembled for a group photograph. These men, some of whom had had long careers with the Wabash, provided the public with excellent food and service, and they did much to make this train a popular travel option between St. Louis and Kansas City. (Author's Coll.)

Despite these successes, management avoided taking a Pollyannaish worldview. It realized that labor and material costs, along with state and federal taxes, were rising and that it was difficult to win regulatory approval, most of all from the Interstate Commerce Commission (ICC), for rate increases and line abandonments. "The volume of revenue traffic for 1946 was the greatest moved by the Company or its predecessor during any peacetime year," remarked Pitcairn in March 1947. "However, due to increased wages and higher costs of fuel, materials and supplies, the relative spread between operating expenses and operating revenues was the smallest since 1932."[2]

The Wabash also confronted formidable competition from motorized vehicles, especially trucks. The ICC had regulated bus lines and motor carriers since the mid-1930s, but now these vehicles posed more challenges because of the end of fuel, tire and other rationing. Truck manufacturers had resumed production of larger, more powerful and better-engineered highway equipment. Also in the postwar years, road construction accelerated. By the mid-1950s, the Ohio and Indiana Turnpikes and hundreds of miles of other high-speed roadways were either under construction or completed. Highway interests, the so-called road gang, one of the most powerful pressure groups in the nation, accelerated their lobbying efforts. In 1956, they realized their greatest triumph with the enactment of the National Defense Highway Act, which would create a high-speed, limited-access interstate highway network of more than 40,000 miles. These roads not only attracted more trucks but also spurred on the purchase and heavy use of private automobiles. Americans' love affair with the car now became an obsession. And state-of-the-art roadways helped the bus industry. Even though failing to retain their war-era load levels, bus firms increased their intercity speeds and began to operate competitive express runs between major cities.[3]

The Wabash also began to encounter meaningful competition for long-distance passengers, most of all business travelers. Several regional and interregional carriers, including American Airlines, Chicago & Southern Air Lines, Ozark Air Lines, Trans World Airline (TWA) and United Airlines, annually siphoned off a growing number of patrons. Following World War II, the airline industry acquired increased capacity and longer range aircraft. In 1946 TWA, for example, flew Lockheed Constellations (51 passengers) and Boeing Stratoliners (38 passengers) along with older Douglas Skyliners (21 passengers). Moreover, creative airline marketing departments introduced a popular two-class fare structure (first-class and tourist), and Chicago & Southern and some others also offered attractive "Family Fare Plans."[4]

Though hardly a moneymaking machine, the Wabash prospered throughout the immediate postwar period, before it felt the real sting of highway competition. Net income burgeoned from $3,674,299 in 1946 to $7,393,274 in 1947 and rose impressively to $10,997,653 in 1948. The short-lived Recession of 1949, however, forced net income down to $5,693,237, but the company continued to pay its $4.50 dividend on each share of preferred stock, and in that year declared a $1.50 dividend for every share of common.[5]

Positive feelings continued after a top leadership change on April 17, 1947. Pitcairn, who had recently turned sixty-five, left the president's office to assume the newly created, largely ceremonial post of chairman of the board of directors. (Ten months later, Pitcairn died after a lingering illness that had baffled diagnosticians.) His successor as president was senior Wabash executive Arthur K. Atkinson, whom the board of directors had groomed to replace Pitcairn. In many ways, Atkinson was an Horatio Alger figure who rose from rags to riches by dint of hard work, determination, pluck and luck. Born on October 19, 1891, in Denver, Colorado, "Art" Atkinson lacked a college education, receiving instead business training at Denver's School of Commerce and Accounts. His first railroad position came in 1909, when he landed a job with the Denver & Rio Grande as an errand boy in the auditing department. Likely his father, who was an express man for the company, provided the needed connections. Atkinson subsequently held various clerical positions in the offices of the auditor of disbursements and the general auditor and later served as statistician, general bookkeeper, traveling accountant and special accountant. In 1920, he left the Denver-based railroad to join the United States Railroad Administration as a field accountant and then took on special accounting assignments. Two years later, Atkinson joined the Wabash as an assistant auditor and advanced rapidly, serving from 1930 to 1942 as secretary and treasurer and also becoming a director. On May 15, 1942, after the corporate reorganization, he became vice president for finance and accounting.[6]

As with any chief executive, Atkinson possessed strengths and weaknesses. No one ever doubted that he knew the business side of railroading. He fully understood the interworkings of financial matters, demonstrating publicly his considerable knowledge before the Wheeler Committee, for example. Throughout his long career with the Wabash, he labored hard and with considerable success to make it a profitable carrier. Individuals both within and outside the industry considered him to be a "good railroader" and admired his high energy level. But, much like Pitcairn, Atkinson was not particularly well liked by underlings. One observer remembered him as being "always crabby."

A confident President Arthur K. Atkinson rests on the front of a Wabash diesel locomotive. Although he possessed considerable knowledge of railroading, especially in matters of finance, he hardly endeared himself to all employees. His ego occasionally "got out of control," which hurt his relationship with subordinates. When in the early 1950s Sverre Elsmo wrote a piece of sheet music called "Riding the Wabash Road," he dedicated it to Atkinson, who "requested that his portrait be there on the cover." (Author's Coll.)

And David P. Morgan, editor of *Trains*, noted in 1950, "It is reliably rumored at Wabash's Railway Exchange Building headquarters in St. Louis that the men about President Arthur Kimmins Atkinson's office suffer from ulcers. Anyone who has witnessed this 58-year-old, Colorado-born executive in action would take as much for granted." Atkinson, however, had the ability to "talk to the average employee and he would." He easily recalled names and seemingly enjoyed his contact with those outside the executive suite. "Some CEOs only talk to their next level of officers, but not Atkinson."[7]

Atkinson's rise to the presidency of a major American railroad only fueled his large ego. He was, without a doubt, a publicity hound. For years he had his private secretary keep scrapbooks of numerous newspaper clippings that told of his public appearances, civic awards and other accomplishments. Atkinson loved to hobnob with important individuals, especially corporate executives and high-ranking Republican Party office holders and functionaries. He also delighted in being around fellow Masons and often spoke at their events. The fraternal organization was a vital part of his life. "Next to my family and my railroad job my Masonic activities claimed the largest amount of my time." The short and stocky Atkinson drank heavily, loved cigars and relished games of poker. He also occasionally attended, "with the better people," an establishment Presbyterian church in St. Louis. He was hardly unique among his presidential peers. George F. Ashby at Union Pacific (UP), Clyde Fitzpatrick at the Chicago & North Western (C&NW) and Lucian C. Sprague at the Minneapolis & St. Louis shared similar personality characteristics.[8]

Whereas Atkinson considered himself "Mr. Wabash" and the personification of progress, the public likely thought differently. If any one thing symbolized dramatically the postwar revival of the Wabash, it was introduction of the lightweight, diesel-powered "streamliner." In the early 1930s the Chicago, Burlington & Quincy (CB&Q) and UP had pioneered these popular and profitable passenger trains. For a nation scarred by doubt and depression, streamliners represented promise for a better tomorrow. Although the Wabash lacked the financial wherewithal to follow the lead of the CB&Q, UP and several other Class I railroads, it could boast of having such equipment by the immediate postwar period. Its first streamlined (or semistreamlined) passenger train would be the *City of St. Louis,* a cooperative arrangement with the UP that would principally serve Midwestern and Western markets.[9]

Long before passengers boarded the *City of St. Louis* at St. Louis Union Station on June 2, 1946, the Wabash had regularly been improving its intercity service. Even in the dreariest prewar years, the company never forgot the paying traveler. Its upgrading of

the *Banner Blue Limited* in the mid-1930s attests to this desire to bolster or at least maintain long-distance passenger business. For many patrons, this attractive and high-speed Chicago–St. Louis service showed that the Wabash cared about the public and that, even in bankruptcy, it remained a competitive carrier.

Prewar passenger train improvements included the Wabash and Pennsylvania (PRR) "sensational new train," the *Red Bird,* between Chicago and Detroit, introduced in July 1941. "There is no Chicago-Detroit train faster than the RED BIRD." This name train would be one of six joint passenger runs that sped daily between its terminal cities via Fort Wayne and that later would be updated and powered by diesel-electric locomotives. Immediately before the war erupted, management had contemplated participating in either a through-train or through-car service between the East and West coasts. The likely partners would be the PRR and UP using the St. Louis and Kansas City gateways. These discussions continued intermittently into the early postwar years and presumably would involve streamlined, diesel-powered trains.[10]

This creative thinking about modern passenger service captured the attention of many associated with the Wabash. At the September 1943 meeting of the board of directors, brick manufacturer Allen P. Green indicated that he wanted management to consider "establishing and maintaining lightweight, streamlined passenger trains between St. Louis and Kansas City, and perhaps other points." He was troubled by the upgraded service provided by the Missouri Pacific (MOP) over its rival route. Three years before, the MOP had introduced the streamlined *Missouri River Eagle,* which served the St. Louis, Kansas City and Omaha markets and in the process increased its share from 43 to 60 percent of the St. Louis–Kansas City business. Pitcairn told Green not to fret, for he was fully "aware of the significance of this new competition," and that "a number of studies already had been made and that further studies were in progress on this subject." The general consensus at that board meeting was that "in the post-war period, conditions would be favorable for profitable operations of fast lightweight passenger trains between large cities."[11]

That would be the Wabash course of action. It wanted to make certain that its twenty-eight major daily trains kept up with the times, recognizing that during the war people overlooked most inconveniences, but sacrifices "for the duration" had ended. As Tom H. Hayes, the company's passenger traffic manager correctly observed, "Travelers today are expecting good, convenient service." There was also the strong sense that the public still wanted to have rail adventures. "People have extra money burning their pockets, people who have always wanted to travel," observed a Midwestern editor in 1945, "so off they go . . . for a train trip to some distant city."[12]

Admittedly, the *City of St. Louis* of June 1946 did not look like the contemporary stainless steel CB&Q *Zephyrs* or the sleek C&NW *400s*, but it was an attractive and mostly diesel-powered train. Initially it used UP diesels, although the agreement called for the Wabash to provide this modern motive power between Kansas City and St. Louis. But the road's first passenger diesel unit, No. 1000, an E-7A type from the Electro-Motive Division of General Motors (EMD), would not be available until August. When necessary because of delays from the West, the Wabash usually responded by assigning one of its 700-series Hudson-type steam locomotives. This conventional power, however, was hardly unattractive. "I still think that Wabash 700s were just about the most regal locomotive that I ever saw," observed

one train watcher. The equipment on the *City of St. Louis,* which featured a mixture of heavyweight and lightweight cars, including a modern six-section, six-roomette, four-double bedroom car, sported the two-tone UP gray paint scheme. Several cars had CITY OF ST. LOUIS in eye-catching silver lettering placed above their windows. Subsequently, the consist would always have diesel power and all lightweight equipment. When in the spring of 1951 the *City of St. Louis* became a through train between St. Louis and Los Angeles, its six yellow and gray train sets rivaled the best trains in North America.[13]

This cooperative relationship between the Wabash and UP predated inauguration of the *City of St. Louis.* The *Pacific Coast Limited,* an earlier train that the *City* replaced, had for some years carried through tourist sleeping cars (open section Pullmans with lavatories at the ends of cars) between St. Louis and San Francisco and also made connections for Los Angeles and Portland. But the replacement train eliminated the necessity of passenger changing cars while en route to Los Angeles, Portland or San Francisco and the old tourist sleepers were removed. "Through Sleepers and Coaches *St. Louis to Kansas City, Denver* and the *Pacific Coast* 16 hours and 15 minutes to Denver, 48 hours and 50 minutes to the West Coast," boasted the Wabash in St. Louis newspaper advertisements.[14]

The *City of St. Louis* enjoyed an immediate positive reception as the first through train from the Gateway City to the West Coast. (The MOP, however, soon offered through service to San Francisco via the Denver & Rio Grande Western and the Western Pacific.) In remarks made at the inaugural ceremonies at St. Louis Union Station, George C. Smith, president of the St. Louis Chamber of Commerce, underscored the importance of this new Wabash-UP train for the city's postwar development. "We have

On June 2, 1946, Wabash officials gathered at St. Louis Union Station to ride the inaugural St. Louis–Pacific Coast train, *City of St. Louis*. Boarding, from left to right, are President Norman B. Pitcairn; Vice President and Secretary Treasurer Arthur K. Atkinson; Vice President and General Manager George H. Sido; and nattily attired Vice President of Traffic Leo E. Clarahan. (Western Historical Manuscript Coll.)

long been aware of the fact that superior service to the West from Chicago meant the continued loss of a trade advantage, rightfully ours historically and geographically. But history and geography are not enough to insure development of or much protection to trade route or markets." Continued booster Smith: "It takes dynamic leadership in these days of uncertainty and change to insure a place in commerce. The Wabash and the Union Pacific officers are demonstrating the kind of leadership needed so badly today." St. Louis mayor A. P. Kaufmann echoed Smith's sentiments: "I am particularly pleased that this train, which should usher in a new day in railroading, was made possible by the farsighted planning and cooperation of a 'home-town' railroad—the Wabash." Everyone cheered when the mayor's wife broke a bottle of water from the Pacific Ocean and the confluence of the Missouri and Mississippi rivers on the locomotive's nose. Early on, passenger volume was good, and likely some business travelers selected St. Louis over Chicago as a stopping place or a departure point for destinations in the East because of the attractiveness and convenience of the *City of St. Louis*.[15]

There is no question that the Wabash strove to make the *City of St. Louis* a train that served the needs of the long-distance passenger. Not only were the equipment upgraded and speeds modestly increased, but over the years the Wabash sought always to make this streamliner accessible to as many riders as possible. One worry involved scheduling. In May 1950, Atkinson personally got involved, telling Arthur Stoddard, his counterpart at UP, "Together, we have spent considerable sums of money to provide excellent equipment and power for the operation of a service between St. Louis and Los Angeles, San Francisco and the North Pacific Coast cities. In the westbound direction especially, this service has met with a particularly gratifying public acceptance." Unfortunately, there had developed a serious problem with arrival time at St. Louis Union Station. "In the east bound direction the response has not been so enthusiastic, principally because the 'City of St. Louis' does not arrive here in time to connect with the Noon departures for points east of St. Louis." Stoddard and the UP passenger department did not ignore this Wabash concern. Schedule adjustments followed, and the eastbound *City*, No. 10, arrived earlier, allowing practical connections with the early afternoon trains for the East.[16]

The Wabash became fully part of the streamliner era on November 24, 1947—regular service began two days later—with introduction of its own *City of Kansas City*. Designed for daytime travel between Kansas City and St. Louis, this new train came from the St. Charles, Missouri, plant of the American Car & Foundry Company and consisted on a baggage car, baggage-mail car, diner,

On November 24, 1947, U.S. Army General Omar Bradley, the most famous former employee of the Wabash, pressed a button in his Washington, D.C., office that released a ceremonial bottle of water that christened the *City of Kansas City* on Wabash rails. (Author's Coll.)

coffee-shop coach, two coaches (or "leg-rest" cars) and an observation-parlor car. A 2,000-horsepower EMD diesel provided power. More so than the original consist of the companion *City of St. Louis,* this was a stunning train. "[It] has been designed and styled to provide an appearance of unity from locomotive to observation end," reported *Railway Age.* "Fluted aluminum sections at the eaves, the lower edge of the letter board, and the sides from belt rail to side sill run the full length of the cars, except across the doors, while the letter boards, pier panels and skirts are Wabash blue."[17]

Ever mindful of positive publicity, the Wabash staged an unusual inaugural event for the *City of Kansas City.* The formal christening of the train at Kansas City Union Station was done by remote control from Washington, D.C. General Omar Bradley, the railroad's most famous former employee, pressed a button that electronically released a ceremonial bottle that contained a mixture of waters from the Mississippi, Missouri and Grand rivers. This vessel broke as expected to the applause from a throng of joyous onlookers and perhaps a cheer or two from a live radio audience.[18]

As with the *City of St. Louis,* the *City of Kansas City* became an instant hit. The train competed effectively with the MOP's *Missouri River Eagle,* its foremost daylight rival between the two Missouri metropolises. Extensive advertising—newspapers, magazines, radio, television, billboards and printed matter—helped to fill regularly nearly all of its 205 revenue spaces. Passengers appreciated the comfort of the "Sleepy Hollow" seats, and then there was the "really sm-o-o-oth ride" that in the morning took five hours and twenty minutes westbound and in the late afternoon five hours and forty minutes eastbound. In order to maintain its popularity, the company in 1952 added a dome coach and at times made other minor upgrades.

The train also made a convenient connection at Centralia with service to Columbia and its large college-student traffic.[19]

Streamliners would not be limited to the St. Louis–Kansas City mainline. The Wabash next turned its attention to the even more competitive St. Louis–Chicago route. The company wanted to meet the challenges posed by the restructured Alton, now the Gulf, Mobile & Ohio (GM&O), and the Illinois Central (IC). The former had had historically the largest share of the passenger traffic, in part because it had the shortest route, operated the most trains, including the streamlined *Abraham Lincoln* and *Ann Rutledge,* and served such important intermediate cities as Alton, Springfield, Bloomington and Joliet. The latter dispatched three daily trains, the same as the Wabash, and offered travelers the luxury of the streamlined *Green Diamond,* although the IC had the handicap of the longest mileage. The Wabash tried to meet its rivals, however, with fast schedules and comfortably modernized, albeit nonstreamlined, equipment, but still "found itself in a difficult competitive position."[20]

The Atkinson administration took enormous pride with its answer to the St. Louis–Chicago passenger conundrum, namely, introduction of the *exclusive* dome streamliner *Blue Bird* on this 286-mile route. This luxury train, which went unpublicized until a week or so before it entered service on February 26, 1950, met the public with traditional fanfare following several days of open display at St. Louis Union Station. At 8:45 A.M. on dedication day, Lynda Atkinson, the eight-year-old granddaughter of the Wabash president, in front of a large crowd at Union Station broke a bottle of champagne against the *Blue Bird*'s dome-observation car. This Budd Company–built train cost approximately $1.5 million and consisted of a EMD 2,000-

horsepower diesel and a stainless steel and dark blue consist: combination baggage-buffet-lounge car, three dome chair cars, a diner-lounge car and a dome parlor-observation car. By scheduling the *Blue Bird* to leave St. Louis at 8:55 A.M. rather than 4:45 P.M. and to arrive at Dearborn Station in Chicago at 2:05 P.M. (fifteen minutes faster than the previously elapsed travel time) and retaining the previous departure time from the Windy City at 4:45 P.M., entering St. Louis Union Station at 10:10 P.M., the company required only a single stream-lined train instead of two sets of standard equipment that it had previously used.[21]

The *Blue Bird* was an immediate sensation. On its inaugural runs that snowy February day, railroad employees beamed. "The hearts of all Wabash railroad officialdom and crews on the new Blue Bird were filled with pride yesterday when they took the maiden round trip spin on their little red wagon between St. Louis and Chicago, both ways on time," commented Bruce Kipp, a

The Atkinson administration took enormous pride with its *Blue Bird,* which in February 1950 entered the competitive market between Chicago and St. Louis. This $1.5 million streamliner offered a domed observation parlor car for which the Pullman Company provided the staff. (Author's Coll.)

staff writer for the *Decatur Review.* Not long after the first trip, a conductor in some awe, told a reporter, "They came just for the ride," referring to a group of passengers who boarded the streamliner in Chicago for Decatur on the afternoon trip to St. Louis. And during the first weeks of operation, hundreds of curious individuals made their way to their local stations or at scattered trackside sites to see the *Blue Bird* whiz by. People wanted to experience something that an industry publication considered to be "among the most beautiful trains in America." It seemed that the Wabash had done everything right, whether an on-board lunch-counter service with its diverse fare of economy food and drink or the comfortable domes that offered commanding vistas of mostly prairie country between the terminals.[22]

Popularity also translated in profits. Even though the *Blue Bird* drew some patronage from the companion *Banner Blue* and possibly from the overnight *Midnight,* the general revenue picture for St. Louis–Chicago service was bright. Indeed, the Wabash drove down the total passenger share of the GM&O from approximately 76 percent to between 60 and 65 percent. Critics that "questioned the wisdom of operating domes in trains in flat prairie country" were shown to be wrong in their thinking. In a May 1952 article, "Trains That Pay," which appeared in *Railway Age,* the *Blue Bird* was singled out as one of the nation's notable moneymakers. The revenue per train-mile amounted to $3.41, while out-of-pocket expenses per train-mile stood at $2.59. The train was so favored that the company added a second dome parlor car, which came in 1952 from Chicago-based Pullman-Standard at a cost of more than $230,000, and like other parlor cars on the Wabash was staffed by employees of the Pullman Company until 1956. Measuring eighty-five feet in length and seating fifty-one passengers, it featured the much-heralded "Blue Bird Room," which gave businessmen an attractive venue for meetings. It even offered a complimentary Dictaphone machine to facilitate these working sessions. Yet neither the Wabash nor *Railway Age* noted that in 1952 conversion of U.S. Highway 66 between Chicago and St. Louis

The Wabash traffic department did not miss a beat with its promotion of the *Blue Bird.* An illustrated brochure gave details about the streamliner that it called "the ultimate in luxury" and emphasized its availability "at NO EXTRA FARE." (Author's Coll.)

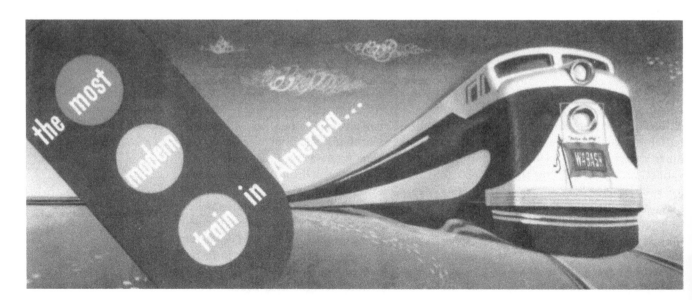

into a four-lane thoroughfare had begun in earnest. In time, this roadway contributed to a substantial drop in passenger train revenues, including those for the *Blue Bird*.[23]

The demand for an additional parlor car hardly vexed management. In July 1951 Atkinson explained to the board the need to expand the train set. "From the inauguration of . . . service in February 1950, it has been evident that one parlor car does not provide a sufficient amount of space at the first-class rail fare and since January 1, 1951, it has been necessary to put a conventional-type parlor car into the northbound train twenty-four times and into the southbound

train eighty-five times to take care of the overflow first-class business demanding space on the 'Blue Bird' and many complaints have been received from passengers who were assigned space in the conventional-type parlor cars that they were not given the kind of accommodations advertised." Added Atkinson, "A considerable amount of new business is being developed from the Southwest as a result of the morning northbound 'Blue Bird' service, and the present parlor car space does not permit assignment of sufficient seats for sale at Houston, Dallas, Little Rock and Shreveport." No board member questioned the president's

In April 1958 prominent railroad photographer J. Parker Lamb caught the speeding Chicago-bound *Blue Bird* near the central Illinois community of Mansfield. (J. Parker Lamb Photograph)

explanation or objected to the hefty expenditure required to enhance parlor car service. They liked that their railroad had raised eyebrows and revenues with its domeliner, which public relations dubbed, "the Most Modern Train in America!"[24]

Introduction of the *Blue Bird* freed two sets of highly serviceable passenger equipment. Management assigned some of the former *Blue Bird* cars to the *Banner Blue,* but the majority appeared in St. Louis–Detroit service. On February 26, 1950, the Wabash with less-than-usual fanfare introduced the "Direct Route of the Diesel Powered Wabash Cannon Ball." In replacing the less attractive *Detroit Special* and *St. Louis Special,* the *Cannon Ball* could offer patrons on this 488-mile line, the shortest between St. Louis and Detroit, "with observation parlor car, deluxe coaches, and dining-lounge car." The publicity department lauded the convenience of this train for Detroit-bound travelers coming from the Southwest: "Your train from the Southwest takes you into St. Louis Union Station from which the Cannon Ball departs. You don't have to make cross-town [Chicago] transfers." The company also considered streamlining this train, but that did not occur, largely because of increased automobile and commercial airline competition. Although the *Cannon Ball* initially operated an hour faster than had the *Detroit Special,* in 1954 it was again speeded up, twenty minutes eastbound and fifty-five minutes westbound, and, by using Delmar Station, the revised westbound schedule allowed passengers to connect with the *City of Kansas City.* But because of heavy "head-head" or mail and express business that needed to be "worked" at more than two dozen stations, it never ran as fast as the premier St. Louis–Chicago and St. Louis–Kansas City trains.[25]

The emphasis on improvement to passenger service involved those trains that traveled long distances and made only limited stops. From the late 1940s into the 1950s, the com-

This early photograph of the *Wabash Cannon Ball,* taken at Logansport, Indiana, on June 11, 1950, shows the Pullman observation car *Embassy.* (Bob's Photo Coll.)

pany won permission to discontinue a number of local and branch line runs. In 1950, for example, the Public Service Commission of Missouri, notwithstanding protests from businessmen in Centralia, Columbia and Hallsville, agreed to allow termination of six daily trains on the Columbia branch, which gave the company an annual savings of nearly $50,000. Six trains remained, however, allowing convenient connections at Centralia for direct service to and from Kansas City or St. Louis. Interstate 70, the future trans-Missouri artery, was not yet even in the planning stage, and Columbia passenger traffic, especially from college students, for a few years remained at acceptable levels.[26]

In August 1958 a north-bound *Banner Blue*, hauling an ancient open-observation car, whips around a curve south of Mansfield, Illinois. (J. Parker Lamb Photograph)

A Wabash photographer made this view of the precast depot at Morrisonville, Illinois, which company employees completed in August 1955. (James Holzmeier Coll.)

The Wabash did not abandon its interest in running passenger specials, especially those to popular football contests. After World War II, games held at the University of Illinois always drew crowds to company trains. "Once John Barrett, the passenger traffic manager, came out [to Delmar Station] from downtown to see how many football fanatics were going to be boarding [for Champaign]," recalled veteran agent O. K. Blackburn. "The station was so crowded he couldn't get in through the regular doors and had to walk along Hodiamont [Avenue] and come in from the tracks."[27]

To complement its new and improved passenger trains and its ubiquitous specials, the Wabash throughout the late 1940s and 1950s paid attention to its station facilities. Its most important large-scale project took place in Detroit. The company joined with fellow tenants Chesapeake & Ohio (C&O) and PRR to extensively remodel the Fort Street Union Station. This Romanesque brick structure, built in 1893, had become "archaic and anachronistic," especially so by the streamliner era. Beginning in 1947, crews dramatically improved the public space by expanding waiting areas and mak-

ing a variety of cosmetic improvements. They also added air conditioning. Indeed, workers even placed air conditioning in the banks of enclosed telephone booths, "believed to be the first installation of its kind." At the public dedication on March 8, 1948, Detroit mayor Daniel J. Van Antwerp lauded the three roads for their "civic mindedness," and everyone seemed pleased with the more than $1 million investment (the Wabash's share being 36 percent).[28]

The Wabash also replaced a number of its small-town depots. An example occurred at Carrollton, Missouri. The existing 22 x 100-foot combination frame structure, built in 1893, had "deteriorated beyond economical repair, and there has been considerable local criticism regarding its condition." In 1956, the company built a smaller standardized depot, one constructed creatively from precast concrete panels. Earlier the company had employed this type of replacement building at New Florence, Missouri, and Morrisonville, Illinois, and it would erect even more of these practical structures.[29]

This dedication to maintaining what would be considered a high level of passenger service for a Midwestern carrier is largely attributable to Atkinson. "The Wabash offered good trains well into the late 1950s because of the community-oriented spirit of Atkinson," explained an observer. "And he knew that the GM&O, IC and especially the Missouri Pacific had made similar commitments and shared that same general public-spirited point-of-view." Atkinson furthermore accepted the premise, which may or may not have been correct, that if happy passengers had freight to ship, they would request that it go by the same carrier that they liked to travel. "I know from letters and conversations that we have pleased many shippers with our new [passenger] trains," noted Atkinson in 1953, "and they know that their freight will receive the same fine and personalized attention." It was also true that trains traveling 250 to 500 miles could complete effectively with propeller-driven aircraft.[30]

This positive outlook on the "New" Wabash found expression in other forms. Atkinson and the board gladly contributed to what would turn out to be a smashing postwar public relations triumph for the industry, the Chicago Railroad Fair of 1948. The company readily paid its share for the overall cost, $37,863, and another $48,617 for participation in the Eastern Railroads' Exhibit. When organizers decided to continue the fair in 1949 because of its unexpected popularity, the Wabash expended an additional $47,000. The Wabash emphasized its modernity by contrasting a full-scale replica of the 1838 *Rogers* with one of its newest refrigerator cars and one of its automobile-carrying freight cars. In seizing every possible advantage, the company hosted for specially invited individuals what it called "Wabash Railroad Day." These guests enjoyed prefair activities at the downtown Union League Club, dinner in the air-conditioned executive lounge of the Eastern Railroads' Exhibit and preferred seating at the evening showing of the "Wheels A' Rolling" pageant.[31]

Whereas the Chicago Railroad Fair was ephemeral, the Atkinson administration sought a more permanent way to honor its postwar triumphs. The medium would be a commercially produced twenty-eight-minute sound and color film, *Once upon the Wabash,* and the message would again be the railroad's remarkable technological progress, most of all since World War II. As the company said in a press release, the "motion picture . . . will portray the history and development of the railroad since its start 114 years ago, . . .[and] will concentrate on the road as it is today." Although the historic *Rogers* replica would be featured, the *Blue Bird* became the real star of this 1952 production. Atkinson approved the format and

coverage, but he was somewhat disappointed with the length. "We would like to have made the film run longer. . . so as to show more of the procedures involved in operating a modern railroad, but realized that an industrial film of this type should be limited to less than a half hour, especially if it is to be shown on television."[32]

The Wabash wanted the best possible promotional film and for it to be widely seen throughout its service territory. A recently launched industrial movie producer in St. Louis—Condor Films, Inc.—received "top dollar" for its work, allowing it to engage professional actors (unusual if not unique for

Management celebrated the impressive postwar development of the Wabash with an expensive and highly promoted motion picture. This 1953 folder describes the background, scope and ways civic groups and others might engage *Once upon the Wabash* for showing. (Author's Coll.)

The Wabash took full advantage of the centennial of railroading in Decatur, Illinois. In May 1954 it circulated hundreds of commemorative aluminum coins that depicted the *Blue Bird* on one side and a Great Western locomotive on the other. (Author's Coll.)

an industrial film at the time) and even to hire an established composer, Lloyd B. Norlin, of Chicago, to create an original musical score. Included, too, were the vocals for the film's theme song, "You Can Bank on the Wabash," written by Thomas S. Hayes, the company's passenger traffic manager, in collaboration with a professional songwriter, and "the peppy hit song, 'Riding the Wabash Road,' by Cy Elsmo." Following the release of *Once upon the Wabash,* the company promoted it vigorously, encouraging civic organizations and clubs to show this "something *different* in railroad motion pictures." The only charge for viewing a print was cost of delivery. There would be scores of takers, ranging from the Huntington, Indiana, Chamber of Commerce to the Bement, Illinois, Centennial Committee. "I was so pleased with this movie and so pleased that the hall was so full of people who liked what they saw," remembered one employee from St. Louis. *Once upon the Wabash* served as an effective public-relations tool.[33]

Once upon the Wabash was released shortly before numerous on-line communities, mostly in Illinois, Indiana and Missouri, celebrated their centennials. Predecessor companies had either founded these towns or had greatly contributed to their development, and the Wabash did not want to miss out on these highly publicized local events. Company representatives loaned the replica of the *Rogers,* brought in modern rolling stock for display and contributed in other ways to enhance these popular festivities.[34]

The grandest of all of centennial celebrations of the 1950s took place in Decatur, the center of Wabash operations and a bustling industrial city. Rather than the customary one day of special events, the Decatur Asso-

ciation of Commerce, the organizing group, decided to create a weeklong celebration in early May 1954 "to signify its appreciation for a century of railroad service." The numerous activities varied from music and theater students at Millikin University presenting a historical pageant to special showings of *Once upon the Wabash* in all local public schools. Even a commemorative aluminum coin, with an image of a Great Western Railway steam locomotive on one side and the *Blue Bird* on the other, was distributed to well-wishers. The main event, however, took place on May 12, when the association of commerce hosted an elaborate "community dinner" for invited guests. Wabash director and Decatur business leader A. E. Staley, Sr., served as toastmaster. James C. Worthy, assistant secretary of commerce in the Eisenhower administration, gave the principal speech, and Atkinson received a community-donated bronze plaque.[35]

There was no question about the success of the Decatur celebrations for enhancing the image of the Wabash. Atkinson, most of all, basked in the spotlight and received hearty, true-felt congratulations. "Like everything you do, Wabash Day on the 12th was a thoroughly delightful and altogether successful event," wrote railroad executive John W. Barriger III. "It typifies the broad array of fine personal and official qualities which underlie the accelerated progress of your administration of this great property. Best wishes for the next 100 years. You are giving the Wabash the momentum to carry it through all of them."[36]

DIESELIZATION

As anyone who watched *Once upon the Wabash* or who attended a centennial celebration immediately realized, creation of the "New" Wabash involved acquiring additional diesel-electric locomotives. Though old reciprocating steam engines might be romantic, the future belonged to these sleek pieces of replacement technology. What had begun as a modest commitment to upgrading yard operations on the eve of World War II, dieselization gathered headway following the conflict. These same trends emerged throughout the industry, although some large coal-hauling Class I carriers did not push dieselization as rapidly as did the Wabash and scores of other roads. These railroads, the mighty PRR included, worried that if they abandoned the iron horse the market for bituminous coal would shrink. To prevent this from happening, several companies, among them the C&O, Louisville & Nashville and Norfolk & Western (N&W), funded projects designed to develop more efficient coal-burning locomotives and even a coal-burning steam-electric turbine engine. This overall research lasted until the mid-1950s, when the last holdout roads finally accepted the inevitability of diesels. They could no longer ignore the advantages of more horsepower, higher fuel efficiency, lower maintenance costs and greater availability. Some railroad officers seemed surprised to learn that a diesel-electric locomotive is never a single diesel-driven generator powering a single electric motor. Rather, a heavy train is always powered with enough components that failure of any one of them will not prevent it from limping home at reduced speed. The old arguments against dieselization rang hollow: diesels required a much larger initial capital investment than steam locomotives; new repair and support facilities, longer passing tracks, better bridges, heavier rail and reconfigured yards were needed to handle longer and heavier diesel-powered freight trains; and employee-training programs for both operating and shop personnel would be essential. The statistics reveal how the diesel revolution swept the industry. In 1941, there were 41,911

steam locomotives and only 1,517 diesels of all kinds in service in the United States. Twenty years later, the latter figure had skyrocketed to 30,123 and the former number stood at a mere 210.[37]

With the return to peacetime, the Wabash focused considerable attention on its motive power. Heavy wartime traffic had taken its toll on rolling stock, including steam locomotives. In June 1946, the board of directors authorized $184,240 to equip ten Class O-1 (4-8-4) freight locomotives with rolling bearings. Management had been delighted with the savings in maintenance due to rolling bearings on its Class P-1 (4-6-4) passenger engines. "There has been an increase of approximately 100% in mileage between shoppings of said locomotives as compared with the Class J-1 [4-6-2] passenger locomotives which are equipped with plain bearings." Improvements for its stable of iron horses, however, would not continue. The company abandoned this conservative approach to motive power and turned its attention to diesels, not for switching purposes but for general road use.[38]

By the latter half of the 1940s, dieselization had fully begun. Not only did the Wabash acquire from various diesel locomotive manufacturers additional switch engines, but it also took possession of its first diesel passenger locomotive in 1946 and its first diesel freight locomotive three years later. Curious about the road's plans for dieselization, a Chicago railroad consultant, David A. Hill, interviewed Atkinson in the spring of 1948. In a confidential report to investors, Hill explained precisely why he

The Wabash family surely appreciated the attention the railroad received in the 1950s when the Post Cereal Company offered children twenty-eight different metal railroad emblems in boxes of Sugar Crisp, including the "Follow the Flag." Post advertised these three-inch-diameter tin signs as being "Easily attached to bike and wagons [and] fine for room decoration. Save 'em—Trade 'em—Wear 'em!" (Author's Coll.)

The advertising department of the Electro-Motive Division of General Motors created an informative card that provided an image (front) and specifications (back) of the 2,000-horsepower passenger locomotive "designed and built for Wabash Railroad." (Author's Coll.)

wanted to speak with the Wabash president: "Frankly, the reason I went to St. Louis to meet Mr. Atkinson was my concern over the fact that this railroad had been so backward, or timid, about adopting Diesel road freight locomotives. I wondered, frankly, whether it had been due to P.R.R. influence." Although there remained stock control by the PRR over the Wabash and the PRR, a major soft-coal carrier, had only a year earlier started what turned out to be the slow process of dieselization, Atkinson denied that Philadelphia called the shots on technology or anything else. "Pennsylvania officials make no recommendations to the Wabash, except in Directors' meetings, where some Pennsylvania men are represented." Atkinson then told Hill that "he personally had been watching the progress of Diesels with great interest and was in favor of adopting them more fully (though some of the staff had not shared his enthusiasm)." In fact, Atkinson could not restrain his excitement that "the road now has on order four (3-unit) 4500 H P Diesel road freight locomotives from Alco; and four (3 unit) 4500 HP road freight locomotives from

Electro-Motive." Though these purchases had not been announced, this "confidential information" pleased Hill and reinforced his belief that the Wabash would be a good place for anyone's investment dollar.[39]

Progress remained steady toward complete dieselization. In October 1950, approximately a year and a half after the real push had started, 100 percent of the passenger train miles were performed by diesels and 89.6 percent of freight train miles. Also in 1950, the Ann Arbor was converted to diesel operation almost overnight by the addition of thirteen new units. By mid-June 1953, the Wabash had become totally dieselized for normal operations with 106 switch engines and 198 freight and passenger road units. These diesels came from all of the major domestic manufacturers, but EMD built the majority. Said Atkinson cleverly in one of his numerous public addresses that covered dieselization: "With apologies to the Coca Cola people I would describe them [diesels] as 'the *power* that refreshes.'" Most of these units had arrived since 1949 and collectively represented an investment of $43.5 million.[40]

In 1953 dieselization came to the Columbia, Missouri, branch. In January a 4-6-2 Pacific rests at the water tank in this Boone County seat, but by fall this 41-year-old locomotive had become junk. In March a GP-7 diesel, new in February 1952, enters the Columbia yard with its mixed consist of freight and passenger cars. (George C. Drake, Sr., Photograph, Gary Roe Coll.)

The steam era is about to end on the Bluffs-Keokuk branch and the Wabash Railroad. On October 18, 1953, the fireman of No. 573 fills the 6,000-gallon water tank of this 1899 Rhode Island–built 2-6-0 Mogul at Mt. Sterling, Illinois. (Don L. Hofsommer Photograph)

In addition to the money spent on replacement motive power, the Wabash invested heavily in a modern diesel repair complex at Decatur. This involved installation of special machine tools, testing equipment and cranes, thus making the facility "one of the most modern and efficient Diesel engine repair shops in the country." Although the company operated its diesels in "pool service," which meant being assigned where needed systemwide, it sensibly

decided to conduct all maintenance work at this centralized location. And at strategic locations the railroad continued to install diesel fuel oil stations, often with 100,000 gallon capacities. Work gangs also began the lengthy task of removing the artifacts of the age of steam: water tanks, coal chutes, cinder pits and the like.[41]

Even though the Wabash could rightly claim to have been fully dieselized by 1953, the iron horse had not entirely disappeared from the property. In 1952 and 1953 the company sold or scrapped a large number of steam locomotives but retained some for standby use. The critical need for additional power during World War II remained fresh in the minds of management, and, although the Korean Conflict was winding down, the cold war was very much a national concern. The question "who knew what the morrow would bring?" explained why in November 1953 the board decided to place thirty-two of the most serviceable and powerful locomotives in mothballs. As the minutes of the directors' deliberations explain, "[These engines will be] retained for standby purposes in case of a national emergency or until such time as this Company has available sufficient diesel power for any emergency."[42]

The last steam locomotives on the Wabash were not be one of the big Mountain types or a handsome Hudson, however, but rather four of the smallest and oldest of engines, Class F-4 and F-5 Moguls (2-6-0), which dated from the 1890s. The reason for these locomotives carrying the final banner of steam was size, not sentiment. The Illinois River bridge at Meredosia on the seventy-six-mile Bluffs-Keokuk branch could not hold the weight of heavier diesels. Explained Atkinson, it was an old structure and "the supports have been struck so often by river boats and barges that weight restrictions have had to be imposed limiting our operation to the lightest weight steam locomotives." But in 1955 the company solved this problem by leasing from the PRR a pair of steeple-cab forty-five-ton diesels, which could manage the weight restrictions on the bridge and then using one of its 1,000-horsepower diesel units beyond to Keokuk. (Within a few years the rickety bridge was removed and the line relocated so as to cross over a new span.) The last official day of steam on the Wabash was June 28, 1955. Then, in August, Atkinson took great pride in donating Mogal No. 573 to the St. Louis Museum of Transport, where he served as board chair. To this day, the steamer remains at this St. Louis County–operated museum on Barrett Station Road.[43]

On October 18, 1953, No. 573 and its eight-car train move along the weedy Keokuk branch near Hamilton, Illinois. This elderly Mogul would be saved; in August 1955 the Wabash donated this historic locomotive to the St. Louis Museum of Transport. (Don L. Hofsommer Photograph)

On September 20, 1956, President Arthur Atkinson dons a cap and gloves at the Decatur shops and ceremoniously takes a welding torch to the last company-owned steam locomotive. (Museum of Transportation)

Technically, one last locomotive, No. 534, a Class B-7 switcher (0-6-0), remained in service until early 1957. It operated not on the Wabash but on its tiny Lake Erie & Fort Wayne subsidiary. By the time of its retirement, this 1906 product of the Rhode Island Locomotive Works was in poor operating condition. "[It] is in urgent need of general repairs, including new flues, the cost of which would be prohibitive." The Wabash logically substituted one of its earliest diesel switch engines, No. 200, which it had acquired in 1941. Continuing to sense the historical value of the iron horse, Atkinson arranged to have the little steamer donated to the city of Fort Wayne for public display. Later, municipal officials leased it to the Fort Wayne Railroad Historical Society, and subsequently it was moved to New Haven, Indiana.[44]

FAST FREIGHTS AND PIGGYBACKS

While the razzle-dazzle of sparkling diesel-electric locomotives, especially those that pulled name trains, captured the public fancy, the more mundane freight operations during the postwar era underwent an unheralded revolution. Because the company had long relied heavily on bridge traffic, about 65 percent of its tonnage in 1950, which included fruits and vegetables and automobiles and automobile parts and other time-sensitive commodities, it needed to expedite freight movements. Moreover, the Wabash lacked an exclusive territory—there was no important traffic center that was not served by one or more trunk lines—and it had few exclusive belt or terminal facilities. Therefore, shipper satisfaction became essential.

To prosper, the road had to attract a large volume of high-rated "time-sensitive freight," and this it did. For example, in 1949 the handling of motor vehicle parts and set-up automobiles produced $7,307,612 in earnings, or more than 8 percent of all freight revenues.[45]

Following World War II, management maintained its freight philosophy of "keeping 'em moving." Operating personnel kept close watch over yards, making certain that they did not become clogged, and were always mindful of adding outbound cars to the appropriate trains as quickly as possible. Employees also carefully adhered to published schedules for manifest freights, which frequently maintained an average speed of more than thirty-five miles per hour. Unlike some competitors, for example the Chicago Great Western, the Wabash would not delay departure until full tonnage was achieved. When necessary, these light time-freights might handle empties or lower-grade traffic. Promises made by freight agents to customers were usually kept, and this synchronized manifest service usually produced smiling faces. Even the PRR became annoyed when Wabash representatives, "with the assured enthusiasm of automobile salesmen," regularly succeeded in having long-distance shippers specify "WAB" for their freight destined to the PRR to travel on Wabash rails between Kansas City and Logansport, Indiana, rather than an interchange at St. Louis. Wabash speed and the avoidance of the congestion of the St. Louis

On the point of a long revenue-producing train that passes historic Wabash grain elevators in North Kansas City, Missouri, is EMD-built freight locomotive 1180A, purchased by the Wabash in 1952. (Wabash Railroad Historical Society)

In the late 1950s, the Detroit-bound *Cannon Ball* departs Tolono, Illinois, passing a freight train headed toward Decatur. (J. Parker Lamb Photograph)

terminal made for an attractive transfer at Logansport. Of course, the company dispatched the necessary main- and branch-line locals, but with diesel power even their speeds were much faster than during the age of steam. "The Wabash has earned a fine fast freight reputation through its ability to highball its manifest traffic, day in and day out, in storm and fair weather," concluded

Kip Farrington in his 1951 book, *Railroading the Modern Way.* "Its operating men, its two-fisted railroaders, rank high on the roster of American railroads."[46]

Second only to dieselization for strengthening freight operations was adoption of "piggyback," or truck trailer-on-flatcar (TOFC), service. Although the Wabash briefly experimented with carrying containers on flatcars during the Great Depression, it and the vast majority of other carriers did not follow the lead of several Class I carriers in the late 1930s and 1940s in developing TOFC operations. There were several reasons. The technology had not been fully developed, and a general lack of standardization existed among those companies that offered piggyback service. Because the existing program nearly always involved loading only one trailer on a flatcar, profits were at best modest. Moreover, some officials feared that truck trailers would merely diminish boxcar loadings. Still others, bound by tradition, considered the concept to be only a "flash in the pan" and were reluctant to make major financial commitments. But by the early 1950s, industry innovators—most of all Gene Ryan, who launched Rail-Trailer Company in 1952—responded effectively to the alleged or real disadvantages of the piggyback concept.[47]

The Wabash began its piggyback service on July 23, 1954, though in a somewhat experimental fashion. It had spent about $36,000 for twenty-four flatcars that would be dedicated to these freight operations. That year saw the first big push for piggyback when more than a dozen roads, mostly from the Midwest, started to handle commercial truck trailers. By the following year, about thirty carriers had joined the not-so-exclusive piggyback club. Initially, the Wabash operated TOFC traffic between Chicago and New York via the Delaware, Lackawanna & Western and Lehigh Valley. Indeed, these two major interchange partners at the Buffalo gateway had requested that the Wabash provide such service, including installation of the appropriate terminal loading and unloading facilities in Chicago. Soon TOFC was expanded with trailers being handled in Detroit and St. Louis.[48]

Even before the end of 1954, pleased with

the financial results and customer responses, the Wabash expanded its piggyback fleet and made adjustments called for by the operations of its initial equipment. Twenty-six flatcars would be modified, and the price per car would be higher "due to the experience gained in operating the first group of cars." Specifically, employees discovered that the "gang-planks between cars were not heavy enough, the wheel chocks, while satisfactory, were too slow and costly to operate, and for safety reasons double instead of single jacks are desirable for the second group of cars, all of which is emphasized by the increasingly heavy loads being received in the trailers."[49]

Expansion followed swiftly, and by March 1955 the Wabash offered piggyback service between Chicago and New York (Buffalo), Chicago and Detroit, Chicago and St. Louis, Chicago and Kansas City, St. Louis and Detroit, Detroit and New York (Buffalo), St. Louis and New York (Buffalo) and St. Louis and Kansas City. The number of trailers handled monthly reflected both its popularity and the expansion:

On August 19, 1954, workers unload from a flatcar the first piggyback trailer to arrive in East St. Louis, Illinois. A Mack-built tractor belonging to Ben Gutman Trucking Service would soon pull this Wabash-owned trailer to its local destination. (James Holzmeier Coll.)

August 1954	4
September 1954	44
October 1954	93
November 1954	96
December 1954	143
January 1955	211
February 1955	235[50]

When it came time to produce the annual report for 1955, management thought it wholly appropriate to feature a cover color drawing of a Wabash truck trailer being loaded on a Wabash flatcar. In this publication "'PIGGY-BACK' SERVICE" received a special section. Readers learned that expansion "has been continuous" and that, "in addition to leased trailers, the Company now owns fifty-five trailers and an order has been placed for sixty additional trailers. Ninety Wabash flat cars are assigned to this service, thirty new flat cars are being equipped, and fifty, 75' flat cars have been ordered." The infrastructure was also taking shape with more fully equipped terminals and trained support personnel.[51]

An important event in Wabash piggyback operations came with its investment in the fledgling Trailer Train Company. Incorporated in November 1955 to furnish railroads inexpensively with the large quantities of special flatcars required for the rapidly expanding business, the firm found the support of the PRR, which quickly acquired 2,500 shares of the 7,500 issued. The N&W, controlled by PRR, became the other early railroad backer. In 1956 the Wabash purchased 500 shares of Trailer Train for $50,000 and joined PRR, N&W and five other new railroad investors, giving Trailer Train a strong level of support and helping to ensure its future in the intermodal business.[52]

Joining Trailer Train and adding to its own fleet of piggyback equipment worked well for the Wabash. As Atkinson told William Harp, financial editor for the *St. Louis Globe-Democrat,* in March 1956, "This new branch of railroading since its inauguration in July of 1954 by the Wabash has doubled and redoubled." And he was pleased that the Wabash was regaining traffic that had been lost to over-the-road truckers. No wonder Atkinson believed—and correctly so—that expansion of piggyback freight was "most promising for the future of the railroad industry." He emphasized the importance of this developing service by indicating that the company had recently established a separate piggyback merchandising department. Just as traffic representatives aggressively sought carload freight, peers would do the same in the TOFC market. Whereas several plans for piggyback service developed, Wabash agents seemed most comfortable with "Plan II," which was fully railroad run, being rated, billed and operated door to door in railroad equipment.[53]

The success of piggyback service was not without problems. Fortunately, the Trailer Train pool usually provided the Wabash with an adequate number of appropriate flatcars, which had become longer as truck-trailer lengths increased. By the late 1950s, the eighty-five-foot car with a capacity for two forty-foot trailers had become the industry standard. The company had to retire obsolete cars and build, modify or lease new equipment. Terminals frequently needed to be increased or expanded. It became apparent, for example, with the growth of piggyback operations at the 12th Street facility in Detroit that it was wholly inadequate to accommodate business. Traffic grew when the ICC made rate adjustments on railroad tariffs that equaled or bettered highway charges on steel moving from Buffalo to Detroit. The terminal could not effectively manage the

7,250 trailers that had entered between July 1, 1956, and June 30, 1957. Because the railroad did not want to lose revenues, the board readily approved the expenditure of $185,084 to construct a replacement facility at Oakwood Yard.[54]

The physical plant was vital to successful fast-freight and piggyback operations. Following World War II, management gave a high priority to revitalizing mainline track, signaling, yards and the like. Wabash annual reports consistently mention the installation of heaver rail, especially new 132-pound steel; improved alignment and grade revisions; longer passing tracks and extension of better signaling best represented by centralized traffic control (by 1958, some 316.16 miles of CTC were in use). The company also installed carrier telephone lines and teletype networks; renewed interlocking plants; upgraded yards (for example, a $4,002,833 expenditure in 1952–1953 at Decatur); purchased modern equipment of various types ranging from Jackson multiple tie tampers to office car-data processing machines and, of course, acquired more freight rolling stock, including scores of all-steel 50' 6"-long box cars equipped with "damage-free loading," or DFL, devices.[55]

Unlike a Great Northern or a UP, the Wabash lacked the financial resources to make every mile of mainline track a speedway. Yet it tried. As the Kansas City–Moberly-Hannibal-Decatur line became more important for fast-freight service, the Atkinson administration realized that the saw-tooth profile of the Hannibal-Decatur District of the Decatur Division posed the greatest operating difficulties. Near the Mississippi River, an eastbound 1.52 to 1.64 percent ruling grade existed along the fifteen miles between the Illinois communities of Baylis and Kinderhook. These grades reduced freight-train speeds, even with diesel power, to a thirty-five-mile maximum. But

Just as the Wabash promoted its named passenger trains, it likewise issued advertising materials, including this 1954 pamphlet, boosting its newly established piggyback service. (Author's Coll.)

in 1950 and 1951, workers relocated more than eleven miles of line and reduced the ruling grade to only 0.6 percent and, in the process, eliminated several sharp curves. A study in 1951 of the Baylis line change revealed that with diesel operation, 30 percent fewer trains were operated, yet they carried 17 percent more tonnage, and the average tons per train rose by 68 percent. The impact was obvious: "The combination of new Diesels and modern roadway engineering thus greatly reduces our costs and at the same time enables us to render faster service to our shippers."[56]

The Hannibal-Decatur line also saw replacement of an elderly bridge over the Illinois River at Valley City together with the necessary track relocations. Construction began in June 1957, and on October 6, 1959, the first trains used these betterments. This project not only replaced the span that stood about 1,200 feet upstream, but also the ancient, low-tonnage bridge at Meredosia on the Keokuk branch. Altogether, the company spent more than $6 million on upgrading the Hannibal-Decatur line. Fortunately, the railroad received some federal assistance, made possible by the Truman-Hobbs Act, which was designed to eliminate obstructions on navigable waterways.[57]

Notwithstanding these improvements, the Hannibal-Decatur trackage continued to challenge train crews. Commented David P. Morgan shortly before the Hannibal cut-off opened: "Even [after the changes] . . . the run from the summit into Springfield will remain a challenge to the power and brake skill of enginemen on 100-car trains." Too much or too little slack could damage cargoes and occasionally cause a train to break in two. It would still hold true that "it is an old and understandable maxim on the Wabash that an engineer on the Hannibal-Decatur haul is qualified for anything on the entire road."[58]

In the postwar era, another sign of the New Wabash involved industrial development. Ideally the company needed to become less dependant on the always competitive and somewhat cyclical bridge traffic, generating a larger volume of freight from on-line businesses. "Local traffic has all the strength of better relative revenue, control by cooperative efforts of railroad with shipper, availability of inbound raw material movement and outbound finished product movement, lesser competitive nature, and valuable trading material in our relations with connecting lines," concluded a company traffic education manual about 1948. Although earlier the company had operated a small but active agricultural department that indirectly promoted farmer-generated shipments, in the late 1930s it turned more attention to making its industrial department an important asset. When Homer McIntyre, a college-trained civil engineer, took charge of the department in 1938, he quickly moved it from being a largely amateurish operation into a more professional agency. Following World War II, it became a dynamic force in bolstering revenues.[59]

Like other railroad industrial development departments, the one at the Wabash carefully explored appropriate sites and promoted them to potential businesses. Mostly trained civil engineers and other college-educated specialists, the staff developed and regularly updated a detailed inventory of potential places for industrial location and expansion. These studies contained a wealth of detailed data, including information about the nature of the soil, local tax structures and availability of a labor supply. Once a firm decided to locate along the Wabash or on its property, representatives provided additional assistance, ranging from suggestions for placement of sidings to contacts with area utilities. Industrial department personnel worked closely with other units of the railroad, in particular the legal, real estate and traffic departments.[60]

Some of work of the industrial department took years to be completed. In 1945, the Wabash correctly sensed the enormous potential for an industrial district in the Hazelwood-Berkeley area, about ten miles northwest of St. Louis. The railroad then acquired various parcels of real estate and began its development work, which it fortunately found not to be too difficult. The site had immediate accessibility to the mainline and what became expanded car-storage space near the Robertson station. Convenient access also existed to abundant supplies of water, natural gas and electric power and good all-weather public roads. In time, the St. Louis Metropolitan Sewer District would serve the industrial park. Moreover, the immediate vicinity offered valuable human assets, namely, "high grade labor and skilled craftsmen." By 1957, approximately a dozen rail users had selected the industrial park, the largest being an assembly plant of the Lincoln-Mercury Division of the Ford Motor Company, which early on had acquired a ninety-nine-acre tract. This facility, which employed 4,000 workers and used the railroad heavily, was unmistakably the crown jewel of this highly successful development project.[61]

The Wabash creatively utilized its resources to attract businesses. To facilitate land development, the company used a dormant subsidiary, the Wabash Motor Transportation Company (WMT). Launched in 1930 to operate coordinated bus-train service between Decatur and East St. Louis, Illinois, because of regulatory and financial restraints this firm never took to the highways. But in 1946 the railroad resuscitated WMT to become an agent for land rental. When in the late 1940s Ford Motor Company representatives scouted possible sites in the Kansas City area for a plant to manufacture aircraft wings, the Wabash became involved. The land ultimately selected, approximately 1,100 acres near Birmingham, would be acquired by WMT and made available to Ford. Construction of this facility at Claycomo (Clay County, Missouri) began in 1950 and opened a year later. Then in 1956, much to the delight of Wabash officials, Ford decided to convert the factory into an automobile assembly plant, and car-making production began the following January. For convenience, tax and regulatory purposes, WMT continued to be a useful part of on-line industrial development. This subsidiary later would also handle equipment leasing, including piggyback flatcars.[62]

Industrial department employees kept their eyes open, and while the best opportunities seemed to be found in metropolitan areas and along main arteries, these "go-getters" did not ignore business opportunities along appendages. For example, during the 1950s they made great strides in increasing traffic along the Streator branch, thirty-seven miles of track in north-central Illinois that left the Decatur-Chicago line at Forrest (running six miles over the Toledo, Peoria & Western between Forrest and Fairbury). Between 1938 and 1958, tonnage rose about 200 percent. The earlier shipments of grain, brick and sewer pipe largely gave way to mill products (oil, cake and meal), chemicals, fertilizer and agricultural limestone. The industrial department's triumphs included the Douglass Company, a producer of mixed fertilizer, and Honegger's & Company, an animal-feed processor. In part because of these successful development, *Railway Age* in 1958 praised this appendage in a feature story, "Why Wabash Branches Pay Off."[63]

NEW RAILROADS

From the early 1930s through much of the 1950s, remarkably stable corporate structures characterized the railroad industry. Architects for greater unification would not become active until the late 1950s, accelerating their work a decade later into what commentators rightly called "merger madness." Still, some ownership changes occurred, and in two cases they involved the Wabash. In the 1950s, the Wabash made substantial investments in two interchange partners, the

Detroit, Toledo & Ironton Railroad (DT&I) and the Illinois Terminal Railroad (IT). Each of these commitments made considerable economic sense.

The DT&I resembled many other small Class I carriers, especially the Ann Arbor. Both properties consisted of several rather woebegone predecessors dating back into the nineteenth century, and both emerged as a conduit for a principal city. The 359-mile DT&I extended on a largely north-south axis south from Detroit through Flat Rock, Michigan, and the Ohio cities of Lima and Springfield, to Ironton, on the Ohio River. The railroad had access to Toledo and operated two important branches, fifty-five miles between Malinta, Ohio, and Tecumseh, Michigan, which originally had been part of its main stem, and thirteen miles between D&I Junction, north of Flat Rock, to Dearborn, Michigan.[64]

Shortly after World War I, the DT&I became a much more important railroad. On July 9, 1920, the Ford Motor Company, the nation's largest automobile maker, acquired control of the carrier for less than $5 million and soon extensively upgraded the hapless property. The most expensive improvement involved construction of the sixty-mile Malinta Cut-Off, built in 1926, which had slight grades and only two curves. In 1923, the DT&I even started an electrification program ("heavy-traction") in the Detroit area. Shortly, sixteen miles of line would be under wire between Flat Rock and the River Rouge plant of the Ford Motor Company, although no additional miles would ever be electrified. Henry Ford, who closely oversaw the workings of his vast manufacturing empire, considered the DT&I a valuable conduit for raw materials, especially coal from newly acquired mines in Kentucky and West Virginia, as well as auto parts into his sprawling River Rouge Plant. It was also an outlet for his motor cars. Indeed, not long after Ford acquired

the DT&I, there were published rumors that suggested that the car czar would purchase two other carriers, the Virginian Railroad, an important Appalachian coal carrier, which through new construction or trackage rights could be extended from Deepwater, West Virginia, to Ironton, and the Wabash, which connected with the DT&I at various points, including Adrian, Michigan, and Delta, Ohio. Ownership of the DT&I, Virginian and Wabash would be more of the vertical business integration that Ford cherished.[65]

But by the late 1920s Henry Ford had tired of railroads. Frustrated most of all by the ICC, he later said, "We [Ford and his son Edsel, who was a DT&I director] had some ideas, but we found we couldn't do the things we wanted." So in 1929 the DT&I was sold to the Pennroad Corporation. Created by major PRR stockholders, this newly formed *independent* financial firm was designed to make investments in the transportation field that would be "sound and profitable" but that would also protect the overall well-being of the PRR. The DT&I met that criteria. Pennroad executives especially fancied the DT&I terminal properties in greater Detroit, and they liked the route structure that crossed all of the major east-west trunk lines, including main stems of the PRR at Lima and South Charleston, Ohio.[66]

Atkinson would play a pivotal role in the Wabash's involvement in the former Ford property. In the summer of 1948, he learned of Pennroad's desire to sell its DT&I securities. He then discussed the matter with his long-time friend and former colleague, PRR vice president (and soon to be president) Walter Franklin, who in the early 1930s had been Wabash president and coreceiver. It did not take long before the two railroaders decided that the Wabash and PRR should acquire the DT&I. Atkinson and Franklin knew the importance of the DT&I to their companies. The DT&I interchanged more than 40 percent of its traffic, which included high-value goods, with the PRR, Wabash and Ann Arbor. As Atkinson would later tell the ICC, "With this close traffic relationship, the road fits naturally into the Pennsylvania system."[67]

On January 26, 1949, the process for the PRR and Wabash to gain control officially began. The two railroads filed a joint application with the ICC for permission to purchase from Pennroad 245,329 shares of DT&I stock. The plan proposed that the Wabash would take a minority interest, 45,329 shares. Part of the request also included the PRR taking over the remnants of a former Ohio interurban (née Springfield, Troy & Piqua Railway), by then a three-mile industrial switching operation, the Springfield Suburban Railroad. This little diesel-powered road, which served the giant Crowell-Collier Publishing Company and several other customers in the Springfield area, connected with the DT&I at Maitland.[68]

Not everyone was happy with the PRR-Wabash proposal. Although no shippers or state regulatory authorities objected, several competing railroads did. The Baltimore & Ohio (B&O), most of all, worried about additional competition from the PRR, especially between Cincinnati and Detroit.[69]

But the B&O's protests were in vain. On May 2, 1950, the ICC gave the green light to the purchase. Federal regulators succinctly expressed their reasoning: "It would be in the public interest for control of Ironton to pass from the non-carrier investment company which no longer desires it, to carrier auspices, and on this record the most logical owners would be the applicants." And, they added, "On the basis of the present interchange their interests are superior to those of any other carrier in the area." The B&O, New York Central and Nickel Plate shortly thereafter filed a complaint in federal court, seeking to set aside the ICC order. In November 1951, a three-judge panel considered the matter, and on February 9, 1951, the panel sustained the purchase. The sale became effective on February 23. Five days later, the Wabash paid Pennroad $4,782,209.50 for its portion of the DT&I stock, the money coming from cash reserves.[70]

Three years after the Wabash invested heavily in the DT&I, it became involved with a somewhat smaller carrier, the 344-mile Illinois Terminal Railroad. Unlike the DT&I, the IT had once been a mighty electric interurban. In fact, as the 400-mile Illinois Traction System ("McKinley System"), the company was the largest Midwestern interurban property to remain directly under a single management for a prolonged period. Through the early part of its existence, the IT did a brisk passenger business, even operating sleeping and parlor cars, and competed with the Wabash between various Illinois communities, especially on the Decatur-Springfield route. But by the late 1920s it had become more dependant on freight revenues. As weaker Midwestern interurbans entered bankruptcy, scaled back their trackage or abandoned altogether, the IT (known after 1928 as the Illinois Terminal) continued to prosper. It did so by increasing its carload freight operations and expanding its terminal facilities in the Alton and East St. Louis areas. To expedite a diversified freight business, largely coal, grain and manufactured goods, it wisely built belt lines around major cities to avoid excessive street running, the bane of most electric roads that handed carload freight.[71]

By the era of World War II, the IT consisted of its principal passenger artery, the 172-mile line between St. Louis and Peoria via Carlinville and Springfield, and two other routes, the 123 miles between Springfield via Decatur and Champaign-Urbana and Danville and the sixty-six miles that linked Decatur via Clinton and Bloomington with the St. Louis–Peoria line at Mackinaw, near

Peoria. In the early 1950s, the IT pared back the Danville line to a point near Ogden, Illinois, and retired much of the Decatur-Mackinaw trackage.[72]

Even with retrenchments and a drastic reduction in remaining passenger service, the largely dieselized IT generated a good income. In 1953, its freight earnings exceeded $10.5 million, but passenger revenues amounted to only $778,000. Indeed, the company claimed to be losing about $500,000 annually on its passenger runs, although it had acquired modern streamlined electric cars. In April 1956, the IT won regulatory approval to shut down its final interurban passenger operations, and maintenance crews removed the overhead trolley wire on the remaining mainlines. Yet for two more years electric streetcars continued to clank along between St. Louis and Granite City.[73]

By 1954, IT stockholders wanted to liquidate. Explained a longtime Santa Fe official, "I suspect that the IT stockholders forecast a downward spiral for their small railroad and just wanted to get their money out." They decided to do so at a good time; there were two would-be suitors. One was the small but ambitious Toledo, Peoria & Western (TP&W) and the other a consortium of nine (later ten) railroads, including several that paralleled portions of the IT (GM&O, IC and Wabash). At East Peoria the TP&W did a brisk interchange business with the IT, and it wished to protect this traffic. The consortium, headed by Atkinson under the banner of the Illinois-Missouri Terminal Railway (I-MT), coveted the East St. Louis–area terminal operations. Even though the TP&W vigorously opposed the sale to Atkinson's group, fearing that the I-MT would scrap most of the trackage north of Edwardsville, the I-MT made the better offer. It bid $20,015,635, enough for the IT, after retiring its first mortgage bonds, to pay $16.50

on each common share, stock that earlier had been selling on the open market for about eight dollars a share. On April 6, 1956, the ICC approved the I-MT bid, and the Wabash became a one-tenth owner of another valuable, adjoining property.[74]

Although neither the DT&I nor the IT appeared on official Wabash maps, management considered other additions and deletions that might require cartographic changes. In September 1946, the Wabash paid a modest price for a remnant of the recently defunct Chicago, Attica & Southern Railroad, a 120-mile Indiana shortline that had never prospered. When the company finally suspended operations in 1946, abandoning its last segment of trackage, thirty-seven miles between Morocco and Veedersburg, the Wabash acquired from the corporate estate about two miles of its industrial spurs in Attica. Because the physical condition was abysmal, it would take about $40,000 to rehabilitate the track and build a proper connection with the Decatur–Detroit line. Still, this appeared to be a promising investment. The Wabash expected to generate about 3,000 cars annually, for gross revenues of about $175,000.[75]

Although line abandonments were negligible, including retirement of the Stroh, Indiana, stub at the end of World War II, the Wabash removed scores of miles of second track along its major lines. In the postwar era, installation of CTC, which "all of the progressive railroads are undertaking," markedly enhanced utilization of single-track arteries. A divisional dispatcher could set trackside signals and switches, allowing for safer and faster meets of opposing trains and for passenger and "red ball" trains to pass slower freights traveling in the same direction. Though CTC projects represented a major capital outlay, the company realized considerable long-term savings by not having to maintain these double-track lines, and it could upgrade trackage elsewhere with the surplus heavy steel, usable ties and other salvageable materials.[76]

Earlier the Wabash had negotiated several trackage-rights agreements that allowed abandonment of line segments, and management continued to explore such money-saving alternatives. In 1950, it proposed retiring nearly all of the 35.5-mile Ottumwa, Iowa, branch, which left the Des Moines stem at Moulton, Iowa, and extended east to Bloomfield before heading north to Ottumwa. Because Ottumwa remained a good source of freight revenues, especially from a John Deere & Company plant in South Ottumwa, the company proposed to send its weekday freight from Moulton north to Moravia and then run east over 27.5 miles of the Milwaukee Road's Kansas City mainline into Ottumwa. The arrangement called for payment of a minimum annual rental of $25,000, and more if per-train mile usage passed a certain level. Company accountants calculated that the Wabash would have saved $50,243 had it used the Milwaukee Road line in 1949. The law department therefore filed the required documents with the ICC for the right to abandon the Ottumwa branch and use the Milwaukee Road.[77]

In a surprising move, on May 21, 1951, the Wabash withdrew these requests. It had come to believe that, if the branch were dieselized and modestly upgraded, especially several of its older wooden deck bridges, it could become economically viable. The deciding factor, however, was anticipation of new business, and therefore "an effort should be made to keep the branch in operation a sufficient time to determine whether or not the additional traffic is developed." This occurred, highlighted by the opening of several strip mines in the Bloomfield area, and trains continued to travel between Moulton and Ottumwa.[78]

CHALLENGES

Events during the postwar period pointed in a positive direction for the New Wabash. Revenues, for example, generally looked good. During the Recession of 1949, net income hit its nadir for the immediate postwar period at $5,693,237, but in the early 1950s made strong showings, reaching $11,192,297 in 1952 and $11,061,984 a year later. Although in 1954 net income slipped to $9,894,190, it came roaring back the following year, climbing to $15,844,920. Operating ratios (the ratio of direct operating expenses to revenues) dipped from an acceptable 76.89 percent in 1954 to an impressive 73.33 percent a year later. "The modernization of the transportation plant in recent years," explained Atkinson, "was largely responsible for this improved efficiency." Although net income slumped to $10,554,814 for 1956, this figure was hardly alarming. The following year the total fell another $1 million, but then the harsh business recession of 1958–1959, which included several major strikes in the manufacturing sector, pushed net income to record lows for the postwar era: $4,124,035 in 1958 and $3,781,487 in 1959. Most financial observers and company leaders expected that the economy would revive by the early 1960s, and they were correct. Recovery from recession began in the spring of 1961 and continued for some time without serious interruption.[79]

Wabash security holders prospered with these strong net income figures. While owners of preferred stock continued to receive their usual $4.50 per share payment, holders of common, most notably the PRR, thrived. In 1947, the dividend rate increased from one dollar to two dollars per share, reached $2.50 in 1948 and jumped to three dollars in 1950. Although common stock shareholders received fifty cents less in 1951, the three-dollar level was restored for 1952. Then substantial increases occurred during the core years of the "Eisenhower prosperity" and even continued into the recession years of the late 1950s: $8.50 in 1955, $12.00 in 1956, $8.40 in 1957, $4.85 in 1958 and $3.50 in 1959. In general, when preferred and common shares traded on Wall Street, they remained high, usually in the $85 to $100 range.[80]

Management of the Wabash could not, however, spend all of its time watching investments grow. There were challenges, one of which involved labor. Since the shopmen's strike of 1922, the railroad's overall labor-management relations had been relatively harmonious. Admittedly, during World War II the company had become part of a national dispute over wages between the industry and operating and nonoperating unions. The mandated wage settlements that ensued cost the Wabash and other carriers dearly, yet they helped employees who had felt the burden of higher prices caused by wartime inflation. Following the conflict, railroad labor again would make demands for wage hikes with the

carriers, and the Wabash would be party to these negotiations and agreements. The company, too, had to deal with National Maritime Union of America, which operated its car floats across the Detroit River and the Ann Arbor car ferries. A brief strike in 1948 had been both bitter and costly.[81]

Fortunately for management, railway unions tied themselves to the American Federation of Labor (AFL) before its merger in December 1955 with the Congress of Industrial Organizations (CIO). The craft-based AFL was basically conservative, with the Brotherhood of Locomotive Engineers being one of, if not the most, Republican unions in the Midwest. Even the CIO affiliates considered AFL railroad brotherhoods to be reactionary, describing them as being "like an 1870 wood burner next to a modern streamliner."[82]

During the late 1940s and 1950s, strikes occasionally erupted against individual railroads, and the Wabash would not be spared this labor unrest. In the latter part of 1948, trouble began to brew when representatives

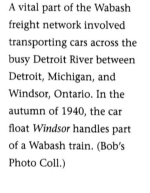

A vital part of the Wabash freight network involved transporting cars across the busy Detroit River between Detroit, Michigan, and Windsor, Ontario. In the autumn of 1940, the car float *Windsor* handles part of a Wabash train. (Bob's Photo Coll.)

The great Missouri River flood of July 1951 badly disrupted Wabash train operations. The station in Carrollton, Missouri, could best be reached by boat or canoe. (Author's Coll.)

of four operating unions, the Brotherhood of Locomotive Engineers, Brotherhood of Locomotive Firemen and Enginemen, Brotherhood of Railroad Trainmen and the Order of Railway Conductors, filed more than 150 specific grievances that involved interpretation of schedule rules, time claims and other issues. Wages, however, were not included. The National Mediation Board (NMB) entered the controversy and forestalled strike actions, first in December and then in January. Labor and management both hoped that these "minor disputes" could be settled, but this did not happen.[83]

A strike came at 6:00 A.M. on March 15, 1949. Approximately 3,500 operating employees on the Wabash and Ann Arbor walked out, and immediately all trains, except those en route before the deadline, rolled to a stop. The system embargoed freight shipments, and connecting carriers and terminal companies rerouted cars. Several on-line shippers closed down almost immediately, including the Sinclair Mining Company near Huntsville, Missouri. In major passenger stations, long lines of stranded Wabash passengers appeared at "special transaction" windows to make alternative travel arrangements.[84]

The March 1949 strike affected more than members of the four operating unions and freight and passenger customers. With board sanction, Atkinson responded by ordering a mass layoff among the approximately 8,500 nonstrikers. The largest group to be furloughed without pay were 1,630 shopmen in Decatur. Only a skeleton workforce remained on the Wabash and the Ann Arbor.[85]

Following these drastic actions by labor and management, the federal government became more heavily involved. This was a disruptive strike action, with hundreds of shippers soon being adversely affected. "They are feeling the pinch, and hard." The NMB quickly asked President Harry Truman to intervene. Specifically, it wanted him to create an emergency fact-finding board as authorized by the Railway Labor Act of 1926. The NMB hoped that formation of this panel would send strikers back to their jobs during the thirty-day investigation period and for thirty days after the report was made. (In past experience, parties to a dispute usually maintained the status quo for sixty days.) President Truman agreed, and late on March 15 he issued an executive order launching an emergency body to investigate the conflict. Fortunately, labor and management negotiators settled about 40 percent of the disputes in conferences, and the unions then signed a back-to-work agreement. On March 22, employees began to return to their posts. It took several weeks, however, to restore normal operations, and for the first time since reorganization the Wabash posted a loss for a single month.[86]

This eight-day strike should not have taken the legalistic and regulatory course that it did. Because the disputes belonged to the minor category, the National Railroad Adjustment Board (NRAB), which had been in existence since 1934, should have resolved the matter. Unlike "major disputes," which involved negotiation of a new or significantly altered basic contract, minor differences centered on controversies dealing with the meaning of an existing collective bargaining agreement and usually with only a single employer. It would not be until 1957 that the U.S. Supreme Court, in *Brotherhood of Railroad Trainmen v. Chicago River & Indiana Railroad Company,* ultimately decided that minor issues were *not* strike material and must be sent to the NRAB for adjudication. At the time of the 1949 stoppage, Wabash operating personnel struck in order to change the work agreement without going through the legally prescribed process. In fact, this would be a common tactic used by railroad labor before it lost the *Chicago River & Indiana Railroad* case.[87]

As well as dealing with labor disputes, the Wabash repeatedly coped with the ravages of nature. On Friday, July 13, 1951, the skies opened over western Missouri on an already saturated watershed, and soon the Missouri River and its tributaries inundated vast sections of greater Kansas City. These unprecedented floods, which rivaled the great flood of 1903, disrupted all freight and passenger operations through the Kansas City gateway and proved to be enormously expensive, causing damages in excess of $1 billion. The company estimated that it lost about $1.4 million in revenues, and damage to its physical plants carried a price tag of $596,309. The cleanup took weeks. Crews faced monumental tasks, ranging from removing silt that had piled up over yard rails and switches to cleaning and repacking journal boxes in freight cars. Luckily, the Wabash and other railroads had time to prepare before the flood waters reached St. Charles and St. Louis, although some damage occurred there, too. For several days the company operated, as a public service, a twice-daily special ten-car "flood-emergency train" between Robertson and St. Charles to accommodate residents who no longer could travel the flooded St. Charles Rock Road.[88]

Other challenges also loomed as the Wabash management coped with growing competition from motor carriers and regulatory and labor issues. Fortunately, piggyback operations promised a reasonable expectation of bringing some truck freight back to the rails. Of course, there was nothing the railroad industry could do about the road-building blitz that followed passage of the National Defense Highway Act of 1956 or America's infatuation with the automobile. Nevertheless, officials became frustrated by the maze of red tape that resulted from stringent regulatory control and the obvious problem of railroad "featherbedding." The latter directly cost the Wabash tens of thousands of dollars annually by having hundreds of unproductive, though well-paid, workers, most of all firemen on diesel locomotives and telegrapher-agents in little-used country stations.[89]

THE NEW WABASH 227

Whereas the Atkinson administration relegated labor "featherbedding" to a back burner except for supporting the national lobbying conducted by the Association of American Railroads (AAR), "unjust regulation" did occupy its attention. Atkinson himself repeatedly lashed out at "horse and buggy-era regulatory restraints" and worried publicly about nationalization of the railroad industry. "Railroad profits are the victim of a squeeze play forced on us by the Government's long standing policy toward our industry," he told the Downtown Optimist Club of St. Louis in April 1949. "Government regulation has been effective in keeping the railroads from making 'too much' money—but has *not* been equally effective toward giving them a chance to earn *enough* despite better service and greater efficiency of operation. The railroad industry wants to serve you better and we are confident we can do so if permitted to operate as private enterprises with an adequate return."[90]

Atkinson did more than go on a speaking crusade complaining about unjust regulations and insisting on the freedom to manage. He spent considerable time personally lobbying friendly politicians, especially after his cherished Republican Party took control of both Congress and the White House in January 1953. Before the elections of 1952, Atkinson also orchestrated a well-publicized mailing campaign to prominent opinion makers. In addition to a personal letter extolling the virtues of less regulation, each envelope contained two shiny pennies. "These two pennies won't buy a newspaper or a stamp for an out-of-town letter but for them last year the Wabash and other American railroads hauled a ton of freight about a mile and a half." And Atkinson, with board authorization, cheerfully paid AAR assessments and made generous contributions to the American Heritage Foundation and other free-enterprise groups. He

seemed to be a man on a mission.[91]

Although it is difficult to gauge the effectiveness of Wabash efforts to cut red tape and defend conservative business values, Atkinson and other industry leaders, such as Fred Gurley of the Santa Fe and Perry Shoemaker of the Delaware, Lackawanna & Western, took considerable pleasure in the passage of the Transportation Act of 1958. Enacted to relieve the "deteriorating railroad situation," this measure failed to be the Magna Carta that the Staggers Rail Act of 1980 would become, but it offered the industry more than a glimmer of hope that the regulatory stranglehold might be significantly loosened. The new law created a less stringent approach to rate making. No longer were charges to be set at a particular level to protect the traffic of other modes of transportation. The act also made it easier to remove unprofitable passenger trains and to retire money-losing branch lines. In addition, it guaranteed loans to carriers in financial difficulties. The law also required ICC regulation of motor carrier rates on some agricultural commodities such as frozen fruits and vegetables that were formerly exempt.[92]

When Atkinson moved out of the president's office on July 1, 1959, to assume less rigorous duties as chairman of the board, he left his beloved Wabash Railroad in good condition. The company was hardly a joke in the industry, business or financial circles, and nothing indicated that it was headed again toward bankruptcy. There existed a general optimism among corporate analysts about an upturn in the economy for 1960 and even for the ensuing decade, although, admittedly, some railroad experts were uncertain what the future held for the industry. As an independent railroad, the Wabash would not see its way through the 1960s. Instead, it would choose to join the ranks of the "fallen flag" carriers, a wise and calculated move in the merger juggling of the day.[93]

A Fallen Flag

ENTER HERMAN PEVLER

If Arthur K. Atkinson was a "Wabash man," Herman H. Pevler, his successor in the presidential suite at the Railway Exchange Building, was a "Pennsy man." Born on April 20, 1903, in the northwestern Indiana village of Waynetown, Pevler graduated in 1921 from high school in another small Hoosier community, Danville, west of Indianapolis. A gifted and hardworking student, Pevler later matriculated at his home state's land-grant college, Purdue University, where in 1927 he received his bachelor of science degree in civil engineering. Immediately after graduation, Pevler joined the Pennsylvania Railroad (PRR) as an assistant in the engineering corps attached to its Philadelphia Terminal Division. Steady employment with the PRR followed, and he advanced through the engineering department, reaching the position of division engineer. In 1939, Pevler transferred to the operating department, however, and assumed the superintendency of the Logansport Division. By 1955, he had become the highly respected vice president and general manager of the Northwest Region, based in Chicago, one of the most im-

Even though some Midwestern railroads allowed their passenger service to decline rapidly after the late 1950s, the Wabash sought to maintain standards, although at times it had no option but to abandon runs. The southbound *Blue Bird* heads toward the Decatur, Illinois, station. Near the end of its life, this train had lost its rounded observation car. And on this particular day, the *Blue Bird* includes a heavyweight Railway Post Office (RPO) car. (J. Parker Lamb Photograph)

portant positions outside the Philadelphia headquarters. It would be the efforts of David Bevan, chief financial officer at PRR, who considered Pevler to be "one of the best operating men in the country," that led to his appointment to the Wabash presidency at age fifty-six.[1]

The white-haired, heavy-browed and bespectacled Pevler was an appropriate replacement for Atkinson. As soon as he arrived in St. Louis, on July 1, 1959, he seized the reins of leadership. Unlike his predecessor, Pevler, never wanting to waste time on what he considered to be unimportant matters, acted quickly. He revealed a more determined side than Atkinson. "He runs a business—and if the 'traditional' way of doing things gets in the way," commented an industry writer, "it's demolished." Usually with a smile, Pevler demanded that subordinates tell the truth and pay heed to company needs. When the Wabash president once passed through Decatur in his business car, he asked the local superintendent if he experienced any problems with the sprawling yard facility. "No sir!" came the response. "We have a perfect yard operation here." So Pevler told his traveling associates, "Pull the pin. I'm going to stay here for a couple of days to observe this perfect yard." As expected, perfection had not been achieved at the Decatur facility.[2]

Whenever a major executive change occurs, not everyone in the ranks is pleased. Those who thrived under Atkinson worried about their status with Pevler, and some found that they had good reason to be concerned. Whether one prospered or foundered, there was a widespread feeling among longtime white-collar Wabash personnel that Pevler was "too much of a Pennsy man," which most of all carried with it a certain haughty demeanor. Even those beyond the Wabash shared similar views. "There was an arrogance associated with these men, including Herman Pevler," opined the former general counsel of the Southern Railway. "They thought that they were gods." Still, one Wabash underling offered probably a fair assessment of the new Wabash president: "He's tough—but he's good."[3]

An immediate priority for Pevler involved operations. Certain aspects bothered him. He thought that the previous regime dispatched too many light freight trains. "The service performed by the Wabash was, in some instances, not that desired by the public." Although Pevler wanted tonnage to move rapidly over the lines and through terminals, he saw the advantage of longer consists. To handle heavier trains, the mechanical department quickly equipped all diesel A units with front jumper cables to permit greater use of three-and four-unit combinations. It soon became rare to see only two diesels on a main-line freight train. Within a short time, these through freights averaged approximately 105 cars, or about eighteen more than on the eve of Pevler's ascendancy. The new Wabash president could take considerable satisfaction that by January 1960 his road achieved one of the industry's best gross ton-miles per train-hour figures, and his performance greatly impressed PRR officialdom.[4]

Train speeds were not overlooked. A continuation of centralized traffic control installations, which by the end of 1962 reached nearly 550 miles, better curve alignments and other track improvements reduced running times. Pevler, however, concentrated on pesky terminal delays, the bane of the railroad industry. He wanted them reduced, and they were. The most effective assault on this problem involved inexpensive logistical changes. By 1960, the company operated several of its principal time-freights with transfer cabooses already cut in behind cars that had been preblocked for delivery to connecting roads. When the train reached the terminal, transfer cuts moved out immediately

By the time of the Herman Pevler administration the Wabash bottom line depended heavily on shipments of raw materials, parts and finished products associated with the automobile industry. In fact, Ford Motor Company achieved the status of being its best freight customer. In the summer of 1959, near Sidney, Illinois, a pair of F7 freight units sped a Detroit-to–Kansas City train with two gondola cars filled with auto frames. (J. Parker Lamb Photograph)

without time-consuming yard delays that involved adding cabooses.[5]

Customers benefited from improved terminal efficiency and faster over-the-road-speeds. Soon the Wabash offered, in conjunction with the Lehigh Valley (LV), second-morning delivery on freight between New York City and St. Louis. This saved one day over previous schedules. Service from St. Louis to Chicago improved so that cars leaving the Gateway City in the evening arrived in time for market openings in the Windy City and early morning connections with Eastern railroads. Moreover, arrangements with the shipper-friendly Erie Railroad accelerated service to various Eastern destinations via the Huntington, Indiana, interchange.[6]

The upgrading of freight operations was

due to more than just additional diesel power, fewer terminal delays and new traffic strategies. Another early priority of the Pevler regime involved reorganization of corporate activities. Not surprisingly, the operating department received first attention. Under the previous administration, the company employed three assistant general managers, one who handled personnel matters and two others who performed operational functions that varied and shifted. This structure posed some real problems. For example, no one had definite responsibility for station operations. Pevler badly wanted "to unconfuse confusion." Effective March 1, 1960, the president, backed by a cooperative board of directors, created four specific departments: transportation, special operations, personnel and stations-motor truck service. A manager headed each of these units and reported directly to the vice president and general manager.[7]

There would soon be a fifth department, known as operations research, or "OR." Although the concept was new for the Wabash, it was hardly novel in the industry, but Pevler and the board thought it was better to be late than never to act at all. They believed that OR would fill a glaring void in the overall running of the company. This unit received broad areas of responsibilities, including operations, traffic and passenger service. Thus, with "factual information" supplied by OR, Pevler expected that his railroad could make decisions that would be based on more than hunches and tradition.

He liked a managerial tool that "uses scientific and mathematical approaches to the solution of business problems."[8]

With a better handle on operations, Pevler next spearheaded reorganization of the traffic department. The concept was to make this unit "more efficient, to put authority and responsibilities out in the territory where the department operates, to create a department to sell all Wabash service." The reorganization proceeded quickly. First, freight and passenger sales operations merged, in part because of the declining importance of the passenger sector. Then all sales activities were divided into nine territories, each with its own traffic manager, who had an office outside St. Louis headquarters. (Heretofore, the supervision of field forces

It is a frigid day in the winter of 1959 as J. Parker Lamb captures a long Wabash freight moving through Tolono, Illinois. By climbing a boxcar, located on a side track, he could demonstrate his exceptional photographic skills. But as Lamb said, "being perched on a boxcar was uncomfortable, to say the least." (J. Parker Lamb Photograph)

had been centrally located and "many travel hours and expense dollars from the territory and miles away from shipper contacts.") Somewhat later, the Wabash and Ann Arbor traffic departments were unified. This meant not only more focused sales efforts but also restructuring resulted in sizeable payroll savings for the Ann Arbor, amounting to more than $200,000 the first year.[9]

There were other changes in the corporate bureaucracy. Pevler liked the idea of streamlining divisional activities, for example. It was decided that the Detroit Terminal Division should be abolished as a separate entity. As of November 1, 1961, it became the Detroit Terminal Division of the Montpelier Division. The change modestly boosted efficiency and reduced operating costs.[10]

Pevler also wanted more than structural alterations; he had other ideas that were part of his improvement road map. One involved offering customers Plan I trailer-on-flatcar (TOFC) service. The original piggyback program covered only so-called Plan II, where the railroad provided all aspects of the operation, including the truck trailer. Plan I, however, involved the shipper dealing directly with the motor carrier that supplied the trailer. The cargo then moved by rail from ramp to ramp, and the trucking company handled pickup and delivery. In time, shipments of new automobiles and light trucks, principally from Ford but also from Studebaker, became a major part of the Wabash involvement with Plan I. At Pevler's insistence, the Wabash also participated in the several other TOFC options.[11]

The activist president perceived another problem at the Wabash, namely, the need for better internal communications. He sought the effective transmission of new ideas. "Yours get twisted going down and theirs never get to you," he told an industry journalist. "We are going to make every effort to improve that situation," and changes

followed. A few months after his arrival, Pevler orchestrated the first "Wabash family meeting" since 1953. The company picked up the tab for a two-day affair at a St. Louis hotel for approximately 400 key employees and their wives. A variety of speakers, including several from outside the railroad industry, participated, and Pevler and Atkinson also addressed the assembled. About the same time, Pevler endorsed creation of a four-page monthly in-house newsletter, appropriately named *The Banner*. It succinctly explained major corporate happenings, frequently providing information that never appeared in either commercial print or broadcast media reports. Headquarters mailed copies to every Wabash household. Only during the 1920s were employees given access to such a publication.[12]

The new regime did not overlook external communications. The company organized a small speakers bureau, designed to improve understanding with shippers, civic and fraternal organizations and the scores of communities the railroad served. This program became particularly important in explaining the company's position in at least one highly publicized and politically charged passenger train "take-off" case.[13]

Following in the steps of Atkinson, Pevler went on the highly caloric "rubber chicken" circuit. He spoke to a variety of groups, usually with a pronounced business orientation. In these presentations, he offered more than paeans of praise for his railroad (which, incidentally, he thought the Atkinson administration had physically overbuilt), but dealt head on with a number of national issues, some of which were highly controversial. Pevler particularly underscored the negative impact employee "featherbedding" (or, as he called it, "the continuance of archaic working rules") had on the Wabash and the industry. He liked to provide illustrations that came from the home areas of his audience.

In a September 1959 address before an assembly of prominent Kansas City area business leaders, for example, he gave them this powerful example of the disconnect between worker performance and worker pay: "The engineer on our passenger train CITY OF KANSAS CITY leaves Moberly at 11:45 A.M., after an early lunch, arrives Kansas City 2:25 P.M., leaves Kansas City at 3:55 P.M., and arrives back in Moberly at 6:15 P.M. in plenty of time for dinner." He then added the clincher: "In a matter of 6½ hours he has accumulated 2½ days' pay without missing a meal at home."[14]

While talk about work rules continued, and the attendant issues would take years to be resolved, the Wabash delayed in seizing several opportunities that were readily available to improve efficiency and reduce costs. It took the company longer than some railroads to embrace three forms of technology that would have a profound impact upon the industry: radios, computers and continuous welded rail. Perhaps a degree of corporate ossification explains the delay.[15]

The Wabash was painfully slow in adopting two-way radios for train use, suggesting to some that it was rather tradition bound. As early as 1951 the Erie, an often-innovative carrier, became the first major railroad to have its entire mainline served by radio. Known as the "four-way train radio-telephone," this VHF system allowed static-free voice contact from train cab-to-caboose, train-to-train, train-to-station and station-to-station. The Erie and other carriers quickly discovered that the radio promoted safety, offered convenience and enhanced efficiency. Although the Wabash in 1955 installed radios on three switch engines at Toledo with the operational center located in the yardmaster's office, it took until early 1962 before the company made a major commitment to this well-proven technology. An initial expenditure of nearly $200,000 resulted in the installation of radio equipment in 162 diesel units and sixty cabooses for freight trains that operated between Decatur and Moberly and St. Louis and Kansas City. Base stations opened in both Decatur and Moberly. Subsequently, the railroad expanded radio communications, including their usage in additional yard operations.[16]

In the 1950s, computers began to appear on railroads. Even in their infancy, they could make major contributions. In 1954 Union Pacific (UP), a transportation leader, installed its first computers, supplied by the International Business Machine Company (IBM), at yard offices in three scattered locations. The devices made tracing car locations easier. It did not take long before computers also allowed UP to manage better its interline-freight accounts, material inventory and payroll. Other railroads joined the computer bandwagon, including the St. Louis–based Missouri Pacific in 1958. If there ever was an industry that could benefit from computers, it was railroads. This technology was to the railroads of the late 1950s and 1960s what diesel-powered streamliners had been in the late 1930s and 1940s. Each produced unexpected economies, often beyond the wildest expectations of management.[17]

In time, the Wabash participated in the fast-evolving computer revolution, although it only dimly glimpsed the radical changes that this technology would create. At the May 24, 1962, board meeting Pevler told directors that "it has been determined that greater efficiencies and economies can be realized within the Accounting Department if certain of its functions were mechanized." He predicted that annual savings would be at least $65,000. With approval in hand, the company acquired IBM 1401 and 1410 data processing systems, which consisted of computers, readers, punches, printers and tape drives. A specially constructed room in the central accounting department, with air conditioning, humidity control and dust-proofing features, housed the expensive new equipment.[18]

The Pevler administration also expanded the railroad's use of continuous welded rail (CWR). As with radios and computers, this type of rail assembly, which significantly reduced maintenance costs and provided a smoother ride by eliminating the familiar "clickety-clack," had been adopted much earlier by other carriers. In the 1930s, the spunky Chicago Great Western had achieved national acclaim for its bold use of welded rail on its core stem in eastern Iowa. Although some CWR was installed during Atkinson's tenure, most appeared on the Wabash after Pevler arrived. The butt-welding plant at Moberly, opened in 1956, experienced much usage. In 1959, for example, thirty-five miles of new 115-pound rail and thirteen miles of relay rail were welded into continuous lengths and laid on the mainlines. Yet, the real CWR revolution did not occur on Wabash lines until after the take-over by the Norfolk & Western Railway (N&W) in 1964.[19]

In the late 1950s and early 1960s the Wabash garnered public attention not for its advances in technology or its general profitability, but rather for cutbacks in its passenger operations. The company could not ignore the bottom line. It had become impossible to justify trains that hemorrhaged red ink. Business travelers were opting for speedy and convenient commercial airliners, and pleasure seekers found high-horsepower automobiles, inexpensive gasoline and superhighways more to their liking. Furthermore, the U.S. Post Office started to rely more on trucks and specially equipped buses to serve as highway post offices (Hypos). The reduction or loss of head-end mail traffic might well turn a marginally profitable passenger train into a real money loser.[20]

The Wabash had certainly tried to serve the traveling public. Even a member of the Illinois Commerce Commission in 1960 admitted that "the Wabash has been very progressive and has done a fine passenger job," as indeed it had. In 1958, for example, the railroad chopped ten to thirty-five minutes from the timetable of its four St. Louis–Detroit trains. This became possible because of more efficient dispatching and the assignment of two rather than one diesel units on these runs. During the twilight years of privately owned long-distance passenger service, the Wabash continued to invest in rolling stock. Most notably, in 1959 it spent $250,000 for a dome coach to be added to the *City of St. Louis* on its journey between St. Louis and Los Angeles. (The Union Pacific acquired five additional dome cars for these train sets.) Moreover, the Wabash trumpeted a host of specials. In the late 1950s it scheduled from Decatur, with usually an intermediate stop at Taylorville, excursions that brought thousands of riders to St. Louis, where they enjoyed the Ice Capades, Broadway musicals and other entertainment. At times, these runs carried as many as 1,500 people. The "Theatre Train," which ran in two sections on September 28, 1957, was packed with passengers holding tickets for a Saturday matinee performance of a stage production of *My Fair Lady* at Kiel Auditorium. The company also continued its popular tradition of operating football specials. In 1959, for example, St. Louisans could take trains to Columbia, Champaign and South Bend to see home games of the University of Missouri, University of Illinois and University of Notre Dame. "The all-expense trip [to South Bend from St. Louis] on Pullmans of $29.25 includes transportation, food, reserved ticket to game and all taxes. The full cost on coaches is $21.75." Thousands of football fans frolicked, and the Wabash benefited.[21]

There were other ways that the Wabash sought to attract passengers. One involved price reductions. On February 25, 1959, it offered a three-cents-per-mile coach and first-class fare for passengers traveling one way between St. Louis, Kansas City and Denver and Cheyenne via the UP and established a round-trip fare at 166.6 percent of the one-way tariff, instead of 180 percent. The company further instituted a special "Family Fare Savings" plan, designed to encourage spouses and children to travel with husbands and fathers. "With Family Fare, only Dad pays full fare; Mom and all the rest of the family pay about half their regular fare; children under five travel free, of course." The railroad appealed to patrons' pocketbooks *and* stomachs when, in 1958, it added its highly touted "Silver Dollar Dinner" to dining car menus (except on the *City of St. Louis*). "You can get for $1 an entree, bread and butter, beverage and dessert," explained a company official. "It is silly to get a man on the train with a low fare and murder him in the dining car." For budget-minded travelers, it was no longer necessary to pack fried chicken, bread and butter sandwiches and a slice of cake, although some thrifty folks still brought along their own "eats." Most important for the Wabash, hungry diners filled tables, and compliments flowed into St. Louis headquarters.[22]

But all was not well on the passenger front. "We will not desert the passengers—the passengers must desert us," declared Pevler in discussing passenger service in September 1959 at a luncheon meeting of the Kansas City Chamber of Commerce. Unfortunately, for those who wanted to maintain passenger service on the Wabash, the latter

One of the lesser trains dispatched by the Wabash during the Pevler years was No. 214, which operated along the more than 400 miles between Omaha and St. Louis. In the early 1960s No. 214 stands at the Montgomery, Missouri, station, and would soon glide into St. Louis Union Station. (Gary Roe Coll.)

seemed to be occurring. Backed by the Transportation Act of 1958, which made it less difficult to end money-losing operations, the company won authority in 1959 to eliminate Trains 12 and 13, which operated between Fort Wayne and Toledo, and Trains 11 and 14, which ran between St. Louis and Des Moines. "These trains are no longer used or needed in the public service," explained Pevler rather tersely to the board. Later he commented, hardly to anyone's surprise, that "development of interstate highway systems and the increased use of automobile transportation and other forms of passenger transportation have largely contributed to the decline in the passenger traffic."[23]

Although the hearings that considered discontinuance of the Toledo and Des Moines trains elicited some public and labor opposition, the Wabash experienced greater objections and endured a more protracted examination in a subsequent abandonment request. On March 9, 1960, it asked the Illinois Commerce Commission for permission to drop Trains 117 and 118, *The Midnight*, its overnight runs between Chicago and St. Louis. Immediately after the formal filing, the company bought newspaper space to explain its action. "Last year [1959] these trains operated at a loss of $325,567. In 1958 the losses amounted to $372,276. No one except the federal government can operate under such conditions." The justification continued: "We are tempted to point the finger at antiquated work rules, federal subsidies to our competitors, and unfair state and federal regulations. More specifically these losses are attributable to increased costs of wages, payroll taxes, terminal expenses, Pullman operating costs and others." The railroad, however, did not fail to remind travelers that it would continue its fine *Banner Blue* and *Blue Bird* trains between these two Midwestern metropolises.[24]

On May 1, 1960, formal hearings on re-moving *The Midnight* began in Springfield. They continued intermittently for several weeks and kept a stenographer busy producing more than 1,400 pages of testimony. Whereas the Wabash presented its evidence in somewhat succinct fashion and with a variety of supporting exhibits, the public response tended to be scattered and poorly documented. Representatives from Decatur, the only large community on the route, complained that their city of approximately 100,000, lacked direct access to an interstate highway and worried what would happen "when the weather gets ornery—when trucks bog down on snow-covered highways and planes are grounded." The witnesses, most of all, wanted *The Midnight*s as back-up transportation during a weather emergency.[25]

At times the testimony elicited more personal objections. The most poignant one involved military veterans, overwhelmingly from World War I, who needed to travel overnight to Chicago. The superintendent of the Veterans' Assistance Commission for Macon County (Decatur) explained why he wanted the Wabash to retain the trains:

THE WITNESS: The effect that this [discontinuance] would have on the veterans in this area is the fact that men who have pensions coming or who are already drawing compensation are requested to appear in the Chicago Veterans' Administration Regional Office for a physical examination.

They are always scheduled at eight o'clock in the morning.

From the Veterans' offices in this county we sent approximately eighty to a hundred men a month. I would say that from 90 to 95 percent of these men take that early morning train; so consequently, that was my basis of the objection. It's because of the inconvenience to the veteran.

Most of these men are elderly men, 65 and over; and to be perfectly frank with you, they would have no other way that I know of to get to Chicago.

They are at the age where they can't drive, and I am a lot younger than most of them and I go from two to three times a year to Chicago for the same purpose; and I refuse to drive from here to Chicago to be there at eight o'clock to take the examination.

Now, this 118, the way it is scheduled, will generally get the men in there to where they are not more than half hour late.

I feel that the removal of this train will not only affect the veterans in this particular area, but it will affect them all the way down the line from East St. Louis on, because the Veterans' Administration Regional Office in Chicago covers that area. . . . It extends to East St. Louis; and if we are sending 80 to a hundred men a month, I know these other areas must be sending men also.

So the way the significance of this train is felt by the veteran, I think it is a crime that this train has to be removed.[26]

Though appropriate deference was paid to the Veterans' spokesperson, the commission quickly decided in favor of the Wabash. It accepted the company position that "there is uncontroverted testimony to the effect that these trains are operated at a substantial loss" and agreed that there is "an abundance of testimony that there is not only diversified substitute transportation by other modes of transportation, . . . but also alternate transportation by the Wabash Railroad over the same line of railroad running between Chicago and St. Louis." It did not take long before the two *Midnight*s made their last runs, leaving the Gulf, Mobile & Ohio with the only overnight service between Chicago and St. Louis.[27]

Unlike some carriers in the Midwest, the Wabash did not exit completely from the passenger business. As late as 1962, it continued to dispatch the *Banner Blue* and *Blue Bird*

(both sported dome cars, although the *Banner Blue* did not receive lightweight equipment until 1960 and carried some heavyweight cars until its discontinuance in 1968) between St. Louis and Chicago; the *Wabash Cannon Ball* and the *Detroit Limited/St. Louis Limited* between St. Louis and Detroit; the *City of St. Louis* and the *City of Kansas City* between St. Louis and Kansas City; the not-so-elegant Trains 211 and 214 between St. Louis and Council Bluffs; and several mixed trains on the Columbia branch. Even after the company entered the orbit of the N&W, this service mostly remained.[28]

Although the Wabash had to forsake some faithful passengers, it certainly did not abandon freight patrons. The company continued its tradition of responding to shipper needs, especially those of its best customer, Ford Motor Company. Beginning in October 1, 1959, for example, the Wabash made its first movement of sixteen set-up automobiles on auto transports from Detroit to St. Louis and soon expanded this service to other Ford assembly plants. In 1962, the company inaugurated its "Cannon Ball Freight Service" with Ford in mind. "It is different from traditional railroad freight service in that emphasis is placed on the needs of the shipper," explained Pevler to his employees, "and Wabash Railroad operations will be tailored, both from a sales and operating angle, for the special benefit of patrons." New locomotives, specialty boxcars and better schedules made Cannon Ball Freight Service effective. Automobile parts, for example, sped from manufacturer to assembler in what would later be called "just-in-time" delivery, thus requiring the maintenance of only a modest inventory.[29]

While piggyback cars moved in the fastest trains, research and traffic personnel discovered that TOFC business could be strengthened if a first-class freight train between Chicago and St. Louis, comprised *only* of

Wabash management did its best to attract and keep freight customers. It creatively advertised its fast, dependable service. This particular promotional copy dates from 1963. (Author's Coll.)

"The Rumble and the Roar"

The old Wabash Cannonball melody has a new refrain now. Efficiency, up-to-dateness, special services mark "Cannonball" Freight Service. It's a modern way of shipping to meet the needs of modern business. Try it . . .

WABASH "CANNONBALL" FREIGHT SERVICE

Contact: Wabash Railroad Co.
(name and phone)

WABASH CANNON BALL FREIGHT · SERVICE

"Follow the Flag"

WABASH

piggyback trailers, could be created and dispatched on a user-friendly schedule. "Studies showed that a fast piggyback train which would be assembled and would depart after normal closing hours would be highly attractive to shippers. And, if shipments could arrive in either city in time for the start of the next morning's business, this, too, would be highly instrumental in attracting new customers." On May 19, 1964, with the requisite publicity, the company introduced "Roadrunner" TOFC service. A pair of trains, the first solid piggyback operations by the Wabash on an advertised basis, left both Chicago and St. Louis in the evening and arrived early the next day at their terminal ramps. These trains maintained rigid schedules, taking only six hours and thirty minutes to complete their runs, not far behind

the *Blue Bird*'s carding of five hours and forty minutes. Roadrunners thrived, and they continued to dash through the night to the satisfaction of both consumer and railroad. These hotshots seldom ran late.[30]

MERGER DANCES

A series of triumphs seemed to mark postwar railroading. For a while, although Americans turned increasingly to their automobiles, many still considered passenger trains as the best means of long-distance pleasure travel. Those who opted for airplanes likely did so because of pressing time concerns, but vagaries of weather might make this a gamble. If one lacked an expense account, air travel was expensive. Railroads such as the Wabash seized the opportunity to exploit travel both for business and pleasure by introducing scores of streamliners. These natty trains symbolized a new era in ground transportation. Although representing enormous capital expenditures, for a decade or so this upgraded service appeared to be a good financial risk. But the far better investment involved dieselization. The economies and efficiencies achieved were staggering, saving large carriers like the Wabash millions of dollars annually. Furthermore, introduction of piggyback service offered hope for reclaiming some traffic that had been lost to truckers, while creation of sophisticated development departments helped to attract shippers to the ever-more-popular "industrial park."[31]

By the late 1950s, however, events altered the mood of the industry into a more negative mode. Optimism about long-distance passenger service faded. State-operated toll roads and newly completed toll-free interstate highways attracted an increasing number of automobiles and trucks whose drivers were not impeded by the congestion of two-lane roads with their ubiquitous traffic lights, slow-moving vehicles and speed traps. Major airlines introduced jet aircraft, and regional firms offered larger, more dependable propeller-driven planes. Cruising speeds also increased, often doubling or even tripling. Air carriers benefited from vast, almost unlimited public expenditures on airports and auxiliary installations. Water competitors siphoned off more freight tonnage, often what motor carriers did not want to haul, the result of government support for inland waterways, including the costly St. Lawrence Seaway project. Then, beginning in the fall of 1957, the national

Until its entry into the Norfolk & Western system, the Wabash spent heavily on freight equipment. A yard switcher has a cut of cars, including a new "hi-cube" boxcar, in this July 1964 photograph of operations in Oakwood Yard in Detroit. (H. G. Goerke Photograph, J. David Ingles Coll.)

economy became sluggish and even depressed in some areas. The rail industry realized that other factors deepened its growing sense of pessimism. Significantly, too, the cost reductions made possible from massive dieselization had largely been realized. "What had once spelled dramatic savings was now a lot less dramatic," argued historian Richard Saunders, "and it was time to look beyond the diesel." Adding to this ever-more-complex sense of pessimism was the problem of overcapacity. Between New York City and Buffalo, for example, five different railroads competed for traffic, and further south three roads battled for business between Washington, D.C., and Chicago.[32]

If railroads were to remain economically viable, mergers increasingly appeared to be the most practical option. Soon the industry generated rumors, speculation and a few announced plans for unification. On August 31, 1957, the first merger in what became a spate of corporate marriages occurred when the 1,043-mile Nashville, Chattanooga & St. Louis Railway (NC&StL) united with the 4,765-mile Louisville & Nashville Railroad (L&N), the latter having had stock control of the former since 1880. Designed to save nearly $4 million annually, the NC&StL-L&N merger claimed to be the initial union designed for *retrenchment*. A combination of line abandonments and elimination of duplicate personnel and support facilities would produce the anticipated economies.[33]

While the unification of the NC&StL and L&N, which was largely a paper transaction, went well, the railroad industry paid closer attention to the even more impressive merger of two *competing* bituminous coal carriers, the 611-mile Virginian Railway (VGN) with the 2,132-mile N&W. Both enjoyed high profitability, being almost like conveyor belts between mines and markets. Even the post–World War II decline in coal usage, especially for home heating, did not seriously hurt either road. Demand for steam coal to generate electricity remained strong for both domestic and export markets, especially in the mid-Atlantic and Midwestern states and Western Europe. Because both of these Pocahontas coal roads were anything but streaks of rust, savings would come mostly from combining managements, shops and yards. And they would be considerable, estimated at $14 million annually. But there would be another bonus: coal would move more expeditiously over the best grades between West Virginia mines and Hampton Roads, Virginia, coal docks, and expensive "helper" locomotives and their crews would no longer be needed. The portions of the former mainlines that had the least attractive profiles could handle empties, while loaded cars could rumble along the easier grades. The VGN-N&W union became effective on December 1, 1959, and helped to prompt merger thoughts among every major Eastern railroad.[34]

The result was that, as the 1960s began, more roads became "fallen flags." A variety of corporate marriages took place, ranging from a parent company adding a subsidiary to forming wholly new units. In 1960 alone, the Atlantic Coast Line Railroad took over its Charleston & Western Carolina Railway affiliate. The Canadian Pacific Railway simply brought together its three American properties—the Duluth, South Shore & Atlantic Railroad, Minneapolis, St. Paul & Sault Ste. Marie ("Soo") Railroad, and the Wisconsin Central Railroad—into the Soo Line Railroad. The giant Chicago & North Western Railway (C&NW) acquired the smaller Minneapolis & St. Louis Railway (M&StL), and the Erie Railroad joined with the Delaware, Lackawanna & Western Railroad (DL&W) to create the Erie-Lackawanna Railroad (EL), a strengthened New York to Chicago trunk line. This trend showed no signs of ending. In fact, it continued, involving some of the nation's largest carriers.[35]

Wabash officials watched the growing merger phenomena with keen interest. As early as November 1957, the board of directors, taking cues from its PRR owners, gave its approval for Atkinson "to participate in studies of benefits to be derived from a merger of the Pennsylvania and the New York Central" and authorized him "to appoint a representative or representatives of this company to participate in such studies." When it became clear that railroad consolidations were in the fast lane, the Wabash paid close heed. While interested in protecting the "Albia Gateway," which might be adversely affected by the C&NW takeover of the M&StL, management showed much greater concern about the proposed formation of Erie-Lackawanna. If approved, the Wabash feared, most if not all of its interchange traffic with the DL&W through the Niagara Frontier, perhaps as much as $1 million annually, would be lost.[36]

PRR officials had their eyes open as well. They had backed the N&W-VGN union, and with the proposed Erie-DL&W marriage they mostly saw an opportunity for strengthening two of their properties, namely, the Lehigh Valley and Wabash. (PRR executives did not believe that the proposed EL itself would pose any real financial threat.) Instead, top brass, including president James M. Symes, hoped that the ICC would force the would-be EL to provide a better physical connection between the LV and Wabash at Buffalo. Specifically, these PRR men wanted the two roads to be able to use DL&W trackage in Buffalo. If this occurred, another potentially profitable route for parent PRR would exist between Chicago and New York.[37]

Because Symes preferred to work behind the scenes, he got Herman Pevler involved in negotiating for a better linkage between LV and Wabash. The Wabash president then discussed Buffalo matters with Erie and DL&W personnel. But, as DL&W president Perry Shoemaker recalled, "We knew he [Pevler] was a stalking horse of Symes and the Pennsy." Prior to the ICC hearings, Pevler asked Harry Von Willer, the Erie president, and Shoemaker to grant concessions. "They were given an ultimatum: give the trackage rights that would make the Wabash-Lehigh route competitive with the Erie Lackawanna or face prolonged harassment." Shoemaker and Von Willer refused. At the ICC hearings, representatives from the LV and Wabash demanded access to Erie-Lackawanna facilities in Buffalo. As Shoemaker later explained his feelings to a group of security analysts, "The . . . opposition . . . from Wabash and Lehigh Valley . . . reflected no credit upon the industry. . . . I know of no precedent for the price of merger being the supplying of property investment and property rights to improve a competitor's product, even if it is a product badly in need of improvement." Continued the DL&W executive, "It was, of course, rejected by us, and much time was spent on what was basically a phony issue having no proper part in the merger proceedings." By April 1960, the two sets of parties reached "terms mutually satisfactory," and the LV and Wabash (and PRR, too) gave the EL merger their endorsement. Said Pevler to Shoemaker and Von Willer, "We on the Wabash feel that your merger is for the good of our whole industry." Fortunately, for what rapidly became "Erie-Lack-of-money," the new railroad did not surrender too much to the two PRR-control roads and it was not forced to "short-haul" itself between Chicago and New York.[38]

EXIT THE WABASH

The Wabash could not remain an interested "outside" party; it had to join in the merger consolidation movement of the 1960s. Unlike a C&NW or an Erie, the company would not act in an independent manner. It was, after all, under the PRR's large wing, and merger activity on the part of the PRR directly affected the Wabash.

The PRR itself had merger plans. As the 1950s wore on, Symes believed that he had the solution to the increasing financial woes of all Eastern railroads, especially those operating in New England and the mid-Atlantic states, namely, giant consolidations. What he personally desired was to have the PRR, the nation's largest transportation enterprise, unite with archrival New York Central Railroad (NYC), the country's second-largest carrier. The other principal trunk roads would also need to unify, particularly the Baltimore & Ohio (B&O) and the Erie that operated in the PRR service territory. Although Symes realized that there would be major obstacles to overcome, the fight for a combined PRR-NYC would be worth the effort. He could be the architect and personal beneficiary of an American rail colossus.[39]

During the fall of 1957, the first steps in the merger process began. Discussions took place between Symes and Robert R. Young, who chaired the NYC but foolishly excluded NYC president Alfred Perlman. On November 1, 1957, the roads jointly announced that they planned to study the possibility of merger. Then in January 1958, Young shockingly committed suicide, despondent over his company's financial problems, and Perlman assumed power. Unfortunately for Symes and PRR managers who wanted to unite with the NYC, Perlman was not interested. If he had his way, the NYC would join the Chesapeake & Ohio Railway (C&O), a prosperous coal hauler that had lines between Chicago and the Virginia tidewater. Indeed, Perlman labored hard to have his road included in the pending merger proposal of the C&O and the less-stellar B&O. Talks therefore ended between PRR and NYC.[40]

Still, Symes wanted to fulfill his pet unification concept. In the interim, he had the

PRR win ICC approval to take total control of the LV. By 1962, the PRR had acquired nearly all of the road's equity, including the 265,469 shares held by Wabash, for which it paid $1,222,485. This would not be a wise financial decision on the part of PRR. The LV would repeatedly require cash infusions, and by 1970 it had consumed about $18 million of the parent's precious assets. But the PRR president argued that, with the LV inside the PRR fold, an important step had been taken in "an overall simplification of the eastern railroad competitive situation." He continued to believe that eventually a PRR-NYC merger would occur.[41]

Symes also liked the idea of an aggressive N&W, and he was not to be disappointed. On March 18, 1960, that carrier, in which the PRR continued to hold a substantial position, announced that merger talks had commenced with the New York, Chicago & St. Louis Railroad, commonly known as the Nickel Plate Road (NKP). Symes and his colleagues at PRR hoped that this would be yet another large Eastern system aborning. N&W president Stuart Saunders wholeheartedly agreed, as did the influential Walter J. Tuohy, president of the C&O, who called it "a constructive and natural step in the unification of the Eastern railroads." Industry experts also believed that the "eastern railroad mess" could be significantly lessened by an enlarged N&W.[42]

The NKP was a logical mate for the N&W. Even though these two companies did not connect physically, they could be tied together through construction or a purchase or lease of existing trackage. The N&W eventually paid top dollar for the PRR's rather decrepit 111-mile Sandusky, Ohio, branch that provided a direct route between Columbus and Sandusky via Bellevue, a strategic contact point with the NKP. From the N&W's perspective, it would gain access to some important terminals in mid-America. The

2,178-mile NKP, headquartered in Cleveland, operated not only its original core between Buffalo and Chicago via Cleveland and Fort Wayne but also the former Toledo, St. Louis & Western ("Clover Leaf Route") and Lake Erie & Western. Later, in the late 1940s, the NKP had leased the Wheeling & Lake Erie Railway, which once had been in the Wabash orbit. Not only did the NKP serve the Buffalo and Chicago gateways, but it reached Peoria, St. Louis and Toledo and other strategic interchange locations. Yet the NKP was not all the same. The most attractive portion was its trackage between Chicago and Buffalo, a fast, largely single-track and centralized traffic–controlled line. The former Clover Leaf Route, which gave the NKP access into St. Louis, however, was an undulating line, much of which originally had been built on the cheap in the 1870s by the narrow-gauge Toledo, Cincinnati & St. Louis Railroad.[43]

With the Eastern railroad networks showing signs of solidifying, the NYC found itself in an awkward situation. After being locked out of any union with the C&O or C&O-B&O, Perlman wanted the NYC included in the N&W-NKP proposal. Stuart Saunders and the N&W, however, did not fancy the NYC, believing that it would be too much of a financial liability. Rather, Saunders thought of including two other Eastern carriers, the Erie-Lackawanna and the Delaware & Hudson (D&H). "The Erie [EL] would put us into New York and the D&H would have put us into Montreal." By late 1961, Perlman decided that the NYC had no other practical alternative but to join the PRR, hardly his first, second or even third choice. In fact, leaders of the powerful C&O had already agreed on this strategy. The reasoning was that "unless something was done quickly, all railroads in the East would be in bankruptcy."[44]

The C&O decision was not made in a vacuum. At a momentous summer 1961 meeting held at White Sulphur Springs, West Virginia, between Walter Tuohy, C&O president, John Kusik, C&O's financial vice president, James Symes, PRR president, and Fred Carpi, PRR's vice president for sales, the C&O decided to endorse a PRR-NYC union. Symes was delighted that he had this crucial support for his highly desired merger. Yet he made a major concession of sorts: the N&W would remain *independent* of these proposed combinations—namely, it would not become part of either the C&O-B&O or PRR-NYC. From the perspective of the Wabash, the most important dimension of the parlay between C&O and PRR executives was that the PRR agreed to terminate its financial interests in both the N&W and Wabash for the right to pursue the "supermerger."[45]

Agreements reached at White Sulphur Springs delighted the hard-driving Saunders. It meant that he could build the N&W on his own, free from the influence of its largest shareholder, the PRR. Still, the PRR would have a say in shaping the merger map. When it earlier had backed the N&W-NKP union, it made it clear that it wanted the Wabash included; however, the PRR favored leasing its profitable affiliate rather than having it corporately fused into an expanded N&W.[46]

The Wabash lease had been hammered out in 1960 between the PRR and N&W, and, not surprisingly, it benefited the PRR. The N&W agreed to do several things: to contribute $1,399,635 a year to allow a dividend of $4.50 on Wabash preferred stock; to expend on the property an additional $7.1 million annually for a six-year period; to award an extra payment if N&W dividends exceeded a certain threshold; to pay federal taxes owed by Wabash and to provide compensation to Wabash security holders for any realized tax credits. The N&W also agreed to, "at its own expense and without deduction from the rent, maintain, manage and operate the leased property and make such extensions, additions, betterments and improvements thereto as it considers necessary or desirable." Furthermore, at a later date, but no sooner than six years or later than fifty years, the PRR would exchange its Wabash stock for N&W shares, which it assumed would be of considerable value. John P. (Jack) Fishwick, a N&W officer who later became president, recalled that his meeting in Philadelphia with the PRR representatives led to "very tough negotiation." He added, "We [N&W] had no bargaining power. All I could do at time was to sit across the table and say that the lease or price offered seemed unrealistic. But we finally got a price." Subsequently, the board of directors of the PRR passed a formal resolution that approved a merger of the N&W with the NKP along with lease of the Wabash. This union would create a 7,400-mile system with promising opportunities.[47]

On December 1, 1960, the public announcement of the Wabash involvement in the proposed merger of the N&W and NKP took place. "The proposal marks a great step forward in meeting the urgent need to strengthen the railroad industry in the public interest," were the words used by Pevler to explain the agreed-upon strategy. Soon executives from the N&W, NKP and Wabash sought to publicize the value of the merger/lease and to assuage fears about major cutback proposals, almost exclusively on the NKP and Wabash. In early January 1961, Saunders went to St. Louis to calm any concerns about his firm's expansion. "It would bring to this city the most prosperous railroad system in the country which will have a tremendous traffic potential and great financial stability." And he added, "St. Louis will be a key point in the operation of this proposed giant new transportation system." Still, Saunders admitted, but in a soothing way, changes would occur. "In all frankness,

I would not want to create the impression that St. Louis will be the headquarters of the proposed new system. As a matter of fact I think that 'headquarters' term will not be of great significance in the contemplated set up." Not to ruffle more feathers than necessary, Saunders told the press that the N&W would retain both the Nickel Plate and Wabash names. This would be done by referring to the lines of these former carriers as the "Nickel Plate Region" and the "Wabash Region" of the N&W. Commenting on the Wabash moniker, Saunders said, "The name 'Wabash' has stood for another fine, dependable line. We do not intend to let these respected symbols of reliable railroading disappear from the scene."[48]

Coinciding with the public pronouncement, the Wabash moved to dispose of its control over the Ann Arbor and the tiny Manistique & Lake Superior Railroad (owned by Ann Arbor). The N&W did not want the Ann Arbor in its expanded system, considering the railroad as only marginally profitable and the lake ferry service a financial albatross. Therefore, the Wabash pursued a buyer. Fortunately, the Detroit, Toledo & Ironton (DT&I), still controlled by the PRR and with some Wabash ownership, took interest, and in early 1961 it offered the Wabash $3 million for its preferred and common stock, which "represents the fair value of the shares of the Ann Arbor." On February 16, 1961, the Wabash board agreed to the sale. Within a few months the DT&I filed its request with the ICC to control the Ann Arbor. Permission came on December 18, 1962, and the effective date occurred nearly nine months later, September 9, 1963.[49]

Although railroad executives could make deals and have their stockholders overwhelmingly concur, the ICC (and occasionally federal courts) ultimately had the final say in any merger arrangements. Admittedly, the ICC had lost its past vitality. Political scientists considered it to be a casebook illustration of a regulatory body that, over a long period of time, had become unduly influenced by the parties that it was mandated to control. Still, the architects of mergers needed to receive the green light from the ICC.[50]

On October 10, 1961, the ICC launched its hearings on the N&W-NKP merger and lease of the Wabash. They would continue intermittently through May 2, 1962. The N&W personnel from corporate headquarters in Roanoke, Virginia, came well prepared. They knew what to tell regulators and had visual aids to underscore their points. The messages were clear: union would end "wasteful duplication" and would be in the "public interest." Saunders, himself, was well versed in his testimony. He stressed that the new railroad anticipated savings of $27 million annually and that it would provide shippers will superior service. But in reality, it would take five to ten years before these reductions could be fully realized. Moreover, this "superior service" already existed. "Every one of Saunders's examples of improved service had to do with the Wabash and the Nickel Plate, not the N&W," noted historian Richard Saunders in his analysis of the hearings. "The 15-hour reduction in Chicago-Buffalo schedules, for example, was nothing more than rerouting Wabash traffic over the Nickel Plate. There was no need for a merger to do this. All shippers had to say was 'Nickel Plate,' and they got the faster service." It was true, of course, that the merger/lease would bolster investor confidence by providing the N&W with a "seamless" distribution for its steam coal to a number of large electric generating plants in the Midwest and would lessen its dependence on export coal. There was merit to the public service arguments that the pooling of equipment, an expanded joint traffic department and state-of-the-art electronic possessing of car-movement data would benefit shippers.[51]

The N&W lined up scores of backers for its unification plans. The states of Illinois and Missouri, the Property Owners' Committee (an organization of Appalachian coal producers) and the West Virginia Chamber of Commerce, for example, intervened in support of the application. Their collective input left no question: consolidation would bolster local and area economies. Many emphasized that a more powerful railroad would increase the attractiveness of the service territory as a location for new or expanded industries. These businesses, among other things, would create jobs, consume more electric power and increase tax revenues.[52]

There were a few participants at the hearings, however, who did not want an expanded N&W. Representatives from a group of communities along the NKP's St. Louis line, who called themselves the "Four Cities Citizens Committee," worried about the likelihood of their hometown freight service being downgraded and presumed that there would be a loss of tax revenues from closed or diminished NKP properties. After all, the Wabash possessed the superior line between Indiana and the St. Louis Gateway and beyond, and Nickel Plate facilities, particularly in Frankfort, Indiana, would not likely be maintained at that current level. Other civic spokesmen fretted about altered patterns of railroad traffic. Governor Nelson Rockefeller of New York, for one, foresaw the historic connections to the Port of New York via the NKP and Wabash being seriously damaged. The Port of Norfolk, on the other hand, stood to gain handsomely from expanded export tonnage. "The N&W merger could do for Virginia what the opening of the Erie Canal had done for New York in 1825—raise it triumphantly ahead of old rival ports."[53]

While the hearings were under way, the N&W and its partners agonized about opposition from the newly created Erie-Lackawanna. This expanded road, whose executives were experiencing difficulty bringing together the Erie and DL&W operations, worried about the loss of interchange traffic if there were to be an enlarged N&W. It unequivocally wanted inclusion. In fact, EL made a cogent argument that a state-of-the-art classification yard at Huntington, Indiana (EL's junction with the Wabash), could produce spectacular savings, possibly exceeding $30 million annually. Understandably, the N&W felt the need to appease EL. "We thought this [support for EL] would be in our interest in the long run," admitted Fishwick, "and we also were interested in getting our merger through, frankly."[54]

EL wisely asked for more than a handshake. On October 12, 1961, the EL, N&W and NKP signed a document in which the EL agreed not to protest at the ICC merger hearings. In return, EL received a concession: "[The companies would] *forthwith, in good faith,* enter into consultations and negotiations in an attempt to agree upon a plan for some form of affiliation of E-L with the enlarged Norfolk system which would be mutually advantageous to the two companies." Twelve days later, the same parties approved a second agreement reaffirming this position. To show their earnestness, N&W and NKP decided to make a modest financial investment in EL securities. By the end of 1962, the former would acquire "not less than $1,000,000," and the latter "not less than $500,000." And big smiles appeared in the EL executive suites in Cleveland's Midland Building when the NKP consented to acquire a half interest in the Bison Yard project in Buffalo, then under construction. This would ensure that the EL would be the route of preference for tonnage arriving in Buffalo on the NKP. Regardless of the outcome of the merger application, the contract between EL and NKP was binding.[55]

Although several other carriers complained and the U.S. Department of Justice fussed, no insurmountable roadblocks appeared. Officials in Roanoke, Cleveland and St. Louis knew that they would triumph. Even though some jobs would be lost because of the merger (mostly among the ranks of white-collar employees), the brotherhoods understood that agreements firmly established from previous rail unifications would provide them with substantial labor protection.[56]

As the Wabash moved closer to union with the expanded N&W, a major leadership change occurred. In the summer of 1963, Pevler resigned the presidency to assume a similar role on the N&W in Roanoke. He succeeded Saunders, who moved to Philadelphia to head the PRR. It appeared that a real bond had already developed between Wabash and N&W. Although not everyone in the N&W hierarchy approved of Pevler, his four-year record at the Wabash revealed his considerable talents. He rightfully took enormous pride in his accomplishments. For one thing, the company in 1962 had achieved one of the best financial gains in the industry. The testimonial provided by the Wabash board was without reservation: "Mr. Pevler devoted himself unsparingly to the important functions of railroad management and, as a result of his effecting many economies and improvements in service, equipment and properties, the System holds a position of prominence among other carriers."[57]

Pevler's successor was expected. On October 1, 1963, Henry Whelen Large took charge in St. Louis. "A very high class fellow," recalled an industry associate, he had stepped into Pevler's shoes as vice president and general manager of the Northwest Region. Born on July 5, 1905, in Philadelphia, he received a quality education, graduating in 1924 from the Lawrenceville School in New Jersey and four years later from nearby Princeton University. Like Pevler, Large had spent his entire railroading career with the

PRR, although in nontechnical departments. One of his major achievements before arriving at Wabash was orchestrating some of the fastest freight service in the country.[58]

The final merger and lease process seemed excruciatingly slow to many observers. After the hearings closed, the ICC needed to deliberate. Not known for its speed of action, it would not be until July 13, 1964, that the ICC approved the union by a vote of ten to one. But there were important conditions. The PRR had to agree to place its N&W stock in trust and to dispose of it over a ten-year period. Also, the EL, D&H and Boston & Maine railroads, who needed "expanded and safe corporate homes," had at some point to be included in the N&W. And as part of the N&W-NKP merger and lease of the Wabash, the N&W took control over two important, though small Class I roads, the 171-mile Akron, Ohio–based Akron, Canton & Youngstown Railroad, which had close traffic ties with the NKP, and the 132-mile Pittsburgh-based Pittsburgh & West Virginia Railway, the old Wabash Pittsburgh Terminal property.[59]

Action quickly followed. On September 14, 1964, the PRR informed the ICC that it would accept the requirement to divest its holdings in the N&W within ten years. Its ownership of these securities had been a roadblock in its efforts to bring about merger with the NYC; the ICC had been sitting on that proposal since March 1962. In essence, the PRR was gambling that savings generated by what would then be the almost-assured PRR-NYC union would more than offset the loss of steady income derived from its investments it the N&W. Of course, money realized from these asset sales could be placed in other high-yielding investments or distributed to shareholders.[60]

Then at 12:01 A.M., on October 16, the merger/lease was consummated. The previous day, the Wabash board of directors abol-

The last president of the Wabash Railroad, Henry W. Large had been a career railroader with the Pennsylvania Railroad before he joined the management team in St. Louis. Because of the N&W merger, Large's tenure with the Wabash was brief, lasting less than a year. (Author's Coll.)

ished "all salaried officer and employee positions" and passed a final resolution: "The Board of Directors wishes to acknowledge, with thanks, the many years of valued and dedicated service of all Wabash officers and employees, both past and present, without whose enthusiastic performance of duties this Company would not have so flourished and prospered." On the first day of united operations five new directors joined the expanded N&W board of directors, including two former Wabash members William S. Lowe, president of the A. P. Green Fire Brick Company, and Raymond Rowland, president and chairman of the board of Ralston Purina Company. (The three directors who represented the PRR had resigned.)[61]

The greatly enlarged N&W possessed much. It sported a fourteen-state 7,800-mile system with 32,324 employees, 1,420 locomotives and 120,316 freight cars, 62,594 stockholders, assets of $2 billion, working capital of $130 million and one of the highest profit potentials of any American railroad. The Wabash had joined with a winner. Its roller-coaster existence, which could be traced back to the Northern Cross Railroad in the 1830s, had concluded on the high end.[62]

But the fate of the Wabash could have been dramatically different. If it had remained under the thumb of the PRR, its final years might have been much less pleasant. Those at PRR who wanted to merge with NYC finally had their wish granted. On February 1, 1968, the 19,459-mile Penn Central Transportation Company, with much hoopla, made its debut. Then, in June 1970, the giant failed, producing one of the most spectacular bankruptcies of the twentieth century. In time, though, the U.S. Congress passed several pieces of "bailout" legislation designed to "save" the railroad enterprise and would sanction placing Penn Central and several other bankrupt Eastern carriers, including the EL, into the specially created quasi-public Consolidated Rail Corporation (Conrail), which began operations on April 1, 1976. The Wabash was lucky to avoid the Penn Central debacle. Ironically, in the late 1990s the Norfolk Southern Railway (NS) (née N&W and Southern Railway) acquired major portions of the former PRR when it and another super railroad, CSX (C&O, Seaboard Coast Line and several other properties), carved up the principal components of Conrail. At that point, some historic Wabash lines might well have entered the Norfolk Southern fold through the PRR. The viable Wabash routes, of course, had already been residing there and adding to the profitability of NS.

Epilogue

Although, from an operational standpoint, the Wabash Railroad in October 1964 joined the Norfolk & Western Railway (N&W), the corporate identity of the Wabash remained. The Pennsylvania Railroad (PRR) had insisted that the railroad be leased rather than sold to N&W, and the Interstate Commerce Commission (ICC) approved this stratagem. For the next twenty-seven years, minimal yearly meetings of the board of directors took place in Roanoke, Virginia, and a skeleton staff prepared a modest annual report and filed the legally required documents with the Securities and Exchange Commission and the ICC. During this period, the N&W itself became involved in one of the monumental mergers of the twentieth century. On June 1, 1982, it consolidated with the Southern Railway Company to form the 18,252-mile Norfolk Southern Railway (NS), which in turn became a subsidiary of Norfolk Southern Corporation. As part of a streamlining process, in November 1991 NS consolidated the Wabash with its N&W unit. Under this arrangement, Wabash security holders, excluding the N&W, received

On April 17, 1968, Norfolk & Western conductor Robert Dempsey asks "Tickets, Please" for the final time on the *City of St. Louis*. After forty-seven years of service with the Wabash and N&W, this veteran trainman retired. Fourteen months later Dempsey's last assigned train would be discontinued. (Author's Coll.)

$75 in cash plus $3.90 for each share of Wabash preferred and $649.97 in cash for each share of Wabash common. From an investor's perspective, this was an attractive settlement.[1]

Not long after the takeover, physical reminders of the Wabash began to disappear. Painters in Decatur and at other N&W shops quickly replaced Wabash markings with those of N&W or entirely repainted locomotives, freight and passenger cars and cabooses in N&W livery. It took longer before maintenance-of-way employees obliterated most Wabash signage, removing "Wabash Railroad Company" signboards from depots, freight houses and other structures. Smaller signs, however, might not be changed, although if they required replacement new markers lettered "N&W" duly appeared in their place. Because Wabash crews had placed WABASH in large letters on scores of steel bridges that crossed public roads, these eye-catching markings usually escaped repainting or destruction, and today a few remain, albeit faint if at all wholly readable. "All of this wanton destruction of the proud Wabash name didn't make me feel very good," remarked a veteran employee of the Des Moines Union Railway, a terminal road that the Wabash had long partially owned. "It wasn't a particularly smart act on their [N&W] part and I heard a lot of old Wabash men complain." Former Nickel Plate Road employees shared similar feelings.[2]

In the seven years between the N&W lease and formation of the National Railroad Passenger Corporation, better known as Amtrak (from *Americans travel by track*), which in May 1971 took over nearly all of the nation's intercity rail operations, several Wabash passenger trains remained. The *Omaha Limited* (and it became "limited" indeed) ran until June 9, 1968, although by the end it had become a mixed train, often consisting of piggyback trailers, and originated not at Union Station in St. Louis but rather at Luther Yard on the north side of the city. Moreover, the train no longer terminated in Omaha at the Union Pacific station but at East Switch Yard in Council Bluffs. The *Banner Blue* and the *City of Kansas City* and *City of St. Louis*, which retained their creature comforts, plied their routes until the late 1960s with the joint N&W–Union Pacific *City of St. Louis* operation dissolving on June 19, 1968. Not long thereafter, N&W received permission to discontinue the *City of Kansas City* (trains 203 and 212), its last trains between St. Louis and Kansas City, and to reduce the *Blue Bird* to a Chicago-Decatur operation. The *Wabash Cannon Ball,* however, continued until Amtrak made its debut, and for a time the N&W combined it with the *Blue Bird* eastbound and the *Banner Blue* westbound on the Decatur–St. Louis segment. Although the N&W made several efforts to terminate the *Cannon Ball,* the ICC wanted to maintain direct passenger train service between Detroit and St. Louis, in part because of rail connections with the Southwest.[3]

These former Wabash trains usually died without much fanfare. On a cold January day in 1970, only one passenger was aboard the *Blue Bird* when it departed from St. Louis Union Station on its final trip to Dearborn Station in Chicago. Barney Wippold, a reporter for the *St. Louis Globe-Democrat,* covered the largely ignored event. "The lone passenger was Thorold Nichols, a hat salesman of 4955 Schollmeyer ave., who said he has used the train frequently during the last 12 years to attend trade shows in Chicago," wrote Wippold. "[Nichols] said he liked the convenience of the train and had no idea of what he would do in the future." Air service between the two Midwestern metropolises, though, was excellent, including flights operated by Ozark and Trans World Airlines.[4]

An exception to the lack of attention did occur with the *Wabash Cannon Ball.* Perhaps the name inspired significant protests and widespread publicity. Surely, the song had given it a special meaning. "I can't image a more American train than this one," explained one of the last riders on the *Cannon Ball*. "It is a legendary train in the country's heartland. I have known 'the jingle, the rumble and the roar' nearly all of my life and this Cannonball song and its namesake train are really special to me." As soon as the media publicized the train's demise, cries of "Save the Cannon Ball" arose. "Everyone is raising hell now," commented an N&W official in April 1971. "There's been more excitement over this train in the last two weeks than in the last 20 years." Even Dizzy Dean, the Baseball Hall of Fame great, lamented the demise of the *Cannon Ball*. During his baseball broadcasts on radio and television in the late 1940s and 1950s, he repeatedly offered a distinctive, albeit popular, rendition of the famous folk song between innings. "I tell you it's a sad thing to hear the clickety clack of the Cannonball is going, but the song will never die. Everywhere I go, they still want me to do it." The *Cannon Ball* train, a big money loser, did go, and on April 30, 1971, another vestige of the Wabash disappeared. There was extensive local, regional and national media coverage, and multiple newspaper editorials and letters-to-the editor decried its demise. The public seemed truly saddened to "watch a legend die."[5]

With the emergence of the rails-to-trails movement, the Wabash railroad name has achieved a degree of grassroots immortality beyond the song. Spearheaded by the Rails-to-Trails Conservancy, which dates from the late 1960s, approximately 10,000 miles of the nation's abandoned railroad rights-of-way have been converted into more than a thousand multipurpose trails. Hikers, cyclists, equestrians and others enjoy these public-use corridors. Two of the nation's

On June 28, 1969, members of the Michigan Railroad Club took a "Farewell Trip" on the Wabash *Cannon Ball* between Detroit and Peru, Indiana. Yet this beloved passenger train lasted until April 30, 1971. In this souvenir folder the organization realized that this would not the final run: "This train is up for discont[inuance] and the decision will be given by the I.C.C.—July 3, 1969 or prior, but not known at this date to us." Added these enthusiasts: "Our thanks to the N&W Railway for keeping the name to this date." (Author's Coll.)

longest rails-to-trails have incorporated former Wabash lines: the sixty-three-mile "Wabash Cannonball Trail," which runs between the Ohio communities of Maumee and Liberty Center and Maumee and West

In the late 1980s Norfolk Southern supervised the lifting of the rails and ties from much of the former Wabash line across northern Indiana. In 1990 only the naked right-of-way remains in the vicinity of Wakarusa. (James Geyer Photograph)

Unity, and the approximately sixty-mile "Wabash Trace Nature Trail," which connects Council Bluffs with Blanchard, Iowa, near the Iowa-Missouri border.[6]

Some former Wabash lines that have been abandoned did not enter the rails-to-trails network and simply disappeared. Hundreds of miles of retired trackage, including major portions of the Decatur–Chicago, Moberly–Des Moines and Chicago–Montpelier routes, have reverted to private ownership. Farmers have extended their fields over sections, urbanites have built or paved over others and vegetation has consumed the rest. At times, it becomes difficult to locate former Wabash rights-of-way, although with a light dusting of snow on the ground and favorable lighting, grades, depressions and other railroad-made features become visible.[7]

Still, trains continue to roll over major sections of the onetime Wabash. Currently, NS freights heavily use the Kansas City–Moberly–Hannibal–St. Louis–Detroit routes. Traffic density maps reveal that some of the busiest parts of the sprawling NS system are former Wabash units, namely, between Kansas City and Moberly and Decatur and Detroit. But NS trains also rattle over

trackage between the Illinois communities of Bement and Gibson City, Bluffs and Meredosia, and Chicago and Manhattan and between the Indiana towns of New Haven and Woodburn.[8]

Moreover, shortline operators maintain service to some former Wabash customers. Although a few of these carriers have failed and all or parts of their trackage have been cast off, others trundle freight cars over economically viable portions of former "Follow the Flag" routes. These low-cost start-up concerns, which include the Appanoose County Community Railroad, Bloomer Shippers Connecting Railroad (Bloomer Line), Chillicothe-Brunswick Rail Authority, Columbia Terminal Short Line Railroad, Indiana Northeastern Railroad, Maumee & Western Railroad and Pioneer Railcorp (Keokuk Junction Railway), operate trackage that NS no longer wanted and gladly sold, sometimes at attractive prices. Yet, with shortline ownership, NS still retains much of this revenue freight business, often being the principal interchange partner.[9]

The shortline scenario also applies to the former Ann Arbor. N&W rejected this longtime Wabash subsidiary, and in 1963 this largely Michigan carrier entered the fold of the Detroit, Toledo & Ironton. But economic woes followed, and in 1974 a federal court judge ruled that as a corporation the Ann Arbor could not be reorganized on an income basis. Yet service continued. The Consolidated Rail Corporation, Conrail, a quasi-public corporation that started in 1976, operated the Ann Arbor for more than a year. Then the state of Michigan acquired the less viable lines northwest of Ann Arbor and leased them to shortline operators who ran the trains. Today the Tuscola & Saginaw Bay Railway runs over the truncated segment. The original core of the Ann Arbor, Toledo to Ann Arbor, is served by another shortline, appropriately named the Ann Arbor Railroad.[10]

It is interesting to note that Amtrak did not opt to use Wabash routes for its passenger service. Although it provided trains between Chicago and St. Louis and St. Louis and Kansas City, the lines chosen were those that traditionally were the strongest, namely, the old Alton Road between Chicago and St. Louis and the Missouri Pacific between St. Louis and Kansas City. Whereas Amtrak riders have not been able to see sights along the former Wabash rights-of-way, commuters who take the Metra SouthWest line of the Northeast Illinois Regional Commuter Rail Corporation can travel between Orland Park (179th Street) and Chicago over a small portion of the one-time St. Louis–Chicago mainline. And riders of the Metrolink light rail in St. Louis who board trains between downtown and Lambert–St. Louis International Airport pass over portions of old Wabash trackage and make a stop beside the Delmar Street Station. Still more testimony that the transportation landscape is forever in flux.

There are other remnants of the Wabash in place. A variety of small-town depots remain, and a few have been faithfully restored, including structures at Monticello, Illinois, Shenandoah, Iowa, and Wakarusa,

Indiana. One, the station at Ferguson, Missouri, has become a popular ice cream parlor and sandwich shop, appropriately called the Whistle Stop. A few larger buildings are still in use. For example, the Decatur passenger depot presently houses an antique mall, and Delmar Station in St. Louis, though vacant, still stands, its exterior in good condition. On abandoned trackage there are an assortment of bridge piers, culverts and foundations. In Monroe County, Iowa, for instance, "Cottonwood Pits" remains a popular local fishing and picnic site, where once Wabash work gangs removed clay and gravel for ballast on the Des Moines and Ottumwa lines.

The memory of the Wabash, a "fallen flag" for nearly forty years, is being kept alive in other ways. The Wabash Railroad Historical Society is a vibrant rail fan organization that publishes a newsletter, maintains a Website and holds annual meetings, usually in former Wabash communities. Modelers and collectors of "railroadiana" show their interests, too. On the electronic auction site, e-Bay, usually a page or two of Wabash-related memorabilia, ranging from scale models of Wabash boxcars to Wabash dining car china, are daily listed for sale. Commercial video companies, too, peddle VHS tapes, including Green Frog Productions' "The Wabash Railroad: From the Camera of Emery Gulash." The Wabash Railroad Memorial Hospital Association is one of the few remaining railroad health maintenance organizations in the country. It serves not only Wabash and N&W retirees, but also active NS employees.

Although the Wabash Railroad has departed the corporate world, it has not been entirely forgotten. Surely as time passes, however, its memory will fade even more, not unlike those dimming Wabash letters on bridge spans. After all, only a few historians, railroad enthusiasts and local history buffs can today identify such onetime, large and vibrant Wabash predecessors as the Toledo, Wabash & Western and the Wabash, St. Louis & Pacific.

Notes

1: THE WABASH EMERGES EAST OF THE MISSISSIPPI RIVER

1. H. Roger Grant, *The North Western: A History of the Chicago & North Western Railway System* (DeKalb: Northern Illinois University Press, 1996), 11; John Luther Ringwalt, *Development of Transportation Systems in the United States* (Philadelphia: Railway World, 1888), 126; Charles M. Eames, *Historic Morgan and Classic Jacksonville* (Jacksonville, Ill.: Daily Journal, 1885), 103.

2. *Illinois State Journal* (Springfield), August 31, 1935.

3. William K. Ackerman, *Early Illinois Railroads* (Chicago: Fergus, 1884), 17–22; A. A. Graham, "The Great Wabash: The Pioneer Railway of the West," *Potter's American Monthly* 13 (July 1879): 1–2.

4. Graham, "The Great Wabash."

5. "Railroads and Canals in Illinois," *American Railroad Journal* 6 (April 1, 1837): 194; Elias Horry, *An Address Respecting the Charleston & Hamburgh Rail-Road; And on the Rail-Road System* (Charleston, S.C.: A. E. Miller, 1833); John F. Stover, *Iron Road to the West: American Railroads in the 1850s* (New York: Columbia University Press, 1978), 7, 10–11; Frederick L. Paxon, "The Railroads of the 'Old Northwest' Before the Civil War," *Wisconsin Academy of Sciences, Arts, and Letters* 17 (October 1913): 247–48; *Michigan Sentinel* (Monroe, Mich.), May 21, 1834; *Detroit Journal and Advertiser* (Detroit, Michigan), December 14, 1835; Alvin Harlow, *Road of the Century* (New York: Creative Age Press, 1947), 247.

6. "Railroads and Canals in Illinois," 194; "Illinois Internal Improvements," *American Railroad Journal* 6 (March 11, 1837): 248–49; Frederick C. Gamst, ed., *Early American Railroads: Franz Anton Ritter von Gerstner's Die innern Communication* (1842–1843) (Stanford, Calif.: Stanford University Press, 1997), 479–508; Newton Bateman and Paul Selby, eds., *Historical Encyclopedia of Illinois* (Chicago: Munsell, 1906), 439.

Likely the Northern Cross name came from a well-known public trail, which it largely followed, the "Northern Crossing," often shortened to Northern Cross.

7. Bateman and Selby, eds., *Historical Encyclopedia of Illinois*, 439.

8. H. J. Stratton, "The Northern Cross Railroad," *Journal of the Illinois State Historical Society* 27 (July 1935): 13.

9. Ibid., 13–14; George M. McConnel, "Recollections of the Northern Cross Railroad," *Transactions of the Illinois State Historical Society* (1908): 147.

10. Stratton, "The Northern Cross Railroad," 15–16.

11. Don Harrison Doyle, *The Social Order of a Frontier Community: Jacksonville, Illinois, 1825–70* (Urbana: University of Illinois Press, 1978), 42–46; Stratton, "The Northern Cross Railroad," 17.

12. Stratton, "The Northern Cross Railroad," 21.

13. Eames, *Historic Morgan and Classic Jacksonville*, 105.

14. *Decatur (Ill.) Review*, November 24, 1901; *History of the Wabash Railroad in Illinois During the '30s* (St. Louis: Wabash Railway Company, n.d.); *Extra Board* 7 (Fall 2002): 2; Stratton, "The Northern Cross Railroad," 22.

15. Stratton, "The Northern Cross Railroad," 22; *Meredosia (Ill.) Budget*, November 8, 1928; *Chicago Daily News*, May 5, 1910; Charles E. Fisher, "The Northern Cross R.R.," *Bulletin of the Railway & Locomotive Historical Society* 84 (October 1951): 58.

16. Robert F. Frey, ed., *Railroads in the Nineteenth Century* (New York: Facts on File, 1988), 340–44.

17. Stratton, "The Northern Cross Railroad," 23.

18. Fisher, "The Northern Cross R.R.," 59.

19. *Springfield (Ill.) Journal*, July 6, 1838.

20. Eames, *Historic Morgan and Classic Jacksonville*, 103–4.

21. Fisher, "The Northern Cross R.R.," 59; *Illinois State Journal*, August 31, 1935; *Meredosia Budget*, November 8, 1928; McConnel, "Recollections of the Northern Cross Railroad," 149–50; Gamst, ed., *Early American Railroads*.

The first locomotive *Illinois*, unfortunately, never reached the Northern Cross at Meredosia, having been lost at sea. Details on the company's motive power can be found in William Swartz, "The Wabash Railroad," *Railroad History* 133 (Fall 1975): 45.

22. Eames, *Historic Morgan and Classic Jacksonville*, 104.

23. *History of Sangamon County, Illinois* (Chicago: Inter-State, 1881), 145.

24. Stratton, "The Northern Cross Railroad," 24.

25. Ibid., 24–25, 43; *History of Sangamon County, Illinois*, 145.

26. Ackerman, *Early Illinois Railroads*, 24.

27. Stratton, "The Northern Cross Railroad," 25–26; Gamst, ed., *Early American Railroads*, 499.

28. Stratton, "The Northern Cross Railroad," 44–45.

29. Ibid., 45–46.

30. Ibid., 46; *Illinois State Journal*, August 31, 1935; Eames, *Historic Morgan and Classic Jacksonville*, 105; *History of the Wabash Railroad in Illinois During the '30s*.

The fate of the *Rogers* differed dramatically from the *Pioneer* of the Galena & Chicago Union, which today remains on public display at the Chicago Historical Society. According to a letter from a Wabash official, "This engine [*Rogers*] was derailed and abandoned at New Berlin, Illinois, in 1843. General [James] Sample, then State Senator, bought the engine and tried to fix it up to carry freight over the prairie without track. However, after considerable trouble and expense in getting said engine several miles from New Berlin, he finally gave it up and the engine was abandoned, the natives dismantling same of such parts as could possibly be used in repairs to farm machinery, etc." H. C. Ettinger to G. F. Hess, March 5, 1930, J. Orville Spreen Collection, Western Historical Manuscript Collection, St. Louis, Mo. (hereafter cited as J. O. Spreen Coll.).

31. *The Great Western Rail Road, in Illinois History* (Jacksonville, Ill.: Morgan Job Office, 1857), 7; *Illinois State Journal*, August 31, 1935.

32. Stratton, "The Northern Cross Railroad," 49; Ackerman, *Early Illinois Railroads*, 105–6.

33. Eames, *Historic Morgan and Classic Jacksonville*, 124; Ackerman, *Early Illinois Railroads*, 106.

34. Eames, *Historic Morgan and Classic Jacksonville*, 124.

35. Stratton, "The Northern Cross Railroad," 50–51; *Report of an Experimental Survey of that Portion of the Northern Cross Rail-Road Extending from Quincy to Meredosia* (Quincy, Ill.: Northern Cross Board of Directors, 1850), 1–2; Eames, *Historic Morgan and Classic Jacksonville*, 103; Charles Fisher to J. Orville Spreen, April 8, 1954, J. O. Spreen Coll.

36. *The Wabash Club Souvenir, Silver Jubilee, 1911–1916* (St. Louis: Wabash Railway Company, 1936), 35; *Illinois State Journal*, January 7, 1850; D. E. Brummitt, "History of the St. Louis, Naples & Peoria Packet Co.," (October 28, 1958), J. O. Spreen Coll.

37. *The Great Western Rail Road, in Illinois History*, 9–10.

38. *Report of the Directors to the Stockholders of the Great Western R. R. Co.* (New York: George Scott Roe, 1854), 4; "Corporate History of the Wabash Railway Company: Compiled Pursuant to and in Accordance with Valuation Order No. 20, Interstate Commerce Commission, Dated May 13, 1915," (June 30, 1919), 6 (hereafter cited as "Corporate History of the Wabash Railway Company"); John F. Stover, *History of the Illinois Central Railroad* (New York: Macmillan, 1975), 56.

39. Stover, *Iron Road to the West*, 13, 116.

40. "Reminiscences of Sullivan Burgess, Surveyor of Great Western R.R. Line (Now Wabash) into Decatur (December 25, 1892)," J. O. Spreen Coll.

41. *Decatur (Ill.) Sunday Herald and Review*, May 9, 1954; O. T. Banton, ed., *History of Macon County* (Decatur, Ill.: Privately printed, 1976), 120–21.

42. Swartz, "The Wabash Railroad," 45; *Report of the Directors to the Stockholders of the Great Western R.R. Co.*, 3.

43. *First Annual Report of the Directors of the Great Western Railroad Company of 1859 to the Stock and Bondholders* (Springfield, Ill.: C. H. Lanphier, 1860), 5.

44. Great Western Rail Road, Time Table No. 17, November 3, 1861.

45. "Corporate History of the Wabash Railway Company," 16, 26; Theodore Gregg, *History of Hancock County, Illinois* (Chicago: Charles C. Chapman & Company, 1880), 982; Richard C. Overton, *Burlington Route: A History of the Burlington Lines* (New York: Knopf, 1965), 15, 35.

46. *First Annual Report of the Directors of the Great Western Railroad Company of 1859*, 5.

47. "Corporate History of the Wabash Railway Company," 17–18; *Report of the Chief Engineer of the Lake Erie, Wabash and St. Louis Rail Road* (Lafayette, Ind.: Cyrus Luse, 1853), 8; "Construction of the Lake Erie, Wabash and St. Louis R.R. Co.," Wabash Railroad Collection, Norfolk Southern Archives, Atlanta, Ga. (hereafter cited as NS Archives); *Exhibit of the Lake Erie, Wabash & St. Louis Railroad Company* (New York: Oliver & Brother, 1853); *Exhibit of the Lake Erie, Wabash & St. Louis and Toledo and Illinois Railroad Companies, March 1, 1854* (New York: Railroad Journal, 1854), 3–4, 7; *Report of the Toledo and Illinois and the Lake Erie, Wabash & St. Louis Railroad Companies* (Rochester, N.Y.: A. Strong & Company, 1855), 3. See also Elbert Jay Benton, *The Wabash Trade Route in the Development of the Old Northwest* (Baltimore: Lord Baltimore Press, 1903).

48. *Report of the Toledo and Illinois and the Lake Erie, Wabash & St. Louis Railroad Company* (New York: Hall, Clayton & Company, 1855), 19.

49. *Exhibit of the Lake Erie, Wabash & St. Louis and Toledo and Illinois Railroad Companies*, 4.

50. *History of Miami County, Indiana* (Chicago: Brant & Fuller, 1887), 289; *Biographical Record and Portrait Album of Tippecanoe County, Indiana* (Chicago: Lewis, 1888), 257.

51. *Report of the Toledo, Wabash and Western Railroad Company, Lately the Toledo and Illinois Railroad Co., and the Lake Erie, Wabash & St. Louis Railroad Company* (New York: George F. Nesbitt, 1857), 7–9; "Abstract Points Leading Up to the Construction of the Wabash through Huntington, Ind.," Wabash Railroad Coll., NS Archives; *Weekly Intelligencer* (Wabash, Ind.), February 13, March 26, November 26, 1856; *Report of the Toledo and Illinois and the Lake Erie, Wabash & St. Louis Railroad Companies*, 5.

52. *Report of the Toledo, Wabash and Western Railroad Company, Lately the Toledo and Illinois Railroad Co., and the Lake Erie, Wabash & St. Louis Railroad Company*, 5; *Biographical Directory of the United States Congress, 1774–1989* (Washington, D.C.: U.S. Government Printing Office, 1989).

53. *Report of the Toledo, Wabash and Western Railroad Company, Lately the Toledo and Illinois Railroad Co., and the Lake Erie, Wabash & St. Louis Railroad Company*, 10; Ronald E. Shaw, *Canals for a Nation: The Canal Era in the United States, 1790–1860* (Lexington: University Press of Kentucky, 1990), 158–59; ? to N. S. Brown, May 7, 1915, Wabash Railroad Coll., NS Archives; "Corporate History of the Wabash Railway Company," 22–24.

54. *Third Annual Report of the Toledo & Western Railway Company* (Toledo, Ohio: Pelton & Waggoner, 1861), 10–11, 15.

55. "The History of the Wabash Railroad," (ca. 1953), Bureau of Railway Economics Collection, John W. Barriger III National Railroad Library, St. Louis, Mo.; "Brief History of the Lines Owned by the Wabash as Existed When It Entered Detroit, Michigan," J. O. Spreen Coll.

56. "Corporate History of the Wabash Railway Company," 28–31; "Toledo, Wabash and Western R.R.," *American Railroad Journal* 21 (July 8, 1865): 651; "Toledo, Wabash and Western Railroad," *American Railroad Journal* 21 (July 15, 1865): 661; "Toledo & Western Railway," J. O. Spreen Coll.; "Toledo, Wabash and Western Railway," *American Railway Times* 17 (August 26, 1865); H. Roger Grant, ed., *Iowa Railroads: The Essays of Frank P. Donovan, Jr.* (Iowa City: University of Iowa Press, 2000), 175, 179.

57. "Toledo, Wabash and Western Railway," *American Railway Times* 17 (August 26, 1865).

58. "Toledo, Wabash and Western Railway," *American Railway Journal* 42 (July 3, 1869): 734.

59. Diary of Claude A. Crommelin, May 30, 1866, in possession of Augustus J. Veenendaal, Jr., Pinjacker, Holland; "Toledo, Wabash and Western Railway," *American Railroad Journal* 40 (October 5, 1867): 968; *Annual Report of the Toledo, Wabash & Western Railway Company to the Stockholders for the Fiscal Year Ending December 31, 1868* (Toledo, Ohio: Blade, 1869), 11.

60. *Annual Report of the Toledo, Wabash & Western Railway Company to the Stockholders, for the Fiscal Year Ending December 31st, 1869* (Toledo, Ohio: Blade, 1870), 9.

61. Ibid., 10; George H. Burgess and Miles C. Kennedy, *Centennial History of the Pennsylvania Railroad Company* (Philadelphia: Pennsylvania Railroad Company, 1949), 292–94; Thomas J. Misa, *A Nation of Steel: The Making of Modern America, 1865–1925* (Baltimore: Johns Hopkins University Press, 1995), 17–22, 31–32; *Railroad Gazette* 5 (September 20, 1873): 378.

62. *Intelligencer* (Edwardsville, Ill.), March 21, 1867; *American Railroad Journal* 40 (December 21, 1867): 1213; *Annual Report of the Toledo, Wabash & Western Railway Company to the Stockholders for the Fiscal Year Ending December 31st, 1868*, 13; *Annual Report of the Toledo, Wabash & Western Railway Company, to the Stockholders for the Fiscal Year Ending December 31st, 1869*, 13–14; "Corporate History of the Wabash Railway Company," 27; *American Railroad Journal* 43 (July 2, 1870); ibid. 43 (October 8, 1870): 1147; *Railroad Gazette* 14 (October 8, 1870): 31.

63. *Intelligencer*, February 6, 1868; "Corporate History of the Wabash Railway Company," 38–42.

64. *Pike County Democrat* (Pittsfield, Ill.), December 21, 1904; M. D. Massie, *Past and Present of Pike County, Illinois* (Chicago: S. J. Clarke, 1906), 129; Hannibal & Naples R.R. Company Records to Dec. 1876, June 15, 1857, 11, Virginia Tech Digital Library and Archives, Blacksburg, Va.; "Corporate History of the Wabash Railway Company," 44.

65. *Commercial and Financial Chronicle* (New York), October 11, 1873.

66. Ibid.

67. Ibid.; "Toledo, Wabash and Western Railway," *American Railroad Journal* 43 (May 21, 1870): 594; *Railroad Gazette* 3 (May 6, 1871); "Toledo, Wabash & Western Railway Report," *Railroad Gazette* 3 (July 22, 1871): 193; ibid. 4 (May 25, 1872): 224–25.

68. *Railroad Gazette* 14 (June 25, 1870): 293; ibid. 14 (October 8, 1870): 3.

69. Ibid. 15 (November 25, 1871): 357; ibid. 15 (March 23, 1972): 131; "Toledo, Wabash and Western Railway," *American Railroad Journal* 42 (July 3, 1869): 734; ibid. 46 (October 25, 1873): 1334.

70. "Toledo, Wabash and Western Railway," *American Railroad Journal*, July 3, 1869, 734; ibid., October 25, 1873, 1334; ibid. 30 (October 10, 1874): 1283; *Travelers' Official Guide of the Railways* (Philadelphia: National Railway Publication Company, 1872), 271; *Railroad Gazette* 3 (May 20, 2871): 94; ibid. 5 (August 23, 1873): 336.

71. *Railroad Gazette* 6 (May 16, 1874): 188; ibid. 6 (December 5, 1874): 479; A. L. Gilbert to [J. E.] Taussig, July 7, 1931, J. O. Spreen Coll.; "Toledo, Wabash and Western Railway," *American Railroad Journal* 46 (October 25, 1873): 1334.

72. George H. Miller, *Railroads and the Granger Laws* (Madison: University of Wisconsin Press, 1971), 82–96; *Railroad Gazette* 6 (May 2, 1874): 167.

73. "Toledo, Wabash and Western Railway," *American Railroad Journal* 30 (October 10, 1874): 1281; *A Statement to the Stockholders of the Toledo, Wabash and Western Railway Company* (New York: Jones Printing, 1876), 4.

74. "Toledo, Wabash and Western Railway," *American Railroad Journal* 30 (October 10, 1874): 1282.

75. Ibid.; *Railroad Gazette* 6 (November 7, 1874): 439; ibid. 7 (March 6, 1875): 99; ibid. 7 (May 8, 1875): 188.

76. *A Statement to the Stockholders of the Toledo, Wabash and Western Railway Company*, 7–8.

77. Ibid., 3, 9.

78. Ibid., 8–9.

79. *Boston Traveler*, December 1, 1876; "Governor Cox Becomes Receiver," J. O. Spreen Coll.; Robert Sobel and John Raimo, eds., *Biographical Directory of the Governors of the United States, 1789–1978* (Westport, Conn.: Meckler Books, 1978), 1211–12.

80. J. Thomas Scharf, *History of Saint Louis and County* (Philadelphia: L. H. Everts, 1883) II: 1189; *American Railroad Journal* 48 (February 27, 1875): 259; ibid. 48 (February 6, 1875): 164; ibid. 49 (April 22, 1876): 541; ibid. 32 (June 17, 1876): 669; *Railway World* 21 (January 6, 1877); *American Railroad Journal* 23 (April 5, 1879): 315; *Railroad Gazette* 9 (January 12, 1877): 20; *Poor's Manual of the Railroads of the United States for 1880* (New York: H. V. & H. W. Poor, 1880), 721.

2: THE WABASH EMERGES WEST OF THE MISSISSIPPI RIVER

1. *St. Louis Globe*, January 5, 1947; John W. Million, *State Aid to Railways in Missouri* (Chicago: University of Chicago Press, 1896), 86; Paul Wallace Gates, "The Railroads of Missouri, 1850–1870," *Missouri Historical Review* 26 (January 1932): 129.

2. Gates, "The Railroads of Missouri, 1850–1870," 131; *Mitchell's*

Traveler's Guide through the United States (Philadelphia: Mitchell & Hinman, 1837), 67.

3. Million, *State Aid to Railways in Missouri*, 6–7; *Mitchell's Traveler's Guide through the United States*, 59–60.

4. Million, *State Aid to Railways in Missouri*, 7; *Historical Statistics of the United States: Colonial Times to 1957* (Washington, D.C.: U.S. Bureau of the Census, 1960), 13; *A Statement in Regards to the Importance, Prospects and Necessities of the North Missouri Railroad Company* (Jefferson City, Mo.: Examiner Book, 1857), 8–10.

5. Gates, "The Railroads of Missouri, 1850–1870," 130–31; Richard C. Overton, *Burlington Route: A History of the Burlington Lines* (New York: Knopf, 1965), 19–21.

6. *Fourth Annual Report of the Board of Directors to the Stockholders of the North Missouri Railroad* (St. Louis: Drake & Co., 1858), 3; "North Missouri Railroad," *American Railroad Journal* 13 (May 23, 1857): 324.

7. *Memorial of the North Missouri Railroad Convention* (Jefferson City, Mo.: James Lusk, 1852); *History of Schuyler County* (Trenton, Mo.: W. B. Rogers, 1909), 77–79.

8. "North Missouri Railroad," *Western Journal and Civilian* 9 (October 1852): 46.

9. *Annual Report of the Directors of the North Missouri Railroad Company to the Stockholders* (St. Louis: Republican Book, 1855), 4; *A Statement in Regards to the Importance, Prospects and Necessities of the North Missouri Railroad Company*, 8.

10. See William Cronon, *Nature's Metropolis: Chicago and the Great West* (New York: W. W. Norton, 1991), esp. chap. 2.

11. See *Memorial of the North Missouri Railroad Convention; Report of the Board of Directors of the North Missouri Railroad Company to the Stockholders* (April 1866), 12. See also "Early Days on the North Missouri," clipping in "Railroad Files" at the St. Louis Public Library, St. Louis, Mo.

12. *St. Louis Intelligencer*, July 30, 1857; "Report on the Internal Commerce of the United States, 1889," Wabash Railroad Collection, Norfolk Southern Archives, Atlanta, Ga. (hereafter cited as NS Archives); "North Missouri Railroad," *American Railroad Journal* 13 (May 23, 1857): 324; Overton, *Burlington Route*, 55; *Report on the Present State and Prospects of the North Missouri Railroad upon Examinations Made by Messrs. Jay Cooke & Co.* (June 1866), Bureau of Railway Economics Collection, John W. Barriger III National Railroad Library, St. Louis, Mo.

13. Gates, "The Railroads of Missouri, 1850–1870," 131–32; *Fourth Annual Report of the Board of Directors to the Stockholders of the North Missouri Railroad*, 4.

14. "North Missouri Railroad," *American Railroad Journal* 13 (May 16, 1857): 313; "North Missouri Railroad," ibid. 13 (December 26, 1857): 818.

15. North Missouri Railroad public timetable, n.d. (ca. 1860); "All-Time Wabash Locomotive Roster," *Railroad History* 133 (Fall 1975): 52.

16. *Report on the North Missouri Railroad,* n.d., NS Archives.

17. No. Mo. R.R. Co. Minutes of Meetings of Stockholders & Board of Directors from June 12, 1861, to May 7, 1872, August 14, 1861, 6, Virginia Tech Digital Library and Archives, Blacksburg, Va. (hereafter cited as No. Mo. R.R. Co. Minutes); *History of Randolph and Macon Counties, Missouri* (St. Louis: National Historical, 1884), 882.

Even though Macon City benefited enormously from the presence of the North Missouri, Macon County claimed distinction of being the only county along the original pre–Civil War line that did not subscribe to either company bonds or stocks. This occurred not because of a lack of interest in the iron horse, but rather because sections of the county fought over the projected routing of the road. See *General History of Macon County Missouri* (Chicago: Henry Taylor, 1910), 75.

18. No. Mo. R.R. Co. Minutes, July 9, 1862, 33.

The reason why the North Missouri did this additional construction work north of Macon City was "to intercept the business coming from above this point before it reaches Macon where this Company has to compete with [the Hannibal & St. Joseph] for the business."

19. James Neal Primm, *Lion of the Valley: St. Louis, Missouri, 1764–1980* (St. Louis: Missouri Historical Society Press, 3rd ed., 1998), 232–38; Robert E. Shalhope, *Sterling Price: Portrait of a Southerner* (Columbia: University of Missouri Press, 1971), 147–59.

20. *A Report of the North Missouri Railroad Co. On Its Affairs in General* (St. Louis: George Knapp, 1863), 13.

21. Richard S. Brownlee, *Gray Ghosts of the Confederacy: Guerrilla Warfare in the West, 1861–1865* (Baton Rouge: Louisiana State University Press, 1958), 14–16.

22. Shalhope, *Sterling Price*, 176–78, 181–83, 202–6, 263–79.

23. Brownlee, *Gray Ghosts of the Confederacy*, 24; *History of St. Charles, Montgomery and Warren Counties, Missouri* (St. Louis: National Historical, 1885), 990; *Eleventh Annual Report of the Board of Directors of the North Missouri Railroad Company to the Stockholders* (St. Louis: George Knapp, 1864), 6.

24. "North Missouri Railroad," Report to Accompany Bill H.R. No. 1231, U.S. House of Representatives, 39th Congress, 2nd Session, (February 28, 1867), 1–2.

25. Brownlee, *Gray Ghosts of the Confederacy*, 34–35; *Eleventh Annual Report of the Board of Directors of the North Missouri Railroad Company to the Stockholders*, 6.

26. *Report of the Board of Directors of the North Missouri Railroad Company to the Stockholders* (St. Louis: George Knapp, 1865), 7.

27. Brownlee, *Gray Ghosts of the Confederacy*, 204–5.

28. Ibid., 216–18; *The War of the Rebellion: A Compilation of the Official Records of the Union and Confederate Armies* (Washington, D.C.: U.S. Government Printing Office, 1893), ser. 1, vol. 41: 417; *Columbia (Mo.) Herald*, September 24, 1897.

29. Brownlee, *Gray Ghosts of the Confederacy*, 218.

30. Ibid., 218–20; *Report of the Board of Directors of the North*

Missouri Railroad Company to the Stockholders (St. Louis: George Knapp, 1866), 7–8.

31. *The War of the Rebellion,* ser. 1, vol. 41: 416.

32. Ibid., ser. 3, vol. 41: 634.

33. Brownlee, *Gray Ghosts of the Confederacy,* 223–25; *Report of the Board of Directors of the North Missouri Railroad Company to the Stockholders,* 1865, 7.

34. *Report of the Board of Directors of the North Missouri Railroad Company,* 1866, 6.

35. *Report on the Present State and Prospects of the North Missouri Railroad upon Examinations Made by Messrs. Jay Cooke & Co.,* 10; George W. Hilton, *American Narrow Gauge Railroads* (Stanford, Calif.: Stanford University Press, 1990), 35; *American Railroad Journal* 40 (August 17, 1867): 773.

36. *American Railroad Journal* 40 (October 26, 1867): 1033; Primm, *Lion of the Valley,* 279–91; Robert W. Jackson, *Rails across the Mississippi: A History of the St. Louis Bridge* (Urbana: University of Illinois Press, 2001), 41–42, 186–87.

37. No. Mo. R.R. Co. Minutes, September 24, 1866, 94–96; November 26, 1866, 232–33; February 19, 1867, 241–42; "The St. Charles Bridge," *Railroad Gazette* 3 (June 3, 1871): 114.

38. "The St. Charles Bridge," 114.

39. "The St. Charles Bridge," 114; "Visit to St. Charles Bridge," *Proceedings of the Grand International Division of the Brotherhood of Locomotive Engineers,* October 16, 1872, 33; *United States Railroad and Mining Register* 16 (June 24, 1871): 1; H. C. Wicker to Maria Wicker, January 28, 1872, Wicker Collection, Missouri Historical Society, St. Louis, Mo.

40. *First Annual Report of the Board of Directors of the St. Louis, Kansas City & Northern Railway Company* (St. Louis: Hugh R. Hildreth, 1873), 6; "The St. Charles Bridge," 114.

41. "North Missouri Railroad," *American Railroad Journal* 22 (May 12, 1866): 459; "Corporate History of the Wabash Railway Company: Compiled Pursuant to and in Accordance with Valuation Order No. 20, Interstate Commerce Commission, Dated May 13, 1915," (June 30, 1919), 49 (hereafter cited as "Corporate History of the Wabash Railway Company").

42. E. M. Violette, *History of Adair County* (Kirksville, Mo.: Denslow, 1911), 315–16; *Ottumwa (Iowa) Courier,* July 30, 1868.

43. Initially, the North Missouri selected Leavenworth, Kansas, as its western terminus. In August 1864 that community voted $250,000 to help underwrite construction. Because Leavenworth battled Kansas City for commercial control over the immediate region, these public funds came with a stipulation: the North Missouri could not pass within three miles of Kansas City. A year later the company, however, wisely decided to build by way of the emerging Missouri metropolis, and immediately Leavenworth withdrew its financial backing. See Charles N. Glaab, *Kansas City and the Railroads: Community Policy in the Growth of a Regional Metropolis* (Madison:

State Historical Society of Wisconsin, 1962), 135.

44. *Moberly (Mo.) Monitor-Index,* September 27, 1943; "Moberly," *Missouri Historical Review* 53 (October 1958): 27–28; *Moberly (Mo.) Daily Monitor,* September 27, 1886.

45. "Moberly," *Missouri Historical Review,* 28; *Bowling Green (Mo.) Times,* February 26, 1891.

46. "Corporate History of the Wabash Railway Company," 47–48; Shalhope, *Sterling Price,* 133–37.

47. "Corporate History of the Wabash Railway Company," 49; *Missouri and Kansas! Homes for All!* (St. Louis: North Missouri Railroad, 1870), 7.

48. Glaab, *Kansas City and the Railroads,* 141–43; *United States Railroad and Mining Register* 16 (June 24, 1871): 1; William J. Dalton, *The Life of Father Bernard Donnelly: With Historical Sketches of Kansas City, St. Louis and Independence, Missouri* (Kansas City, Mo.: Grimes-Joyce, 1921), 90–91; "North Missouri Railroad," *American Railroad Journal* 42 (May 1, 1869): 1; J. Pik, *De Amerikaansche Spoorwegwaarden: Bijdrage tot de kennis der te Amsterdam verhandelde fondsen* (Groningen, Holland: Erven B. Van Der Kamp, 1879), 127.

49. "Corporate History of the Wabash Railway Company," 137; A. J. Roof, *Past and Present of Livingston County, Missouri* (Chicago: S. J. Clarke, 1913), vol. 1: 130.

50. "Corporate History of the Wabash Railway Company," 141–43; A. O. Cunningham to Henry Hatch, November 11, 1919, NS Archives; Henry Hatch to A. O. Cunningham, November 21, 1919, NS Archives; "Synopsis of Articles of Association September 25th, 1873," Minute Book, Brunswick & Chillicothe Railroad Co., Virginia Tech Digital Library and Archives, Blacksburg, Va.

51. "North Missouri Railroad," *American Railroad Journal* 42 (May 1, 1869): 1; ibid. 44 (September 16, 1871): 1039; *Third Annual Report of the Board of Directors of the St. Louis, Kansas City & Northern Railway Company* (St. Louis: J. McKittrick, 1875), 17; *Fourth Annual Report of the Board of Directors of the St. Louis, Kansas City & Northern Railway Company* (St. Louis: Woodward, Tiernan & Hale, 1876), 7; "History of St. Joseph and St. Louis R.R. Co. Under control of the Wabash R.R. Co. during Years 1874 to 1886, respectively," NS Archives.

52. Earle D. Ross, *Iowa Agriculture: An Historical Survey* (Iowa City: State Historical Society of Iowa, 1951), 61–70; Dorothy Schwieder, *Black Diamonds: Life and Work in Iowa's Coal Mining Communities* (Ames: Iowa State University Press, 1983), 6–7.

53. "Corporate History of the Wabash Railway Company," 90; *Ottumwa Courier,* January 18, 1866; April 4, 1867; June 11, 1868; "St. Louis and Cedar Rapids R.R.," *American Railroad Journal* 41 (July 25, 1868): 720.

54. "Corporate History of the Wabash Railway Company," 90; *American Railroad Journal* 46 (November 18, 1871): 1291.

As soon as the North Missouri became reorganized as the St. Louis, Kansas City & Northern, commercial interests from southern

Iowa lobbied the St. Louis carrier for additional railroad construction, particularly a twenty-seven-mile extension from Moulton northward to Albia, seat of Monroe Country and the new southern terminus of the Central Railroad of Iowa, which was completing an important north-south trans-Iowa route. See *Railroad Gazette* 4 (May 4, 1872): 197.

55. *Ottumwa Courier*, July 21, 1870.

56. "Corporate History of the Wabash Railway Company," 117; *Missouri Statesmen*, (Columbia) May 4, 1866; November 1, 1867.

57. "St. Louis and its Railroads," *Locomotive Engineers' Monthly Journal* 2 (February 1869), 70.

58. Gene V. Glendinning, *The Chicago & Alton Railroad: The Only Way* (DeKalb: Northern Illinois University Press, 2002), 90–92; *United States Railroad and Mining Register* 16 (August 10, 1871): 1.

59. *St. Louis Daily Globe-Democrat*, February 28, 1926; *Report of the Board of Directors of the North Missouri Railroad Company*, 1866, 8, 11, 27; "North Missouri Railroad," *American Railroad Journal* 47 (November 25, 1865): 1118.

60. "Corporate History of the Wabash Railway Company," 50; *Railroad Gazette* 14 (June 11, 1870): 246; ibid. 14 (February 25, 1871): 512; Dolores Greenberg, *Financiers and Railroads, 1869–1889: A Study of Morton, Bliss & Company* (Newark: University of Delaware Press, 1980), 44–45; "Morris Ketchum Jesup," *Dictionary of American Biography* (New York: Charles Scribner's Sons, 1933), vol. 10: 61–62; Henry V. Poor, ed., *Manual of the Railroads of the United States for 1872–73* (New York: H. V. & H. W. Poor, 1872), 568–69.

61. *American Railroad Journal* 45 (January 13, 1872): 67; ibid. 45 (September 21, 1872); Robert L. Frey, ed., *Railroads in the Nineteenth Century* (New York: Facts on File, 1988), 358–62; Glendinning, *The Chicago & Alton Railroad*, 68.

62. Henry A. Hull, ed., *America's Successful Men of Affairs: An Encyclopedia of Contemporaneous Bibliography* (New York: New York Tribune, 1895), vol. 1: 336.

63. *Railroad Gazette* 4 (January 20, 1872): 77.

64. *First Annual Report of the Board of Directors of the St. Louis, Kansas City & Northern Railway Company*, 9–11.

The Moberly shops complex was truly impressive. "The buildings will require 2,750,000 bricks, 4,000 cubic yards of stone work . . . , and about 1,000 window sills." An Alton, Illinois-based firm did most of the construction. See *Railroad Gazette* 4 (June 29, 1872): 268.

65. *Second Annual Report of the Board of Directors of the St. Louis, Kansas City & Northern Railway Company* (St. Louis: Woodward, Tiernan & Hale, 1874), 12.

66. *Railroad Gazette* 10 (December 27, 1878): 630; "Corporate History of the Wabash Railway Company," 143; "Memorandum on St. Louis, Council Bluffs & Omaha Railroad," n.d., NS Archives; "From a Brief History of Malvern, Iowa, by John D. Paddock," NS Archives.

67. *Fourth Annual Report of the Board of Directors of the St. Louis,* *Kansas City & Northern Railway Company*, 4; "St. Louis, Kansas City & Northern," *Railroad Gazette* 8 (June 16, 1876): 270; *Fifth Annual Report of the Board of Directors of the St. Louis, Kansas City & Northern Railway Company* (St. Louis: Woodward, Tiernan & Hale, 1877), 7.

68. Alexander H. Waller, *History of Randolph County Missouri* (Topeka, Kan.: Historical Publishing, 1920), 215; *Fifth Annual Report of the Board of Directors of the St. Louis, Kansas City & Northern Railway Company*, 4; Glendinning, *The Chicago & Alton Railroad*, 108–10.

69. "The St. Louis, Kansas City & Northern Railway," *Railroad Gazette* 4 (January 27, 1872): 40; ibid. 7 (June 19, 1875): 261; ibid. 7 (October 30, 1875): 453.

70. *Railroad Gazette* 7 (March 6, 1875): 98; ibid. 7 (August 14, 1875): 340; *History of Audrain County, Missouri* (St. Louis: National Historical, 1884), 297.

71. *Travelers' Official Railway Guide for the United States and Canada* (Philadelphia: National Railway Publication, July 1874), 317; St. Louis, Kansas City & Northern Railway public timetable, n.d.; St. Louis, Kansas City & Northern Railway public timetable, December 1875.

72. J. A. Dacus and James W. Buel, *A Tour of St. Louis or, the Inside Life of a Great City* (St. Louis: Jones & Griffin, 1878), 165.

73. *Moberly (Mo.) Headlight*, July 20, 1876.

74. *Railroad Gazette* 5 (March 22, 1873): 123; *Second Annual Report of the Board of Directors of the St. Louis, Kansas City & Northern Railway Company*, 8.

75. Dacus and Buel, *A Tour of St. Louis*, 167; Pik, *De Amerikaansche Spoorwegwaarden*, 126–28; *Second Annual Report of the Board of Directors of the St. Louis, Kansas City & Northern Railway Company*, 5; *Manual of the Railroads of the United States for 1876–77* (New York: H. V. & H. W. Poor, 1876), 673; ibid. *1879*, 849; *American Railroad Journal* 49 (January 15, 1876): 91; ibid. 50 (February 10, 1877); *Sixth Annual Report of the Board of Directors of the St. Louis, Kansas City and Northern Railway Company* (St. Louis: Woodward, Tiernan & Hale, 1878), 7; Maury Klein, *The Life and Legend of Jay Gould* (Baltimore: Johns Hopkins University Press, 1986), 233.

76. Klein, *The Life and Legend of Jay Gould*, 232.

3: THE JAY GOULD YEARS

1. The two leading biographies of Jay Gould are Julius Grodinsky, *Jay Gould: His Business Career, 1867–1892* (Philadelphia: University of Pennsylvania Press, 1957), and Maury Klein, *The Life and Legend of Jay Gould* (Baltimore: Johns Hopkins University Press, 1986).

2. H. Roger Grant, *Erie Lackawanna: Death of an American Railroad, 1938–1992* (Stanford, Calif.: Stanford University Press, 1994), 3–6.

3. "Erie Improvement," *Railroad Gazette* 14 (February 25, 1871): 512; Klein, *The Life and Legend of Jay Gould*, 116–29.

4. See Kenneth D. Ackerman, *The Gold Ring: Jim Fisk, Jay Gould*

and Black Friday, 1869 (New York: Harper & Row, 1988); Klein, *The Life and Legend of Jay Gould,* 3.

5. Maury Klein, *Union Pacific: The Birth of a Railroad, 1862–1893* (Garden City, N.Y.: Doubleday, 1987), 307–22, 388–99, 426–40.

6. Robert L. Frey, ed., *Railroads in the Nineteenth Century* (New York: Facts on File, 1988), 141–43.

7. Grodinsky, *Jay Gould,* 252–67; R. E. Riegel, "The Missouri Pacific, 1879–1900," *Missouri Historical Review* 18 (January 1924): 178; Frey, ed., *Railroads in the Nineteenth Century,* 143.

8. Klein, *The Life and Legend of Jay Gould,* 233; Julius Grodinsky, *The Iowa Pool: A Study in Railroad Competition, 1870–84* (Chicago: University of Chicago Press, 1950), especially 53–67.

9. Grodinsky, *Jay Gould,* 192; *New York Daily Tribune,* July 9, 1879; "Wabash Control of the St. Louis Roads," *Railroad Gazette* 11 (November 21, 1879): 622.

10. Grodinsky, *Jay Gould,* 192; Klein, *The Life and Legend of Jay Gould,* 233; *Chronicle,* November 30, 1878; Meeting of Directors Record, Wabash Railway Company, May 15, 1879, Norfolk Southern Archives, Atlanta, Ga. (hereafter cited as NS Archives).

11. *Railroad Gazette* 11 (January 17, 1879): 39; Meeting of Directors Record, Wabash Railway Company, May 15, June 5, 1879, NS Archives.

12. *Railway World* 22 (December 7, 1878): 182; Meeting of the Directors Record, Wabash Railway Company, July 19, 1879, NS Archives; "Corporate History of the Wabash Railway Company: Compiled Pursuant to and in Accordance with Valuation Order No. 20, Interstate Commerce Commission, Dated May 13, 1915," (June 30, 1919), 65–66 (hereafter cited as "Corporate History of the Wabash Railway Company"); *Prospectus of the Chicago & Paducah Railroad* (New York: Howes & Macy, Bankers, 1872), 10–11, Bureau of Railway Economics Collection, John W. Barriger III National Railroad Library, St. Louis, Mo.

13. *Railroad Gazette* 10 (November 29, 1878): 579.

14. Meeting of the Directors Record, Wabash Railway Company, June 5, 1879, NS Archives; "Corporate History of the Wabash Railway Company," 69; *Chronicle,* November 23, 1878; "Wabash Ry.— History," J. Orville Spreen Collection, Western Historical Manuscript Collection, St. Louis, Mo. (hereafter cited as J. O. Spreen Coll.); Minute Book, Chicago & Strawn Ry. Co., 23–24, Virginia Tech Digital Library and Archives, Blacksburg, Va.

Within a few years the WStL&P changed its terminal in Chicago, becoming a tenant in the Dearborn Street Station, when that large facility opened on May 1, 1885.

15. Klein, *The Life and Legend of Jay Gould,* 233–34; Grodinsky, *Jay Gould,* 196.

16. Klein, *The Life and Legend of Jay Gould,* 235.

17. *American Exchange* (New York), July 9, 1879; *Chronicle,* April 19, 1879; April 17, 1880; *Public,* July 10, 1879; clipping from *Bayonne (N.J.) Evening Journal,* 1900, in J. O. Spreen Coll.

18. Frey, ed., *Railroads in the Nineteenth Century,* 208–11.

19. "How Mr. Joy Came to be on the Wabash Board," *Railroad Gazette* 16 (October 24, 1884): 773; *New York Daily Tribune,* July 25, 1879; *Railroad Gazette* 11 (May 2, 1879): 247; ibid. 11 (May 23, 1879): 291; ibid. 11 (June 27, 1879): 361; *Public,* June 19, 1879.

20. Richard S. Simon and Francis H. Parker, *Railroads of Indiana* (Bloomington: Indiana University Press, 1997), 125; Richard S. Simons, "The Eel River and Its Railroad," *National Railway Bulletin* 53 (No. 6, 1988): 28, 30; *Chronicle,* August 30, 1879; *Railroad Gazette* 11 (October 10, 1879): 547.

21. "Memorandum Re: Corporate History of The Detroit, Butler & St. Louis Railroad Co.," February 8, 1921, in J. O. Spreen Coll.; "Corporate History of the Wabash Railway Company," 61–64; Vance C. Lischer, Jr., to author, July 14, 2002, based on 1880 ledger book of the Detroit, Butler and St. Louis Railroad in possession of Lischer.

22. *Railroad Gazette* 13 (July 15, 1881): 394; ibid. 13 (August 19, 1881): 461; *Chronicle,* August 20, 1881.

23. *Railroad Gazette* 13 (March 25, 1881): 176; ibid. 19 (June 17, 1887): 411.

24. *First Annual Report of the Wabash, St. Louis and Pacific Railway Company For the Year Ending December 31, 1880* (New York: Jones Printing, 1881), 1; *Manual of the Railroads of the United States for 1880* (New York: H. V. & H. W. Poor, 1880), 723; *Railway World* 24 (April 3, 1880): 321; *Railroad Gazette* 13 (March 25, 1881): 176

25. Elmer G. Sulzer, *Ghost Railroads of Indiana* (Indianapolis: Vane A. Jones, 1970), 33; *Railroad Gazette* 33 (March 20, 1891): 10.

26. H. Roger Grant, ed., *Iowa Railroads: The Essays of Frank P. Donovan, Jr.* (Iowa City: University of Iowa Press, 2000), 241; George W. Hilton, *American Narrow Gauge Railroads* (Stanford, Calif.: Stanford University Press, 1990), 397; *Railway World* 25 (September 3, 1881): 861; *Manual of Railroads of the United States for 1883* (New York: Henry V. Poor, 1883), 674.

27. *Railway World* 25 (October 8, 1881): 980; ibid. (November 5, 1881): 1076; ibid. 23 (May 31, 1879): 516; Jean Strouse, *Morgan: American Financier* (New York: Harper Collins, 1998), 196–97; *Manual of Railroads of the United States for 1883,* 674; Richard R. Wallin, Paul H. Stringham and John Szwajkart, *Chicago & Illinois Midland* (San Marino, Calif.: Golden West Books, 1979), 53, 56.

28. Hilton, *American Narrow Gauge Railroads,* 389; "Estimate of Wabash, St. Louis, & Pacific, for 1881," J. O. Spreen Coll.

Gould personally did not endorse the narrow-gauge doctrine, but, when appropriate, he willingly acquired these slim roads. See Hilton, *American Narrow Gauge Railroads,* 524.

29. *Railway World* 25 (July 23, 1881): 714; Pennsylvania Railroad Minutes of the Board of Directors, vol. 9, May 25, 1881, 267, Pennsylvania Railroad Collection, Hagley Museum and Library, Wilmington, Del. (hereafter cited as PRR Coll.); H. W. Schotter, *The Growth and Development of the Pennsylvania Railroad Company* (Philadelphia: Pennsylvania Railroad Company, 1927), 202; Taylor Hampton, *The*

Nickel Plate Road: The History of A Great Railroad (Cleveland: World, 1947), 53.

30. *Third Annual Report of the Wabash, St. Louis and Pacific Railway Company for the Year Ending December 31, 1882* (New York: Jones Printing, 1883), 3–4; *Railroad Gazette* 14 (November 10, 1882): 697; ibid. 14 (January 20, 1882): 34.

31. *Railway World* 25 (March 19, 1881): 276; *Railroad Gazette* 15 (July 6, 1883): 456; Frank P. Morse, *Cavalcade of the Rails* (New York: E. P. Dutton, 1940), 279.

32. *Railroad Gazette,* 25 (March 21, 1881): 171.

33. *New York Daily Tribune,* October 13, 1880; November 8, 1880; November 10, 1880; *Chronicle,* November 13, 1880; unidentified clipping in Spreen Coll.

34. *Chronicle,* March 24, 1883; Charles Elliott Perkins to John Murray Forbes, May 11, 1880, Chicago, Burlington & Quincy Railroad Collection, Newberry Library, Chicago (hereafter cited as CB&Q Coll.).

35. Richard C. Overton, *Burlington Route: A History of the Burlington Lines* (New York: Knopf, 1965), 110, 171–72, 187; Richard C. Overton, "Why Did the C.B.& Q. Build to Denver?" *Kansas Quarterly* 2 (1970): 11.

36. J. F. Joy to Elijah Smith, September 16, 1880, J. O. Spreen Coll.

37. *Railroad Gazette* 12 (September 24, 1880): 512; ibid. 15 (January 19, 1883): 52; Solon Humphreys to Charles Elliott Perkins, September 13, 1880, CB&Q Coll.; Overton, "Why Did the C.B.& Q. Build to Denver?" 12; *Second Annual Report of the Wabash, St. Louis and Pacific Railway Company For the Year ending December 31, 1881* (New York: Huxton & Skinner, 1882), 8.

38. Overton, *Burlington Route,* 186; Overton, "Why Did the C.B.& Q. Build to Denver?" 12; *Railway World* 25 (June 18, 1881): 597; *Iowa State Register* (Des Moines), January 27, 1881.

39. John Lauritz Larson, *Bonds of Enterprise: John Murray Forbes and Western Development in America's Railway Age* (Cambridge, Mass.; Division of Research, Graduate School of Business Administration, Harvard University, 1984), 168; Frey, ed., *Railroads in the Nineteenth Century,* 145.

40. *Report to the Stockholders of the Missouri Pacific Railway For the Year 1883* (New York: Evening Post Job Printing Office, 1884), 3; Broadside, Wabash, St. Louis & Pacific Railway, April 19, 1883, in J. O. Spreen Coll.; *Railway World* 27 (April 28, 1883): 399.

41. *St. Louis Post Dispatch,* April 9, 1883; newspaper clipping in J. O. Spreen Coll.

42. "To the Bondholders of the Wabash, St. Louis and Pacific Railway Company," May 28, 1884, in J. O. Spreen Coll.; *New York Herald,* July 19, 1884.

43. Arthur S. Dewing, "Theory of Railroad Reorganization," *American Economic Review* 8 (December 1918): 784–85.

44. *Railroad Gazette* 16 (June 6, 1884): 438; *Financial News* (London), November 22, 1884.

45. "A Chapter of Wabash," *North American Review* 146 (February 1888): 185; Bradley Hansen, "The People's Welfare and the Origins of Corporate Reorganization: The Wabash Receivership Reconsidered," *Business History Review* 74 (Autumn 2000): 380–81; *New York Herald,* August 7, 1884; *Railroad Gazette* 16 (August 15, 1884): 612.

46. "A Chapter of Wabash," 188; *Chronicle,* June 21, 1884.

47. *Chicago Tribune,* July 14, 1884; *Financial News,* August 9, 1884; December 24, 1884; Hansen, "The People's Welfare and the Origins of Corporate Reorganization," 382; *Railroad Gazette* 16 (August 29, 1884).

48. *Railroad Gazette* 18 (July 30, 1886): 534; Hansen, "The People's Welfare and the Origins of Corporate Reorganization," 381; William Larrabee, *The Railroad Question: A Historical and Practical Treatise on Railroads, and Remedies for Their Abuses* (Chicago: Schulte, 1893), 212; *Railway Register* (St. Louis), May 18, 1889.

49. *Wabash, St. Louis & Pacific Railway, Solon Humphreys and Thomas E. Tutt, Receivers, Report of the Receivers, March 1, 1883 to May 31, 1885* (St. Louis: Nixon-Jones Printing, 1885); *Report of the Purchasing Committee of The Wabash, St. Louis & Pacific Railway Company* (New York: Evening Post Job Printing, 1891), 8; *Railroad Gazette* 19 (March 18, 1887): 12; "Cash Expenditures by Wabash, St. Louis & Pacific On Lines Lost," Box 3, Wabash Railway Collection, Virginia Tech Digital Library and Archives, Blacksburg, Va.

50. Eel River Rail Road Company Minute Book, 35, 37, PRR Coll.; Craig Berndt to author, December 7, 2002.

51. Eel River Rail Road Company Minute Book, November 25, 1886, 38–39.

52. *Paris (Mo.) Mercury,* January 8, 1886; *Moberly (Mo.) Daily Monitor,* January 5, 1886; January 6, 1886.

53. Dewing, "The Theory of Railroad Reorganization," 786–87; *Railroad Gazette* 21 (March 29, 1889): 188.

54. Hansen, "The People's Welfare and the Origins of Corporate Reorganization," 385–86.

55. See *Moberly Daily Monitor,* February 3, 1886; February 23, 1886.

56. *Railroad Gazette* 14 (August 18, 1882): 516; *St. Louis Post Dispatch,* March 13, 1882.

57. See George James Stevenson, "The Brotherhood of Locomotive Engineers and Its Leaders, 1863–1920." PhD diss., Vanderbilt University, 1954; and Walter Licht, *Working on the Railroad: The Organization of Work in the Nineteenth Century* (Princeton, N.J.: Princeton University Press, 1983).

58. Norman J. Ware, *The Labor Movement in the United States, 1860–1895: A Study in Democracy* (New York: D. Appleton, 1929), 18–373.

59. Ruth A. Allen, *The Great Southwest Strike* (Austin: University of Texas Publications, 1942), 25; Harry J. Carman, Henry David and Paul N. Guthrie, eds., *The Path I Trod: The Autobiography of Terence V.*

Powderly (New York: Columbia University Press, 1940), 117.

60. Carmen et al., eds., *The Path I Trod*, 30–31. See also *New York Sun*, March 7, 1885.

61. Klein, *The Life and Legend of Jay Gould*, 357; Arthur E. Holder, "Railroad Strikes Since 1877," *American Federationist* (July 1912): 530; Allen, *The Great Southwest Strike*, 33.

62. Klein, *The Life and Legend of Jay Gould*, 358; Carroll D. Wright, "An Historical Sketch of the Knights of Labor," *Quarterly Journal of Economics* 1 (January 1887): 156.

63. Harry Frumerman, "The Railroad Strikes of 1885–86," *Marxist Quarterly* (1937): 399; Carman et al., eds, *The Path I Trod*, 114; Klein, *The Life and Legend of Jay Gould*, 358–59; F. W. Taussig, "The South-Western Strike of 1886," *Quarterly Journal of Economics* 1 (January 1887): 191–95.

64. *Moberly Daily Monitor*, March 5, 1886; Klein, *The Life and Legend of Jay Gould*, 360; *The Official History of the Great Strike of 1886 on the Southwestern Railway System* (Jefferson City, Mo.: Tribune Printing, 1886), 90–92; Robert V. Bruce, *1877: Year of Violence* (Indianapolis: Bobbs-Merrill, 1959).

65. Klein, *The Life and Legend of Jay Gould*, 361–62; Frumerman, "The Railroad Strikes of 1885–86," 404; *New York Times*, April 30, 1886; Taussig, "The South-Western Strike of 1886," 208–11.

66. Ray Ginger, *Altgeld's America, 1890–1905* (New York: Funk & Wagnalls, 1958), 35–60. For the best study of the Haymarket Square Riot, see Paul Avrich, *The Haymarket Tragedy* (Princeton, N.J.: Princeton University Press, 1984).

67. Allen, *The Great Southwest Strike*, 116–18.

68. *Moberly Daily Monitor*, June 16, 1886.

69. *Railroad Gazette* 16 (August 12, 1884): 660; ibid. 19 (September 2, 1887): 576; Murat Halstead and J. Frank Beale, Jr., *Jay Gould: How He Made His Millions* (n.p.: Edgewood, 1892), 81.

70. *Munn v. Illinois*, 94 U.S. 113 (1877); Ali and Olive Hoogenboom, *A History of the ICC: From Panacea to Palliative* (New York: W. W. Norton, 1976), 7–8.

71. Richard C. Overton, *Perkins/Budd: Railway Statesmen of the Burlington* (Westport, Conn.: Greenwood Press, 1983), 37–48. See also George H. Miller, *Railroads and the Granger Laws* (Madison: University of Wisconsin Press, 1971) and D. Swen Nordin, *Rich Harvest: A History of the Grange, 1867–1900* (Jackson: University Press of Mississippi, 1974).

72. *Wabash, St. Louis & Pacific Railway Co. v. State of Illinois*, 118 U.S. 557 (1886).

73. Ibid.

74. *Moberly Daily Monitor*, October 26, 1886.

75. Hoogenboom, *A History of the ICC*, 8–17.

76. Klein, *The Life and Legend of Jay Gould*, 73–74, 423, 481–82; *New York Times*, December 3, 1892.

77. Minute Book No. 1, Wabash Railroad Company, December 2, 1892, 203, NS Archives.

4: THE WABASH MATURES

1. *Second Annual Report of the Directors of the Wabash Railroad Co. For the Fiscal Year Ending June 30th, 1891* (St. Louis: Woodward & Tiernan, 1891), 2–3; *Railroad Gazette* 24 (September 16, 1892): 696; *Third Annual Report of the Directors of the Wabash Railroad Co. For the Fiscal Year Ending June 30th, 1892* (St. Louis: Woodward & Tiernan, 1892.

2. George Rogers Taylor and Irene D. Neu, *The American Railroad Network, 1861–1890* (Cambridge, Mass.: Harvard University Press, 1956), 83.

3. Craig Berndt to author, November 12, 2002; *Railroad Gazette* 22 (February 21, 1890): 136; ibid., 813; *Peru (Ind.) Tribune*, September 26, 1956.

4. *Travelers's Official Railway Guide for the United States and Canada* (New York: National Railway Publication Co., June 1892), 103.

5. *Railroad Gazette* 29 (June 11, 1897): 406; ibid. 29 (November 11, 1897): 742; Richard S. Simons and Francis H. Parker, *Railroads of Indiana* (Bloomington: Indiana University Press, 1997), 211–13; *Eel River R. Co. et al. v. State ex rel*, Supreme Court of Indiana (57 N.E. 388).

6. *Auburn (Ind.) Courier*, October 11, 1900; "Corporate History of the Wabash Railway Company: Compiled Pursuant to and in Accordance with Valuation Order No. 20, Interstate Commerce Commission, Dated May 13, 1915," (June 30, 1919), 104, 129 (hereafter cited as "Corporate History of the Wabash Railway Company"); Craig Berndt to author, December 7, 2002; George W. Hilton and John F. Due, *The Electric Interurban Railways in America* (Stanford, Calif.: Stanford University Press, 1960), 277; Simons and Parker, *Indiana Railroads*, 213.

7. George S. Morison to O. D. Ashley and James F. Joy, June 1, 1891, in Minute Book 1, n.p. Wabash Railroad Company, Norfolk Southern Archives, Atlanta, Ga. (hereafter cited as NS Archives).

8. Ibid.

9. Ibid.; *Railroad Gazette* 24 (March 11, 1892): 199; *United States Railroad and Mining Register* 16 (November 11,1871): 2; Minute Book, Montpelier & Chicago Railroad Co. of Indiana, 16–17, Virginia Tech Digital Library and Archives, Blacksburg, Va.; *Third Annual Report of the Directors of the Wabash Railroad Co. For the Fiscal Year Ending June 30th, 1892*, 7; *Goshen (Ind.) Democrat*, November 20, 1872; *Goshen (Ind.) Weekly News*, April 4, 1890; June 6, 1890; Vicki L. Brown Comstock, *Journey into the Past: History of Olive Township, Elkhart County, Indiana* (Nappanee, Ind.: Evangel Press, 2001), 527; *Waterways Journal* 2 (April 16, 1892): 10.

10. Comstock, *Journey into the Past*, 528.

11. *Railroad Gazette* 24 (November 18, 1892): 871; ibid. 25 (April 28, 1893): 328; broadside in J. Orville Spreen Collection, Western Historical Manuscript Collection, St. Louis, Mo. (hereafter cited as J. O. Spreen Coll.).

12. "The Wabash Railroad Company, Detroit & Chicago Extension," J. O. Spreen Coll.; Simons and Parker, *Railroads of Indiana,* 126.

13. Minute Book 1, Wabash Railroad Company, June 28, 1893, 213, NS Archives.

14. Ibid.

15. See H. Roger Grant, *Self-Help in the 1890s Depression* (Ames: Iowa State University Press, 1983), 6–8.

16. *Poor's Manual of Railroads 1897* (New York: H. V. and H. W. Poor, 1897), 816; *Fourth Annual Report of the Directors of the Wabash Railroad Company For the Fiscal Year Ending June 30th, 1893* (St. Louis: Woodward & Tiernan, 1893), 5, 8.

17. Minute Book 1, Wabash Railroad Company, March 26, 1894, 229–30, NS Archives; ibid., April 25, 1894, 230; ibid., December 5, 1895, 260; *Moberly (Mo.) Sunday Democrat,* January 26, 1896.

18. Ray Ginger, *The Bending Cross: A Biography of Eugene Victor Debs* (New Brunswick, N.J.: Rutgers University Press, 1949), 92–96; Nick Salvatore, *Eugene V. Debs: Citizen and Socialist* (Urbana: University of Illinois Press, 1982), 115–18.

19. Albro Martin, *James J. Hill and the Opening of the Northwest* (New York: Oxford University Press, 1976), 415–16; O. D. Boyle, *History of Railroad Strikes* (Washington, D.C.: Brotherhood, 1935), 47–50; Ginger, *The Bending Cross,* 102–18.

20. Liston Edgington Leyendecker, *Palace Car Prince: A Biography of George Mortimer Pullman* (Niwot: University Press of Colorado, 1992), 221–23; Salvatore, *Eugene V. Debs,* 125–29.

21. Ginger, *The Bending Cross,* 118–19, 121.

22. Ibid., 127, 140–43; See also Almont Lindsey, *The Pullman Strike: The Story of a Unique Experiment and of a Great Labor Upheaval* (Chicago: University of Chicago Press, 1942).

23. *Fifth Annual Report of the Directors of the Wabash Railroad Co. For the Fiscal Year Ending June 30, 1894* (St. Louis: Woodward & Tiernam, 1894), 20; *Sixth Annual Report of the Directors of the Wabash Railroad Co. For the Fiscal Year Ending June 30th, 1895* (St. Louis: Woodward & Tiernam, 1805), 4, 17–18.

24. Robert D. Sampson, "'Honest Men and Law-Abiding Citizens': The 1894 Railroad Strike in Decatur," *Illinois Historical Journal* 85 (1992): 75.

25. Ibid., 76.

26. Ibid., 77, 79.

27. Ibid., 80, 83.

28. Ibid., 84, 86.

29. Ibid., 86.

30. Ibid., 87–88.

31. *Fifth Annual Report of the Directors of the Wabash Railroad Co. For the Fiscal Year Ending June 30, 1894,* 18; *Sixth Annual Report of the Directors of the Wabash Railroad Co. for the Fiscal Year Ending June 30, 1894,* 4; *Kirksville (Mo.) Democrat,* July 13, 1894.

32. *Poor's Manual of Railroads of the United States* (New York: H. V. & H. W. Poor, 1902), 408.

By the dawn of the twentieth century, the general offices of the Wabash Railroad were housed in the Lincoln Trust Building in St. Louis, located at the corner of Seventh and Chestnut streets. Prior to the spring of 1899, the company rented space in the city's Century Building.

33. *Eighth Annual Report of the Directors of the Wabash Railroad Company For the Fiscal Year Ending June 30th, 1897* (St. Louis: Woodward & Tiernan, 1897), 5; *Ninth Annual Report of the Directors of the Wabash Railroad Company For the Fiscal Year Ending June 30, 1898* (St. Louis: Woodward & Tiernan, 1898), 6.

34. Minute Book 1, Wabash Railroad Company, 372–73, NS Archives.

35. *St. Louis Republic,* December 10, 1905; *Railroad Gazette* 39 (December 29, 1905): 604–6; ibid. 40 (April 20, 1906): 400–1; ibid. 42 (January 25, 1907): 102–3.

36. *St. Louis Post Dispatch,* December 6, 1903.

37. *Railroad Gazette* 29 (June 11, 1897): 420; *Buffalo Courier,* June 1, 1897; Minute Book 1, Wabash Railroad Company, February 9, 1898, 297, NS Archives; "General Notice, The Wabash Railroad Company, Vice-President and General Manager's Office, March 1st, 1898," J. O. Spreen Coll.; Wes Dengate, "The Wabash in Canada: The Buffalo Division," *Banner* (October 2001): 3–4.

38. *Tenth Annual Report of the Directors of the Wabash Railroad Company For the Fiscal Year Ending June 30th, 1899* (St. Louis: Woodward & Tiernan, 1899), 8; Minute Book 1, Wabash Railroad Company, April 13, 1898, 301, NS Archives; Dengate, "The Wabash in Canada," 3.

39. Minute Book 1, Wabash Railroad Company, April 13, 1898, 302–3; December 23, 1899, 373, NS Archives.

40. *Railroad Gazette* 33 (September 13, 1901): 640.

41. "Corporate History of the Wabash Railway Company," 78–79.

42. ICC Valuation Docket 906, October 29, 1926, 14–15; Minute Book 1, Wabash Railroad Company, December 6, 1898, 331, NS Archives.

43. Ibid.

44. Richard C. Overton, *Burlington Route: A History of the Burlington Lines* (New York: Knopf, 1965), 164; *Poor's Manual of Railroads of the United States* (New York: H. V. & H. W. Poor, 1896), 314.

45. Minute Book 1, Wabash Railroad Company, November 16, 1898, 331, NS Archives.

46. *Railroad Gazette* 31 (June 30, 1899): 462; Minute Book 1, Wabash Railroad Company, September 6, 1898, 325; January 3, 1899, 335, NS Archives.

In the process of determining its routing strategy, the Wabash received an offer from Iowan G. D. Braman to build 24.5 miles of line from South Ottumwa, Iowa, westward to Albia and a connection with the DM&StL. While this construction would unite Wabash properties, it lacked the directness of the Moulton-Albia route, and the board logically rejected the proposal. See Minute Book 1, Wabash Railroad Company, April 13, 1898, 319, NS Archives.

47. *Railroad Gazette* 31 (March 31, 1899): 236; *Friday Union* (Albia, Iowa), November 24, 1899; *Tuesday Union* (Albia, Iowa), November 28, 1899.

48. "Corporate History of the Wabash Railway Company," 115–16; *Thirteenth Annual Report of the Directors of the Wabash Railroad Company For the Fiscal Year Ending June 30th 1902* (St. Louis: Woodward & Tiernan, 1902), n.p.

49. Minute Book 2, Wabash Railroad Company, May 29, 1906, 303, NS Archives.

50. Kansas City, Excelsior Springs and Northern Railway Company file, NS Archives; *Kansas City Times*, March 23, 1973.

51. H. Roger Grant, ed., *Iowa Railroads: The Essays of Frank P. Donovan, Jr.* (Iowa City: University of Iowa Press, 2000), 246–47; Ben Hur Wilson, "Abandoned Railroads in Iowa," *Iowa Journal of History and Politics* 26 (January 1928): 46–48; Minute Book 3, Wabash Railroad Company, December 29, 1909, 103, NS Archives; Otha D. Wearin, "The Tabor and Northern Railroad," *Annals of Iowa* 38 (Summer 1965): 427–30.

52. Grant, ed., *Iowa Railroads*, 247; Wilson, "Abandoned Railroads in Iowa," 46, 48; J. W. Kendrick, *A Report upon the Wabash Railroad* (Chicago, 1912), 24–25.

53. Kendrick, *A Report upon the Wabash Railroad*, 25.

54. Minute Book 1, Wabash Railroad Company, March 1, 1898, 299, NS Archives; William Edward Hayes, *Iron Road to Empire: The History of 100 Years of the Progress and Achievements of the Rock Island Lines* (New York: Simmons-Boardman, 1953), 162–63, 174.

55. Kendrick, *A Report upon the Wabash Railroad*, 24; Richard S. Simons, "St. Joseph Valley Railway," *National Railway Bulletin* 52 (1987): 28–36.

56. Hilton and Due, *The Electric Interurban Railways in America*, 22–23, 255, 275, 335.

57. Ibid., 146, 264, 363; H. Roger Grant, "The Excelsior Springs Route: Life and Death of a Missouri Interurban," *Missouri Historical Review* 45 (October 1970): 37–50; Bob Sell and Jim Findlay, *The Teeter & Wobble: Tales of the Toledo & Western Railway Co.* (Blissfield, Mich.: Blissfield Advance, 1993), 19–20.

58. Hilton and Due, *The Electric Interurban Railways in America*, 346–47; Minute Book 2, Wabash Railroad Company, November 13, 1906, 355, NS Archives.

59. Hilton and Due, *The Electric Interurban Railways in America*, 24; Minute Book 2, Wabash Railroad Company, March 26, 1907, 370, NS Archives

60. Hilton and Due, *The Electric Interurban Railways in America*, 104; "Electric Railways," Wabash Railroad Company, NS Archives.

61. John L. Cowan, "Freeing a City from a Railroad's Control," *World's Work* 9 (January 1905): 5712, 5722; *New York Times*, January 3, 1943.

62. Walter C. Fine, "Chasing Rainbows," *National Railway Bulletin* 21 (1956): 25, 27; Cowan, "Freeing a City from a Railroad's Control," 5712–13.

63. Keith L. Bryant, ed., *Railroads in the Age of Regulation* (New York: Facts on File, 1988), 168–69); *Railroad Gazette* 33 (1901): 262.

64. John A. Rehor, *The Nickel Plate Story* (Milwaukee: Kalmbach, 1965), 318; Burton J. Hendrick, "The Passing of a Great Railroad Dynasty," *McClure's Magazine* 38 (March 1912): 497.

65. "Joseph Ramsey, Jr.," *Railway Age Gazette* (July 14, 1916): 65; Edward M. Killough, *History of the Western Maryland Railway Company* (Baltimore: Western Maryland Railway, 1940), 110–11.

66. Howard V. Worley, Jr., and William N. Poellot, Jr., *The Pittsburgh & West Virginia Railway: The Story of the High and Dry* (Halifax, Penn.: Withers, 1989), 36, 38.

67. Ibid., 38; Cowan, "Freeing a City from a Railroad's Control," 5713.

68. Worley and Poellot, *The Pittsburgh & West Virginia Railway*, 38.

69. "The Wabash Pittsburgh Terminal Investigation," *Decisions of the Interstate Commerce Commission of the United States* (Washington, D.C.: U. S. Government Printing Office, 1918), 97–98; Joseph Frazier Wall, *Andrew Carnegie* (New York: Oxford University Press, 1970), 780.

70. George H. Burgess and Miles C. Kennedy, *Centennial History of the Pennsylvania Railroad Company, 1846–1946* (Philadelphia: Pennsylvania Railroad, 1949), 513–14.

71. Minute Book 2, Wabash Railroad Company, October 8, 1901, 23, NS Archives; Worley and Poellot, *The Pittsburgh & West Virginia Railway*, 39.

72. Rehor, *The Nickel Plate Story*, 318, 324; Worley and Poellot, *The Pittsburgh & West Virginia Railway*, 40.

73. Jean Strouse, *Morgan: American Financier* (New York: Harper Collins, 2000), 400–4; *Chronicle*, August 1, 1901; Worley and Poellot, *The Pittsburgh & West Virginia Railway*, 38, 42–44; Burgess and Kennedy, *Centennial History of the Pennsylvania Railroad Company*, 515–16.

Labor historian Colin Davis has shown that during the early part of the twentieth century the PRR made it extremely difficult for labor organizers to gain much of a footing with Cassatt's road. In 1916 a company official admitted to a Congressional committee that in order to control unwanted labor agitation it "spent $800,000 annually on its spy system and employed five hundred gunmen armed with high-powered rifles and revolvers." See Colin J. Davis, *Power at Odds: The 1922 National Railroad Shopmen's Strike* (Urbana: University of Illinois Press, 1997), 25, 183–84.

74. Clipping, December 11, 1901, in Pliny Fisk Collection, John W. Barriger III National Railroad Library, St. Louis, Mo. (hereafter cited as Pliny Fisk Coll.); Cowan, "Freeing a City from a Railroad's Control," 5717; Worley and Poellot, *The Pittsburgh & West Virginia Railway*, 49.

75. Worley and Poellot, *The Pittsburgh & West Virginia Railway*, 45, 48; Robert L. Frey, ed., *Railroads in the Nineteenth Century* (New York: Facts on File, 1988), 39–40; *The Pennsylvania System of Railroads in Greater Pittsburgh and Vicinity* (Philadelphia: Pennsylvania Railroad Company, 1909).

76. Worley and Poellot, *The Pittsburgh & West Virginia Railway*, 48–49, 56, 59; John A. Droege, *Freight Terminals and Trains* (New York: McGraw-Hill, 1925), 324–25; H. Roger Grant, Don L. Hofsommer and Osmund Overby, *St. Louis Union Station: A Place for People, a Place for Trains* (St. Louis: St. Louis Mercantile Library, 1994), 63–67; *Railway Age* (March 23, 1906): 412; *Railroad Gazette* 40 (April 27, 1906): 427–32.

77. *Travelers' Official Railway Guide* (New York: National Railway Publication, July 1904), 111; Worley and Poellot, *The Pittsburgh & West Virginia Railway,* 62–63, 65.

78. Undated clippings, Pliny Fisk Coll.; *Railroad Gazette* 42 (February 22, 1907): 259; *Poor's Manual of Railroads of the United States* (New York: H. V. & H. W. Poor, 1908), 484; *New York Herald,* March 20, 1907.

79. Minute Book 2, Wabash Railroad Company, October 2, 1903, 89, NS Archives; "The Wabash Pittsburgh Terminal Investigation," 97–98, 106–9; *Poor's Manual of Railroads 1906* (New York: H. V. & H. W. Poor, 1906), 423; Augustus J. Veenendaal, Jr., *Slow Train to Paradise: How Dutch Investment Helped Build American Railroads* (Stanford, Calif.: Stanford University Press, 1996), 77–78.

80. These observations are based on letters and other papers found in the Pennsylvania Railroad Collection, Hagley Museum and Library, Wilmington, Del.

81. General Superintendent to G. L. Peck, General Manager, July 9, 1904, Pennsylvania Railroad Collection, Box 1309, Hagley Museum and Library, Wilmington, Del.

82. *Toledo Blade,* June 29, 1905; Wabash Pittsburgh Terminal Railway public timetable, January 8, 1905; Hartley M. Phelps, "Palace Depot for Two Trains a Day," *Technical World Magazine* 19 (March 1913): 94–96.

83. *Poor's Manual of Railroads 1900* (New York: H. V. & H. W. Poor, 1900), 180; George H. Drury, *The Historical Guide to North American Railroads* (Milwaukee: Kalmbach, 1985), 349–50; undated clippings, Pliny Fisk Coll.

84. *Wall Street Journal,* February 12, 1902; Harold A. Williams, *Western Maryland Railway Story: A Chronicle of the First Century, 1852–1952* (Baltimore: Western Maryland Railway, 1952), 90–92.

85. *Railroad Gazette* 35 (September 4, 1903): 636; ibid. 37 (February 5, 1904): 89.

86. Williams, *Western Maryland Railway Story,* 95–96.

87. Drury, *The Historical Guide to North American Railroads,* 350; Harold H. McLean, *Pittsburgh and Lake Erie R.R.* (San Marino, Calif.: Golden West Books, 1980), 75; George M. Leilich, "The Western Maryland: A Corporate History," *Railroad History* 155 (Autumn 1986): 72, 74–75.

88. Minute Book 2, Wabash Railroad Company, December 28, 1903, 103, NS Archives.

89. Maury Klein, *The Life & Legend of E. H. Harriman* (Chapel Hill: University of North Carolina Press, 2000), 418.

90. Ernest Howard, *Wall Street Fifty Years after Erie* (Boston: Stratford, 1923), 17–18l; Edwin P. Holt, *The Goulds: A Social History* (New York: Weybright and Talley, 1969), 248.

91. Clippings April 22, 1905; April 26, 1905, in Pliny Fisk Coll.; Hendrick, "The Passing of a Great Railroad Dynasty," 487.

92. "Debenture and Stock holders of the Wabash Railroad Company," J. O. Spreen Coll.; *New York Times,* October 1, 1905.

93. Minute Book 2, Wabash Railroad Company, October 2, 1905, 243; ibid., October 5, 1905, 245, NS Archives; "Joseph Ramsey, Jr.," *Railway Age Gazette,* 65; Carl Snyder, *American Railways as Investments* (New York: Moody Corporation, 1907), 724; Killough, *History of the Western Maryland Railway Company,* 111.

94. Synder, *American Railways as Investments,* 723; Undated clipping, Pliny Fisk Coll.

95. Bryant, ed., *Railroads in the Age of Regulation, 1900–1980,* 107–8.

96. Undated clippings, Pliny Fisk Coll.; Maury Klein, *Union Pacific: The Rebirth, 1894–1969* (New York: Doubleday, 1989), 150–51.

97. "The Wabash Pittsburgh Terminal Investigation," 147; Worley and Poellot, *The Pittsburgh & West Virginia Railway,* 73–75.

98. Ibid., 75; Rehor, *The Nickel Plate Story,* 334.

99. *Twenty-First Annual Report of the Directors of the Wabash Railroad Co. For the Fiscal Year Ending June 30, 1910* (St. Louis: Woodward & Tiernan, 1910), 4; *Twenty-Second Annual Report of the Directors of the Wabash Railroad Co. For the Fiscal Year Ending June 30, 1911* (St. Louis: Woodward & Tiernan, 1911), 4–7.

100. Clippings in Pliny Fisk Coll.

101. "The Wabash Pittsburgh Terminal Investigation," 144.

102. Hendrick, "The Passing of a Great Railroad Dynasty," 498; clipping, December 27, 1911, in Pliny Fisk Coll.; Rehor, *The Nickel Plate Story,* 325.

103. Clipping, June 21, 1904, in Pliny Fisk Coll.

104. *Railway Age* 64 (February 8, 1918): 341.

105. Kendrick, *A Report upon the Wabash Railroad,* 5.

In time John D. Rockefeller bought control of the Western Maryland and Wheeling & Lake Erie and coal-mining magnate Frank E. Taplin took possession of the Pittsburgh & West Virginia, née WPT.

5: "FOLLOW THE FLAG"

1. John Day, *95 Years with John "Jack" Day the Orphan Nobody Wanted: An Autobiography* (Mahomet, Ill.: Mayhaven, 1997), 127, 150.

2. "Address of N. S. Brown," *The Wabash Club Souvenir* (St. Louis: Wabash Club, 1923), 23, 25; James A. Ward, "On the Mark: The History and Symbolism of Railroad Emblems," *Railroad History*

153 (Autumn 1985): 17–74; G. H. Burck, "Railroad Trade-Marks," *Railroad Man's Magazine* 7 (December 1931): 57.

3. "Address of N. S. Brown," 25.

4. Ibid.; *Decatur (Ill.) Sunday Herald and Review*, May 9, 1954; "Follow the Flag," *Extra Board* 7 (Fall 2002): 1–2; *Railway and Engineering Review* 45 (July 29, 1905).

On occasion in the twentieth century, the Wabash used another advertising phrase. The words SERVING SINCE 1838 appeared under WABASH, most commonly in newspaper advertisements for its passenger service.

While hardly as well known as the "Follow the Flag" phrase or even "Serving Since 1838," railroaders for years used the word "Wabashing." Apparently it originated in the 1880s in the company's East St. Louis yards and came to mean the "smashing of cars in an effort to push them in some place where they couldn't possibly fit." At times, too, Wabashing meant to move at breakneck speeds. See B. A. Botkin and Alvin F. Harlow, *A Treasury of Railroad Folklore* (New York: Crown, 1953), 308–9.

5. Norm Cohen, *Long Steel Rail: The Railroad in American Folksong* (Urbana: University of Illinois Press, 1981), 374; interview with Robert Green, Clemson, S.C., July 25, 2002.

6. L. A. Brown to Henry B. Comstock, November 1, 1946, J. Orville Spreen Collection, Western Historical Manuscript Collection, St. Louis, Mo. (hereafter cited as J. O. Spreen Coll.); Botkin and Harlow, *A Treasury of Railroad Folklore*, 462–63; "The Omaha Cannon Ball," J. O. Spreen Coll.

7. Interview with Arthur D. Dubin, Highland Park, Ill., January 8, 2003; Wabash Railroad public timetable, October 1, 1898; *The Official Guide of the Railways* (New York: National Railway Publication, January 1903), 124; *Railroad Gazette* 30 (June 17, 1898): 441.

8. *St. Louis Republic*, April 11, 1902; Charles E. Fisher to J. O. Spreen, May 17, 1954, J. O. Spreen Coll.

9. Interview with Arthur D. Dubin, Highland Park, Illinois, January 21, 2003; *The Official Guide of the Railways* (New York: National Railway Publication, October 1904), xxix; H. Roger Grant, ed., *Brownie the Boomer: The Life of Charles B. Brown, an American Railroader* (DeKalb: Northern Illinois University Press, 1991), 129; Gene V. Glendinning, *The Chicago & Alton Railroad: The Only Way* (DeKalb: Northern Illinois University Press, 2002), 138–39.

10. *Poor's Manual of the Railroads of the United States* (New York: Poor's Railroad Manual, 1906), 420; "Passenger Trains" (1915), Norfolk Southern Archives, Atlanta, Ga. (hereafter cited as NS Archives).

11. "Passenger Trains" (1915), NS Archives.

12. *The Official Guide of the Railways* (New York: National Railway Publication, June 1904), 121; *The Orland Story: From Prairie to Pavement* (Orland Park, Ill.: Orland Heritage Books Association, 1991), 61–62.

13. *Travelers' Official Guide of the Railway and Steam Navigation Lines in the United States and Canada* (New York: National Railway Publication, May 1890), 87.

14. *St. Louis Globe-Democrat Sunday Magazine*, February 16, 1930.

15. *Champaign-Urbana (Ill.) Courier*, February 16, 1954; *Sunday Morning Democrat* (Moberly, Mo.), March 12, 1922; *Moberly (Mo.) Daily Monitor*, August 13, 1886; *Moberly (Mo.) Monitor-Index*, September 12, 1935.

16. See, for example, "Many Dead in Fatal Wreck on Wabash," ca. 1910, clipping in Miami County Museum, Peru, Ind. (hereafter cited as Miami County Museum); *Missouri Statesman* (Columbia), June 11, 1890.

17. Grant, ed., *Brownie the Boomer*, 125–26.

18. Wabash Railroad Co., Train Order No. 12 [Form 31], September 19, 1901, J. O. Spreen Coll.

19. "A Few Facts for Visitors to the Columbian Exposition," Wabash Railroad Company, 1893; "The World's Columbian Exposition, Transportation" (St. Louis: Passenger Department, Wabash Railroad Company, 1893).

20. Minute Book 1, Wabash Railroad Company, May 4, 1891, 124, NS Archives; John F. Stover, *History of the Illinois Central Railroad* (New York: Macmillan, 1975), 217–21.

21. Minute Book 1, Wabash Railroad Company, June 26, 1900, 397; July 12, 1900, 401, NS Archives.

22. Wabash Railroad public timetable, June 1901; "The Pan-American Exposition in Buffalo" (St. Louis: Wabash Railroad Company, 1901); "Pan-American Exposition, Buffalo, New York, May 1st to November 1st, 1901" (Buffalo: Pan-American Exposition Company, 1901).

23. Minute Book 1, Wabash Railroad Company, July 12, 1900, 401, NS Archives; J. Ramsey, Jr., to David R. Francis, May 6, 1901, in "Complimentary Trip to the Dedicatory Exercises of the Pan-American Exposition Tendered to the Louisiana Purchase Exposition Directors by the Wabash Railroad, May 20th, 1901," Missouri Historical Society Library, St. Louis; Minute Book 2, Wabash Railroad Company, December 31, 1903, 106, NS Archives; Minutes of Meetings of Executive Committee, Board of Directors of the TRRA, March 14, 1904, Pennsylvania Railroad Collection, Hagley Museum and Library, Wilmington, Del. (hereafter cited as PRR Coll.).

24. Timothy J. Fox and Duane R. Sneddeker, *From the Palaces to the Pike: Visions of the 1904 World's Fair* (St. Louis: Missouri Historical Society Press, 1997), 26.

25. *St. Louis Globe-Democrat*, April 30, 1904; May 1, 1904; *Travelers' Official Railway Guide* (New York: National Railway Publication, July 1904), 116; The Wabash Railroad Company, Circular No. 72–1904, J. O. Spreen Coll; A Paper Prepared by Mr. J. J. Turner for the 1904 Annual Dinner Given by the Board to the President: "The Pennsylvania Railroad Exhibit at the St. Louis World's Fair," Box 113, PRR Coll.; *Official Catalogue of Exhibitors, University Exposition, St. Louis, U.S.A. 1904--Department G Transportation* (St. Louis: Louisiana Purchase Exposition, 1904), 20–21; *History of the LPE* (St. Louis: Universal Exposition, 1905), 582.

26. Fox and Sneddeker, *From the Palaces to the Pike*, 237; Grant, ed., *Brownie the Boomer*, 124; J. W. Kendrick, *A Report upon the Wabash Railroad* (Chicago, 1912), 35; "Report on the St. Louis World's Fair" (1905), NS Archives.

27. See Roy V. Scott, *Railroad Development Programs in the Twentieth Century* (Ames: Iowa State University Press, 1985).

28. *Schedule of the Special Lecture Train Operated by the Wabash Railroad, March 21 to 23, 1911, in Connection with The College of Agriculture and State Board of Agriculture* (n.p., n.d.), 1, 3, 9.

29. Scott, *Railroad Development Programs in the Twentieth Century*, 54–55; Minute Book 2, Wabash Railway Company, April 4, 1922, 99, NS Archives; Minute Book 3, Wabash Railway Company, September 11, 1929, 323, NS Archives.

30. Minute Book 3, Wabash Railway Company, June 12, 1929, 240, NS Archives; newspaper clipping, ca. 1930, John W. Barriger III Papers, John W. Barriger III National Railroad Library, St. Louis, Mo.; "Wabash Poultry Car," *Railway Age* 88 (April 5, 1930).

31. *Moberly Daily Monitor*, February 23, 1886; *Moberly (Mo.) Evening Democrat*, March 4, 1896.

32. Grant, ed., *Brownie the Boomer*, 127–28, 131, 146; John F. Moore, *The Story of the Railroad Y* (New York: Association Press, 1930).

33. Moore, *The Story of the Railroad Y*.

34. Grant, ed., *Brownie the Boomer*, 127; Celeste Andrews Seton, *Helen Gould Was My Mother-in-Law* (New York: Thomas Y. Crowell Company, 1953), 67–69.

35. "Reception to Miss Helen Miller Gould at the Railroad and City Young Men's Christian Association Building, Peru, Indiana, March 13th, 1912," Miami County Museum.

36. *The Wabash Club Souvenir* (St. Louis: Wabash Club, 1916), 9, 11, 13.

About 1900, several Wabash officials in St. Louis spearheaded organization of the Wabash Veterans' Corps, and within a few years it boasted a membership of approximately 250 members. This type of group, usually meeting on an informal basis, continued after the 1964 merger with the Norfolk & Western.

37. Maurice A. Phillips, "The Wabash Club—Historical Review," *The Wabash Club Souvenir* (St. Louis: Wabash Club, 1916), 111–12.

38. *Moberly Evening Democrat*, January 23, 1923; *St. Louis Globe-Democrat Sunday Magazine*, December 28, 1930; *Kansas City (Mo.) Call*, January 28, 1922.

39. Minute Book 7, Wabash Railroad Company, October 16, 1947, 115–18, NS Archives; *The Wabash Club Souvenir* (St. Louis: Wabash Club, 1930), 25; C. H. Stinson to E. E. Pershall, May 12, 1922, T. J. Moss Collection, Western Historical Manuscript Collection, University of Missouri—St. Louis; Financial Secretary to T. J. Moss, May 6, 1922, in ibid.

40. *St. Louis Globe-Democrat Sunday Magazine*, December 28, 1930; Minute Book 7, Wabash Railroad Company, October 16, 1947.

41. *Decatur (Ill.) Review*, June 3, 1935; interview with Ollie Blackburn, St. Louis, June 23, 2002 (hereafter cited as Blackburn interview).

42. *Railway Age* (July 23, 1897): 605; *Decatur Review*, September 6, 1972.

43. Untitled typescript history of the Wabash Employe's Hospital Association, Wabash Memorial Hospital Association Archive, Decatur, Ill. (hereafter cited as WMHA Archive).

44. Mark Aldrich, "Train Wrecks to Typhoid Fever: The Development of Railroad Medicine Organizations, 1850 to World War I," *Bulletin of the History of Medicine* 75 (2001): 257; interview with Augustus J. Veenendaal, Jr., Pijnacker, Holland, May 2, 2003; *Railway World* 58 (June 1914): 468–69; Barbara Young Welke, *Recasting American Liberty: Gender, Race, Law, and the Railroad Revolution, 1865–1920* (New York: Cambridge University Press, 2001), 98–99.

45. George F. Beasley, "The Wabash Surgical Association; Its Beginning and Its Officers," n.d., n.p., 1, 3; Aldrich, "Train Wrecks to Typhoid Fever," 265; Ira M. Rutkown, "Railroad Surgery: A Forgotten Chapter in the History of American Surgery," *Archives of Surgery* 137 (May 2002): 624.

46. "History of WEHA," WMHA Archive.

47. *Railroad Gazette* 18 (November 19, 1886): 800; "Proceedings of the Surgeons of the Wabash, St. Louis & Pacific Railway;" (1884); "Proceedings of the Surgical Association of the Wabash Railway," (1888); "Proceedings of the Surgeons of the Wabash Railroad," (1907).

When Wabash surgeons gathered for their annual meeting on November 10, 1904, at the Southern Hotel in St. Louis, they adjourned early to "give [themselves] . . . an opportunity to attend the World's Fair," a decision that surely enhanced good feelings and increased bonds of commitment to the society and the railroad.

48. Aldrich, "Train Wrecks to Typhoid Fever," 258–59; "History of the WEHA;" R. O. Woolsey, "The Modern Railway Hospital and Its Management," *Official Proceedings St. Louis Railway Club* 18 (August 8, 1913): 135.

49. Aldrich, "Train Wrecks to Typhoid Fever," 262–63; "Dues," WMHA Archive.

50. "History of the WEHA;" *Peru (Ind.) Republican*, September 4, 1885; *Miami County Sentinel* (Peru, Ind.), April 30, 1885; August 27, 1885.

Dr. E. B. North, this first head of Wabash's Peru hospital, was a beloved member of his community. In July 1887 when he attempted to break up a domestic dispute, "one James Christiansen, a worthless Dane who lived near the hospital," shot North at point-blank range, although he did not die until a few days later. Police officers immediately arrested Christiansen and placed him in the Miami County jail. Townspeople, however, became so enraged at this violence that they broke into the Christiansen's cell and dragged him by a rope through the streets to the Wabash Railroad bridge. The *Peru Republican* of July 6, 1887, reported the final events of this gruesome lynching: "When near the bridge the mob in charge of the affair started on a double quick when the prisoner fell down and the men supporting him on each side fell over him. The men in front pulling the rope, did not stop until the prisoner was choked considerably. He was finally hustled to the middle of the bridge, a guard being planted across the entrance to keep the crowd back. The rope was passed over a beam and the prisoner was asked to plead in his own behalf. His words were inaudible to the outside crowd. A vote was taken on the question of hanging him which resulted in a unanimous and emphatic 'aye.' He was then drawn up, but his hands not being tied, he grasped the rope and drew himself up. The mob then seized his legs and held him down until he was strangled."

51. *Moberly Monitor-Index & Evening Democrat,* April 6, 1997; Blackburn interview; Sister M. Clarella, O.S.F., to George M. Bruck, September 18, 1965, Miami County Museum.

52. *Minutes of Meetings Board of Trustees and Board of Managers* (St. Louis: Wabash Employe's Hospital Association, 1929), 18; *Minutes of Meetings Board of Trustees and Board of Managers* (St. Louis, 1923), 4–5.

53. *First Annual Report of the Wabash Western Railway Co.* (St. Louis: Woodward & Tiernam, 1888), 19; *Minutes of Meetings Board of Trustees and Board of Managers* (1929), 17–19; A. H. Ulmer to George M. Bruck, August 24, 1965, Miami County Museum; "The Wabash Hospital at Peru," *Railway Age* (July 23, 1897): 605; newspaper clipping, n.d., Miami County Museum; *Peru Republican,* November 27, 1896.

54. *Decatur (Ill.) Daily Review,* September 9, 1902; *Decatur Sunday Herald and Review,* May 9, 1954.

55. Untitled typescript history of the Wabash Employe's Hospital Association; *Report of the Wabash Employe's Hospital Association* (St. Louis: Wabash Employe's Hospital Association, 1927), 9; *Minutes of Meetings Board of Trustees and Board of Managers* (St. Louis: Wabash Employe's Hospital Association, 1917), 25.

56. *Minutes of Meetings Board of Trustees and Board of Managers* (St. Louis: Wabash Employe's Hospital Association, 1932), 17; newspaper clippings, WMHA Archive.

Although it is generally assumed that members of the First Church of Christ, Scientist belonged to the ranks of the upper and middle classes, recent scholarship indicates that at one time the faith attracted a sizeable number of believers from the working class. See Rolf Swensen, "Pilgrims at the Golden Gate: Christian Scientists on the Pacific Coast, 1880–1915," *Pacific Historical Review* 72 (May 2003): 229–263.

57. Laurie C. Dickens, *Wreck On The Wabash* (Blissfield, Mich.: Made for Ewe, 2001), 33–57.

Dickens is highly critical of the Wabash for underestimating the number of passengers killed. Yet there is no evidence that the company deliberately falsified the list of fatalities. An accurate account was impossible, because of the large number of Italian immigrant passengers onboard, with ticket records inexact. There is no question that the Wabash responded nobly to the disaster, providing a medical relief train from Detroit and a high-speed run from the crash site to its well-equipped hospital in Peru, Indiana. Moreover, it was not unusual for a railroad not to know the precise number of fatalities. In the deadliest accident in Vermont history, for example, which occurred on February 7, 1887, the Central of Vermont Railway estimated the deaths in the derailment of the *Montreal Express* at thirty. Various nonrailroad accounts, however, listed thirty, thirty-one, thirty-four and thirty-seven. See *Vermont Sunday Magazine (Rutland Herald),* August 11, 2002.

58. *Report of the Wabash Employe's Hospital Association For the Fiscal Year Ending June 30, 1913* (St. Louis: Wabash Employe's Hospital Association, 1913), 1; *Report of the Wabash Employe's Hospital Association For the Fiscal Year Ending December 31, 1927* (St. Louis: Wabash Employe's Hospital Association, 1928), 10.

59. *St. Louis Globe-Democrat,* December 14, 1960; *Moberly Monitor-Index & Evening Democrat,* April 6, 1997; Wabash Employe's Hospital Association Circular, October 1, 1960, J. O. Spreen Coll.; *Peru Republican,* May 21, 1965; *Peru (Ind.) Daily Tribune,* July 1, 1976.

60. *Decatur Review,* July 25, 1972; July 28, 1972.

61. Interview with Robert W. Kimmons, Decatur, Ill., August 22, 2002.

62. H. Roger Grant, *The North Western: A History of the Chicago & North Western Railway System* (DeKalb: Northern Illinois University Press, 1996), 122–24; *Railway Age Gazette* 53 (July 19, 1912): 127; ibid. 53 (October 25, 1912): 796–97; ibid. 57 (November 13, 1914): 914; B.C. Winston, "Safety Always," *The Wabash Club Souvenir* (1916), 81, 83.

6: REORGANIZATION, WAR, BOOM AND BUST

1. *Report of the Board of Directors of the Wabash Railway Company to the Stockholders For the Eight Months Ended June 30, 1916* (St. Louis: Wabash Railway Company, 1916), 2; "The New Wabash Railroad," (New York: A. A. Housman, December 15, 1915), 1, 3, Pliny Fisk Collection, John W. Barriger III National Railroad Library, St. Louis, Mo. (hereafter cited as Pliny Fisk Coll.); "Wabash Railway," Dow, Jones & Co. September 16, 1916, Pliny Fisk Coll; *Railway Age Gazette* 58 (February 12, 1915): 256–57.

2. "The Wabash Reorganization," Norfolk Southern Archives, Atlanta, Ga. (hereafter cited as NS Archives).

3. *Address to Hon. Elliott W. Major By Edward B. Pryor, Receiver, Wabash Railroad, October Nineteenth, 1914,* Missouri Historical Society Library, St. Louis (hereafter cited as *Address By Edward B. Pryor*).

4. Albro Martin, *Enterprise Denied: Origins of the Decline of American Railroads, 1897–1917* (New York: Columbia University Press, 1971), 113–15, 183–93; "Important Developments in the Trans-

portation Field," *Railway World* 57 (June 1913): 439.

5. *Address by Edward B. Pryor.*

6. *Railway Age Gazette* 53 (August 16, 1912): 318; ibid. 55 (August 1, 1913): 211; ibid. 57 (November 13, 1914): 914; William Swartz, "The Wabash Railroad," *Railroad History* 133 (Fall 1975): 78–80; Wabash Railroad public timetable (ca. 1914), 51–52.

7. "The Wabash Reorganization Plan," *Railway Age Gazette* 58 (May 7, 1915): 978; *New York Times*, October 22, 1915; "Wabash Plan of Reorganization, Statement of Joint Reorganization Committee," Union Pacific Railroad Archives, Omaha, Neb.; *Railway World* 59 (August 1915): 649; Margaret L. Coit, *Mr. Baruch* (Washington, D.C.: Beard Books, 2000), 128–30.

8. *Historical Statistics of the United States, Colonial Times to 1957* (Washington, D.C.: U.S. Bureau of the Census, 1960),429; George W. Hilton and John F. Due, *The Electric Interurban Railways in America* (Stanford, Calif.: Stanford University Press, 1964), 186.

9. Albro Martin, *Railroads Triumphant: The Growth, Rejection, and Rebirth of a Vital American Force* (New York: Oxford University Press, 1992), 354–55; Maury Klein, *Union Pacific: The Rebirth, 1894–1969* (New York: Doubleday, 1989), 218.

10. "Edward F. Kearney," NS Archives; Minute Book 1, Wabash Railway Company, March 19, 1919, 307, NS Archives; *The Biographical Directory of Railway Officials of America* (Chicago: Railway Age Company, 1906), 327.

11. *Philadelphia Public Ledger*, July 22, 1924; *St. Louis Globe Democrat*, October 15, 1931; "William H. Williams Dies," *Railway Age* 91 (October 17, 1931): 605; Keith L. Bryant, Jr., ed., *Railroads in the Age of Regulation, 1900–1980* (New York: Facts on File, 1988), 259; *Barron's National Financial Weekly*, January 7, 1935; *New York Daily Investment News*, November 20, 1929.

12. *Railway Age Gazette* 63 (December 7, 1917): 1025; Swartz, "The Wabash Railroad,"84; *Second Annual Report of the Wabash Railway Company For the Fiscal Year Ended December 31, 1917* (St. Louis: Wabash Railway Company, 1918), 10.

13. Minute Book 1, Wabash Railway Company, January 3, 1918, p. 200, NS Archives; K. Austin Kerr, *American Railroad Politics, 1914–1920* (Pittsburgh: University of Pittsburgh Press, 1968), 72–91.

14. Eugene L. Huddleston, *Uncle Sam's Locomotives: The USRA and the Nation's Railroads* (Bloomington: Indiana University Press, 2002), 1–3; John F. Stover, *The Life and Decline of the American Railroad* (New York: Oxford University Press, 1970), 161; Richard Saunders, Jr., *The Railroad Mergers and the Coming of Conrail* (Westport, Conn.: Greenwood Press, 1978), 35–37.

15. Huddleston, *Uncle Sam's Locomotives*, ix–xi. See also Aaron A. Godfrey, *Government Operation of the Railroads, 1918–1920* (Austin, Tex.: Jenkins, 1974).

16. Minute Book 1, Wabash Railway Company, February 19, 1919, 301; ibid., June 19, 1919, 341, NS Archives.

17. Swartz, "The Wabash Railroad," 80,82; *Fourth Annual Report*
of the Wabash Railway For the Fiscal Year Ended December 31, 1919 (St. Louis: Wabash Railway Company, 1920), 7; "Notes on Engines," ca. 1919, NS Archives.

18. Minute Book 1, Wabash Railway Company, August 15, 1917, 167; ibid., April 5, 1920, NS Archives.

19. Interview with Ollie Blackburn, St. Louis, Mo., June 23, 2002 (hereafter cited as Blackburn interview); Minute Book 1, Wabash Railway Company, insert, n.d., NS Archives.

20. Minute Book 1, Wabash Railway Company, insert, n.d., NS Archives; Eric Arnesen, *Brotherhoods of Color: Black Railroad Workers and the Struggle for Equality* (Cambridge, Mass.: Harvard University Press, 2001), 45–48.

21. *Seventh Annual Report of the Wabash Railway Company For the Fiscal Year Ended December 31, 1922* (St. Louis: Wabash Railway Company, 1923), 12.

22. Minute Book 1, Wabash Railway Company, March 19, 1919, 307; ibid., June 19, 1919, 341, NS Archives; James L. Minnis to Otto H. Kahn, June 9, 1919, Maury Klein Papers, John W. Barriger III National Railroad Library, St. Louis, Mo.

Minnis was correct that Williams received annual income from other carriers, including the Delaware & Hudson, Missouri Pacific and Texas & Pacific.

23. *The Biographical Directory of the Railway Officials of America* (New York: Simmons-Boardman, 1922), 611–12; *St. Louis Globe-Democrat*, November 28, 1925; Ollie Blackburn interview.

24. Douglas Wixson, *Worker-Writer in America: Jack Conroy and the Tradition of Midwestern Literary Radicalism, 1898–1990* (Urbana: University of Illinois Press, 1994), 53–54.

25. Colin J. Davis, *Power at Odds: The 1922 National Railroad Shopmen's Strike* (Urbana: University of Illinois Press, 1997), 30–39; William Norris Leonard, *Railroad Consolidation Under the Transportation Act of 1920* (New York: Columbia University Press, 1946), 53–54.

26. Leonard, *Railroad Consolidation Under the Transportation Act of 1920*, 40–63; Robert H. Zieger, *Republicans and Labor, 1919–1929* (Lexington: University of Kentucky Press, 1969), 118–21, 192.

27. Davis, *Power at Odds*, 57–62.

28. Ibid., 62–63.

29. *Moberly (Mo.) Evening Democrat*, November 20, 1921; April 28, 1922.

30. *Moberly Evening Democrat*, June 29, 1922; *Sunday Morning Democrat* (Moberly, Mo.), July 2, 1922; Davis, *Power at Odds*, 67–68.

African Americans did not show much enthusiasm for the shopmen's strike. C. A. Franklin, a leading journalist in the black community, thought that railway unions should fight to increase the wages of the lowest paid railroad workers, lamenting that black coach cleaners made only $18 per week. See *Kansas City (Mo.) Call*, July 15, 1922.

31. *Moberly Evening Democrat*, June 29, 1922.

32. *Sunday Morning Democrat*, July 9, 1922; Davis, *Power at Odds*,

chap. 4; Wixson, *Worker-Writer in America,* 80–81.

33. *Moberly Evening Democrat,* July 7, 1922; *Sunday Morning Democrat,* July 9, 1922.

34. *Sunday Morning Democrat,* July 9, 1922.

35. *Moberly Morning Democrat,* July 11, 1922; July 16, 1922; William E. Hooper, "General Atterbury's Attitude toward Labor," *World's Work* 44 (September 1922): 507; James N. Giglio, *H. M. Daugherty and the Politics of Expediency* (Kent: Kent State University Press, 1978), 146–49; Davis, *Power at Odds,* 130–33.

Although few shopmen belonged to the Communist Party, the Central Executive Committee of the Communist Party of America told strikers to "DEFY THE INJUNCTION! This injunction is a blow at the working class. Down with the injunction! On with the Strike. Resist the terror of the master class. Make the Strike General!" See Pennsylvania Railroad Collection, Box 1047, Hagley Museum and Library, Wilmington, Del. (hereafter cited as PRR Coll.).

36. *Sunday Morning Democrat,* August 20, 1922.

37. Davis, *Power at Odds,* 103–10; David M. Vrooman, *Daniel Willard and Progressive Management on the Baltimore & Ohio Railroad* (Columbus: Ohio State University Press, 1991), 45–47.

38. *Moberly Evening Democrat,* July 25, 1922; July 28, 1922; *Decatur (Ill.) Herald,* October 3, 1922; Wixson, *Worker-Writer in America,* 78–79, 81, 84.

39. *Moberly Evening Democrat,* August 9, 1922; November 7, 1922.

40. Ibid., August 16, 1922; *Sunday Morning Democrat,* October 15, 1922; *Moberly Evening Democrat,* October 19, 1922; October 20, 1922; November 19, 1922.

41. "Decatur Car Shops Seniority List as of July 1, 1935," Wabash Memorial Hospital Association Archive, Decatur, Ill. (hereafter cited as WMHA Archive).

42. Davis, *Power at Odds,* 102; *Sunday Morning Democrat,* February 11, 1923.

43. "Strike Memories," WMHA Archive; Wixson, *Worker-Writer in America,* 72, 83–84.

44. W. N. Jennings to M. W. Clement, August 26, 1941, PRR Coll.

45. I. Leo Sharfman, *The American Railroad Problem: A Study in War and Reconstruction* (New York: Century, 1921), 397–431; Ari and Olive Hoogenboom, *A History of the ICC: From Panacea to Palliative* (New York: Norton, 1976), 94–97.

As with other Class I roads, the Wabash found it expensive to meet the demands imposed by the Valuation Act of 1913. By 1924, this progressive era reform measure, designed to determine "original cost" of individuals railroads, had cost the Wabash $1,049,313.98. Because the ICC could never fully discover original costs, much of these fact-finding activities became merely a time- and money-draining experience for the carriers. See *Eighth Annual Report of the Wabash Railway Company for the Fiscal Year Ended December 31, 1923* (St. Louis: Wabash Railway Company, 1924), 11.

46. Leonard, *Railroad Consolidation under the Transportation Act of 1920,* 64–83, 299–310; William H. Williams to Albert R. Erskine, June 8, 1929, Wabash Railway Collection, Virginia Tech Digital Library and Archives, Blacksburg, Va. (hereafter cited as Virginia Tech Coll.).

47. Leonard, *Railroad Consolidation under the Transportation Act of 1920,* 311–36; Minute Book 3, Wabash Railway Company, June 28, 1929, 263, NS Archives; Richard Saunders, Jr., *Merging Lines: American Railroads, 1900–1970* (DeKalb: Northern Illinois University Press, 2001), 66–67; Herbert H. Harwood, Jr., *Invisible Giants: The Empires of Cleveland's Van Sweringen Brothers* (Bloomington: Indiana University Press, 2003), 187.

48. "Control of Ann Arbor R.R. Co. By Wabash Ry. Co., Finance Docket No. 4942, Interstate Commerce Reports, 1925," 43–44; John Uckley, "To Be or Not to Be," *Rail Classics* 14, No. 2, 55; *Poor's Manual of Railroads* (New York: Poor's Manual Company, 1913), 620–21.

49. Allen Johnson, ed., *Dictionary of American Biography* (New York: Charles Scribners' Sons, 1928), 389–90; Henry E. Riggs, *The Ann Arbor Railroad Fifty Years Ago* (n.p.: Ann Arbor Railroad Company, ca. 1947.), 5.

50. *Twenty-Sixth Annual Report of the Ann Arbor Railroad Company For the Fiscal Year Ended December 31, 1924* (Ann Arbor, Mich.: Ann Arbor Railroad Company, 1925), 34.

51. Ibid.

52. Edward Ringwood Hewitt, *Those Were the Days: Tales of a Long Life* (New York: Duell, Sloan and Pearce, 1943), 259; Riggs, *The Ann Arbor Railroad Fifty Years Ago,* 6, 18–19; *Owosso (Mich.) Argus-Press,* June 30, 1936.

53. Graydon M. Meints, *Michigan Railroads and Railroad Companies* (East Lansing: Michigan State University Press, 1992), 15; Thomas William Scott, "Lake Michigan Trainferries and Their Freight Traffic." PhD diss., University of Illinois, 1967, 13, 16–17.

54. Riggs, *The Ann Arbor Railroad Fifty Years Ago,* 32–33

55. Ibid., 11; A. M. Schoyer to G. L. Peck, December 4, 1905, Box 1298, PRR Coll.

56. Clipping (May 21, 1902) and notes, 1902, Pliny Fisk Coll.

57. *Twenty-Fifth Annual Report of the Ann Arbor Railroad Company For the Fiscal Year Ended December 31, 1923* (n.p.: Ann Arbor Railroad Company, 1924), 6; ICC Finance Docket No. 4942, 44–46; "Wabash to Benefit From Owning Ann Arbor," *Railway Age* 78 (June 26, 1925): 1542.

58. Minute Book 2, Wabash Railway Company, November 10, 1925, 379; *Railway Age* 79 (November 14, 1925): 907; *Moody's Manual of Investments: Railroad Securities* (New York: Moody's Investors Service, 1933), 1814.

59. ICC Finance Docket No. 4942, 47–48.

60. A. J. County to General Atterbury, February 10, 1931, PRR Coll.

While the 1920s saw the Wabash take stock control of the Ann Arbor, rumors persisted in 1922 that Henry Ford would purchase both the Virginian and Wabash railroads. He wished to protect his coal supplies and understood the importance of the Wabash in connecting his Detroit and branch automotive plants with major markets. See *Moberly Evening Democrat* October 6, 1922; October 11, 1922, and Julius Grodinsky, *Railroad Consolidation: Its Economics and Controlling Principles* (New York: D. Appleton and Company, 1930), 4–5.

61. Whereas the Ann Arbor acquisition materialized, efforts by the Williams administration to strengthened its Canadian position and to widen its presence in Michigan failed. In 1926, the Wabash sought to acquire from the Canadian National Railways (CN) its double-track line between Windsor and Glencoe and the single trackage between Glencoe and Welland Junction; Welland Junction and Niagara Falls, Ontario; and Welland Junction and Bridgeburg. The price tag of $14,070,214 was too high. Similarly, Williams's proposals to the CN for the Wabash to gain trackage rights over CN subsidiary Grand Trunk Railway between Detroit and Grand Haven and Detroit and Muskegon never moved beyond the discussion stage. The former was inspired by the failure of CN to maintain adequately the Buffalo line and the latter by the desire for additional connections with Great Lakes shipping. See Henry W. Thornton to W. H. Williams, October 20, 1926; December 3, 1928; W. H. Williams to Henry W. Thornton, July 28, 1927, both in Virginia Tech Coll.

62. *Moody's Manual of Investments and Security Rating Service: Railroad Securities* (New York: Moody's Investors Service, 1926), 1649; *The Biographical Directory of the Railway Officials of America* (New York: Simmons-Boardman, 1922), 676–77; *St. Louis Globe-Democrat,* October 15, 1931.

63. Ian S. Haberman, *The Van Sweringens of Cleveland: The Biography of an Empire* (Cleveland: Western Reserve Historical Society, 1979), 65–88; Harwood, *Invisible Giants,* 27–85.

64. Saunders, *The Railroad Mergers and the Coming of Conrail,* 50–52.

65. W. H. Williams, "The D&H and Wabash Ry. Co.," ca. 1926, NS Archives; *Railway Age* 82 (March 5, 1927): 659.

66. *St. Louis Globe-Democrat,* April 19, 1932.

67. Bryant, ed., *Railroads in the Age of Regulation, 1900–1980,* 265–66.

68. Ibid., 266; *Railway Age* 84 (May 5, 1928).

General Atterbury gave Loree an opportunity to create his cherished Fifth System. "The shrewd Atterbury had little to lose and much to gain," concluded one historian. "Probably knowing that Loree's chances of consummating all his plans were slim, he let him play out his hand." See Harwood, *Invisible Giants,* 147.

69. *St. Louis Star,* April 28, 1928.

70. *Wall Street Journal,* October 16, 1929.

71. "Six-System Plan for Eastern Roads Proposed by Wabash," *Railway Age* 87 (July 6, 1929): 17–21; Minute Book 3, Wabash Railway Company, June 28, 1929, 263, NS Archives; *Detroit News,* De-

cember 23, 1929; *Kansas City Star,* December 24, 1929.

72. Memorandum to General Atterbury, November 11 (?), 1929, PRR Coll.

73. "Penna. Control of Wabash and L.V. Disapproved," *Railway Age* 89 (December 13, 1930): 1275–76.

74. *Wall Street Journal,* June 4, 1930; *Railway Age* 96 (March 24, 1934): 453; *Moberly (Mo.) Monitor-Index,* March 19, 1934; March 23, 1934.

75. *Railway Age* 81 (September 18, 1926): 526; "Wabash Freight Traffic a Record," *Railway Age* 86 (May 4, 1929): 1055.

76. *Eighth Annual Report of the Wabash Railway Company For the Fiscal Year Ended December 31, 1923,* 9–11; *Ninth Annual Report of the Wabash Railway Company For the Fiscal Year Ended December 31, 1924* (St. Louis: Wabash Railway Company, 1925), 9–10; "Banner Blue Limited Uses New Decatur Bridge," *Wabash News* 2 (March 1, 1927): 1.

Although the Wabash felt the impact of cars on its short-haul and branch-line passenger revenues, it took advantage of the automobile age as much as possible. The railroad benefited from the transportation of automobiles and parts to and from manufacturing plants, most of all those operated by the Ford Motor Company, and the hauling of cement, asphalt and other road-building materials for highway construction and improvement projects. The company even encouraged the post–World War I "Ocean to Ocean Trail" scheme. In 1921 when citizens of Meredosia, Illinois, asked that this highway be allowed to use the Wabash Railroad bridge over the Illinois River, the company agreed. The railroad planked the bridge at a cost of about $12,000 and charged $6,000 in annual rental fees. Residents agreed to maintain the approaches and to charge tolls for both motor vehicles and pedestrians. See Minute Book 2, Wabash Railway Company, November 29, 1921, 81; January 29, 1924, 277, NS Archives.

77. Minute Book 2, Wabash Railway Company, April 23, 1923, 181, NS Archives.

78. Wilbert P. Williams, "The Wabash—Kingshighway to Maple," 8–14, Missouri Historical Society Library, St. Louis; J. E. Taussig, "A Reply to a Recent Statement Attributed to Mayor Miller," n.d., in ibid.

79. *St. Louis Globe Democrat,* June 19, 1928; *St. Louis Star,* June 19, 1928.

80. *Decatur (Ill.) Sunday Herald and Review,* May 9, 1954; "New Wabash Coach Shops Marked by Effective Use of Space," *Railway Age* 78 (January 24, 1925): 269–72; "New Passenger Car Repair Shops and Stores Buildings for Wabash Railway," reprint from *Railway Age,* February 7, 1925, J. Orville Spreen Collection, Western Historical Manuscript Collection, St. Louis, Mo. (hereafter cited as J. O. Spreen Coll.).

81. "Wabash Employs Novel Plan to Enlarge Locomotive Shops," *Railway Age* 83 (November 19, 1927): 969–72.

82. "New Fruit Auction Facilities in St. Louis," Wabash Railway

Company, June 15, 1928, J. O. Spreen Coll.; "Railroads Build Modern Produce Terminal at Detroit," *Railway Age* 87 (December 28, 1929): 1463–68; Minute Book 3, Wabash Railway Company, June 28, 1928, 25; ibid., September 25, 1928, 54; January 30, 1930, 411, NS Archives.

83. *St. Louis Post-Dispatch*, February 19, 1928; "Start from Delmar Boulevard Station," Wabash Railway Company, n.d.; *St. Louis Globe-Democrat*, November 23, 1929.

The Wabash also showed pride with the replacement passenger facilities in Chicago. On December 21, 1922, fire destroyed much of the thirty-eight-year-old brick and wood Dearborn Street Station, temporarily leaving homeless eight railroads, including the Wabash.

84. *Wabash News* 4 (August 1, 1929): 1,4; James M. Symes to [General Manager Western Region], October 4, 1929, PRR Coll.

The PRR considered using the Delmar Station for its St. Louis service; however, as James Symes noted in his letter of October 4, 1929, "There is no question but what we could get some passengers on our trains via this route, I am convinced that we would not get enough additional travel to warrant the delay and no doubt the cost of securing tracking rights over the Wabash would be prohibitive."

85. Clipping, J. O. Spreen Coll.

86. "The New Banner Blue Limited," clipping in J. O. Spreen Coll.; *St. Louis Globe-Democrat*, September 28, 1925; *St. Louis Star*, December 9, 1927; *Omar D. Gray's Sturgeon (Mo.) Leader*, January 19, 1928.

87. *Railway Age* 86 (June 8, 1929): 1350; "New 'Central States' Limited," clipping in J. O. Spreen Coll.; *The Official Guide of the Railways* (New York: National Railway Publication, March 1932), 254.

Another, albeit less glamorous, name train, which operated in 1929, the *Radio Special,* only briefly traveled between St. Louis and Omaha.

88. *Wabash Summer Trips* (St. Louis: Wabash Railway Company, 1930).

89. "[Wabash] Fast Freight Means Business," (ca. 1925), WMHA Archive.

90. Swartz, "The Wabash Railroad," 82–84; W. A. Pownall, "Operation of Three-Cylinder Engines on Wabash," *Railway Age* 80 (February 27, 1926): 527–29.

91. *Railway Review*, January 10, 1925, clipping in J. O. Spreen Coll.

92. *Railway Age*, 84 (February 4, 1928): 291–92.

93. *Chicago Daily News*, March 3, 1927; "Wabash Uses Tractors and Trailers," *Railway Age* 82 (April 23, 1927): 1303–4.

94. *Moody's Manual of Investments and Security Rating Service: Railroad Securities* (New York: Moody's Investors Service, 1926), 1662; "The NJI&I Railroad Co.," NS Archives; *Railroad Magazine* 42 (April 1947): 54; Richard S. Simons and Francis H. Parker, *Railroads of Indiana* (Bloomington: Indiana University Press, 1997), 197.

The objective of enhancing freight and passenger service prompted the Wabash to consider building its own line across On-

tario. Following World War I, the Canadian National, successor to the Grand Trunk, had allowed the line between Bridgeburg and Glencoe to become poorly maintained, prompting numerous slow orders. But improved Canadian trackage and other priorities caused the Wabash to abandon any plans for construction in Canada. See *St. Thomas (Ontario) Times-Journal*, August 22, 1927. See also note 61.

95. Minute Book 2, Wabash Railway Company, April 23, 1923, 181, NS Archives; *Eighth Annual Report of the Wabash Railway Company For the Fiscal Year Ended December 31, 1923*, 13.

96. "Wabash Freight Traffic a Record," 1055; *Moody's Manual of Investments and Security Rating Service: Railroad Securities* (New York: Moody's Investors Service, 1933), 1803; Charles P. Kindleberger, *The World in Depression, 1929–1939* (Berkeley: University of California Press, 1973), 83–170.

97. "Wabash Working on System Plan," *Railway Age* 88 (February 22, 1930): 467; "Wabash Asks Control of W. & L. E.," ibid. 88 (May 10, 1930): 1139–40; *Wall Street Journal*, February 15, 1930; Minute Book 3, Wabash Railway Company, April 24, 1930, 479; Minute Book 4, Wabash Railway Company, June 10, 1930, 15, NS Archives.

98. *Wall Street Journal*, May 6, 1930; "Wabash Purchases Twenty-Five 4-8-2 Type Locomotives," *Railway Mechanical Engineer*, 104 (April 1930): 203–6; "Mountain Type Locomotives for the Wabash," *Railway Age* 88 (April 5, 1930): 821–22; "Wabash Operates 4-8-4 Types in Freight Service," ibid. 90 (February 14, 1931): 374–75; Minute Book 4, Wabash Railway Company, November 28, 1931, Exhibit II, NS Archives.

99. Minute Book 3, Wabash Railway Company, March 14, 1930, 443–44; ibid., April 22, 1930, 461, NS Archives; *Moberly Monitor-Index*, May 30, 1934; Minute Book of the Pennsylvania Railroad, No. 33, June 12, 1929, 47, PRR Coll.

100. *Conference of Officials* (St. Louis: Wabash Railway Company, 1931), 76.

101. Minute Book 4, Wabash Railway Company, September 2, 1931, 353, NS Archives.

102. Ibid., December 1, 1931, 421, NS Archives; *Moody's Manual of Investments and Security Rating Service* (1933), 1802; *U.S. Daily* (Washington, D.C.), December 3, 1931; *Investigation of Railroads, Holding Companies, and Affiliated Companies*, U.S. Senate, Report No. 25, April 24, 1939, 2–6; "Wabash in the Hands of Receivers," *Railway Age* 91 (December 5, 1931): 859.

103. *St. Louis Globe-Dispatch*, December 2, 1931; Memorandum for General Atterbury, n.d., Box 218, PRR Coll.

104. "Wabash in the Hands of Receivers, 859; *St. Louis Globe-Democrat*, September 10, 1931; October 15, 1931; January 3, 1932; *St. Louis Post-Dispatch*, October 15, 1931.

Williams went down swinging in his efforts to fend off the Van Sweringens' Alleghany Corporation from capturing the Missouri Pacific. His considerable ego and the heavy dependence of the Wabash on interchange business with the Missouri Pacific does much to explain his feistiness. See Harwood, *Invisible Giants,* 170.

105. *Investigation of Railroads, Holding Companies, and Affiliated Companies,* 48–49, 51.

106. "W. S. Franklin Elected President of Wabash and Ann Arbor," *Railway Age* 91 (October 31, 1931): 679; *St. Louis Post-Dispatch,* October 27, 1931.

107. *Who's Who in Railroading in North America* (New York: Simmons-Boardman, 1940), 478.

7: DEPRESSION, REBIRTH AND WORLD WAR II

1. *St. Louis Globe-Democrat,* October 20, 1933; *Moberly (Mo.) Monitor-Index,* November 19, 1933; "Pitcairn Appointed Co-Receiver of Wabash," *Railway Age* 95 (October 28, 1933): 646.

2. *Moberly Monitor-Index,* November 24, 1933; *St. Louis Globe-Democrat,* January 7, 1932; *Nineteenth Annual Report of the Wabash Railway Company For the Fiscal Year Ended December 31, 1934* (St. Louis: Wabash Railway Company, 1935), 14; H. Roger Grant, *The North Western: A History of the Chicago & North Western Railway System* (DeKalb: Northern Illinois University Press, 1996), 154–55.

3. *Moberly Monitor-Index,* July 25, 1933; October 18, 1933; June 22, 1934; *Railway Age* 95 (August 12, 1933): 255; *St. Louis Globe-Democrat,* July 30, 1933; *Railway Age* 109 (November 30, 1940): 843.

4. *St. Louis Globe-Democrat,* January 10, 1932; *Railway Age* 92 (January 16, 1932): 143; *Moberly Monitor-Index,* June 22, 1934.

5. C. H. Hitchborn, "Railroad Livestock Traffic Dwindles," *Railway Age* 92 (June 25, 1932): 1056–58.

6. Minute Book 4, Wabash Railway Company, September 7, 1932, 474–75, Norfolk Southern Archives, Atlanta, Ga. (hereafter cited as NS Archives); Minute Book 5, Wabash Railway Company, May 3, 1934, 57; January 7, 1936, 177, NS Archives; Minute Book 6, Wabash Railway Company, June 16, 1938, 154; May 31, 1939, 239, NS Archives; *Moberly Monitor-Index,* September 9, 1933.

7. Frank P. Donovan, Jr., "The Wabash in Iowa," *Palimpsest* 45 (October 1964): 395–96; Minute Book 4, December 20, 1933, 517, NS Archives; Minute Book 5, June 21, 1934, NS Archives; *Twentieth Annual Report of the Wabash Railway Company For the Fiscal Year Ended December 31, 1935* (St. Louis: Wabash Railway Company, 1936), 15.

8. Donald Steffee, "The Detroit Arrow," *Railroad Magazine* 26 (July 1939): 77; "Wabash Routes Chicago-Detroit Trains over Pennsylvania," *Railway Age* 94 (April 1, 1933): 485, 488; ibid. 98 (May 25, 1935): 832.

9. "Regional Coordinating Committee—Western Railway Group Consolidation of Major Shops—Western Region Locomotive Shop," n.d., Gulf, Mobile & Ohio Railroad Collection, John W. Barriger III National Railroad Library, St. Louis, Mo.

10. Minute Book 4, Wabash Railway Company, December 28,

1932, 482, NS Archives; Minute Book 6, Wabash Railway Company, June 28, 1939, 260, NS Archives.

11. *Decatur (Ill.) Herald Review,* May 19, 1935.

12. John Day, *95 Years With John "Jack" Day the Orphan Nobody Wanted: An Autobiography* (Mahomet, Ill.: Mayhaven, 1997), 50–51.

13. Minute Book 4, Wabash Railway Company, March 17, 1931, 178, NS Archives; Minute Book 5, Wabash Railway Company, January 7, 1936, 187, NS Archives; *Railway Age* 100 (March 14, 1936): 483.

14. Charles P. Kindleberger, *The World Depression, 1929–1939* (London: Penguin Press, 1973), 183; *Moberly Monitor-Index,* October 16, 1933; *Railway Age* 120 (January 5, 1946): 85.

15. *St. Louis Globe-Democrat,* February 14, 1932; *Moberly Monitor-Index,* December 29, 1933; *Railway Age* 97 (September 1, 1934): 269; "Examiner's Report," Reconstruction Finance Corporation Railroad Division, February 19, 1935, John W. Barriger III Collection, John W. Barriger III National Railroad Library, St. Louis, Mo. (hereafter cited as Barriger Papers); *Moody's Manual of Investments: Railroad Securities* (Moody's Investors Service, 1935), 905–6.

16. *Moberly Monitor-Index,* February 26, 1934.

17. James Holzmeier, "The Saint Charles Bridges," *Banner* (Summer 1999): 3–5; *St. Charles (Mo.) Journal,* October 8, 1959.

18. *St. Louis Globe-Democrat,* October 14, 1936; "Completed: The Great Wabash Bridge across the Missouri River at St. Charles is Finished," Wabash Railway Company, 1936; Scrapbook no. 33, Barriger Papers.

19. Holzmeier, "The Saint Charles Bridges," 7; *Daily Cosmos-Monitor* (St. Charles, Mo.), October 30, 1936; *Souvenir of Inspection of New WABASH BRIDGE over Missouri River at St. Charles, Missouri* (St. Louis: Wabash Railway Company, October 29, 1936); S. M. Smith, "Cantilever Bridge Erected From One End," *Engineering News-Record* (November 12, 1936): 690–92; "Wabash Completes New Missouri River Crossing at St. Charles," *Railway Age* 101 (December 5, 1936): 821–24.

20. *Railway Age* 98 (May 18, 1935): 780; Grant, *The North Western,* 157–59.

21. *Decatur Herald-Review,* May 19, 1935; *St. Louis Globe-Democrat,* June 12, 1935; R. J. Ruddy to L. W. Bade, June 3, 1935, Museum of Transportation, St. Louis, Mo. (hereafter cited as MOT Coll.); David S. Oakes, "All Aboard-r-d." *Central Manufacturing District Magazine* 19 (July 1935): 12.

22. *Decatur Herald-Review,* June 3, 1935.

23. L. W. Bade to H. E. Watts, June 3, 1935, MOT Coll.

24. *Railway Age* 102 (January 16, 1937): 161; *St. Louis Star-Times.* May 20, 1935; *GM&O Historical Society News* (2001): 26–31.

25. *St. Louis Globe-Democrat,* May 29, 1932; September 22, 1938; *Moberly Monitor-Index,* June 4, 1934; *Chicago Herald and Examiner,* June 16, 1936; *Railway Age* 97 (November 10, 1934): 584; *Detroit News,* May 26, 1935.

26. *Moberly Monitor-Index,* June 6, 1933; September 7, 1933; November 4, 1933; November 27, 1933; December 1, 1933; *St. Louis Globe-Democrat,* October 8, 1936; March 19, 1939.

27. *Moberly Monitor-Index,* August 18, 1933.

28. Jim Geyer, "Growing Up Alongside the Wabash Railroad (North Branch): A Lifelong Love for Railroads in Words and Pictures" (privately printed, 2002).

29. *St. Louis Globe-Democrat,* May 20, 1932.

30. *Moberly Monitor-Index,* January 3, 1934; February 16, 1934; *Railway Age* 96 (May 12, 1934): 699.

31. H. Roger Grant, *The Corn Belt Route: A History of the Chicago Great Western Railroad Company* (DeKalb: Northern Illinois University Press, 1984), 119–121; "Co-ordinated Fast-Freight Handling System Developed," *Railway Age* 97 (December 15, 1934): 791–92; John H. White, Jr., "The Magic Box: Genesis of the Container," *Railroad History* 158 (Spring 1988): 73–93.

32. *Nineteenth Annual Report of the Wabash Railway Company,* 14.

33. *Moberly Monitor-Index,* July 7, 1934; July 23, 1934.

34. *Moody's Manual of Investments, 1935,* 900; *Twenty-Third Annual Report of the Wabash Railway Company to the Stockholders For the Year Ended December 31, 1938* (St. Louis: Wabash Railway Company, 1939), 9.

35. Patrick D. Reagon, "Recession of 1937–1938," in James S. Olson, ed., *Historical Dictionary of the New Deal: From Inauguration to Preparation for War* (Westport, Conn.: Greenwood Press, 1985), 408–10.

36. David M. Kennedy, *Freedom From Fear: The American People in Depression and War, 1929–1945* (New York: Oxford University Press, 1999), 363–80.

37. See Paul F. Healey, *Yankee from the West: The Candid, Turbulent Life Story of the Yankee-born U.S. Senator from Montana, Burton K. Wheeler* (New York: Octagon Books, 1977).

38. Alonzo L. Hamby, "'Vultures at the Death of an Elephant': Harry S Truman, The Great Train Robbery, and the Transportation Act of 1940," *Railroad History* 165 (Autumn 1991): 9–10.

39. Ibid., 10–11.

40. Ibid., 15; Ian S. Haberman, *The Van Sweringens of Cleveland: The Biography of an Empire* (Cleveland: Western Reserve Historical Society, 1979), 154–55; Herbert H. Harwood, Jr., *Invisible Giants: The Empires of Cleveland's Van Sweringen Brothers* (Bloomington: Indiana University Press, 2003), 287.

41. *Investigation of Railroads, Holding Companies, and Affiliated Companies* (U.S. Senate Report No. 25, part 6, April 24, 1939), 49.

42. *Investigation of Railroads, Holding Companies, and Affiliated Companies* (U.S. Senate Report No. 25, part 23, November 25, 1940), 10–20; John T. Flynn, "Other People's Money," *New Republic* 96 (October 5, 1938): 240; *St. Louis Globe-Democrat,* November 26, 1940.

43. "I.C.C. Suggests Recovery of W. H. Williams' Salaries," *Railway Age* 95 (July 29, 1933): 199; "Senate Hearing of Wabash Is Con-

cluded," ibid. 104 (March 5, 1938): 429–30.

44. *Investigation of Railroads, Holding Companies, and Affiliated Companies,* November 25, 1940, 27–33.

45. Flynn, "Other People's Money," 240.

46. Hamby, "'Vultures at the Death of an Elephant,'" 23–34.

47. William James Cunningham, *The Present Railroad Crisis* (Philadelphia: University of Pennsylvania Press, 1939), 16–22; George W. Hilton, *Monon Route* (San Diego: Howell-North, 1978), 153.

48. *Railway Age* 104 (March 19, 1938): 541.

49. *Wall Street Journal,* February 16, 1938; Patrick B. McGinnis, ed., *Guide to Railroad Reorganization Securities* (New York: Pflugfelder, Bampton & Rust, 1941), "Wabash Railway Company."

50. *Wall Street Journal,* July 15, 1937.

51. *Wabash Railway Company Receivership,* ICC Finance Docket No. 13010, 591–92; *New York Herald Tribune,* July 5, 1940.

52. McGinnis, ed., *Guide to Railroad Reorganization Securities; Railway Age* 110 (March 22, 1941): 546.

53. *Railway Age* 110 (February 15, 1941): 335; *Wall Street Journal,* January 13, 1941; February 15, 1941.

54. *Wall Street Journal,* April 9, 1941.

55. "N.Y. Central Opposes P.R.R. Acquisition of Wabash," *Railway Age* 110 (May 17, 1941): 863–64.

56. "N.Y.C. and P.R.R. Agree on Wabash," *Railway Age,* 110 (June 21, 1941): 1125, 1130; *St. Louis Globe-Democrat,* May 5, 1942.

57. *New York Times,* August 7, 1941.

58. *St. Louis Globe-Democrat,* May 5, 1942.

59. *Railway Age,* 111 (September 13, 1941): 434; *St. Louis Post-Dispatch,* December 1, 1941; *Wall Street Journal,* January 7, 1942.

60. "Pitcairn Elected President of the Wabash," *Railway Age* 112 (May 30, 1942): 1075, 1087; interview with Ollie Blackburn, St. Louis, June 23, 2002; Minute Book 2, Wabash Railroad Company, September 25, 1942, 195, NS Archives.

61. "Right-of-Way," 16 mm film produced by the Office of War Information, 1943, National Archives, Washington, D.C.

62. *Historical Statistics of the United States: Colonial Times to 1957* (Washington, D.C.: U.S. Department of Commerce, 1960), 430–31.

63. *Fourth Annual Report of Wabash Railroad Company Year Ended December 31, 1945* (St. Louis: Wabash Railroad Company, 1946), 27, 33; *First Annual Report of the Wabash Railroad Company For the Year Ended December 31, 1942* (St. Louis: Wabash Railroad Company, 1943), 28; *Third Annual Report of the Wabash Railroad Company For the Year Ended December 31, 1944* (St. Louis: Wabash Railroad Company, 1945), 28.

64. Rose Roelke to "Memories," August 27, 1985, Memories Project, St. Louis Union Station Coll., John W. Barriger III National Railroad Library, St. Louis, Mo.

65. James H. Billington, ed., *I'll Be Home for Christmas: The Library of Congress Revisits the Spirit of Christmas During World War II* (New York: Delacorte Press, 1999), 171–77.

66. Minute Book 3, Wabash Railroad Company, April 15, 1943, 83; June 17, 1943, 144; October 21, 1943, 241, NS Archives; Minute Book 4, Wabash Railroad Company, December 21, 1944, 182; April 19, 1945, 293, NS Archives; *Moberly Monitor-Index*, November 9, 1943.

67. *Moberly Monitor-Index*, January 19, 1943; September 13, 1944; David P. Morgan, "Wabash: Traffic," *Trains* 10 (July 1950): 17.

68. *Third Annual Report of the Wabash Railroad Company*, 15; *Moberly Monitor-Index*. July 28, 1944.

69. *Fourth Annual Report of the Wabash Railroad* Company, 14; *Moberly Monitor-Index*, September 16, 1944.

70. Minute Book 2, Wabash Railroad Company, July 28, 1942, 172, NS Archives.

71. "Three-Cylinder Power Rebuilt as Freight-Passenger Locomotives," *Railway Mechanical Engineer* 117 (December 1943): 585, 587; "Wabash Rebuilds 3–Cylinder Steam Locomotive at Decatur Shops," *Railway Age* 115 (October 23, 1943): 637–38; Minute Book 3, Wabash Railroad Company, September 16, 1943, 186, NS Archives; *Third Annual Report of the Wabash Railroad Company*, 12.

72. *St. Louis Globe-Democrat*, August 5, 1942.

73. Ibid., March 21, 1939; Minute Book 2, Wabash Railroad Company, May 15, 1942, 35, NS Archives; William Swartz, "The Wabash Railroad," *Railroad History* 133 (Fall 1975): 89–90; Wes Dengate, "The Wabash in Canada: Motive Power and Operations on the Buffalo Division." *Banner* (Winter–Spring 2002): 22–23.

74. Donald J. Heimburger, *Wabash* (Forest Park, Ill.: Heimburger House, 1983), 241; Swartz, "The Wabash Railroad," 100; Minute Book 3, September 16, 1943, 200, NS Archives.

Motor 4000 became Maintenance-of-Way car 4297. Motor 4001 finally left the Wabash in 1951. This combination passenger-baggage car of all-steel construction became the property of the Consolidated Railway Equipment Company of Chicago. See Minute Book 11, Wabash Railroad Company, January 18, 1951, 6, NS Archives.

75. *First Annual Report of the Wabash Railroad Company*, 12;Minute Book 2, Wabash Railroad Company, July 28, 1942, 175, 177, NS Archives; Minute Book 4, Wabash Railroad Company, February 15, 1945, 246, NS Archives.

76. *M-K-T Employees' Magazine* (February 1945): 10; Minute Book 3, Wabash Railroad Company, April 15, 1943, 76–77, NS Archives; *Third Annual Report of the Wabash Railroad Company*, 10; Morgan, "Wabash: Traffic,"15.

77. *Second Annual Report of the Wabash Railroad Company For the Year Ended December 31, 1943* (St. Louis: Wabash Railroad Company, 1944), 13–14; *Third Annual Report of the Wabash Railroad Company,* 14.

78. *Second Annual Report of the Wabash Railroad Company*, 7–8, 14; *Fourth Annual Report of the Wabash Railroad Company*, 7, 14.

79. Minute Book 3, May 20, 1943, 128, NS Archives.

8: THE NEW WABASH

1. *Fifth Annual Report of Wabash Railroad Company Year Ended December 31, 1946* (St. Louis: Wabash Railroad Company, 1947), 8, 13; *Sixth Annual Report of the Wabash Railroad Company Year Ended December 31, 1947* (St. Louis: Wabash Railroad Company, 1948), 5;

2. *Fifth Annual Report of Wabash Railroad Company Year Ended December 31, 1946*, 5.

3. H. Roger Grant, *Ohio on the Move: Transportation in the Buckeye State* (Athens: Ohio University Press, 2000), 21–24. See also Mark H. Rose, *Interstate: Express Highway Politics, 1941–1956* (Lawrence: Regents Press of Kansas, 1979).

4. R. E. G. Davies, *Airlines of the United States Since 1914* (London: Putnam, 1972), 324–54.

5. *Wabash Railroad Company Seventh Annual Report Year Ended December 31, 1948* (St. Louis: Wabash Railroad Company, 1949), 7.

6. "Atkinson and Pitcairn Assume New Wabash Positions," *Railway Age* 122 (May 3, 1947): 900; Minute Book 7, Wabash Railroad Company, February 19, 1948, 236, Norfolk Southern Archives, Atlanta, Ga. (hereafter cited as NS Archives); *St. Louis Globe-Democrat*, April 18, 1947; February 17, 1948; Résumé, Arthur Kimmins Atkinson, Arthur K. Atkinson Papers, Museum of Transportation, St. Louis, Mo. (hereafter cited as Atkinson Papers).

7. Interview with Willis Goldschmidt, St. Louis, Mo., June 13, 2002 (hereafter cited as Goldschmidt interview); David P. Morgan, "Wabash: Traffic, *Trains* 10 (July 1950): 17; interview with Vance Lischer, Olivette, Mo., June 14, 2002.

8. Goldschmidt interview; "Address of Arthur K. Atkinson at the Scottish Rite Reunion Banquet Bloomington Consistory, Bloomington, Illinois, on November 12, 1954," Atkinson Papers.

9. John F. Stover, *American Railroads* (Chicago: University of Chicago Press, 2nd ed., 1997), 212, 215.

10. *St. Louis Globe-Dispatch*, July 27, 1941; "History of Through Train and Car Service via St. Louis and Chicago Gateways," Pennsylvania Railroad Collection, Box 341, Hagley Museum and Library, Wilmington, Del. (hereafter cited as PRR Coll.).

11. Minute Book 3, Wabash Railroad Company, September 16, 1943, 214, NS Archives; Wayne Kuchinsky, "Kansas City: Her Trains, Her Railroads, Her Stations," *Passenger Train Journal* 19 (October 1988): 29.

12. *St. Louis Globe-Democrat*, September 16, 1946; "What the Public Thinks of Us," (Wabash Railroad Company, 1947), 4, Bureau of Railway Economics Collection, John W. Barriger III National Railroad Library, St. Louis, Mo.; *Oelwein (Iowa) Daily Register*, July 7, 1945.

13. "Agreement, made and entered between Union Pacific Railroad Company and Wabash Railroad Company, May 24, 1946," Union Pacific Collection, Omaha, Neb. (hereafter cited as UP Coll.); *Railroad Magazine*, 103 (February 1978): 50; *St. Louis Globe-Democrat*,

June 2, 1946; Lawrence N. Thomas, "Going to California On the Overland Route," *Terminal Railroad Association of St. Louis Historical and Technical Society* (Spring–Summer 1996): 4, 6, 8, 14.

14. Thomas, "Going to California On the Overland Route," 4; *St. Louis Globe-Democrat,* April 20, 1938.

15. "Remarks of George C. Smith, President, St. Louis Chamber of Commerce, Sunday, June 2, 1946, 3:30 P.M.," Museum of Transportation, St. Louis, Mo. (hereafter cited as MOT Coll.); "Remarks of Mayor A. P. Kaufmann Christening of Wabash–Union Pacific 'City of Saint Louis,' Union Station, Track Three, Sunday, June 2, 1946, 3:40 P.M." MOT Coll.; *St. Louis Globe-Democrat,* June 3, 1946.

16. Arthur K. Atkinson to A. E. Stoddard, May 8, 1950, November 7, 1950, UP Coll.; Tom H. Hayes to C. J. Collins, February 23, 1951, UP Coll.

17. "'City of Kansas City' Placed in Service," *Railway Age* 123 (November 29, 1947): 52; "Wabash Installs 'City of Kansas City,'" ibid. 123 (December 27, 1947): 40.

18. *Kansas City Star,* November 25, 1947; *St. Louis Globe-Democrat,* November 25, 1947.

19. *St. Louis Globe-Democrat,* August 8, 1947; August 15, 1947; Case No. 16,323, November 9, 1967, Missouri Public Service Commission Collection, Jefferson City, Mo.

The *City of Kansas City,* which was a turn out of St. Louis Union and Delmar stations, operated in a loop fashion through Kansas City. It usually ran westbound by way of the Harry S Truman Bridge and Sheffield, continuing through Kansas City Union Station, and eastbound via the Hannibal Bridge.

20. "The 'Blue Bird' Brings Happiness to the Wabash," *Railway Age* 129 (December 30, 1950): 30; Gene V. Glendinning, *The Chicago & Alton Railroad: The Only Way* (DeKalb: Northern Illinois University Press, 2002), 211–13.

21. James R. Holmes, "The Blue Bird," *Banner* (Winter–Spring 1995): 4; *St. Louis Globe-Democrat,* February 24, 1950; February 27, 1950; May 17, 1950; *Railway Age* 128 (February 25, 1950): 56; "Budd Builds Six-Car 'Blue Bird' for Wabash," *Railway Age* 128 (April 1, 1950): 42–47.

The *Blue Bird* name was not a Wabash original. On January 13, 1929, the Chicago Great Western Railroad introduced its unique *Blue Bird* streamliner. This home-built motor train operated between Minneapolis and Rochester, Minnesota. Earlier the company had dispatched a name train known as the *Red Bird* over the same route. See H. Roger Grant, *The Corn Belt Route: A History of the Chicago Great Western Railway Company* (DeKalb: Northern Illinois University Press, 1984), 94–95, 117.

22. *Decatur (Ill.) Review,* February 27, 1950; "Dome-Car Streamliner For the Wabash," *Modern Railroads* 5 (April 1950): 30–32.

23. Interview with Stephen T. Parsons, Sparta, Ill., March 17, 2003; "Trains That Pay," *Railway Age* 132 (May 19, 1952): 97; *Trains & Travel* 13 (November 1952): 7; *Railway Age* 133 (August 25, 1952):

13; *A Study of the Gulf, Mobile and Ohio Railroad Company* (New York: Hayden, Stone, 1957), 8; *The Official Guide of the Railways* (New York: National Railway Publication, June 1951).

24. Minute Book 11, Wabash Railroad Company, July 19, 1951, 212–13, NS Archives; *St. Louis Globe-Democrat,* November 7, 1950.

25. Tom H. Hayes to C. J. Collins, June 15, 1951, UP Coll.; interview with Stephen T. Parsons, St. Louis, Mo., June 14, 2002 (hereafter cited as Parsons interview); "Direct Route of the Diesel Powered Wabash Cannon Ball," J. Orville Spreen Collection, Western Historical Manuscript Collection, St. Louis, Mo. (hereafter cited as J. O. Spreen Coll.); Don Sarno and Norbert Shacklette, "St. Louis: Pre-Amtrak Railroads and their Trains, *Passenger Train Journal* 21 (July 1990): 31; "Wabash 'Cannon Ball' On Faster Schedules," *Railway Age* 136 (May 17, 1954): 9.

26. *St. Louis Globe-Democrat,* July 1, 1950.

By the mid-1950s the Wabash wanted to end passenger operations on the twenty-six-mile Columbia "Cannon Ball branch." Although it proposed to the Missouri Public Service Commission that it substitute buses for connecting trains at Centralia, it later won regulatory approval only to downgrade service, providing both passenger and "mixed" train service. See *St. Louis Globe-Democrat,* April 18, 1954; March 24, 1955; September 8, 1955; September 16, 1955; Wabash Railroad Company public timetable, April 29, 1962.

27. *St. Louis Post-Dispatch,* April 9, 1991.

28. Minute Book 5, Wabash Railroad Company, December 20, 1945, 168, NS Archives; O. E. Hager, "Revamping Gives Old Station New Look," *Railway Age* 125 (August 28, 1948): 412–17; ibid. 124 (April 17, 1948): 758.

29. Minute Book 17, Wabash Railroad Company, May 24, 1956, 184, NS Archives; "Small Standardized Station Built of Precast Concrete Panels," *Railway Age* 139 (November 14, 1955): 55–57.

The Wabash also painted a number of structures and installed new signage. Probably because of the Green family in Mexico, Mo., (A. P. Green, Jr., served on the Board of Directors as had his father) the company in 1954 spent more than $35,000 "to provide a more pleasing appearance" for the passenger depot, including the addition of canopies and grading and surfacing of the parking lot. Minute Book 15, Wabash Railroad Company, May 20, 1954, 144, NS Archives.

30. Parsons interview; "The Passenger Train Today," n.d., Atkinson Papers.

31. Minute Book 7, Wabash Railroad Company, April 15, 1948, 314, 330, NS Archives; Minute Book 9, Wabash Railroad Company, May 19, 1949, NS Archives; *Railway Age* 125 (August 14, 1948): 78; *Chicago Journal of Commerce,* July 20, 1948; *St. Louis Star-Times,* July 16, 1948; October 4, 1948; "Program-Wabash Railroad Day," J. O. Spreen Coll.

32. *Railway Age* 133 (October 20, 1952): 60; " Modernizing the Wabash: Address by Mr. Arthur K. Atkinson, President of the

Wabash Railroad Company before the St. Louis Railroad Diesel Club," June 9, 1953, MOT Coll.

33. "Modernizing the Wabash;" "Once upon the Wabash," pamphlet in MOT Coll.; interview with Ollie Blackburn, St. Louis, Mo., June 23, 2002.

34. See "Wabash Centennial" folders in J. O. Spreen Coll.; *Peru (Ind.) Republican,* September 27, 1956.

Flush with funds and having varying events to commemorate, numerous railroads in the late 1940s and early 1950s decided to bolster their corporate images through "centennial" celebrations. The Wabash was hardly unique with its centennial-related activities. See H. Roger Grant, "Celebrating a Century," *Classic Trains* 2 (Fall 2001): 68–73.

35. *Railway Age* 136 (May 3, 1951): 11.

36. John W. Barriger III to A. K. Atkinson, May 18, 1954, John W. Barriger III Papers, John W. Barriger III National Railroad Library, St. Louis, Mo.

37. Maury Klein, *History of the Louisville & Nashville Railroad* (New York: Macmillan, 1972), 463–64; Maury Klein, "Replacement Technology: The Diesel as a Case Study," *Railroad History* 162 (Spring 1990): 109–20; Stover, *American Railroads,* 214.

38. Minute Book 5, Wabash Railroad Company, June 20, 1946, 341, NS Archives.

39. David A. Hill, "Confidential Report of my Visit to the St. Louis Office of the Wabash Railroad Company, April 7, 1948." Railway & Locomotive Historical Society Archives, Sacramento, California.

40. *Tenth Annual Report Wabash Railroad Company Year Ended December 31, 1951,* 13; Minute Book 10, Wabash Railroad Company, December 21, 1950, 240, NS Archives; Minute Book 13, Wabash Railroad Company, October 16, 1952, 83, NS Archives; "Modernizing the Wabash;" William Swartz, "The Wabash Railroad," *Railroad History* 133 (Fall 1975): 89–92, 94–98.

41. "Wabash Prepares for Diesel Era," *Modern Railroads* 8 (August 1953): 81–83, 87, 89–90; *Eleventh Annual Report Wabash Railroad Company Year Ended December 31, 1952* (St. Louis: Wabash Railroad Company, 1953), 11; Minute Book 14, Wabash Railroad Company, May 21, 1953, 90, NS Archives.

42. Minute Book 13, Wabash Railroad Company, February 19, 1953, 196; November 19, 1953, 268, NS Archives.

43. Minute Book 14, Wabash Railroad Company, December 17, 1953, 303, NS Archives; *Railroad Magazine* 65 (October 1954): 9; *Trains* 15 (August 1955); *Decatur Review,* July 8, 1955; *St. Louis Post-Dispatch,* August 11, 1955.

44. Minute Book 18, Wabash Railroad Company, March 21, 1957, 110, NS Archives; J. David Conrad, *The Steam Locomotive Directory of North America, Volume Two: Western United States and Mexico* (Polo, Ill.: Transportation Trails, n.d.), 63.

45. "Wabash FAST Freight," *Railway Age* 130 (January 8, 1951):

36–37; Arthur K. Atkinson, "Operation of a Bridge Line," *Investment Dealers' Digest* (March 14, 1955): n.p.

46. "Wabash FAST Freight;" Morgan, "Wabash: Traffic," 15–17; S. Kip Farrington, *Railroading the Modern Way* (New York: Coward-McCann, 1951), 27–34.

47. Grant, *The Corn Belt Route,* 119–20; David J. DeBoer, *Piggyback and Containers: A History of Rail Intermodal on America's Steel Highway* (San Marino, Calif.: Golden West Books, 1992), 21–25, 27–31.

48. "Piggyback Today," *Railway Age* 137 (December 13, 1954): 61; Minute Book 15, Wabash Railroad Company, May 20, 1954, 146; June 17, 1954, 168, NS Archives; "'Piggy-Back' Now More Than Ever As Close As Your Shipping Room Door," Wabash Railroad, 1957; DeBoer, *Piggyback and Containers,* 43.

49. Minute Book 15, Wabash Railroad Company, December 16, 1954, 317, NS Archives; Minute Book 16, Wabash Railroad Company, March 17, 1955, 105, NS Archives.

50. Minute Book 16, March 17, 1955, 105.

51. *Wabash Railroad Company Fourteenth Annual Report* (St. Louis: Wabash Railroad Company, 1956), cover, 9.

52. DeBoer, *Piggyback and Containers,* 44, 70; Minute Book 17, Wabash Railroad Company, May 24, 1956, 186, NS Archives.

53. *St. Louis Globe-Democrat,* March 30, 1956.

54. Minute Book 18, Wabash Railroad Company, July 18, 1957, 243, NS Archives.

55. *Twelfth Annual Report Wabash Railroad Company Year Ended December 31, 1953* (St. Louis: Wabash Railroad Company, 1954), 8. See also "Manual Block Remote Control Developed on the Wabash," *Railway Signaling* 38 (July 1945): 440–49; "How Loudspeakers Expedite Yard Operations On the Wabash at Moberly," *Railway Age* 131 (August 13, 1951): 42–45; "How Wabash Speeds Yard Moves with Interlocking and Communications," ibid. 136 (March 8, 1954): 69–71; "Tailor-Made Freighthouse Keeps Auto Parts Moving," ibid. 142 (April 1, 1957): 44–46; "New Yard Speeds Chicago Service," ibid. (November 18, 1957): 14–15, 18; Edward T. Myers, "Wabash Steps Up Car Reporting," *Modern Railroads* (August 1957): 70–72, 74.

56. *Tenth Annual Report Wabash Railroad Company Year Ended December 31, 1951* (St. Louis: Wabash Railroad Company, 1952), 11; "Talk by Mr. Arthur K. Atkinson, President of Wabash Railroad System, at Wabash Family Meeting Held Wednesday Morning, September 16, 1953, at Hotel Statler, St. Louis, Mo.," Atkinson Papers.

57. *Eighteenth Annual Report Wabash Railroad Company* (St. Louis: Wabash Railroad Company, 1960), back cover.

58. Morgan, "Wabash: Traffic," 20.

59. "Wabash Traffic Education Manual," ca. 1948, MOT Coll.; Farrington, *Railroading the Modern Way,* 318–24.

60. "The Role of the Industrial Department at the Wabash R.R. Co.," n.d., MOT Coll.

61. "Wabash Wraps a 700-Acre Package," *Railway Freight Traffic* 5 (May 1957): 29–31.

62. "Wabash Organizes Motor Coach Operating Company," *Railway Age* 88 (May 24, 1930); Minute Book, Vol. 1, Wabash Motor Transit Company, NS Archives; Minute Book, Volume 4, Wabash Motor Transit Company, NS Archives; *Annual Report Wabash Motor Transit Company For the Year Ended December 31, 1950* (St. Louis: Wabash Railroad Company, 1951); *Ninth Annual Report Wabash Railroad Company,* 13; *Fifteen Annual Report Wabash Railroad Company* (St. Louis: Wabash Railroad Company, 1957), 9.

63. "Why Wabash Branches Pay Off," *Railway Age* 147 (July 27, 1959): 13, 16.

64. Don L. Hofsommer, *Grand Trunk Corporation: Canadian National Railways in the United States, 1971–1992* (East Lansing: Michigan State University Press, 1995), 83–84.

65. "Henry Ford's Railroad Experiment," *Railroad Magazine* (July 1938): 9–28; William D. Middleton, "Henry Ford and His Electric Locomotives," *Trains* 36 (September 1976): 22–26; Scott D. Trostel, *Henry Ford: When I Ran the Railroads: A Chronicle of Henry Ford's Operation of the Detroit, Toledo & Ironton, 1920–1929* (Fletcher, Ohio: Cam-Tech, 1989), 83–94; *Moberly Evening Democrat,* October 6, October 11, 1922.

66. "Henry Ford's Railroad Experiment," 27; George H. Burgess and Miles C. Kennedy, *Centennial History of the Pennsylvania Railroad Company, 1846–1946* (Philadelphia: Pennsylvania Railroad Company, 1949), 638–41.

67. *Detroit, Toledo & Ironton Railroad Company et al. Control, etc.* Finance Docket No. 16426, Interstate Commerce Commission, May 2, 1950, 471–72; *St. Louis Globe-Democrat,* April 20, 1949.

68. "Pennsylvania and Wabash Would Buy D.T.& I. from Pennroad Corp.," *Railway Age* 126 (January 29, 1949): 46; George W. Hilton and John F. Due, *The Electric Interurban Railways in America* (Stanford, Calif.: Stanford University Press, 1960), 260.

69. *Railway Age* 126 (March 12, 1949): 108; ICC Finance Docket No. 16426, 483–85.

70. ICC Finance Docket No. 16426, 487–94; "Would Let P.R.R. and Wabash Buy D.T.& I. from Pennroad," *Railway Age* 127 (October 29, 1949): 781; *Ninth Annual Report of the Wabash Railroad Company Year Ended December 31, 1950,* 14; Minute Book 11, Wabash Railroad Company, March 15, 1951, 82, NS Archives.

71. See Paul H. Stringham, *Illinois Terminal: The Electric Years* (Glendale, Calif.: Interurban Press, 1989).

72. Hilton and Due, *The Electric Interurban Railways in America,* 348–49.

73. Ibid., 349; *Moody's Transportation Manual* (New York: Moody's Investors Service, 1955), 60.

74. John Shedd Reed to author, September 5, 2003; "Illinois Terminal: To Be or Not to Be," *Trains* 15 (February 1955): 7; Robert McMillan to author, July 17, 2003; Minute Book 15, Wabash Railroad Company, August 13, 1954, 307, NS Archives.

75. Richard S. Simons and Francis H. Parker, *Railroads of Indiana* (Bloomington: Indiana University Press, 1997), 172; Minute Book 6, Wabash Railroad Company, September 19, 1946, 33, NS Archives.

76. "CTC on the Wabash Railroad," (ca. 1954), MOT Coll.

77. Minute Book 10, Wabash Railroad Company, November 11, 1950, 202, NS Archives.

78. Minute Book 11, Wabash Railroad Company, June 21, 1951, 184; July 19, 1951, 206, NS Archives.

79. *Ninth Annual Report Wabash Railroad Company Year Ended December 31, 1950,* 4; *Thirteenth Annual Report Wabash Railroad Company* (St. Louis: Wabash Railroad Company, 1955), 2; *Wabash Railroad Company Fourteenth Annual Report,* 3; Moody's *Transportation Manual* (New York: Moody's Investors Service, 1961): 759.

80. "An Analysis of Wabash Railroad Co. Securities from 1946 to 1961," PRR Coll.

81. *Third Annual Report of the Wabash Railroad Company For the Year Ended December 31, 1944* (St. Louis: Wabash Railroad Company, 1945), 14; Minute Book 8, Wabash Railroad Company, September 9, 1948, 82, NS Archives.

82. "Pullman Workers" broadside (July 9, 1946), Pullman Company Collection, Newberry Library, Chicago, Illinois.

83. *St. Louis Globe-Democrat,* January 19, 1949; "Strike Halts Wabash Trains," *Railway Age* 126 (March 19, 1949): 607.

84. *St. Louis Post-Dispatch,* March 15, 1949; March 19, 1949.

85. *St. Louis Star-Times,* March 19, 1949.

86. *Wabash Railroad Company Eighth Annual Report Year Ended December 31, 1949* (St. Louis: Wabash Railroad Company, 1950), 13; "Eight-Day Wabash Strikes Ends," *Railway Age* 126 (March 26, 1949): 102; *St. Louis Globe-Democrat,* March 24, 1949.

87. "Wabash Board Calls Strike 'Damaging' to Cause of Labor," *Railway Age* 126 (April 16, 1949): 78–79; interview with D. Keith Lawson, Rogers, Arkansas, October 18, 1980.

88. *Wabash Railroad Company Tenth Annual Report Year Ended December 31, 1951,* 5; *Railway Age* 131 (July 30, 1951): 23; *St. Louis Globe-Democrat,* July 17, 1951; July 22, 1951; January 2, 1952; Kuchinsky, "Kansas City," 31.

For a full account of the great flood of 1951, see Kenneth S. Davis, *River on the Rampage* (Garden City, N.Y.: Doubleday, 1953).

89. "The Problems We Face," n.d., Atkinson Papers.

90. "The Threat of Nationalization to the Transportation Industry—A Talk by Arthur K. Atkinson, President Wabash Railroad Company before the Downtown Optimist Club of St. Louis," (April 29, 1949), 13–14, Atkinson Papers.

91. *Trains & Travel* 13 (November 1952): 12; Minute Book 15, Wabash Railroad Company, January 21, 1954, 19, NS Archives.

92. George W. Hilton, *The Transportation Act of 1958: A Decade of Experience* (Bloomington: Indiana University Press, 1969), 3, 10–14, 186–207; *New York Times,* January 16, 1958.

93. "Mr. Atkinson Retires," *Banner* 1 (June 1960): 1.

9: A FALLEN FLAG

1. *Who's Who in Railroading in North America* (New York: Simmons-Boardman, 1959), 501; *St. Louis Post-Dispatch,* May 22, 1959; *New York Times,* May 23, 1959; Stephen Salsbury, *No Way to Run a Railroad: The Untold Story of the Penn Central Crisis* (New York: McGraw-Hill, 1982), 90; John Shedd Reed to author, September 5, 2003 (hereafter cited as Reed letter).

2. "Wabash Revamps for Prosperity," *Railway Age* 148 (June 6, 1960): 35; interview with Edward A. Burkhardt, Milwaukee, September 25, 1992.

3. Interview with Ollie Blackburn, St. Louis, June 23, 2002 (hereafter cited as Blackburn interview); interview with James A. Bristline, St. Louis, September 28, 2001; "Wabash Revamps for Prosperity,"35.

4. "Wabash Revamps for Prosperity," 35–36.

5. *Twenty-First Annual Report Wabash Railroad Company* (St. Louis: Wabash Railroad Company, 1963), 5; "Wabash Revamps for Prosperity," 36; *Railway Age* 149 (December 12, 1960): 52.

6. *St. Louis Post-Dispatch,* February 25, 1960.

7. "Wabash Revamps for Prosperity,"34–35.

Pevler also endorsed acquisition of the Indiana Northern Railway Company. In late 1959 the New Jersey, Indiana & Illinois, a Wabash subsidiary, acquired for $90,000 from the Oliver Corporation this 6.57–mile South Bend switching road. The Indiana Northern served Oliver, Studebaker and ten other local industries. Wabash Railroad Company press release, November 2, 1959, Bureau of Railway Economics Collection, John W. Barriger III National Railroad Library, St. Louis, Mo. (hereafter cited as BRE Coll.).

8. Ibid., 35.

9. Ibid., 36; Minute Book 22, Wabash Railroad Company, May 19, 1960, 116, Norfolk Southern Archives, Atlanta, Ga. (hereafter cited as NS Archives).

10. *Twentieth Annual Report Wabash Railroad Company* (St. Louis: Wabash Railroad Company, 1962), 6.

11. David J. DeBoer, *Piggyback and Containers: A History of Rail Intermodal on America's Steel Highway* (San Marino, Calif.: Golden West Books, 1992), 39–41; "Wabash Revamps for Prosperity," 36; *Banner* 3 (January-February 1960): 3.

It was hardly surprising that Pevler pushed industrial development, whether the river-rail terminal complex on the Illinois River at Meredosia, Illinois, or the Willow Run Industrial District near Detroit, "Big City Advantages at Farm Land Prices." See "Railroads Continue to Site Development Pace," *Industrial Development* 131 (July 1962): 56, and *Railway Age* 153 (August 6, 1962): 65

12. "Wabash Revamps for Prosperity," 36; *Railway Age* 147 (November 30, 1959): 88.

13. Clipping in J. Orville Spreen Collection, Western Historical Manuscript Collection, St. Louis, Mo. (hereafter cited as J. O. Spreen Coll.); Blackburn interview.

14. Herman H. Pevler, "The Changing Railroad Picture," September 9, 1959, Museum of Transportation, St. Louis, Mo. (hereafter cited as MOT Coll.).

15. Blackburn interview.

16. H. Roger Grant, *Erie Lackawanna: Death of an American Railroad, 1938–1992* (Stanford, Calif.: Stanford University Press, 1994), 52; "Train Radio on Wabash Freight Trains Benefits Shippers and Improves Safety," *Banner* 4 (March 1964): 1; Minute Book 24, Wabash Railroad Company, April 19, 1962, 143, NS Archives.

17. Maury Klein, *Union Pacific: The Rebirth, 1894–1969* (New York: Doubleday, 1989), 507–9; H. Craig Miner, *The Rebirth of the Missouri Pacific, 1956–1983* (College Station: Texas A&M University Press, 1983), 24–25.

18. Minute Book 24, Wabash Railroad Company, May 24, 1962, 180, NS Archives; "New 1410 Data Processing Systems Installed for Wabash's Accounting," *Banner* 3 (December 1962): 1.

19. H. Roger Grant, *The Corn Belt Route: A History of the Chicago Great Western Railroad Company* (DeKalb: Northern Illinois University Press, 1984), 119; *Eighteenth Annual Report Wabash Railroad Company* (St. Louis: Wabash Railroad Company, 1960), 5; Clipping in J. O. Spreen Coll.

20. Blackburn interview.

21. Illinois Commerce Commission, Docket No. 46645, Illinois Commerce Commission Archives, Springfield, Illinois (hereafter cited as ILCC 46645); *Railway Age* 144 (March 3, 1958): 43; *St. Louis Globe-Democrat,* September 14, 1958; December 14, 1958; September 27, 1959.

22. *Railway Age* 146 (January 26, 1959): 7; Wabash Railroad public timetable, October 26, 1958; *St. Louis Globe-Democrat,* September 11, 1958; ILCC 46645, 63.

The silver dollar meal offer lasted for three years, ending in September 1961.

23. Pevler, "The Changing Railroad Picture;" *St. Louis Globe-Democrat,* September 10, 1959; Minute Book 20, Wabash Railroad Company, February 9, 1959, 194; April 16, 1959, 269, NS Archives.

24. Blackburn interview; *St. Louis Globe-Democrat,* March 11, 1960.

25. ILCC 46645, 14.

26. Ibid., 814–16.

27. Ibid., 1422, 1424; *St. Louis Globe-Democrat,* March 27, 1960.

28. Wabash Railroad public timetable, April 20, 1962; Don Sarno and Norbert Shacklette, "St. Louis: Its Railroads and Trains," *Passenger Train Journal* 21 (July 1990): 31; interview with Steve Parsons, St. Louis, Mo., June 14, 2002.

29. "Wabash Railroad Inaugurating Cannon Ball Freight Service," *Banner* 2 (March-April 1962): 1.

30. "Overnight Service by Hotshot Piggyback," *Railway Age* 156 (June 8, 1964): 16–17; "'Roadrunner' Popularity Increasing with St.

Louis and Chicago Shippers," *Banner* 4 (June 1964): 1.

For commentary on how Wabash crews at Landers yard in Chicago managed Roadrunners and contributed greatly to their on-time performance, see Richard Kukac, "Humpin' at the Wabash," *Trains* 62 (February 2002): 69–71.

31. Interview with Gregory W. Maxwell, Moreland Hills, Ohio, February 19, 1988.

32. Richard Saunders, Jr., *The Railroad Mergers and the Coming of Conrail* (Westport, Conn.: Greenwood Press, 1978), 87.

33. Maury Klein, *History of the Louisville & Nashville Railroad* (New York: Macmillan, 1972), 485–86; Richard Saunders, Jr., *Merging Lines: American Railroads, 1900–1970* (DeKalb: Northern Illinois University Press, 2001), 138–41.

34. E. F. Pat Striplin, *The Norfolk and Western: A History* (Roanoke, Va.: Norfolk & Western Railway Company, 1981), 220–24; Saunders, *Merging Lines,* 145–46.

35. See Gus Welty, ed., *Era of the Giants: The New Railroad Merger Movement* (Omaha, Nebr.: Simmons-Boardman, 1982).

36. Minute Book 19, Wabash Railroad Company, November 21, 1957, 61; *St. Louis Globe-Democrat,* November 7, 1957; Minute Book 20, Wabash Railroad Company, February 19, 1959, 214, NS Archives; Saunders, *Merging Lines,* 174–75; *St. Louis Globe-Democrat,* October 21, 1959; interview with Perry M. Shoemaker, Tampa, Florida, August 19, 1989 (hereafter cited as Shoemaker interview).

37. Shoemaker interview; Saunders, *Merging Lines,* 176.

38. Grant, *Erie Lackawanna,* 94–96.

39. Salsbury, *No Way to Run A Railroad,* 76–77.

40. Ibid., 82–84; Saunders, *Merging Lines,* 245–60.

41. Salsbury, *No Way to Run a Railroad,* 84; Minute Book 23, Wabash Railroad Company, March 15, 1961, 78, NS Archives.

42. Striplin, *The Norfolk and Western,* 245–48; Salsbury, *No Way to Run a Railroad,* 84; Saunders, *Merging Lines,* 186–90; interview with Charles Shannon, Arlington Heights, Ill., October 1, 1988; *Trains* 21 (February 1961): 4.

43. The most comprehensive study of the Nickel Plate Road is John A. Rehor, *The Nickel Plate Story* (Milwaukee: Kalmbach, 1965); George W. Hilton, *American Narrow Gauge Railroads* (Stanford, Calif.: Stanford University Press, 1990), 473–75.

44. Saunders, *Merging Lines,* 186–88; Striplin, *Norfolk and Western,* 248–49; Grant, *Erie Lackawanna,* 120, Salsbury, *No Way to Run a Railroad,* 85.

45. Salsbury, *No Way to Run a Railroad,* 85–86.

46. Striplin, *Norfolk and Western,* 250; Shoemaker interview; Saunders, *Merging Lines,* 242, Minute Book 43, Norfolk & Western Railway Company, 15,639–15,640, Norfolk Southern Archives, Atlanta, Ga.

47. Striplin, *Norfolk and Western,* 251; Minute Book 23, Wabash Railroad Company, March 2, 1961, 62, NS Archives; *Norfolk and Western Railway Company Unification and Related Proceedings, Finance*

Docket Nos. 21510–21514 & 21567 (n.p., n.d. 2 vols.) I: 26–31, 51 (hereafter cited as *N&W Unification*).

48. *Decatur (Ill.) Daily Review,* December 1, 1960; *St. Louis Globe-Democrat,* January 11, 1961, September 15, 1964; Wabash Railroad Company press release, August 28, 1963, BRE Coll.

49. Minute Book 23, Wabash Railroad Company, February 16, 1961, 57, NS Archives; Scott D. Trostel, *The Detroit, Toledo and Ironton Railroad: Henry Ford's Railroad* (Fletcher, Ohio: Cam-Tech, 1988), 221.

50. For useful insights into the historic workings of the ICC, see Marver H. Bernstein, *Regulating Business by Independent Commission* (Princeton, N.J.: Princeton University Press, 1955), and Ari and Olive Hoogenboom, *A History of the ICC From Panacea to Palliative* (New York: W. W. Norton, 1976).

51. "Wabash Railroad-Nickel Plate Railroad, Savings Resulting from Consolidation of Operations, June 27, 1960," Pennsylvania Railroad Collection, Hagley Museum and Library, Wilmington, Delaware; Saunders, *Merging Lines,* 200–7; Shoemaker interview; Michael Conant, *Railroad Mergers and Abandonments* (Berkeley: University of California Press, 1964),84.

52. *N&W Unification,* I: 7–8; II: 20–21.

53. Ibid.: 64–65; Saunders, *Merging Lines,* 203–4.

The Four Cities Citizens Committee included civic, shipper and railroad labor representatives from Charleston, Granite City and Madison, Illinois, and Frankfort, Indiana.

54. Saunders, *Merging Lines,* 204–5; Grant, *Erie Lackawanna,* 120.

55. Grant, *Erie Lackawanna,* 120.

56. Saunders, *Merging Lines,* 206–8.

57. *St. Louis Globe-Democrat,* September 5, 1963; Minute Book 26, Wabash Railroad Company, September 19, 1963, 38, NS Archives.

58. Reed letter; *Who's Who in Railroading in North America,* 368; *St. Louis Globe-Democrat,* September 9, 1963; Minute Book 26, Wabash Railroad Company, September 4, 1963, 2, NS Archives; *New York Times,* December 19, 1999.

After his tenure with the Wabash ended, William Large took a position as an executive vice president with the PRR, retiring from Penn Central in 1970. He died on December 9, 1999, at his home in Blue Bell, Pennsylvania.

In an interesting aside, John Shedd Reed, former president of the Atchison, Topeka & Santa Fe and a graduate of Yale University, recalled, "My family was not enthusiastic about my idea of becoming a railroader. I think they may have thought railroaders were 'roughnecks.' So when they heard about Henry Large, they suggested I get acquainted, because I think he was considered an 'aristocrat,' having grown up on the Philadelphia Main Line plus an Ivy League education." Reed Letter.

59. "Railroads: Toward a Big Three," *Time* (July 24, 1964): 78; *Norfolk and Western Railway 1964 Annual Report* (Roanoke, Va.: Norfolk & Western Railway, 1965), 5, 7, 22.

60. Striplin, *Norfolk and Western,* 266.

61. Minute Book 27, Wabash Railroad Company, October 15, 1964, 122, 149, NS Archives; *Norfolk and Western 1964 Annual Report,* 16.

62. *Norfolk and Western Railway 1964 Annual Report,* 4.

EPILOGUE

1. *Wabash Railroad Company, Annual Report Pursuant to Section 13 of THE SECURITIES AND EXCHANGE ACT of 1934 for the Fiscal Year Ended December 31, 1990;* James B. Burns, *Railroad Mergers and the Language of Unification* (Westport, Conn.: Quorum Books, 1998), 94.

2. Interview with George Niles, Indianapolis, September 29, 2000.

3. Don Sarno and Norbert Shacklette, "St. Louis: The Pre-Amtrak Railroads and Their Trains," *Passenger Train Journal* 21 (July 1990): 31; Wayne Kuchinsky, "Kansas City: Her Trains, Her Railroads, Her Stations," *Passenger Train Journal* 19 (October 1988): 33; Sam L. Manley memorandum, April 11, 1969, Missouri Public Service Commission Collection, Jefferson City, Mo.; interview with Stephen T. Parsons, Sparta, Illinois, April 5, 2003.

The *Banner Blue,* trains 110 and 111, made their final runs on September 9, 1967.

4. *St. Louis Globe-Democrat,* January 9, 1970.

5. Clipping from *Peru (Ind.) Daily Tribune,* n.d., Miami County Museum; *St. Louis Globe-Democrat,* April 29, 1971; *St. Louis Post-Dispatch,* April 30, 1971; Craig Sanders, *Limiteds, Locals and Expresses in Indiana, 1838–1971* (Bloomington: Indiana University Press, 2003), 175–77.

6. Greg Smith and Karen-Leey Ryan, *700 Great Rail-Trails: A National Directory* (Washington, D.C.: Rails-to-Trails Conservancy, 1995), 37, 92.

7. System Map, Norfolk Southern Railway, 1999 (hereafter cited as NS map).

For suggestions on how abandoned railroad rights-of-way can be located, see H. Roger Grant, *Getting Around: Exploring Transportation History* (Malabar, Fla.: Krieger, 2003), 109.

A fascinating account of how Kirksville, Mo., sought to retain freight service and what happened after the last local Norfolk Southern train trundled through this county-seat community on April 24, 1993, is found in Joseph P. Schwieterman, *When the Railroad Leaves Town: American Communities in the Age of Rail Line Abandonments* (Kirksville, Mo.: Truman State University Press, 2001), 163–67.

8. NS map; Harry Ladd, *U.S. Railroad Traffic Atlas* (Orange, Calif.: Ladd Publications, 2000), 91–92.

9. Edward A. Lewis, *American Shortline Railway Guide,* 5th ed.(Waukesha, Wis.: Kalmbach, 1996), 26, 46, 82–83, 87–88, 159.

10. *Moody's Transportation Manual, 1977* (New York: Moody's Investors Service, Inc., 1977), 407; Lewis, *American Shortline Railway Guide,* 24, 315–16; Tom Shedd, "A.A.: The Customer Is Priority One," *Modern Railroads* 44 (January 1989): 23–25.

Index

BOOKS BY H. ROGER GRANT

The Country Railroad Station in America (with Charles W. Bohi)

Insurance Reform: Consumer Action in the Progressive Era

Self-Help in the 1890s Depression

The Corn Belt Route: A History of the Chicago Great Western Railroad Company

Spirit Fruit: A Gentle Utopia

Kansas Depots

Living in the Depot: The Two-Story Railroad Station

St. Louis Union Station: A Place for People, A Place for Trains
  (with Don L. Hofsommer and Osmund Overby)

Railroad Postcards in the Age of Steam

Erie Lackawanna: Death of an American Railroad, 1938–1992

Ohio's Railway Age in Postcards

The North Western: A History of the Chicago & North Western Railway System

Ohio in Historic Postcards: Self-Portrait of a State

Railroads in the Heartland: Steam and Traction in the Golden Age of Postcards

Ohio on the Move: Transportation in the Buckeye State

Getting Around: Exploring Transportation History

Books edited by H. Roger Grant

Years of Struggle: The Farm Diary of Elmer G. Powers, 1931–1936 (with L. Edward Purcell)

We Got There on the Train: Railroads in the Lives of the American People

We Took the Train

Brownie The Boomer: The Life of Charles P. Brown, an American Railroader

Iowa Railroads: The Essays of Frank P. Donovan, Jr.